Going to Iran

ALSO BY KATE MILLETT

Sexual Politics
The Prostitution Papers
Flying
Sita
The Basement

✻ ✻ ✻ GOING

KATE MILLETT

TO IRAN * * *

with photographs by Sophie Keir

COWARD, McCANN & GEOGHEGAN

NEW YORK

LIBRARY OF CONGRESS CATALOGING IN PUBLICATION DATA

Millett, Kate.
  Going to Iran.

  1. Feminism—Iran. 2. Iran—Politics and government—
1979–   . 3. Women—Iran. 4. Millett, Kate.
5. Feminists—United States—Biography. I. Title.
HQ1735.2.M53   1981   305.4′2′0955   81-17272
ISBN 0-698-11095-1   AACR2

The text of this book has been set in Baskerville.

Printed in the United States of America

FIRST EDITION

For the women of Iran,
for their freedom,
for the hope
of the Iranian revolution.

Going to Iran

PART I

1 ❋ ❋ ❋

DAMMIT, the telephone. The resin is all mixed, the catalyst is in it already. The fat lady lies sunning herself, moved yesterday from the garage to her spot under the tree. Two more coats on her topside, the fun of spreading it on her breasts, her belly, the cement working out nicely, a good thixitive, a natural color, not that awful plastic look I've been avoiding for two years now. And if she can take the weather. Yes—it is the phone. More resin on Deana's white Hollywood telephone, hardly the perfect guest's way to repay her hospitality.

And this may not even be for me. It's Deana's house, lovely old Spanish ramble in a quiet neighborhood, terrace, the works, and though I only rent the garage as a studio, Deana lets me sleep in the spare bedroom and pay my rent in drawings. Studio West I call it, the perfect place to sculpt, so I am fond of my trips out here to repair the irascible old fat-lady sculptures which are always yelling for help. But the last few days, once people know I'm here, the phone keeps interrupting my peaceful chemistry. Resin doesn't like to wait. Endless interruptions, arrangements for the next trips, the ones ahead on the way back east, they keep calling from the University of Pittsburgh; Ohio too, still haven't settled those airplane reservations, even Sophie's getting calls about it back home at the Bowery. Two speeches on the way back east. But first the journey to St. Paul, the family, making peace with my aunt after all these years. Twenty years ago she sent me to Oxford. I promised to go alone and not with that "divorcée," the clandestine pervert love affair, romance of college girl and graduate student that made both sides of the family quake with horror. Both Mother and the Milletts. The graduate student was a woman; this sort of thing was unheard-of in St. Paul. Mother weeps, the Milletts arrange summit conferences. The money for me to study at Oxford will only be forthcoming if I give up "this woman." Okay, I say, a poor relation, and ahead of me this one big chance; I would earn my lover's fare. So I go to Oxford. But with the woman. Discovered a few years later by a friendly visitor looking in on us. A blow-up with the Milletts, they explode in wrath and dismember me. And it's been all over for two decades now, both the lover and the aunt; the first had already left me, the other will never return. Unless I can make peace somehow, go there, apologize, be accepted again, any terms at all, admit my fault, receive her blessing. She is old. And ill, my sister says. I've got to make this trip, for all my dread. The chill in her voice, this aunt, queen of my childhood, appointing to meet me in a public restaurant, not at the house I love, not even a chance to see the rooms I love; the Chinese horse on the mantel, the pictures. Rooms I dream still, and her in those rooms.

Well, maybe the next day, you're staying a week. At a motel. Her voice, taking that in. "Why not at your mother's?" Indeed, how absurd it must sound. Because I'm coming to court you, and I want to demonstrate my utter availability by detaching myself even from my mother. Because your two bloodlines have been at class war since my childhood. Because my mother might even forgive my being in St. Paul and not staying with her, and because you will probably never forgive me for going to Oxford with a lover, a lesbian. I brought it up again when I called for this rendezvous, my Great Aunt Christina's voice running from Mayo County west of Ireland ease over into reproach and then suddenly hardening into ice. I have all that ahead of me. And only a day and a half to finish this fat-lady sculpture—I need every minute of it if I'm going to leave her outside to test the new surface, a whole series of airplanes ahead of me when all I'd like to do is sculpt at my leisure . . . and then the phone rings.

I can hear the voice beginning. Deana's taped message is over. Now the stranger starts off. A man. An accent. "This is Khalil from New York CAIFI." Well, if it's "Caifi" I've got to pick it up. The resin is just beginning to congeal, have to mix another batch, but if it's Caifi, it's important. Caifi, the Committee for Artistic and Intellectual Freedom in Iran, is one of the most important things I've done in the last years. Angela's imprisonment became prisoners and then political prisoners, those in Chile and the rest of Latin America, but somehow—I can never remember quite how it started, someone described the situation of political prisoners in Iran to me one day in terms I could not ignore. It is as much an appeal to the imagination as it is to the moral sense, the way you become committed to things, and the description centered on the tortures used, on torture itself. Listening I became angry in that way that anger builds in the stomach, the way I was angry over Sylvia Likens' death, the way anger can make you brood if there's nothing to be done, or can make you act if there is everything to be done. We have been doing what we could for years now. There were times it seemed futile, one college audience after another listening to us describe what the Shah has made. Utter disbelief, stupefaction, inability to comprehend emotionally, and perfect intellectual indifference. Either they don't believe us or they don't care.

Their minds running on sheepishly believing: everybody should obey the government. If you have a despotic government it's too bad. In America we have our civil rights, or most of them; we deserve them. People in other countries probably don't deserve them, or value them as we do, would find them odd. Anyway, they got this guy and the papers here say he's great. Wonderful uniform in the Sunday magazine section, photographed in stunning color. I have been seduced by those icons myself. At their age I was a ski bum waiting tables at Sun Valley, Idaho, and once served lunch to this Majesty. The days of Soraya. Even tried to address the imperial presence in my school French, French appearing to be the language of the court. Five big CIA guards who had to ski with revolvers in their pockets. And one State Department type. Majesty does not talk to waitresses, so I was answered in stinging English by a functionary and returned in shame to the kitchen. What dessert will you choose? "Dessert" is a funny word. In French, it seems even closer to "just deserts," but enjoying the shimmer of royalty, for we all thought him handsome then, a playboy prince, a hell of a skier (in every way; he went straight down the slopes, veering neither to right nor left and terrifying his guards, professional-class skiers but endangered by their guns as much as by his skiing). There was a kind of ebullience in seeing him seated at your table, like Gary Cooper for breakfast, Cary Grant last week.

And to the puzzled faces of American college students you must convey some remembrance that we are a republic and kings were tyrants once to us; that the Shah of Iran is not just another jet-setter, like the movie stars, the athletes they admire, the American pantheon of media—the television is still a better authority to them than their textbooks. These are not the students of the late sixties when you were becoming a radical at Columbia and SDS was at hand with the facts.

Consider most of your friends whom you bore with the political history of Iran, the CIA coup in fifty-three, routing Mossadegh's constitutional democracy which had deposed the illiterate colonel who was calling himself Shah, a brute and criminal who had stolen the throne and then sided with the Nazis. So the big Western powers replaced him with his own son, the present Shah. An upstart too, but called, compliments of the oil majors (Mossadegh was not to be "depended" on, he began to nationalize oil) and the Central Intelligence Agency of the United States, called now the Shah of Shahs, the Shadow of God.

Called what, one wonders, in his prisons by those screaming in pain? Along the table at my side, Reza Baraheni is patiently teaching the students the history of his country; a poet one hundred days under torture, carefully and lovingly outlining the lost constitution. They look on, unable to imagine life without the freedoms and guarantees his very words caress; bored in consequence. They are not very sure where Iran is. They have never given a thought to its constitution. When the CIA is mentioned, some look guilty, others incredulous. Nemat or one of the regular Caifi members will speak next or has already spoken. They are precise, informative, the least able to move our audience. Reza's eloquence does more, the fact that he has suffered, they have never heard torture described, still less by one who has suffered it. But his reticence, his honor, his superb literary taste prevent him from really shocking them into understanding. If he were to read those terrible, complex, ambivalent poems on torture he has read in private, reading with Ginsberg once at a good literary evening, almost an Iranian party though it had been ambitiously touted as a "benefit" for Caifi, it would confuse them further; the relationship of tortured to torturer, intimacy almost sexual, time surely eternal, surreal world where terror becomes ordinary, routine. They would never comprehend, become more confused, misled into a sadomasochist curiosity obliterating the moral sense, difficult enough to stimulate in them. All right, I'll do it. I'll tell them about torture when it gets to be my turn—I know that this is the only way to reach them. Through their new political alienation, their new smugness, their new imperialist anomie. Eyes on a job now, they can't afford activism so they call it despair; a waste of time, they say, unwilling to exercise the enormous power still within their hands. The most privileged class in the country, able, having both the time and the mysteriously acquired authority, to bring universities to a standstill, affect the course of international war, change the relation between races, sexes, classes. A few days' effort and they could utterly divest South Africa of the major source of its American holdings. If no one finds this worth doing, why do we imagine we can fire them over political prisoners in Iran? Four other groups have probably assailed them over four other kinds of political prisoners this very week. The meetings were even more scattered in attendance than ours.

And ours is packed with Iranian students. Who will probably disrupt in the next two minutes. Calling Reza a traitor, a CIA spy, a member of Savak. The first time this happened, I didn't know what to do. Was never so surprised in my life. Who are these guys? I whisper along the table as the catcalls pierce our speaker's flow; Reza's calm deliberate English, his dignity swelling to nobility under this brutal attack. Finally you hear nothing at all but the screaming of his detractors. Beats the Zaps of the sixties, beats the deliberate disruption of certain leftist factions who'd throw free speech or the other fellow's right to his opinion right out the window. But even then, you could hear something being said, the audience would demand one speaker have a turn and then the other; it was a dialogue in comparison to this deluge of noise. Hundreds of angry male faces spitting words at us.

Are they Savak? Do the Iranian secret police show up in South Bend, or Austin or Bloomington, just to shout down our Committee for Artistic and Intellectual Freedom, small, well-run as it is, devoted, efficient in its way, but hardly a threat to the vast machinery of the Shah's prisons, agents, informers? "Probably it's Savak somewhere," Nemat would answer. "Probably some of these guys are Savak. Watch them. Pick out the faces that are too old for graduate school, that don't look like students. See if you can spot a Savak look." "The one over there, who seems to start them off." "Maybe." "The one in the coat." "Probably." "Nemat, no one in graduate school ever wore that kind of coat." "Well, they dress down too." "The one in the sweatshirt?" "Probably. But you see, they are really, the majority of them, students. Some may be misled by Savak agents whose orders are to provoke this way, but the rest of them also have ideas of their own. They're a political faction. They have them on this campus, on a number, in fact; in most places where there is a large group of Iranian students. There are several factions, and this one calls itself the Revolutionary Communist party." "Never heard of them before." "They call themselves Maoists." "Are they?" "As far as I can tell they don't read Mao very much. And what they're doing now is counterproductive—if they hate the Shah, and they claim to—but in disrupting our meeting they are preventing us from denouncing him to a wider audience, namely the American students and faculty. We have a lot of trouble with them. They start fights too."

Nemat is trying to be fair, but he also knows the dangers here: "It's possible some are interrupting Reza because they actually believe he compromised to get out of Iran, and no matter how he contradicts this slander, you see they have no interest in hearing him. But if he can be libeled as a traitor . . . our most effective speaker, both on his reputation as a writer here and at home, and on television since he did that thing with Barbara Walters, as well as in the press . . ." "Yes, that long piece on torture in *The New York Times,* that's our greatest coup to date." "Sure, and if they can slander him bad, everything we've won can be lost." For Reza has been able to organize them at PEN, the *New York Review of Books* crowd, the literary politicos, Arthur Miller, Kurt Vonnegut. Doctorow wrote a splendid introduction to the book Reza has published.

As a writer, I've been much less successful here. The only thing I ever published was an essay on the collusion of the American universities with the Shah in accepting the enormous grants he was offering them, but the reason I wrote it is the same one that caused me to urge our academies to have nothing to do with this largess—torture. I was nearly sick with rage that day in Berkeley when I typed its conclusion:

> The London Sunday *Times* reports that fresh from a trip to Iran where they had the rare opportunity to attend one of the generally secret and closed trials of a political prisoner, two French lawyers heard the defendant whisper to them in English, "Mister, Mister" and then pull up the sweater he was wearing to reveal that "the whole of the middle of his chest and stomach was a mass of twisted scars from very deep burns."[1] The lawyers, Henri Libertalis and Nuri Albala, reported to Philip Jacobson of the Sunday *Times* that the prisoner was displaying the marks of his torture: "They looked appalling . . . his back was even worse. There was a perfect oblong etched and he fell into a coma. He was then untied and left with the oblong the skin was again covered in shiny scars from burning." It seems that the secret police, who are under the direct and personal control of the Shah, whom Chancellor Young of the University of Southern California has described as "an engaging person with a strong personality who has done a great deal in the last fifteen years in terms of social development in Iran," have invented an iron frame covered with a wire mesh called the "hot table" which is heated to "toast" its victims. Further evidence of what this "strong personality" has done is an eyewitness account by a fellow prisoner of the

torture of Asgar Badizadegan: "He was slowly burned by means of the electric fire while his hands and legs were tied to a bed. He was so badly burned in the lower lumbar area that it reached some of the vertebral bones and he fell into a coma. He was then untied and left with his wounds in a putrid state, so much so that the stink of his infected flesh filled our cell and nobody else would come near it. He was then transferred to prison hospital and underwent several operations. But he can no longer walk, only crawl on all fours."[2]

I am in Caifi as a feminist. And I have always wished for a greater interest on the part of feminists in the issue of Iran. But lately NOW has been persuaded to endorse Vita Tabrizi as a political prisoner, seven years under torture until she ceased to menstruate, lost all sensation in her hands and feet, developed a severe heart condition. How much do torture victims experience heart attack, despair, heartbreak? Vita Tabrizi disappeared seven years ago on her way home from the university. It's the way there. It is how things happen. You are coming home about seven, it is just beginning to get dark. A car stops. You are quietly abducted. You are never seen again. Your family is not notified. They ask the police, imagining you are a missing person. Maybe they admit to having you in custody, maybe they don't. If the latter, it is possible you are in some private custody, as in Argentina, where right-wingers run their own private places of detention, torture and murder. But it is even possible that the civil police would not know what the political or secret police do to those they capture; or wouldn't know for quite a time. Until trial. And then what is tried is a relic of what was once a person. Vita's trial was secret. It was a military trial. Her people did not come to it, it was not open to any member of the public. Its verdict was settled in secrecy, probably by judges whose identity was also secret. The verdict was guilty of "crimes against the state and its safety."

Vita Tabrizi was a professor of sociology at the University of Tehran. Her specialty was the ethnic minorities, the Kurds, Azerbai-

[1], [2] Both quotations regarding torture in Iran are from the long and very well documented account by Philip Jacobson in the London Sunday *Times* of January 19, 1975. Only the Berkeley campus paper and one other student publication in the Middle West would publish my free essay. The *Village Voice* told me I should cut out the material about torture and my "rhetoric about immorality" because the editor felt I "lecture the reader a bit too much."

janis, Turks, groups which taken together comprise the majority of the population of Iran, deprived of their language and culture, forced to speak Farsi (Persian), ruled by a Persian minority (the Shah himself more fluent in French than in Farsi; Farsi is nevertheless the state's mandatory tongue), the only route of what little literacy remains in Iran after twenty-five years of the Shah's rule, a rule ruinous to education. And to literate communication as well, the Shah having suppressed ninety-five percent of publications during the course of his reign, as well as all political opposition parties. What ideas did Vita Tabrizi have that brought her into collision with this state of affairs? Was her field of study in itself subversive? Reza, a Turk, once got in trouble for an essay which advocated literacy in Turkish, the rights of Turkish-speaking Iranians to use their own language, even to compose and read in it. Did Vita sign something, a petition or some such thing, at the university? There must have been some dissent, even under that blanket of silence. There were even guerrillas in the hills. But few of them, and little likelihood that she would be aligned with them.

It may even have been that she was one of the thousands who get arrested "by mistake" in police states. A neighbor informed, a neighbor who quarreled or disapproved or held a grudge. In a nation of informers, virtually anyone can inform on anyone else. Estimates of the number of Savak were as high as 100,000. But take the informers together with them, for anyone can inform, and you may conclude, as Reza did, that one out of eight persons was part of the system. There are Savak everywhere in society, almost everyone knows someone in Savak, is even related to Savak members. Rather like the military at home, "the service."

And then one day, after all our plodding, some six years of it in Caifi, we began to feel the earth move. We even hoped we had helped to bring it about. That in informing the West through the universities and through publications and television and creating a very different image of the Shah from that which the media here had fostered for years in virtual collusion with our own Central Intelligence Agency's activities in planting a dictatorship—in airing all this we had made a little difference. Perhaps even in spurring on the dissent of Iranian students abroad, students in the United States, France and England; our pickets in New York and Washington during the Shah's visit, Farah's unscheduled visit to New York City which cost two and a half million dollars in police security, a figure we rejoiced in griping over in the streets, a picket line I joined one cold winter night with Arthur Miller, other literary folk who showed up, a few feminists who never miss anything.

And thousands of angry Iranian students in masks in whose ranks I marched out of curiosity for an hour and because I couldn't find my Caifi friends. Caifi is pacifist and not politically aligned. Though we always had some members with Trotskyite sympathies from the Socialist Workers Party, we were in fact a human-rights group pure and simple, whose whole object was to free political prisoners and stop the torture. Our hope was also the overthrow of the Shah and the reinstatement in Iran of constitutional democracy, but our mission was the prisoners. Caifi had never taken on itself the bloodlust I heard in those other marchers, the fury against the Shah, the cries for his death, his blood, his heart, his gizzard. I found these demonstrators heady and wonderful for a while; then I found them a bit less wonderful, and the Caifi line of old comrades a relief—they were friends. When they said "Down with the Shah," I knew what they meant.

But it was being said everywhere in the world now. To the Shah himself on his last visit to Washington. In Paris. It was almost being said in Iran. At great poetry readings. Odd that the first meetings in open dissent should be vast poetry feasts at Aryamehr University. Mammoth audiences listening to verses increasingly insubordinate, seditious. Then the crowds attacked by the military, people beaten, murdered. But they kept coming. They kept meeting, massing themselves. In a culture where there is actual legislation forbidding assemblages of more than three people. In a place so careful to prevent dissent that one of the few places one could foment it was in a mosque. Where everyone must go. Where the courts of the mosques began to take on the character of debating grounds.

Also where the mullahs could subvert dissent into reaction.[3] I

---

[3] Caifi had in fact put out a mailing on Khomeini on December 11, 1978, urging that the French government not renege on its hospitality to him after he took refuge there upon being asked to leave Iraq. French governmental authorities were anxious that Khomeini might advocate violence to Iranian demonstrators, and Caifi repeated Khomeini's assurances that he was nonviolent, as well as his acknowledgment that his followers have armed themselves. The mailing also quoted Khomeini's endorsements of democracy and free speech. "We deplore the French government's attitude toward Ayatollah Khomeini . . ." as always, we supported the rights of the dissident. What I did not know then, and indeed did not see documented here until my return from Iran, was the careful way that Khomeini prepared for his takeover, even from Paris, using all the methods for the dissemination of propaganda, direction, and control afforded him by the religious organization of the populace in Iran. This is Jim Crockroft's Decem-

remember lunching on that issue with a tableful of Caifi men, my oldest friends in the organization. We were somewhere, some unlikely Ramada Inn breakfast room, one of those places you go in college towns on the prairie, where along with the motel bed and a shag rug you get ice water and paper doilies and chicken salad. The conversation had an unreal quality even then—the streets of Tehran bloodied by students in revolt, the Shah's troops, the four hundred burned to death in the cinema at Abadan—and they blamed it on dissenters. Nemat is furious—it was Savak. How can we know? "Who else? They do everything and then blame it on the people." "All right, but what will happen if the mullahs come to power?" "Oh, don't worry, they won't." "If they do, what will happen to women?" "They won't, don't worry, the mosques are only centers of dissent, it is the people's dissent. Ordinary people. The people in the demonstrations are not religious fanatics, they're workers. Did you know that the oil workers are now calling for the release of political prisoners? It's one of the demands of their strike." "And the other people striking, did you know," Hamid is telling me, "did you know they were postal workers, bank tellers? Clerical workers are not going to be Moslem pietists either. They are demanding democratic freedoms, not a return to religious reaction." "I know, I read it, but I wonder. Women are talking now. They are afraid of the resurgence of Mohammedanism, what that will do. For women. For everyone, for that matter. What if the old codes were imposed again?"

"Don't be silly, that will never happen. The mullahs lead because the mosques are the centers of organization now. That will change with the formation of the Komiteh. You know the Komiteh?" "Explain." "Everyone will be organized by neighborhood, by profession. Place of work, craft, whatever." "What will that do for women? They don't have those affiliations." "Don't worry about it. It is a grass-roots kind of democracy. It will work. It is working." Yes, it sounds very good. I like the sound of it.

One man after another explains. "And the people will rule them-

ber 27, 1978 report on Khomeini's operation in France: "Across the street from Khomeini's small family residence was a bungalow which served as his headquarters, linked by one phone to Iran. To that phone was connected a tape recorder; nearby was a tape duplicating machine. In Iran, similar equipment was hooked up. In just hours, taped cassettes of Khomeini's messages would be played in 80,000 mosques and countless bazaars, converting strategy concocted privately in Khomeini's home into public practice." *Seven Days*, February 23, 1979, Vol. III, No. 1, page 17.

selves. This is the way we can get around those bureaucratic functionaries the Shah set up. Even with him gone, you see, all that could just
go on. And that is by no means a radical social change. Until the
constitution is in force again and the people have elected their
representatives, the Komiteh is the perfect way to reorganize society, I
mean shake it up . . . entirely." None of the men have my misgivings.
Nemat comes in: "Anyway, it isn't our job. Remember, our job is the
prisoners. The victims of that society. Until the prisons are open—we
concentrate on that. Until we've exposed the crimes of that regime.
The manner of the uprising is out of our hands." "But if new forms of
reaction set in—women are already uneasy," I waver. "Predicting
power to the mullahs is a trick of the Western press. They would love
to say the Shah was falling to some wild-eyed reactionary Muslim
fanatics."

"You don't think that's happening?" "No, it is the ordinary people
who demonstrate every day. Don't you see their pictures?" "Yes I do. I
imagine they are students or leftists or liberals, people with regular
jobs who live in apartment houses and are risking their lives by going
out after curfew." "Precisely." "But look, already this seems to be
subverted." "There are thousands of women demonstrating too."
"Right. You don't see their pictures much in our papers." "But you
saw them in ours—the pictures we've printed." "Yeah. I saw the
chador too." "That's in solidarity with Islamic culture, against Western
imperialism." "I understand. But why university women would take it
on again voluntarily still seems strange to me." "It's the symbolism." "I
get the symbolism. I'm afraid it's a trap." "But you got to admit it's
really a terrific cover in a demo." Hamid laughs in a delighted child's
recognition of both the humor and the sense of what he has just said. I
would think it's perfect; anonymity, protection—it has a drama and
grandeur in the pictures. Files of them. "Kate, look at this picture. The
women are leading the protest, they are actually leading it."

"That's why I worry." It is impossible to explain just why. They are
so delighted, these men, they are so sure it's going to be all right. And
I should be a good Westerner and not make obnoxious objections; I
should be a good woman and go along with the struggle of the people
even though I already suspect that at its outcome the "people" will be
men and not women. It must be a creation of the Western press—this
new upsurge of mullahs, of piety, of placing the opposition to the
Shah in xenophobic terms of nationalism, Islam, nationalist Muslim
struggle against imperialism. Who would deny there was imperialism—the Shah is there because of it. But a return to Islam, the chador,
the advisability of this or that holy man leading the masses back to

Islamic piety . . . When the object was a return to the constitution, the democracy they had enjoyed or begun to, under Mossadegh. Why not that direction instead?

"The mullahs will only be around until the Shah is gone. Then the people will make their own democracy, their own solution. There's the Komiteh. And the Army will revolt, they can arm the people. It will be as we say." "Yes, I hope so. It's just that so many women are uneasy now."

At Robin Morgan's, eating dinner a week later, we were very uneasy. Ayatollah Khomeini was pronouncing from France. I defended as my Caifi brothers had advised me. He was, after all, a man brave enough to denounce the Shah. All these years when the rest of the hierarchy had truckled. We had, ourselves, devoted years to freeing the Ayatollah Tolerani from the Shah's prisons; all religious dissenters were political prisoners of conscience, even if not physically imprisoned. And Khomeini with his wonderful face, his wrathful beard, his haunted eyes, seemed to us, at this point, like some reembodiment of Gandhi hurling imprecations on the Shah, adamant that he abdicate, refusing reforms, deals. A man of principles, a man of ideas, above politics. A holy man. Monarchy must go—it was a principle with him that this anathema finally be extirpated after all these two thousand years. The inference would be democracy, and that indeed was what he was saying to us from his retreat in France.

"There will be no democracy for women, I promise you," Robin predicted. "When you see it, kid, remember I a tole ya." I laugh along with her other guests, laugh at this silly pun, and we begin the soufflé. She has invited a diplomat, an Irish man from the United Nations. He corrects me: far from reinstituting democracy, the Ayatollah Khomeini plans to establish an Islamic republic. What would that be? I wondered. "Your guess is as good as anyone else's but you can bet it won't be very democratic. Are you acquainted with the ideas in the Koran? With Islamic legal practices? They can be pretty awful, you know. The right hand of the thief, that sort of thing." "Saudi?" "Maybe not that bad. But hardly what your leftist and student demonstrators have in mind." "Or the women. They're flocking into the streets, you know. They're really taking part in this." "Yeah, and they're gonna get screwed like we always do," Robin says. "How many times have we put ourselves at the barricades for male revolutionaries, imagining it was going to be our freedom won right along with theirs. Remember Algeria?" "Yes, but it isn't like that. It won't happen." "An uprising can end in anything, look at history," our diplomat says. "No," I argue, "the women have taken too many chances, everyone has. And the general strike, the old socialist dream—it's actually worked there. This is really a popular uprising." "And anyone can grab it," he points out. "The Shah will leave in a matter of days. Khomeini will land from Paris." "The airports are closed." "They'll open them. There has been no outside interference—Russia, China, maybe even Uncle CIA is leaving it alone. All with their best regards and brotherly love to the Shah, mind you." "China is certainly disappointing here," I grumble, "still sending brotherly greetings to the Shah." "Politics, my love; big fat-cat international border politics, never mind oil." "Oil's a mirage. But talk to Brooklyn about the price of heat this winter," Robin puts in.

"And the Ayatollah lands"—the diplomat folds his napkin—"and there you are. He takes over." "How can he? The people will have ousted the Shah by themselves. They don't need him." "Ah, but he enters a vacuum, very little political opposition has ever formed under repression, years and years of it." "Surely they can get it together and elect somebody there, some person of reputation, conscience, lay persons, civil libertarians." "Not the charisma." "But surely an ayatollah, a bishop or whatever that would be, is not going to take office." "He won't even need to; rule through willpower. Edict. Papal bull. Pronunciamento." The diplomat's wife is in the fray now; the sound of religion has set her off against the Pope in a humorous way. She works for birth control in South America. "The Pope in Ireland is worse than the weather," she crows. A good deal more to drink. Sophie looks on amused. Robin's husband, Kenneth Pitchford, is talking poetry to her right, a young black man is flirting with her to her left. Our diplomat hitches up his chair and goes for me. And Robin. "What would you do; you're strategists in the women's movement, tell me, what would you do to incite mass protest among the women in Iran?" I've no idea. This is precisely the sort of question I find most ridiculous. Even in theory. Even at a dinner party. Even in a male diplomat whose goodwill never covers his unconscious condescension. Robin will go for it—she will make it a game.

"Protests. Got to have protests. Enormous. Take to the streets. Only way we ever get anything done." "But they can't, they'd be prevented." "They already got some training, sure they could. Been in the streets for weeks now, best possible exercise of rights." "Wouldn't you think of guerrilla tactics?" he pursues. Now it's past a joke. Robin and I should lecture him, drink more, change the topic. How can they do anything, the women there, if it turns against them, I wonder, the righteousness of male insurrection, leftist or reactionary; its fervor, nationalism, tribalism, xenophobia, ethnic and religious narrowness. "Without organization . . ." I begin, and the thing seems more impossible than ever. Even spontaneous protest can be put down. The women in the countryside, the women who've worn chador all their lives, the women under religion. Yet consider, if they marched against the Shah, they can march against anything. If the men let them: "How much autonomy, how much organization, how much consciousness can a colonial class . . ." "Exactly. That's just the problem I'm setting you." I could wave this man away if he weren't so big, so right next to me, if he weren't so experienced in politics, so much my elder. And if he weren't perfectly serious. Because the question can hardly be serious. We are Americans. We can't do one damn thing about the plight of women in Iran. It's their movement, if they make one. Even to discuss it seems absurd. Because we've never heard of a women's movement there. Ashraf, the Shah's hideous twin sister, went around pretending to be a feminist, her representation alone enough to discredit the idea if she were not so cleverly fraudulent; actually got herself appointed head of a UN commission on women's rights years ago. A disgraceful event in itself. Then tried to invite world feminism to Tehran for the second International Women's Year meeting following that in Mexico City. An invitation declined even before history intervened.

But how are women in Iran to build a women's movement at this juncture, admittedly a moment they desperately need one? How, against all the forces now unleashed in that society? Admittedly a state-co-opted feminism is gone, and that's a step. No more Ashraf. No more the Shah's pretensions, the window dressing of Westernization, the token education, token representation in the professions, perhaps even in government, the high bourgeois ladies in collusion with money and family and the system, the court, wealth, technocracy, modernism. True, young women in the universities, the women who have earned some education—the vanguard would be there. But at the moment, many of the best of them are at the service of the revolution. And the very real possibility that it will betray them. Yet to have rid Persia of its Shah is a high mission and perhaps takes precedence over any new social order building.

But the women a little older, the ones Robin has been talking to, they already see the future as a curtailment: their competence, their education, their achievements will all backfire. They may be called bourgeois, reactionary, out-of-date; having fought one form of discrimination all their lives, they may live to fight others, more blatant, more brutal. They say they are losing what little they had. That religious reaction will negate their very existence. That they hated the old order, but hate still more having to hate a new one as well. Everything in it hating them into extinction. "It was the Shah's father, don't forget, who took the veil off the women, you know," the diplomat pursues. "Tore it off them, really, exposing them at first to rape, spittle, insults, blows, stonings. Very complicated, the monarch's response to the West, its customs." "He sure didn't do it for women," Robin comes in. "Why this endless manipulation of us? Why patriarchy, why power, why, maybe most of all, the manic hostility with which we are dealt, a subject people after all? Our subversive magic maybe," I muse. "What do you suppose the veil meant once?" Robin wonders aloud. Did we invent it? Did men just take it over, invert its original meaning, turn its mystery into cruel fact as well as symbol of our fallen state. Abject, conquered?

The diplomat wants an answer to his examination question: how shall the women in Iran rise and restore their rights if they should be denied them? Robin returns to the streets, I return to organization, a base of consciousness. Methods we have seen and experienced at home. Having no relevance in Tehran tonight, having no connections with feminism there, having, in fact, no hope even.

So it's odd that on the fourth ring, I hear a young man named Khalil earnestly explaining that everyone at Caifi has gone home to Tehran, leaving only himself and another young man named Nersi in charge of the depleted New York office, and that he's calling me on a matter of great urgency. Am I ready? The resin has just hardened in the bowl. Of course. "It's a mission. Really. You have never seen Iran." "Of course not. They'd put a bag over my head at the airport, you know that," I laugh at him. But already I'm excited. "Kate, your sisters need you in Iran." It does sound a bit melodramatic. But it also sounds grand. Would that one's sisters ever needed one anywhere. Of course, they don't, they can cope just beautifully by themselves. They may want you around for the fun of it, or because they have a job of work for you to do. Khalil, however, is a delightful young man, I have decided already, and decidedly enthusiastic. "The women in Iran are going to celebrate International Women's Day, March 8, they want you to come and speak." "Wonderful. I'm enormously honored. Who are they?" "You remember Kateh?" I try to remember Kateh. There were women in Caifi at the end, more and more visible, but often shy. Once in the wife/girlfriend class, one saw them more and more at the end as speakers, organizers. A few. I remember one at Southern Methodist University. Good speech. Very competent. A row of them at a party later, there or some other school, the South running into the Middle West sometimes as we stumped one hopeful gathering after another; the women at the party still shy, hard to get through to. Was Kateh the outspoken one that night, bright sharp eyes? "She is very beautiful," Khalil says, "you must have met her somewhere, Indiana or Chicago maybe. She was also in the New York office." But I know the road better than the office. "Well, Kateh was the secretary of the New York office. When Nemat went back, he had a press conference at Tehran airport. And he said that now that the political prisoners are freed, now that Evin and Quasr are finally opened . . ." I hear this news in a dizziness of joy. Evin and Quasr prisons, the huge bastions where thousands of political prisoners suffered torture, opened, the demonstrators pouring in, releasing the Shah's victims at last. I ended speeches with the screams in Evin prison tonight, trying to make other Americans care, hear them, know they exist—they have existed in my mind for years.

"So Nemat says that Caifi, as a civil-rights organization, regards the condition of women as the gravest problem in Iran and the focus of its attention from now on since its return." Good for him. Male feminists, wonderful thing. Caifi brothers were always very special. "And Kateh is forming a group with some other Caifi women, I mean women who were in Caifi here and worked against the Shah—there are other women too, there aren't very many of them." "How many would you estimate?" "Really it's only about twelve to start with. But they have a lot of experience. Kateh's awfully good. So are the others. I think you'll recognize them. Resa. And Asa. They're setting this thing up as a rally. So they've called open meetings of women to participate in the organization of the day. This will bring in others." "Where will it be held?" "Well, they're not sure of that yet. They hope to be able to do it in a university." I imagine Tehran University, scene of so many bloody struggles. Demonstrations of students put down by gunfire. But the danger is past now. The Shah is in exile. The prisons are open. The universities there are holy soil now; they are, for me, the home of the revolution in Iran, those first meetings, the poetry readings, the first outrages against and by tyranny—how fitting the women's movement would make its first stand there.

I have no illusions about our size or our status there. And yet I do. However tiny. Beleaguered. Of course, it could be dangerous. "We will provide you an escort," Khalil promises, "Nersi or I will go with you." It seems the oddest gallantry. I have not heard that phrase or responded to its chivalry since I was a girl going to dances in St. Paul. My amusement settles only when I realize the escort is because of difficulties, language, customs; perhaps even they think it's dangerous. It's absurd to think that way. It's also absurd to keep pursuing this with Khalil, when in fact I am scheduled to speak at the University of Pittsburgh on the eighth of March and at Ohio University on the seventh. Feminists are in demand around International Women's Day.

Could I get out of these gigs, would they give me leave, will I be sued, breach of contract, reviled as an adventurer? "Let me call my friend Sophie and see if I can cancel the things I was supposed to do that day." "I've already talked to Sophie. She thought you could." This guy Khalil is sharp; he's also determined. Nothing, no prospect in years, has excited me as this one does. I'm a goner. The resin corrodes in the bowl, hardly noticed. A day and a half to finish my fat lady; I need eighteen hours' drying time. Still a few days to go to St. Paul, lunch with my aunt. Not the great reunion I fantasized, not days and days of reintegration with the place, exploring my father's blueprints, old friends, his fellow engineers, reminiscences with the good civil-rights lawyers who saved me from the loony bin, when my mother, differing over "life-styles," had the misjudgment to have me committed on the brash advice of a doctor whose scientism she was impressed by—the things an Irish family amuses itself with over whiskey in aftertimes. The geography of St. Paul pulls as hard as it can, has been pulling for months. Hell, I'm in the middle of a book about growing up there. Would I lose this precious trip by having another one?

"When would we have to leave, Khalil?" "As soon as possible, maybe three days. The airport is closed a lot of the time. You might have to land in Karachi and come back. We're not sure we can get a plane. They're heavily booked and many airlines have canceled their flights. The place is still in an uproar, you know. We think the Pan Am flight on the third might really get you there by the eighth." "Hmm, I was going to go through a place called St. Paul on my way back east. I was born there." "I'm from Isfahan. I want you to visit there. My brother will be there. He's in Caifi too." "What's his name?" "Saïd. You've met him. He has a mustache." I try to remember mustaches. Caifi has so many of them. "You can stay with my family. It's a wonderful city. Saïd will take care of you. You'll have time to visit the countryside." It is irresistible. After all these years of eating and sleeping Iran through the exclusive channel of prisons, to imagine there is a whole country, a countryside, pictures and music and rugs and mosques, and that we could be friends, not just comrades in the struggle, not always in some motel or on some college podium or in offices full of leaflets, but celebrating something achieved—there at last.

"You must come. You must see my country. Your friends are waiting for you there. We want to show you everything." To eat real meals, Persian meals, to be in their own place with these people, to be at home with them. It begins to creep over me—to see Persia. To have this once-in-a-lifetime chance. Even, the insidious, insistent whisper in the radical's subconscious, to see a revolution. You've always wanted to. . . .

I have carried the quart-size tub of resin into the kitchen and set it on the dishwasher that no one ever uses, next to this morning's chilly coffee, the familiar shape of the mug. The telephone line stretches from the study with its glass table and immaculate chrome-and-leather chairs (a terrible danger when holding something as messy as resin). I look around Deana's agreeable old-fashioned kitchen, big, easy to work in, lovely old tiled walls, it even crosses my mind to pour a glass of water from the sink—this phone call is changing my life. Just file the trip to St. Paul for a moment, there may still be time to slip in a weekend—don't even consider the possibility of surrendering it yet. Go for the first obstacles: Pitt, Ohio.

"Khalil, look, I'll talk to Sophie. We'll see what we can do about canceling or postponing these engagements. Actually they're paying me, the universities are paying for these lectures, the way sometimes we even got paid on Caifi stuff if the students could pull it off with the administration. Anyway, these gigs are how I make my living, you know, so if I have to cancel, I'm losing the money that was going to get me through the summer or something. But I think we can work something out. As soon as we know, we'll call. Or easier still, just keep in touch with my friend Sophie at the Bowery."

"My friend Sophie," my odd, reticent little phrase for Sophie Keir, friend, lover, the person who lives with me, my better self, more organized, efficient, mature, rational, witty. A writer too, and her book, which was to speed along in my absence, recently interrupted by a flood on the roof, a heavy snowfall and a sudden thaw, whereupon all the leaks in the Bowery tarpaper we had just patched began again; the water was two feet high and must have weighed tons on the old structure. She and Michael Bakaty, our neighbor, the sculptor who lives on the fourth floor, were up there all one morning bailing it out. The lady who supervises our semiderelict building for the City of New York happened to be walking by just then and we have some hope of repairs. If this weren't enough, Sophie woke up two nights ago to hear a man tampering with the lock on the door of the loft. Medeco lock my friend Ruth put on for me. Sophie called Michael. The police. Who arrive in a squadron and corner the guy on the roof. "It's him," a sergeant exults. "Who's him?" Sophie inquires. "Lady, this guy raped and murdered a woman over in Queens last night." Sophie said she didn't inquire how. This is the only time I've ever heard her frightened, her friends staying near her, Ruth from around the corner, Fumio. The neighborhood. But how rotten not to be there to help. Now this, wonder how she'll take this.

Remarkably well. She's even decided to go with me. "I'll do an article for *Ms.* Robin thinks it's a good idea too. They should go for the ticket anyway, don't you think? Caifi and the women's group in Iran are staking you a ticket. Let *Ms.* stake me. I'll give them all my material, photos, interviews, everything." Sophie is a photojournalist, reporter on Mideastern economic affairs and politics for papers in Canada and Britain. Spent years all over that part of the world. "Sophie, you've persuaded me." "Let's see how I do here in New York. I bet I can get photo commissions before I leave. Hardly anybody is permitted into Iran right now. Pictures should be very valuable." "And you can come with me . . ." Suddenly I realize I hadn't wanted to go alone. Suddenly the possible danger, strangeness, the language barrier, customs, whatever—it all seems so much friendlier with a companion. The perfect companion, delightful Sophie. And she knows her stuff. Making tapes, everything would be so much easier too. "We could film it." "Relax. Let's just see if we can get there. Ohio and Pitt gave you permission, by the way." "I mean, we could do just little stuff, film the rally or something. It's archives, that sort of stuff." "You better hurry home and get ready." "I could bring messages from everybody I can think of. Imagine how delighted they'd be. De Beauvoir, Angela, the groups in France. I'll call Sabatini in Italy. They'll all be so happy to greet Iranian feminists. It's the birth of a movement there." "None too soon." "Khalil says the situation is very discouraging for women now. Even though the Shah is gone finally, the miracle we waited for, ignoring much else."

"What's Khalil say about the Ayatollah?" "Khomeini's power seems to be enormous, as great as the official provisional government's, greater maybe. And he's holding on to it. It really doesn't appear very progressive." "Will they even let us do our thing?" "It seems in flux now, a great many opinions side by side," Khalil says. "The left still seems able to say what it likes. I got the impression that this is the time for women to speak out or else." "It could be a great moment to see the place." "Come home and pack." "I'm trying to make my reservations and still get to see my aunt." "You may have to sacrifice that." "I'm trying not to." "I'll call you back as soon as Khalil and Nersi find us a flight. Then you'll know your perimeter."

2 ✳ ✳ ✳

THE LATE-AFTERNOON SUN. The fat lady is covered. One more coat tomorrow before the students pick you up for a panel at UCLA. Figure out your life. The lists on the glass table in the study. Airplane reservations. Pitt and Ohio have vanished, along with their complicated landings and departures, and set topics. There remains the Minnetonka Inn, hopefully inscribed, complete with telephone number, cost of rented car. And the luncheon on Friday. "Right in the village," she had said, her village not being mine, her village being Wayzeta. The house on the lake. Her lawn. Her trees, the damages done over the winter. I had just finished writing a conversation between us about her trees and my trees in the new book. I have even read it or the section near it at a private gathering of women, a little premier of this book, projected first as a book about my father and my childhood, but becoming one about my aunt. I am living in the middle of a book again. Risky. Not since *Flying* have I taken on that madness, not after the fact, but during it. *Sita* was over before I saw it as a book, though half of its pages were written as it occurred; they were private exercises, journals, whatever. The full rabbit run of living in a book, I had tried to avoid that after *Flying*. And now, because I am visiting my aunt, while writing about her, I am living in a book. If she rejects me, I have to write that.

And fail to achieve the resolution that I want. Happy ending? No, but how bitter if she won't forgive me and I have to live with that. You're stuck with what happens, after all. She has her reasons. She was wronged by her terms. All very well for your terms: good students already twenty-one years old really should get an education promised regardless of whether they sleep with folk the folks don't like. But the money had a string to it. Give up that woman. You never planned to, spent the whole summer earning her passage yourself. And you did lie. This lie is going to haunt me the rest of my life. And your Aunt Christina, your beloved aunt is seventy years old; if you let this go, you're taking a chance.

Iran is an adventure, it isn't a book. I don't want to go there as a journalist. But in going to St. Paul, I'm in a book. A book I'm supposed to finish through this spring, writing in happy, intense little spurts at the Bowery, writing the way I've been writing. Third of the way through it now. If you go to Iran, when do you do the other book? This is getting serious now, rearrange a schedule, postpone a visit home, but to throw off the whole plan of a book—my god. Well, you could do it next fall or winter. Book tour for *Basement* in the fall, might go to France if they were ready with the translation. The winter, then. Give it the whole winter. But look, when do you see your Aunt Christina? This is life, not just a goddamn book. This is a real woman, aging, angry, whose feelings you hurt twenty years ago. And who frightens me to death, but whom I adore. This Iran thing . . .

A few hours later, Deana's fireplace going, the martini generous and clear, that essence of Atlantic freshness—one clear lemon peel floating in the crystal gin, the rocks piled high—the spirit of the Atlantic at sunset, I always call it, Provincetown in August every evening of your life no matter where you are. They laugh at me. Deana was born out here, a Hollywood education from the first, pinups in the bathroom that go back to her childhood. A lovely spirit, a wonderful generosity, and a love of music that keeps us up all night drinking Fundador and comparing passages. Sally Fiske is also there. "If I were going to Iran, I'd be out of my mind. What an assignment." "But I'm not a journalist. And you are." "Until I got too much for them to handle, but just watch, I'll be back." During the Briggs Amendment crisis here, Sally had the integrity to mention on a debate that she was gay. Even in "objective" reporting a Jew or black has the right to state that fact about himself when being Jewish or black is under discussion, the thing by no means obvious in the first case, but in the second, where it would be obvious, considered no bar to an informed and valid opinion. Forced to resign as a television inter-viewer, she threw herself into the campaign against this vicious amendment which would have purged homosexuals and even those who sympathize with them from the teaching profession. Sally helped to defeat it in California. Now she's trying her hand at public relations while itching to be back as a reporter. Eyeing me and my fat assignment.

Sophie calls to say we must be ready to leave on Sunday, the fourth of March. Did I ever renew my passport? Idiot oversight in a radical, ever to be without a passport, the thing lying on my desk all summer at the farm, the convenient pink mail-in application for renewal right next to it—all I ever lacked was a few hours to go into town and have a passport photo made. But there were always the big barns to convert into studios, always a new floor to lay in the little barn, always work and a whole placeful of people needing me to be there. To be the chief carpenter, the cook, the errand girl who goes to H. G. Page for more nails or some sheetrock. And never an afternoon rainy enough, empty enough, organized enough to remember such a banal detail as two inches of passport photo. I distinctly remember actually remembering it once; driving out of town after closing the deal on the new land, the additional seventy-three acres that would make it possible to call it a colony in the making, not just my homestead, farmhouse, three barns, and a pond, the seven original acres that came with it at purchase nine years ago. Now I had bought the rest, paid for part of it with *Basement*. There were people waiting back at the farm that day, a picnic, champagne in the wildflowers to celebrate the acquisition, the new land. The dream, the colony, utopian Valhalla of women artists. I was even dressed up, a better picture than that miserable one done last time here in Poughkeepsie after escaping the loony bin and returning to play eccentric lady in Dutchess County; wore a long dress and the most miserable expression. I have hated that picture ever since I saw it, bore it like an affliction through several visits to France. But I'm not going to France again till next fall, I thought, and everybody's waiting for me to start the party. Painting the walls of the barn will take place first, is still taking place now, and the sooner I get home the less painting my friends will have to put up with. It's rude to make them wait. I'll do it some other time.

Fatal error, it now appears. "Look, if you have to get a passport, we may need more time. The weekend comes in, you know, offices aren't open. Friday's the only day you've got." "Friday I was to have lunch with my aunt." "Call her and explain." "I've been trying to all my life." "Well, now you have to choose. We can get our visas in one day. We've special permission from the Iranian government. Let's hope your Americans are as cooperative. Or we can't go. Khalil says the Pan Am plane on Sunday is the only one we can count on. Stops at Rome and Istanbul and lands us in Tehran the evening of the fifth. Anything later is booked or might fail to arrive in time for the eighth of March if we're rerouted." "That's it, Sophie?" "Yes, I'm afraid that's it."

The fire is still warm red roaring, the perfect Hollywood solution to a fire—a gas jet. It is always the thirties in this room. Deana is showing off a recording, Sally is savoring my golden opportunity, and I am lost in that little sadness when you have already relinquished something— a reconciliation, a lover, a book. A plan, a scheme that took weeks building, nervous evenings getting up the grit to telephone this distant lady, once as much mother as aunt, godmother, one more powerful in influence than anyone around me except my parents themselves, and greater always than they, mere mortals to her distant divinity, hauteur, romance. I would go humbly and be further humbled; no, I would storm her affections, seduce her—I wince, remembering the strange erotic dreams I have had night after night out here, fantasies of the wildest incest; encouraged as a form of mental health, synthesis, apotheosis, the obvious realization of a lifetime's inclination: I have married my father to his sister I would smile on awakening and managed to be both child and lover to each. Without spending a cent on analysis or wasting a single afternoon recounting the obvious course of domestic affection.

"What are you thinking about?" "Sally, I'm beginning to realize I need a passport photo." "That's the girl. Now you're talking sense. Let go of the rest. You've really got to make that trip. I happen to know an all-night photomat on Hollywood Boulevard." Of course there'd be one. Right there with the stars' names in bronze stars set in the sidewalk; you can step on the great, memorize the names of bygone directors, dead comics, faded actresses, their specialty indicated by a symbol. I only remember the symbol of the camera itself, the shiny tripod. And parked over it like a car, the photomat. Producing the terrible little pictures without which you cannot travel from one government to another. Not countries or lands anymore, but governments. Governments now running everything, everyone. Controlling them through papers. Paperwork. Bureaucracy. Currency. "Did you know that people didn't need passports at all until this century? Only czarist Russia, I believe." We have reached the photomat; it's the middle of the night. I know that this little monster is coin-fed and it's highly unlikely we will have eight quarters between us, but that's what it demands. "Two dollars in quarters?" We both laugh. "I have some at home. It's only a few blocks."

I wait in the car on a little lane and feel California in the night flowers and a car, a convertible—Sally is a romantic and has an old convertible—and decide, not to lose a moment, to chop off a few examples of this unbeatable California ivy just to see if I can grow it at the farm. I want variety, shadow, ground cover. The work of years. I have never done a big garden; the rest of the landscape is complete and even mowed now, the area around the pond where the deer show themselves, eleven white birch, the willows on the banks. Keep it nicely mowed and let the cinquefoil come back, keep the loosestrife for the heather, it makes that heavenly ring of purple all summer—"You're here."

"With seven dollars in quarters. That ought to do you." These pictures are even smarmier than my old one; "Hollywood wouldn't cast me in anything but a tabloid murder." "Still, it will save you one whole step in the process. You might have had to run all over Manhattan to get that." And it's a symbol. We both know it. Standing on Hollywood Boulevard at two A.M., we know I'm on my way to Iran.

3 ✳ ✳ ✳

NEW YORK AGAIN. "If we don't get out on the street in a half-hour and get that visa . . ." "You're right. We don't even have money, did you know that? I got to see if I can move a little around." "You mean to tell me you don't have a savings account in New York?" "Well, I used to, but I guess I've loaned that money to various friends and got repaid in drawings and so forth." "You've hoarded it up in Pough-keepsie." "Keeps it safe out of reach." "How can we go, then? *Ms.* isn't good for my ticket. I'm going to have to borrow it from you." "I'll ask the country banker, he'll move savings over to checking, and then I'll ask my agents if they'll cash a check for two thousand for me. That should do the ticket and our expenses."

And so in the vault of the Chemical Bank a lady gives us permission to cash a check on my agents' guarantee, and we count the bills beside a policeman and the American flag. When you count the money, you're going someplace. When you buy Sophie's ticket at Pan Am, you are really going. Somehow it's unlike other tickets, other countries, trips to France or England. It's almost as monumental as going to Japan was once. It is sufficiently grave to warrant a smallpox vaccina-tion, something that always makes me sick. I wait while Sophie stays in line at Pan Am. Queasy. It's a big step, this trip. When we talked to Khalil this morning, he was worried about our visa, had premonitions about the Caifi letter of invitation they have spent the entire day composing—my official document. Sophie's is an uncomplicated sentence from *Ms.* promising nothing, not even to print what she produces, but professing a vague interest in it—enough, they say, to get her in as a journalist. *The New York Times* is also uninterested in sponsoring her, wanted to know if she'd like to talk to the style editor. Women, Iran—would you like to speak to someone in fashion? Other magazines might like a look at pictures, but my agent cannot arouse any solid response from the media. No commissions, no sponsorship, no defraying of expenses. Sophie's going on her own. I'm going to make a very short address—I'll be one of many speakers at the March 8 rally—and deliver a few greetings from other Western feminists. We are rather silly. The expense alone.

Now it's Sophie's turn. I have been mulling it over in my mind, in full recognition of the horrific cost of this ticket, the depletion of savings and so forth, I have even been remembering that there's still eight hundred dollars in an account in California, the money I was to live on this month—why not throw it in too, write a check for the airline ticket (bank's open, they can clear it) and keep the two thousand for the trip itself—or rather, let's go the whole way . . . for stuff for the trip. Tape recorders, tape, still film—the worm of a movie crawling through my mind. Your little archive document thing, not cinema but historio-record. Maybe just 'cause nobody wants us as reporters, investigators, documentors of what we see—that in itself ought to make it important to record. The hell with the media's version of reality—a movement is being born in Iran. When ours came into being we were all of us too busy doing it to record it, too busy talking to run a tape recorder, too busy to film. And the plupart of what little was filmed was done so by the media. Even if filmed, it is not in our possession. Now a few of us do record our own events, but in a threadbare way often and without means yet to distribute. We could do a lot over there, we'd be free to observe and record, since we're too useless to help in other ways, not even speaking the language, and illiterate to boot. For years I have wanted to see all this done, made puny little stabs at it, a movie company that failed, a camera never in use, snatches of footage, schemes that don't get shot or stay in the can uncut, the women's music festival at Sacramento, for example; the thousands of examples of unfinished projects. Time, money, discouragement. Maybe we could do something useful.

Bravely writing a check. The ticket is born. Sophie can go. Two of us can do more than one and Sophie can do more than hundreds and we still have two thousand bucks. Bursting into the rain on Fifth Avenue past Rockefeller Plaza and St. Patrick's—juncture of church and state—there's no time for lunch, Nersi awaits us at the Iranian consulate. But first, it's just on the way, Sophie insists I have a proper photograph, "Just right in here, I know the lady who does it, she did me." She is a perfectionist and is determined to give me a handsome photo for a passport even though I already have a crummy one, which is really sufficient. Sophie parks me with the lady photographer, an elderly Turkish refugee, while she goes off to consult her Canadian government, and returns to find me beautifully photographed and the lady and I indulging in rugs. Here in her photo parlor in the grimiest corner of New York, we have spread out in our minds Tabriz and Isfahan and I am really faking because I do not know that much and never get anything except what I can afford from my man in Berkeley, Omar Khayyam, which is not his name but the name of the shop; I love it so I call him that too. He pinches my cheek and we drink strong coffee and we bargain. It takes all day. We both love it because we get to look at so many rugs this way; it is rather like looking at pictures, the long afternoons going over drawings with someone who for a hundred dollars is a patron and therefore deserves a big martini and an entire evening's consideration. The photographer lady deals in the big stuff, or rather, she visits it. Deploring the rise in prices, a thing any collector can do in one sentence, while declaring in another they are priceless, beyond price, all art is expensive. "What is eight square feet of an Andy Warhol," I venture, "what would you pay for a large Jasper Johns, a canvas equivalent to a four-by-six? Did it take him longer to make it, was it more work?" "Exactly, and this. . . . I saw the other day, it was exquisite, the green, you never saw such a green in a carpet. . . ."

We have also spied a copy of *The New York Times* on her bench and beg to have it. Josef Ibrahim, a different man from our usual correspondent, has written a very literate article on the curtailment of civil rights under the Ayatollah, chapter and verse. We need to read this. We need to tell Khalil and Nersi, our very optimistic brothers. Though more pessimistic throughout the course of the day, they now wonder if my visa will be granted, since the personnel at the consulate, specifically the visa section and Immigration, are exactly, they claim, the same ones who used to give them all such a hard time as student dissenters against the Shah. Nersi is now rewriting the letter again. They will meet us there, it's just upstairs from the American Passport Office.

Where everything goes wrong from the start. Today is of course Friday. Tomorrow is Saturday, the next day is Sunday, and so forth. The plane, however, the one plane that will get us there, is on Sunday as well. Saturday the office is closed. We have today and only today and it is not the custom to complete passports in one day. That's all. "But we have permission." "Stand in Line One." In Line One things go pretty well for a while until my completed form reveals a change of name. "Your last passport says you are Katherine Millett Yoshimura." "Yes, well, that's my husband's name." "You are still married." "Well, as a matter of fact, yes." Why bother to get married when you can live in sin? Until the government intervenes and offers to deport your sweetheart. So you get married for Immigration. But for whom should we bother to get divorced? "Separated," seizing on the term. "Well, you will have to fill out an affidavit, have two blood relatives sign it, takes several days." One blood relative in New York. Mallory. Probably too busy, probably out of town or something. My mother in Minnesota, my sister the lady lawyer in Nebraska. This is ridiculous.

Sophie sure thinks so. "What the hell do you care what name?" "No, this is, believe it or not, important to me. They made me take Fumio's name three passports ago, and we were in a hurry then too and capitulated to them; this time I'm not gonna." The bitter hurry of it, before the trip to England, the first trip out after twelve years of starving artist and graduate student. Going to England as the author of *Sexual Politics*. Brand-new celebrity, VIP treatment on British Airways, publisher pays, the little burst of becoming somebody after thirty-five years of obscurity, twelve of them in a broken-down loft on the Bowery. I would see England and France again having achieved something in the years of apprenticeship, the years since I was an Honours School Oxonian trying to buy cigarettes in Paris mortified by the sound of my own French deliberately misunderstood. I could go back again. A new uncertainty: a women's-libber, the lunatic-fringe, a nut for journalists to ridicule carrying the infection of my *Time* magazine and television notoriety to Oxford. Under an assumed name? Feminist author called Mrs. Fumio Yoshimura. Thanks to the Passport Office. It was Friday then too, I surrendered.

"But we may not be able to go, Nersi is waiting for us upstairs. It's getting late." "Let me give it a try." Actually I foresaw all this upon entering the room. On my way to Line One and deliberately filling out my own name on the form, I already knew the chance—and wanted to take it. I want my name back. In fact, I never lost it, except on my passport. Mallory thought it was a fun disguise in case I ever had to blow the country—passport with an airtight name—Katherine Yoshimura, what an alias; also very euphonic. Back in the late sixties when Mallory thought I ought to keep money in a Swiss bank just in case I had to "pull an Angela Davis," as she called it. You forget, Mallory, Angela never even went as far from her heart's desire as Canada; radicals hate exile.

It appears that this one even dislikes disguise; somehow it seems odd for Kate Millett to be going to Iran to speak on feminism under the government-assigned name of Katherine Yoshimura. Days when Sita and I would disappear in Mexico under husbands' names on passports—partly amused, partly humiliated. But this is different. I go as a feminist, I better wear my own name. The Iranians, if they had second thoughts, might even claim my patriarchal pseudonym was disingenuous. I have that fevered buzz of the gambler or the incipient smallpox victim filling out the form, presenting it, arguing my case, insisting, standing in another line—bigger shot. Finding an angle—I was given my husband's name against my will the first time, never changed my bank account, Social Security, dragging out my driver's license, sticking by my guns. Sophie back and forth between Iranian and American, two floors apart; Nersi is nervous.

Clearly I should give up this little stand, every ounce of common sense demands compromise here—quit it, it's ruinous, you won't get to Iran at all. But I don't want to lose, fold myself up and be what I am not for another five years. So change it when you get home. No, be patient a little, the new guy has given me another form. The new guy is young. Oriental. I explain. I have been married to a Japanese. I even try out a little Japanese. All the wrong tack—he's Chinese. But he has a sense of humor, and finds my error amusing. He could find it a great deal worse; we discuss the Japanese invasion of China in the time of the Second World War. We agree on its crimes and excesses. I am absolved of my marriage. Fumio would love all this—Fumio is the one who taught me his country's wrongs on this occasion, and has charm enough to win over this guy too if he ever met him; he disarms even Koreans. I must remember to tell him this story before I leave. And so the young Chinese official of the U.S. Immigration releases me from my marriage to a Japanese I have always adored but never wished to be married to in the governmental sense and have not even lived with for the last six years, though he is my best and always friend. Liberated and rejoicing, Sophie and I bring the approved document to another desk for processing.

We arrive upstairs at Iranian Immigration at three o'clock. My American passport cooks away somewhere getting done by four. The Iranians close at four-thirty. It's Friday afternoon. This is cutting it close, but it's still possible we may do it. No plane leaving after Sunday could guarantee to get us there by the eighth of March. We sit down with Nersi and wait upon the officials. Sophie is okay. She's a *Ms.* reporter. Or a free-lance journalist to whom *Ms.* has promised nothing but a vague interest in what she may write. A mere formality. It suffices. A lady processes us. She does not wear a veil or even a headscarf, the bureaucratic equivalent. The Ayatollah's picture is everywhere, very new looking. I wonder what happens to the Shah pictures, destroyed or hidden somewhere. The place has a new-order feeling, imparted by a number of crude-looking rented American security guards. They inspected us suspiciously. They reinspect me every time I come back from checking to see if my passport has emerged from the bureaucratic machinery downstairs. Time and again, I run down. The Iranian lady clerk cannot accept my application for a visa until I have my passport in order. One thing has already emerged, however: Nersi would prefer that I didn't present my letter of invitation from Caifi. What then? Get another letter from *Ms.* magazine then. But I'm not a reporter. "We think it wiser. These people hate Caifi. We are in nearly as much trouble now as under the Shah." Nersi has a nearly perfect Persian face, beautiful carved beard, tall, circumspect. He was educated in France, where his parents still live. He is an architect, a gentleman, a scholar. He is reserved, even shy somewhere, but determined. "Khalil and I have discussed it all day—if they make obstacles for us, we will take the easier course. We think it wiser."

I think it most unwise. I'd like to say so, but we can't talk in front of the official. I think it is disingenuous to use *Ms.* as a cover. Good enough way to get a press pass into Angela Davis' trial, and *Ms.* was kind enough to give me one, uncertain whether I'd even write about it or not. And since I went as a supporter, not a reporter, I rather thought I wouldn't. Or thought so at first, until what I saw made me want to write in Angela's defense. But I am not in fact going to Iran as a journalist: part snoop, part free communications—the media as they are; I'm going on a mission to and for my sisters in Iran—and I want that designation.

Nersi makes it plain that the new order is the old order and the lady makes it plain by saying that if I go as anything but a journalist I must stay over till Monday and have a full interview with the consul or his assistant, persons who have already left for the day. An invisible man in an office, a man we never meet and communicate with through her visits to him, does, however, have sufficient authority to grant me a visa as a journalist. Am I not a journalist? The lady probably understands it all, seems quite sympathetic, so does another young woman filling out forms at a desk—we are women, we communicate in vibrations. Nersi is a nervous wreck. In a half-hour—since it's three-thirty by now—can we get a letter from *Ms.* across town? I call Robin Morgan. Sure. We'll call a messenger service. A messenger is not quite certain enough. Nersi has bounded out the door already in pursuit of a piece of paper safer than the one he spent the entire day composing on Caifi stationery, together with the Caifi news release that I am going to speak at International Women's Day at the invitation of Iranian feminists, a release available to all, the Iranian consulate as well as the mass media of the world. No one ever appears to have read it.

I go down to check on my passport; it is a quarter to four. Still not done. I explain the urgency. To a reluctant black woman. She sends me to a white Irish male. He refers me to an older Wasp male. He calls up the processors. Be ready at four. Reassurance. Further waiting with Sophie and the Iranian until Nersi bounds back in. He wears a long blue coat and carries an umbrella, he has the paper, *Ms.* magical trademark—a logo that covers half of the page, and under it one sentence of possible interest in what I may possibly write; this flimsy thing will get me into Iran. Whereas the long careful diplomatic letter of Caifi, the Iranian freedom fighters I've worked with all these years, cannot even be presented. It is a dubious morality, altogether. But I go as a feminist, and a line from a feminist magazine will give me a visa. That or else. Nersi gives me a significant look.

Yes, yes, here's my paper. I present it and plunge downstairs to find my passport just about done—harder, trickier than a baked potato this thing—breathing my desperation at the same black woman who opposed me last time, pleading my case, telling my story, plane's on Sunday, so hard to get into this country, you see. She weakens and calls up another black woman. It's on its way down. "Honey, you just sit on that bench and wait for it." I sit. I wait. They will save me. It comes, at four-fifteen it emerges from some chute and I am an American entitled to go abroad. Under my own name. Upstairs again. I wouldn't dare use the elevator I am in such a panic, and have more or less memorized the elaborate staircase. (Though I did find myself facing German Immigration once instead of United States.) Upstairs again with the Iranians I am finally an American entitled to travel abroad as Kate Millett. Girl reporter for *Ms.* magazine.

A whole day with governments—how soon can we get a drink? It is infuriating, terrifying. Their total power over you, it must be that which fills their offices with such tension, the clerks dispensing fascist regulations, overseeing the tension of the sad bitten faces of the mobs that wait, their stomachs writhing in an anger they cannot even permit themselves to feel. Did the Founding Fathers rid us of a king to bring us to this? Power, the ability to humiliate, refuse, destroy, government's own power, now assumed by the clerk with a perfect and absolute rigidity under the cloak of correct behavior—raise your voice in understandable anger or even humor in these places and look a cop in the face—there is even a line to stand behind in American Immigration—fifteen feet back from the clerk or you're in trouble. Know your place. Responsibility and service right out the window; grace, civility, civilization. Poof.

An anarchist's blood boils. Something must cool it: humor, a glass. Where in god's name is a bar? Bureaucracy must contribute enormously to alcoholism. We must find a way to laugh at this, to talk out of the side of our mouths which have had to shut up for fear of our lives these hours. Nersi was attacked in the hallway at the Iranian consulate; fifteen fanatical followers of Khomeini recognized him. As Caifi, the hated libertarian outfit. Caifi fought against the Shah seven years. While they probably did nothing at all. Fulminated at best, were silent at worst. But now have the voice of raw new power. They would have killed him, he felt, if he were not in a public place. He is very shaken. Wouldn't mind a drink either. We wander around, in the manner of political radicals trying to find a cab but walking six blocks through town traffic, so busy with pent-up conversation and confusion that no one ever calls us to order to remind us to flag the taxi or tell the waiter what we want—a familiar experience but still disconcerting in view of our needs. Or the waiter's sore feet. At last we collect ourselves: Sophie with the documents, Nersi with his gentlemanly overcoat, his umbrella for what has become a sunny day, I with my arm out to waylay a taxi. We are halfway downtown before we decide where to go; but at least we're downtown. So displaced that familiar streets are unfamiliar.

First we'll collect Khalil at the Caifi office and tell him the news and inspect the first draft of the press release and drink deli coffee which arrives just as we've decided a drink is better. The office is Caifi plus Hector Moroquin, plus all the Latin-American prisoner-support groups crowded into one small room and one other very small room and a toilet. Caifi is closing down—a thing I deeply regret—the need of it is urgent now. But Nersi is going home, Khalil is going home. Everyone else is home already. "Remember you said we should wait and see if rights still needed protection from abroad? Don't they?" "We can't stay anymore." The two of them like boys missing a football match. The revolution proceeding without them into they don't quite know what yet. And homesick. Exile is long. They have already lost their professions (architecture and engineering) to years of political activity. Khalil feels alone carrying the office with less political experience than Nemat and his other predecessors. He feels young. Green. Scared. Confused. And yet his press release is competent, his arrangements seem in order. This is a hard day for him. His young American wife is perched on a desk, says she saw me in Houston. I wonder how the years of struggle for Iranian rights have been for her; Khalil is never home. He is now on his way out to have a drink with us at my studio, the Bowery. No, she doesn't want to come with us. Nersi has told Sophie that Khalil's wife is leaving him tomorrow morning. I guess he needs a drink.

As we pass out, I see a beautiful poster, stark black and white—a superb design. Elegant Persian script on a pure background. "That's our last one," Khalil says. "We threw all the others away. The prisoners are free now." But the poster . . .

Walking through the Village down from Union Square, knowing I am going to Iran. Every street precious, piquant somehow against the light of the adventure we enter. We consider taking a cab, but prefer the walk, for talking, for relaxing. Nersi walks with Sophie, in whom he appears to have taken some gallant interest; Khalil is my escort, the word "escort" recurring to me from his invitation—that we should have an escort. A humorous thought. It seems years since I promenaded with a man escorting me. Yet it appears that we shall be unescorted to Iran; Nersi must go first to France and will not be leaving for a week; Khalil will be in New York at least a month before he closes up the office. Like many of Caifi's initial arrangements, the escort falls by the board, disregarded; we never needed an escort anyway, as far as I could see; Caifi people will be meeting our plane. Kateh will put us up. Her parents' house; it sounds comfortable. And Khalil is in ecstasy that I should go to Isfahan and stay with his parents and his brother, old-world hospitality, mosques and museums. We ramble from the political situation and the article in the *Times,* to tourism, art and architecture, consultation with Nersi on what buildings to look out for, what shrines he most admires. What the weather will be.

By the time we're at the Bowery, Khalil, who is trying out a martini for the first time, is sure there will be blossoms. It will be spring. We should bring the Persian poets with us. The two of them, these gentle handsome men, joined by Sophie's closest friend, Pamela, and my dear Fumio, the group gathered on rugs and cushions around the low pine table before the Franklin stove at the Bowery, the fire in our glasses, the lamplight—as I approach them, observing them all with love, bringing more ice and just putting the bottle nakedly on the table—seem to constitute every vestige of civilization in which our terrible day has been deficient.

But now we are triumphant. Safe in our fortress, surrounded by our artifacts, books, pictures, sculptures. We have not only survived, we have come off victorious. Humbled we were, scared, almost we were beaten. But we came off with the magic amulet for the journey, the correct talisman demanded by the dragon and the ogre. Sophie and I are now being blessed by those who love us. Those who send us to their own. Those of our own who bid us a good time and plenty of excitement. We are going. We have the visas. We are celebrating.

We are also getting pissed. As Sophie later described it. Perhaps some debauch was a necessary corrective. Nersi and Khalil hold forth about Iranian history, the 1906 revolution, Mossadegh, this Shah, his old man, the one before, the ones all before that. They are in a fine republican fervor. They rehearse the insurrection, their friends' reports, the excitement of those days in February. Pamela and Sophie fill in on the Near East, their adventures as journalists there, their passports seized once, the agony of South Africa, where Pamela was raised, educated, though she is forbidden to reenter it as an enemy of the apartheid state and has wandered from England to America and will be back there again if she can't get a residency here, the state of her case, further tribulations with Immigration. Fumio's early difficulties in coming to America because he had taught an art course for railroad workers, which once struck the American officials as proof of communist subversion. "We are all somehow in transition," Sophie laughs, "dependent somehow on your government." Looking at me. Indeed, we all suddenly notice I am the only American in this New York Bowery loft where we all belong and are having a glorious time—how silly it is.

Khalil describes how he and his brother Saïd have managed to go on studying abroad and doing radical politics at the same time, the fine line his parents in Iran must tread thereby, the finer line between the errant sons and their more conservative sire—"Times, we just blackmail him," he laughs. Parents in general. Nersi, even more homesick than Khalil, and moodier, gradually morose, increasingly dogmatic, Marxist intransigence. Pamela and Sophie, who have been lovers and are still the closest of friends, discuss friends in England. Fumio and I grow giddy, he puts on my terrible Irish ballad record, always a signal for my decline. We are in our cups.

By now a happy chaos, Fumio and I wander off to debate art in some declamatory manner I could not even remember the next day, nor just why I got so mad at him because the sculpture I left in his leaky warehouse in Tokyo got thrown out by the family, or even how much his mother liked the Mexican shawls I sent with him on his last visit home this month. But that a whole roll of my drawings had just disappeared from the shed, seem to have just vanished—this did get to me. "You remember the ones on heavy rice paper? A whole roll. I have only six left in the world—I had hundreds." "You sold some." "No more than ten." "What does it matter, you make millions of drawings." "These were valuable to me." "You'll get better." "Listen, they were even good."

I am still berating him for it when everyone stumbles off into the dark in front of Phoebe's—it is necessary to eat sometimes—where Pamela claims to have supported both Nersi and Khalil into a cab, leaving Sophie and Fumio and me to a Phoebe dinner, which I disturb by hectoring Fumio for having been so critical of my last sculpture show. Though tonight he permitted himself to admire a print of mine: a huge brushline breast with a large cherry at the top of the ice-cream-sundae-type nipple, and the legend "There are times when you're on top of the world." "Not so bad," he says, brat grin of a little brother. Or perhaps an eternal elder brother, smarter male. Or general smart aleck, critical of everything. Even himself. When he is nearly satisfied with his own work, "not so bad" is still all he says. We made friends at my studio in Tokyo, when leafing through the place he looked at all the sculpture (sculpture I heard he later praised extravagantly), saying to Yoshiko, his first wife, "kind of interesting." I ended up renting his studio when he came to America, and when Yoshiko died I ended up falling in love with him and living with him. I am still trying to learn how fifteen years later. He still thinks he's smarter than god. I still find him charming for every other reason but exasperating for this one. His charm, the boy quality, the naughtiness. That is the thing with Fumio—that you can never really get mad at him because of his grin, because at the next moment he will surprise you with a compliment, a kindness, a lad's surreptitious fling of sewing a button on your coat while you were out of town and waiting to see if you notice it. We are becoming friends. It will take us all our lives.

Then I guess I got over being mad and we had a nice coffee and Drambuie and were maudlin and reminiscent, but I don't recall very much beyond saying good night to him at Third Street and marching fiercely home past all the Bowery drunks, almost sober myself and now thoroughly happy. Going to Iran. Going to Sophie. We are going to Iran.

4

TODAY WE ARE on our way. The laundry will be ready at three-thirty, Nersi and Khalil come to take us to the airport at a quarter to four.

A thousand things to do before Khalil and Nersi arrive. At least we got the tape recorder, hitting Lafayette just as they closed and the man from whom I so recently bought an expensive tape deck refuses to open up for five minutes to sell me something portable. "We've got the cash, we know just which model." He shakes his head, adamant,

"Mean, really, they never were any good to us," Sophie says. "Let's try the place up the block." "If it's still open." It is and they are glorious to us, kind, gentle, painstaking, they explain everything perfectly, testing each piece of equipment as they give it to us; they know we can't come back for some inconsequential adapter or gadget without which . . . and they have entered into the spirit of our adventure. They know where we're going, they know what we need. The electricity over there is 220; they figure with this adapter you're okay. "But no recharge, I'm afraid." They tease us to be careful over there, they send us out of the store ready to embrace them. How different one experience can be from another, even commercial ones, purchases, how unpleasant or how delightful. So we are wired up for sound, a big machine for interviews, audio track, stable occasions, and a little machine I call my whisper box, into which I can breathe my thoughts, substitute for a notebook. We're all right for tape, in fact we have been taping already, farewells and feminist messages, the fifteen different telephone conversations to France to obtain Simone de Beauvoir's unlisted number. Never obtained. Irony that I should have her address and visit her in Paris, send her flowers upon every arrival, have lunch with her upon fortunate occasions—but never, since I approach her with our old-world St. Paul courtesies, never have had occasion to ring her on the phone. And need her now, with more urgency than a telegram.

But everything is urgent today. Nersi and Khalil will be here in an hour to take us to the airport, and the laundry has not arrived. It is our good fortune to have a laundry man a block away, who is, because an Orthodox Jew, closed on Saturday, yet actually open on Sunday. He has promised it would be ready, he knows we're going out of the country, we mustn't worry, we've been together fifteen years. There are other, more urgent problems. Ruth is buying us film, both still film and movie film. It would not be a problem, buying on Sunday, our filmmaker friends assured us. Willoughby's. But of course there are problems. We should have done it yesterday. Instead of books, for god's sake. But yesterday, we were still not sure. The Eclair at the farm is too heavy, we needed a Bolex. Rent it? They never work. And it's too late to rent one now, the weekend. Who would loan one to us? Then my friend Susan who made *Three Lives* with me came through. She has been teaching us her camera all afternoon between calls to France and scattered attempts to pack without underwear, socks, shirts, the laundry man's contributions.

Sophie learns the camera. I say good-bye to my younger sister Mallory, who assures me the Iranians are the most beautiful people in the world. "I mean the most physically beautiful. Their faces. Everyone in the whole damn country is beautiful. The men. The women. Everywhere you look, these wonderful faces. I'm a photographer, I almost went crazy looking at them." "You're the first encouraging note I've heard. Our elder sister Sally thinks I'm crazy; Mother's worried to death." "Usual thing. Never mind, you'll love it. I've got to get off the phone now because the washing machine's making its 'I'm done now' noises." "Lucky you, we haven't got any laundry at all." "Don't worry, it will all work out. How I envy you guys. Have a great time, get an eyeful."

Ruth keeps calling from Willoughby's. "They're out of the color you wanted. They have only twenty rolls of Tri-X in cans, what shall I do?" "Get what you can. Get more tape." "You have a lot of tape already, don't you?" "There's never enough tape. How much more money do you have?" "I've spent four hundred on movie stuff and about two on still stuff." "Spend the rest, spend it all. And get back as soon as you can. Nersi and Khalil are here already, we're going to have to leave."

Fumio appears. Nersi, Khalil and Fumio try to talk politics while Sophie and I try to pack. Without the laundry. It must be done now, they were going to deliver it, but they still don't come. Fumio goes off to pick up the laundry. His laundry man too, fifteen years in America. He is Ruth's as well, the whole neighborhood is here helping us, help without which it is obvious we would never be able to leave, dubious still if we will. So disorganized. The film isn't here yet. Fumio returns to say the laundry is closed, the doors locked, padlocked. Impossible. Sophie is mad with wrath, betrayed; I begin to wonder if she'll still go. "Three weeks without underwear"—a tirade from a gentle spirit driven past her limits. We all try hard not to laugh. "I guess we'll just have to go anyway. But jeans!" "Right, how can you even be an American without jeans?" Fumio is delighted. I'm not. I'm stuck with all these long dresses I now have to cart instead. "Why on earth are you bringing that along?" Sophie asks. "Short speech, may be a lot of socializing." Everyone tells me you're supposed to be feminine or old-fashioned or something over there. Expectations of parties, polite ladylike gatherings, early feminism; I'm just trying to do the right thing. "They don't like women in pants maybe?" I make a face at her. "No, it's about the chador, silly, not dresses." "This is the only manner of conformity my imagination can arrive at." Sophie, who travels, has banged all over the Near East being a journalist, has packed a little suitcase, light as a feather. I have an enormous duffel bag on loan, weighted down with books and notebooks, art and architecture, history and politics and a hundred changes of dignified costume all getting hopelessly wrinkled. "You'll regret it." "I already do. But what with no jeans, turtleneck pullovers, etc., what can I do?" "You can hurry."

There is an urgency settling in on all of us. We stop laughing and resume packing. We are leaving, we have to leave. It is happening. Without the laundry. Almost without the film, but Ruth arrives in the nick of time, loaded with cellophane bags of thirty-five-millimeter, cans of sixteen, more tape, further batteries, receipts. We've gone the whole way, spent every cent we dared. While Sophie and Susan pack the film and catalog it, I sit Nersi down to count what is left of our two thousand stash after technology has taken its toll for the work we will do. "Count the money into two piles, please, I've got to finish packing." He looks disturbed. "In case anything does go wrong, Sophie and I will have the same amount of money; in case we get separated." He probably thinks my paranoia and quiet vehemence are crazy, but it is at this moment that I begin to realize we are going into what really may after all be trouble. Not when my mother moans on the phone or my friends give my arm a squeeze and tell me to take it easy over there, be careful, but now at the moment Nersi says we have each four hundred and forty-seven dollars. And that's all. Three weeks on four hundred dollars doesn't buy you much hotel or dinner, and three weeks is a long time in a very foreign and rather expensive country. Hopefully our friends will take care of that, are meeting us at the airport, Khalil assures us he's taking care to call them, we mustn't worry about a thing.

The two piles of bills side by side. Us. Sophie and I. Our destiny. Having spent all the rest on film and tape—the means of making the record. Susan straps up the camera bag, my Nikon and Pamela's old reflex which Sophie's shot with for years, the Bolex with the turret lenses, Susan's own treasure she is generously sending along with us. My duffel bag just outside the dressing room strewn with clothes, Sophie's neat suitcase. That's it.

Nersi is now emptying the garbage, his perfect composure, his elegance even at this moment. Khalil has succeeded in hooking up the mysterious answering machine to the telephone; the wizardry I succumbed to and bought in California, like Deana's but now more complicated in New York than it ever was out there. It pays to have an engineer around. Fumio is engaging everyone in political conversations, he almost seems lonesome. I wish he'd put the car in the parking lot so it wouldn't get towed away. But I'm loath to ask him. Like Ruth, he has been such an angel, has already done so many favors. He thinks of it himself, having thought of everything today, even the names of obscure figures in early-twentieth-century history, Iranian and Japanese. It is a wrench every time he goes down the stairs, leaving him. Ruth, beatifically doing the dishes: "You shouldn't leave the place like this. I'll do them for you. Teresa will water the plants the second week, I'll do it the first, don't worry about putting a message on, you haven't time, I'll do it." Ruth's message begins: "Hello, Kate is unable to come to the phone just now." "My god, Ruth, it sounds like I'm just in the can or something." "Say you're out of town and they'll rob your house, this neighborhood, believe me I know." "You should, you damn near run the place by now." Ruth whom we all coaxed out of a respectable address so she could have a loft and really become a sculptor is becoming the scourge and savior of the Lower East Side, has organized every artist in the district to save their studios from the wrecking ball. I look around my own studio, not Bohème, the old one which the city wrecked, the gaping hole where it was sits just out the window on the corner, but this is, I must confess, even better than the old one, this is the best studio I ever had in my life and probably the only one I ever want and I love it, the work of my own hands. It's a strange hurt to say good-bye to the place.

It's that or you miss the plane. Following Fumio and Sophie and Ruth and Khalil and Nersi, everybody carrying, hugging, hurrying us into a cab. The four of us. Sophie and I and our Iranian escorts. Ruth and Fumio disappear on the curb, big and little figures, her mass and height, his slender and trim little figure, two arms waving and waving passing out of sight before the funny tall loft building, tallest in the block, its absurd big sign on the ground floor proclaiming Intergalactic Art, some kid artist who lived on the first floor four years ago and never paid the rent having conceived this, commissioned its execution in letters eighteen inches high. Somehow no one has ever taken it down. Home is gone now, we're off.

PART II

1 ✻ ✻ ✻

THE FIRST SIGHT of them was terrible. Like black birds, like death, like fate, like everything alien. Foreign, dangerous, unfriendly. There were hundreds of them, specters crowding the barrier, waiting their own. A sea of chadori, the long terrible veil, the full length of it, like a dress descending to the floor, ancient, powerful, annihilating us. And the men beside them too, oddly enough, nondescript in their badly cut Western suits, a costume that had none of the power of an Arab robe. And in giving themselves this bit of "Westernism," this suit that looks, like the suits on men in Japan, never really right since it is an adopted clothing, a deference to the wealth and political force of another section of persons, the men announce their alliance with the "new," the world of business and technology, currency and bureaucratic forms and industrialism. Relegating women to the old, the traditional, the tribal garment. In Japan it is ceremonial and decorative, here merely punitive and abject. The men control them, insignificant as they appear, hardly visible before the splendor and drama of the chador.

Yet if the women were alone they would be wonderful; awesome, even frightening—for there is a mana of antiquity in the sight of their chador, the length, the ferocity of that fall of black cloth, the masses of them like the chorus in Greek tragedy. You would never be close to it; these women seem utterly closed to women. Here in this public place

49

defended by their robes, the fabric held tightly under the chin, much of the face hidden by the fold of cloth as it peaks over the forehead or is folded hard against forehead obscuring it altogether. And the hair hidden, the friendliness of hair, from woman to woman, its personality, its sexual innocence, the signal of animal humanity.

Yet the chador is theater, some theater of women so old I no longer know it. Before this garment was forced upon us for our shame, it must have been our pride; before it was compelled upon us, we must have worn it out of self-love, vanity, grace, thoroughly conscious how glamorous it could be in evening, how seductive. A glance thrown from it, the way it frames the face, reveals the bones, accentuates, turns every face into mystery, eyes, eyebrows speaking. Effective. As all frames are. As all costume heightens. And it is surely costume, the thrill of theater in it. But the threat too.

Look at them and they do not look back, even the friendly curiosity with which women regard each other. Still wearing the cloth of their majesty, they have become prisoners in it. The bitterness, the driven rage behind these figures, behind these yards of black cloth. They are closed utterly. The small, hardly visible men in their suits have absolute control here.

I wonder if the women on the airplane on the way here have ducked back into their headscarves or have dared to enter this crowd without them. I understand now their fear. This is real, and I had only thought they were squeamish, sissy. The crowd before us is adamant, like an ancient obdurate wall of conformity. And behind them you already see the guns. Big ones. Machine guns carried in the arms of militia, some in uniform, some not, but equally ferocious, insanely proud of the object they hold, its authority; new, superbly new, the importance it gives them, the masculinity in a country now in a paroxysm of masculinity. Here is the crowning emblem. Always just about to go off. From the way they hold it you doubt their knowledge of the weapon, are sure it is recently acquired. Their fingers are on the trigger, actually on the trigger, they even carry it and walk along with their fingers on the trigger, naive belief in the magic of the safety catch. Out hunting I once nearly shot a friend by that sort of credulity. The way guns are carried here, displayed, the arrogance of it, the swagger, has even in the half-hour going through customs made me angry and frightened ten times over. How oppressive the size of these weapons, not your policeman's little pistol covered by a holster, but huge, bigger than carbines, faster, more delightful to their possessor, more intimidating to all others.

There are guns everywhere, and when you look around, you discover that they are often pointed at you. In a moment our friends will appear, we'll be out of this, our eyes darting along the faces at the barricade. That moment of truth when you reach the barricade after customs and your friend calls out your name and you smile and people watch you and you are both self-consciously embarrassed and delighted. And saved, crossing over into their arms, you become a private person, no longer stared at, but claimed. For everyone stares at us, we are foreigners, foreign women, the men staring in thousands of ways, the women staring inscrutably from the chador but when we look at them they look away; shut, disapproving.

We are even becoming something of a public spectacle; the fact that we are not being met is becoming public knowledge, the fact of our being unclaimed. When it is so obvious we expect it, our look of anticipation, our assurance that Kateh will be here, that Khalil will have called her. An article of faith to us. And of course she won't be wearing a chador, she'll look like us, she'll be easy to recognize. The people are pressing behind us, we cannot stand here forever searching the crowd behind the barrier, examined and rejected by each of them as we scan one after another for a fellow spirit. Perhaps Kateh sent someone else, Caifi are always doing things like that, one person's busy, another one is dispatched to an airport to pick up an arrival. Who looks the right type? Sort of hip, radical, young, studentlike, the appropriate clothing. There are only two young women without chador in the whole crowd. We are examining it from the back now, having so spectacularly failed the applause moment of being greeted before the throng. In fact we are trying to disappear in it, so intense are the stares.

I stand by the bags, feeling absurd in my English bobby's cape, in shape a chador without a hood, my head an object of reproach, my very existence somehow an affront. The happy traveler. With a submachine gun trained on her from the guard at the front door. He is actually pointing this thing at me, I say to myself, Sophie gone off to page our friends; here is your adventure in Iran you were so crazy to have against all your friends' better judgment, your mother's warning, trying to grin at the guard, trying to be so obviously harmless he will dismiss me and get on to something better.

Travelers are trying to leave through his door, he is giving them the runaround, insisting they use another door, strutting his petty power, being a nuisance, exciting himself to wrath with that weapon in his hands. His superior comes over, dashing type in a jumpsuit, smaller but more glamorous gun, probably Air Force paratrooper, the crack troops here, they armed the insurgents on the great day of the Revolution—21 Bahman (February).

See it all historically; a newly armed populace of course will be fascinated, even childishly fascinated with its weapons, the power they represent, having been shoved around for years by creeps with guns, they will all too easily strut and be insolent having their own—but not in the same entire abuse of power. These are the militia, not the Shah's Savak. You would never have been permitted to enter this airport at all in the old days; and you are an oddity, so calm down. Sit down, in fact, if you want to stop drawing attention. There are other unfortunates whose friends have failed to arrive, it's probably just traffic. I console myself with tobacco and smile at the woman on the next bench. She smiles back. We have arrived in the late evening, the exchange is closed, we have no Iranian money, only one phone number and address in Tehran. If this is not just a little mix-up, it could be a dead end. Rather humbling. Very frightening.

Sophie says it's a little more serious than that, she has begged a coin to use the phone; Kateh's mother had no idea we were coming, Kateh isn't home. Though she speaks little English, Kateh's mother has conveyed her sense that we are dangerous, she recognizes her daughter knows us but it is unwise to speak on the phone, and it would be more graceful perhaps to betake ourselves to a hotel and straighten everything out in the morning. Well, all right, a hotel, I seem to have forgotten that there are hotels, though without money it may be hard to get to one. Sophie dispatches me to the travelers' aid, where a good-looking man with a gun hears my sad tale and changes a twenty-dollar bill. He is going to "The States" in two weeks, he can use the money. Going to Virginia, he says. I tell him Virginia is lovely just now, the blossoms should be out. He says they won't be out here for quite a while, it's been a very cold winter. We are getting along famously, it is almost normal.

Even the guns and the checkpoints on the way to the hotel he has sent us to seem plausible. The hotel itself is overly so—a Sheraton. All one's fantasies of real Persian hotels, beautiful and subtle as Japanese inns—all that out the window. That we have a roof over our heads, running water, a bed after two days of airplane. That is enough. Though it sets the teeth on edge to look at the Arya Sheraton. Awful monumental concrete pile, American anonymous modern transported here, in fact the whole neighborhood is such, and in the days after, as we drove through the city we discovered more dismal "new" buildings than I have ever seen anywhere else in the world. The Shah was in a rage of producing this stuff, to make an entire city of totalitarian modern, a monument to himself, to the conquerors who sponsored him, a tribute to Western imperialism, destroying all indigenous buildings, leaving only these skeletons of half-built towers we see through the windows of our room.

The Sheraton is sandbagged in front. More sandbags in the lobby. Young men with machine guns lolling about to "defend" it from some anonymous attackers. The hotel is nearly deserted. Merely a dozen guests lost in its towers. The hotel staff seem unhappy. Under guard. This is no way to run a place of hostelry, they seem to say. One is even quite open with Sophie over his dissatisfaction. We call Kateh again. She had not expected us, or certainly not so soon. Khalil had waited till the last moment to call Tehran and say we were coming. His paranoia, his precaution, his plain old error, perhaps—but arriving like this, unexpected, or not expected for several days, seems to make us a bit less welcome, a bit of a nuisance. There is little room at Kateh's house, they are crowded with family, her brother Khosrow and his wife and children, Kateh herself and her husband, Babak, are there as well; but we are welcome to sleep on the floor. Awkward. We should stay here, even though we hate it and can't really afford it. Nor did we come all the way to Tehran to live in a hotel; a friend's floor is better. It would be better to be with Kateh tonight; she thinks there is still someplace open where we can all get dinner. "No, on second thought, eat at your hotel and we will send someone to pick you up there when you're finished."

A man comes to bring us towels and we mistake him for a subversive force, howling, "Holy, holy, holy," outside our door. We say we don't want any. Further awkwardness in checking out, the room immaculate, still without towels. At the elevator we meet the towel man having another go at it. A go at us too, elaborate attempts to shake our hands, then to kiss us; we tire of international goodwill and close the elevator door, expecting the worst from the management. Our sudden departure. Explain it as best we can.

Dinner is in the basement, Sheraton's Italian-grotto motif, arranged somewhere else for somewhere else or nowhere at all. The swimming pool just outside the windows is equally "international" in flavor, equally flavorless. Its invitation to the sun, to drinks by poolside, to languor and relaxation, are now only symptoms of decadence. It is also decadent to ask the waiter for a drink. "Alcohol is no longer served," he rebukes me. "But it's on the menu." Until a few days ago you could have a drink here, now it's against the law. Doesn't that seem a pity? I ask him, acknowledging the power of the state over our lives, but curious to know if there is any sense of how arbitrary it all is. Doesn't he think many of the people having dinner here would like to have a beer or a glass of wine with their food, even a little whiskey beforehand? Does he drink himself, does he know how it relaxes you when you're tired, nervous, frustrated? What will it do to a whole population to be without this little pleasure, to have it made against the law? I wheedle, but he's not buying any. The very fact that I dare to discuss Muslim law is impiety. The people at the next table stare and then smile; they are in agreement with us probably as he reports our scandalous remarks.

We suffer through dinner: everything one would hate about a Western multinational corporation is here: the mediocre tasteless food (neither Western nor Eastern nor food), the showy swimming pool to intimidate the poor, the hot, the dusty, the millions who would never be permitted in the door, even the phony decor. And nothing redeemable is left either; the food seems deliberately disimproved and carelessly served, the pleasure of the pool is lost forever since you are sure they will never fill it again. Two corny Western-style bars and you can't have even one drink. As if everything that might be fun is now governmentally interdict. What an odd way to liberate a place. Instead of confiscating the imperialist fat-cat stuff and democratizing the enjoyment of it—instead, what few pleasures it offered have all been forbidden. To everyone.

The just resentment against foreign things, foreign money, foreign arrogance has run its course to a kind of xenophobia. The young militiamen surround us up at the desk and demand to know where we are going. Are we American? Sophie is quick to claim her Canadian dispensation. I answer that I am American, as if it were a crime for which I am expected to take responsibility. Why are we going out at night? Our friends are coming to get us. We are bourgeois foreigners according to them. We ask if they are socialists, leftists. We get little satisfaction here. They are the Islamic revolution, they are from the Komiteh. An earlier bunch—they have just changed guard—had felt like leftist students; these now feel like Khomeini types, the good boys at the mosque who Khalil says are replacing the leftists—but to a woman both give off the same threat, the same obdurate male stance. I ask them about the women. Becoming suspicious thereby. Why ask about that? I want to know what the women will gain by the revolution. "We got rid of the Shah." "Of course, and the women helped to do it, but what will it be like for women now?" "Our women are happy. They do what we want." Another laughs. How easy and infuriating this humor over women, how universal. "That's happiness?" "Why you ask about this?" a third demands, gun in hand. "Because I'm a feminist." A dangerous thing to say, but I risk it, having talked to them long enough now to have established contact, they are unlikely even to arrest me.

We are waiting for our friends, hours of waiting; we still don't know it, but it is only the beginning of our days of waiting. Sophie is talking to the desk clerk, a very different conversation from mine with the militia. Pouring out to her all his detestation of the new regime, his frustration and that of his colleagues—no one comes to the hotel anymore, no one wants to be bossed by the soldiers, denied a drink. The Intercontinental is getting all their business, it is still almost a hotel rather than a branch of the police and the state, it still sells alcohol, it is full of reporters. Sophie makes a mental note to stay at the Intercontinental if she is ever in need of a hotel. She's a reporter; he must tell her what it's like here. And listens to the man's woes. He develops a great interest in her. Becoming inquisitive, becoming forward, offering his services, would we like him to act as our interpreter during our visit here? Sophie decides he's a spy. I decide our friends are never coming long before one of them, Bahram, calls to say there are thirty-two checkpoints to get through between us, and they think it too dangerous. It has taken them this long just to locate a car.

"Are they always this inefficient, these friends of yours in Caifi?" Sophie is miffed. We have been two hours in the lobby exposed to hotel clerks and soldiery. The humiliation of reregistering lies ahead of us; having checked out, we must now check in again. "I can't understand what's the matter, they're always wonderful to work with." Trying to imagine what it means to get through thirty-two check-points; coming here, they didn't stop our cab, but would they stop Caifi, search, question? Thirty-two times. Of course they couldn't come. We are being inconsiderate, we are failing to notice that this is a country under armed guard only a few weeks after an insurrection; if we are not in the midst of a revolution, we are at least in the midst of a counterrevolution, which, because so much is still in flux, might still come out all right.

We have only to wait and see, we have only to be patient, going to bed at the Sheraton, talking into our tape recorder, the day a confusing mass behind us. We are rather alone in Tehran.

I turn to Sophie. We turn together to our tape recorder and summarize. The first sounds it emits much later: "My god," then another exhausted "My god." Then I hear myself:

"Listen, I don't know about you, but I was frightened."

"I wasn't scared, I was just angry nobody was there, after traveling all this way, all that trouble. After everything went so smoothly at the other end. There we were, stranded, hopeless. Helpless." Poor Sophie, I got her into all this.

"Did look bad. Did you think we'd have to turn around and go back?" Sheepish laughter before a nightmare prospect.

"I thought of that. I thought we could stay overnight at the airport and then book home again."

"Can you imagine showing up again at home?" Further laughter.

"We'd have to hide out at the farm. But the laundry might be done by now."

"I was also afraid we just might get shot. All the time you were off at travelers' aid, I was stuck there in my bobby coat conspicuous by this pillar and trying not to tremble. This gun pointed right at me."

"Just for being a foreign lady and looking him in the eye."

Leftists and their guns, the boys from Columbia, the boys from the left, the antiwar movement, the Che killer-hero boys one grew up knowing in America, in France, Latin America, now here finally armed and no longer merely posing. The ones downstairs at the hotel, the second bunch looking pious and even fiercer, religion behind the barrel of a gun. No one knowing even how to hold one. And the failure of the left here, the vacuum into which Khomeini has stolen to snatch away the triumph of the insurrection. There isn't any real left. The Fedayeen are too small. The Tudeh (old-line Stalinist party) are compromised, have backed the mullahs. Nobody right now, or rather no group, is holding out for democratic rights. "Compare how well a French or Italian Communist party could handle this," Sophie points out. "But isn't there an official provisional government that has that to look after?" "And also an unofficial government, Khomeini, who holds no office and therefore no responsibility and rules through decrees, directives, a really perfect situation for dictatorship."

"There was a man following us down to dinner and then back to the desk," Sophie observes, "and I think it would be better if you don't ask for ice, ask for ice water. We make ourselves a little bit less obvious thereby for drinking." "But it was the clerk's idea, he suggested I order some ice and just give it all up for today. I was thinking of going to bed. You know, the younger fellow—he said to me all he'd like to do is just enjoy his life. I told him I was an artist and I couldn't agree with him more. In a way, he's the very person for whom the revolution is supposed to be made."

Our glasses tinkle months later and six thousand miles away on the tape as we mull over the practice of flagellating people for drinking, deciding hopefully it's in the provinces, some little village mullah making himself important. What do they do to women? we wonder.

"They probably have no idea what to do with women. I suspect that lady journalist is the only acceptable occupation for us, otherwise it would be 'Where's your husband?'"

"The clerk actually did ask me that. I told him I did have one but we got along much better after we'd separated. He thought that was a very peculiar answer but he rather liked it when he thought about it. Do you think we're bugged?"

"I've been bugged. Not only in the Near East. In Montreal once. Went right into my room to set it up. I realized when I saw they'd left the cap off my deodorant. I'd never do that." Sophie's exactitude. "I confronted security at the Holiday Inn there and they insisted they had every right to do it under the martial law, FLQ days, you know, I'd talked to someone in the FLQ and they felt perfectly all right about listening."

"Sophie, today when we hit that wall of chadori, that wall of women—you know, later on, they looked like nuns—but at first they were terrifying, hostile, ancient, alien. We just came out of customs laughing like college girls, dragging that foolish duffel bag of mine, and there they were. After the women on the plane, I never expected these women, full chador, full barrier." "Everything seems to be about clothing. What clothes mean." "You know Swift's *Tale of a Tub*? It's a joke about Dissenters and Christianity, about making a coat correctly and Jack cut it one way, Peter another, some other guy doing it on the jib—and they're floating around the ocean arguing and yelling and screaming about this coat. Symbol becomes reality and people will kill for it. Big Endians and little Endians."

"The enormous hostility of women, their closedness." "That whole wall of black figures, that's all I saw until the gun pointing right at me. And no one to meet us." "Well, I was mad." I feel apologetic listening to Sophie, for having thought this up. "I vowed I would never get myself into this sort of situation again after the last time when I was going to be put in prison in Syria. And when I saw the women in veils, afraid to speak to us—that woman I asked a question, actually just how to use the telephone. Waiting for her husband who'd gone off for a moment and was coming back. She was afraid to death of being seen with me. Yet there's a silent kind of communication: she knew that I knew she was intimidated. And when she left she snuck me a little glance and a smile. Like, "Forgive me, I can't manage any more than this now." "It's familiar, isn't it? From home, from women every-where."

"You know the women on the plane, getting ready to put back on that headscarf—it's like striptease in reverse—the headscarf is the last thing to go, the most important symbol they have. They can emerge out into the world when they leave this country and behave like you and I, and then, coming back . . ."

"What is so volatile about a woman's hair? You know, when I was a child growing up, there was St. Paul and what St. Paul had to say about covering your hair in church. There were veils we wore, hats, those hats were powerful. I forgot mine once, completely forgot it, went right through mass, and walking home I touched my head and realized I'd heard the whole mass with a bare head—I felt I'd committed the greatest sacrilege. I'd been naked, my head, my hair was naked."

"Looks like you're out of the same mold."

"I'm telling you it's everywhere, this taboo. But after I'd been in the airport awhile and had seen the chador from behind, I began to hallucinate they were nuns. Almost felt like going up to them to ask 'Sister' for permission for something or other, use the toilet maybe. I started to realize the veil is continuous. All through our world and across the East, the babushka in Russia and the Slavic countries, shawls in Spain. Remember those hats our mothers wore—with veils?"

"Yes, and the Greeks, the folks in the biblical-times pictures," Sophie's voice.

"The veil stretches all the way from the Near East and Islam across the West and Christianity."

"It still existed in our childhood. At least to wear a hat and be a proper lady."

"Pulling your forelock is what it is. Submission, subjection, abnegation, conformity. The women on the plane, their babushkas, their French *foulards,* do not satisfy the requirement in any real sense. But some genuflection has to be made."

"But the women on the airplane—I don't think I'm being paranoid—you remember, as the time drew near . . . Well, you know how friendly they had been—they were the ones who started the conversation—but when they knew why you had come, to speak at the rally, they got strange."

"But one said 'thank you,' you know, the one we called the French one 'cause she wore this funny Simone de Beauvoir toque thing as her little genuflection. We had a great conversation in French and she told the others. She actually said thank you—she kept on giving me the fist, you know, 'right on.'"

"But as we were about to land, they reversed themselves."

"In the airport they didn't want to know us."

"Right, I tried to speak to one going through customs, I asked her the right time because that's about all I'm ever sure of in French." Sophie's French, the bane of her existence. "At the roundabout, picking up the luggage, I asked her where she was living. And she said Naples."

"She was very lively in the plane, when they were talking about Khomeini."

"They all were, pounding the backs of the chairs on the plane—remember how they were?"

I remember very well, feeling at the time that these were gestures of women who have been given education, energy, argument, logic—all that education means. And individual identity—yet it all went away when we entered. We would see it again, and love it, knowing how hard it was to maintain here, knowing how deeply it was forbidden in public, in the traditional behavior public places now demanded, more even than they had before.

Sophie has noticed another thing about that disputation—that when women dispute, they tend to move their hands in a circle while making a point, rather than shaking a finger in the strident way of men, the particularly strident manner of male leftist exhortation; instead there is something pacific, conciliatory, agreeable in the circular motion of the woman's hand in speech, it persuades rather than dictates.

"You remember the tarts, though?" I suddenly remember them myself, how these two amazing females in the brassiest outfits had taken the whole somber airport by storm. So strumpet. Their costume actually a costume, out-harloting every cliché and arriving at a work of art. Highest heels, the flimsiest skirts, hair dyed and flying in the wind as they raced in and shouted the names of their arrivals. Nothing in the world intimidated them, not the chador, not the guns.

"Real outlaws, I loved them."

"You see them somewhere else and you'd think—my, how ridiculous."

"Like Punkers," Sophie muses. "Like punk rock and CBGB they looked."

"The lipstick, the tight clothes. Nail polish. They become gestures of defiance, not just imperialist Western decadence and so forth. For them, in that room, that uptight atmosphere, the guns and the chador—they're a way to say, 'Fuck you.' Man, when they went through that airport, they defied. Everything. You and I are just in the wrong place with the wrong clothes on. They actually got *dressed up* to do that number."

"Like faggots wearing a dress to a parade."

"It's deliberate, subversion. Revolutionary. And that wonderful one welcoming her lover, she jumped right up on his waist, with her legs around his waist, he twirled around and around and they kissed and kissed. Beautiful outrageousness. They were so happy, compared with everyone else. Because every person you see here is so sober, so miserable. These two gorgeous apparitions, this Marseilles tart and her sailor man, were like the circus, like fun, like it could be fun to be alive and untied and celebrate a revolution and dance in the street if that fool with his machine gun would move away from the door." I hardly realize yet the depth of misery in this country.

Though as I got used to it people seemed less crazed with force and repression and tension; there were little kids, everyone's relatives coming home, old women out to see the students return.

"But little girls in chador, did you see them, little things five and six, looking through the bars at us?" Sophie is profoundly moved by the power of the veil as well. Repelled. The men are another thing to her. "Have you seen how affectionate the men are with one another? They really kiss one another. Passionately sometimes. I was watching a group of men who were greeting a fellow who'd come off our flight. He went round them each in turn. And they hung on to one another. Kissing one another on the lips."

"An advance over our town. Doesn't seem to be much affection reserved for our own sex, though."

"And as for this hotel, I reckon there are only about a half-dozen people in it tonight. And twelve machine guns to guard the place, a whole row of sandbags. And us."

"And the funny man downstairs in striped trousers trying to keep up the act. And that agent type who follows us around."

"He's English-speaking, he reads the English Tehran *Journal* while waiting around."

"What day is it? Is it already the sixth of March? Past midnight, it must be, we've been two days in the air. Only a week since I was in California. Long way from here to planting marigolds around a fat lady."

"I think your Caifi friends' notions of security are a bit overdone; if Khalil had called them in time, they would have been expecting us, this is silly. I hope they show up tomorrow sometime."

The checkpoints are real enough, we saw them coming in the cab, cars drawn over to the side of the road, people with their hands up before headlights. "Do you want us dragged over to the side of the road thirty-two times, you and me cowering in the backseat? Not to mention the contraband brandy from the duty-free shop in Rome. You've seen how they carry on with these machine guns."

"One of them even extended his for me," Sophie laughs, "got it up as it were; far more unpleasant at its full length."

"When Bahram said thirty-two checkpoints, 'That would certainly be a nuisance,' I said. 'That is hardly the point,' he said. 'Then it's dangerous,' I said. 'That is precisely the point.' Obvious of course, and I shouldn't have said it over the phone. Things are not as settled and easy as Khalil and Nersi imagined. Over here, it's an armed camp. And if Caifi act like paranoiacs, they probably have good reason." But still we feel small and lonely. A little embarrassed, as if we were in the way, an inconvenience.

"When is checkout time in this place?"

"Noon maybe, capitalist tool, same rules everywhere." Showering and addressing the Sheraton multinational corporation, I point out the wallpaper is crummy, though the bathroom is okay. "Twin beds," Sophie notes brightly. "The twin beds," I say, "are lousy," imagining it an oversight. But the room is twenty dollars less than the first one we rented a few hours ago. Checkout time is not till three. Our friends come at eleven. Hopefully a quiet day to study, work on my speech. Studying Islamic architecture, in my twin bed I fall asleep with a book and not with Sophie. Having checked in, found our friends, checked out again, had dinner, lost our friends and checked in again, I feel a bit like an orphan but at least I'm in a bed falling asleep amid the mosques of a picture book, while outside the Shah's towers rise to be arrested by an insurrection promising to be a revolution but falling quickly into counterrevolution. Though not fallen yet.

2 ✳ ✳ ✳

IT'S NOON. Sophie is very dissatisfied with my friends. I am a little puzzled as well, but cheering myself up with what remnants of the Near Eastern library I have managed to smuggle into the odious duffel bag. Fresh coffee and a book. The comfort of books: all my life I have read when I found life disagreeable and in this way even became a scholar. I'll play scholar this morning; what else is there to do? If it goes on I may even feel moved to work on my speech some more, nice little desk over in the corner. Checkout not till three. Something's bound to happen. We are becoming acquainted with a phenomenon we begin to call "Persian Time."

The first person to arrive is not the Caifi escort who is to take us to where we shall live, but Khosrow, Kateh's handsome young academic brother who has come to "apologize on behalf of his family." Apologies of any sort are irresistible and his concern is genuine, his sense of honor. I adore this sort of manners and in a moment we are having a lovely time. He fascinates me, a proper bourgeois, the son of the house, a family who harbor in Kateh a firebrand they don't entirely understand or approve of. "She is gone all the time and we never know where. Phone calls for her constantly. They worry our mother. We don't always find her friends very polite, yet they are always staying overnight and we are at the moment terribly crowded. I hope you will forgive us in this respect; we are a large family and there are a number of children. In these times we seem to be all packed in. Babak and Kateh may be getting another apartment, but they never seem to have time to do anything—they are always at meetings. Then a whole bunch of them show up at three in the morning and want something to eat. Like children, don't you know? There are times I can't imagine what to make of them. Whatever they're doing is probably dangerous, and Mother is very worried. It was this way before, but then they were out of the country and we didn't live with it so close up, don't you see."

However puzzled he is, it is clear he loves his younger sister a great deal too. Though there is still much common ground, their politics parted ways years ago. Babak, who is a committed leader of the Socialist Workers party, is perhaps still more inaccessible to Khosrow. But he is a brother-in-law, family. Khosrow is a liberal, a junior professor of French, a member of the academic Komiteh for his university, and mightily concerned with purging the place of reactionaries from the old regime. I wonder where they will go if they are fired. He is less concerned with that than with the fact that they should no longer be in power. I remember academia and teachers who got sacked, radical ones like myself, but also boring ones who were competent but would be thrown out if the students had their way. A woman who taught Milton and failed to entertain the students; I remember her agony, riding the subway with her one night and after a long day. My own course had been underregistered due to the manipulations of a chairman who wanted to fire me, was preparing his case to do so. And she was there too, also in trouble for her job. I pleased the students and wanted a department where they would love every course, I had always wanted to weed out the professors who paled, who drove students away from the subject. And then I had to watch her pain for twenty-six stops, sit next to her and hear about her husband the painter and how they danced in the kitchen and I saw she was not only a lovable woman, but a good scholar and probably a good teacher too if she didn't feel so beaten. And I am beaten too, because if my course goes on with only six students it may be canceled or I may be and teaching is then my life and my livelihood. So I hear Khosrow with a certain trepidation. What if the university is now to be reformed according to the correct political opinion? Is that better than all those other criteria by which the conservatives themselves have ruled it for generations, Columbia or Tehran?

And what now is correct? Islam or the left? At the university it is still the left, but Khosrow is very worried it will soon be Islam and another wave of fuddy-duddies—having just gotten rid of the Shah and Savaki supervision, he will have to cope with Islamic correctitude and religious rule. He walks about the hotel room in the sun with his brows furrowed, his smart, almost French costume, shirt, trousers and an ascot. He is very appealing, both as brother and as young scholar, but he is also very advantaged, and when Siamak Zaharie appears from Caifi to pick us up, Khosrow seems very bourgeois as well, next to Siamak's solid socialist line. Siamak is Babak's own brother, Babak is Kateh's husband and therefore Khosrow's brother-in-law, so there are a thousand connections between them, university and class origin may even be one of them, but as soon as we start off in Tehran with Siamak, one is aware of enormous divergences.

Siamak is ecstatic over the insurrection; he is even very pleased with what has followed. On the whole. His analysis, as we drive along, takes great account of the organized workers, chiefly those in petroleum. The backbone of the uprising, their share in the general strike the lion's share. And should religious leadership turn into religious repression, Siamak will look to the organized workers to set it right. As for the Fedayeen, the revolutionary cadres of guerrillas, they and the Muhajadeen, an Islamic guerrilla faction who have separated them-selves off into a unit of their own on rather leftist grounds—these two groups are the main hope of curtailing Khomeini. "Nemat will get you up-to-date, we're going to meet him at Bayram's and have some lunch. Then we'll find a place for you to stay. Maybe you can stay there, Bayram's parents are out of town now."

At the moment Siamak is enthusiastic about Kurdistan, there's a lot of promise there, autonomy from Khomeini, strikes. Siamak has been fifteen years out of the country. When he left, the little ditches Sophie inquires about at the side of the road still brought fresh water from the mountains. "Isn't it a matter of the people creating the insurrec-tion and Khomeini having taken that over, the people now having to take it back?" I ask him. Siamak is more optimistic. "Khomeini is *trying* to take it over." "So who wields power now?" Sophie asks. "Good question," Siamak laughs.

I like him. His burly big-chested mensch quality. We notice a great many unveiled women, a totally different impression from that of the night before, at the airport. Perhaps reunions are formal affairs. And this is daytime, there is less need for protection or even conformity. I spot a mosque and long secretly. Fewer women are wearing the veil now, Siamak tells us; to wear it during the insurrection was a symbol against the Shah. To go without it now shows the women's dislike of

Khomeini. Too simple, I think. "Women have to fight back now, it's the moment everyone here defines the future, the time for them is now," he says. "You see, there was never a successful bourgeois revolution in this country as there was in the United States and Europe. So everything is going to have to combine, transform, everything at once, just now as it is taking place. If they don't finish it off altogether, it will go back to things as they were before. The women have to move in now, become absorbed in the process of decision. Before, the problem was only to get rid of the Shah. That's done. Now everybody wants their rights and is speaking up. The workers say the factories are ours now, out with the foreign capitalists. Everyone needs better education. There's now the possibility for an *independent* women's movement. Now. Not before."

There are signs of protest. But on the other hand, Khomeini has started attacking the Komiteh, their original grass-roots and neighborhood composition is giving way to his picked religious. But one group stood out, a group Siamak translates as "The People's Sacrifice." During the rising they gave arms to the people. They also came out for democratic rights and set up a day for a demonstration. Khomeini came down hard against them, accused them of subverting the revolution. They pulled back, made it a rally, not a demonstration. But a lot of people came, one hundred and fifty thousand. It was a setback, of course, that they didn't turn it into a fight for democracy. "They had the possibility and the popularity and failed to use it," Siamak regrets.

Siamak sees hopeful evidence everywhere: for example, even though the Socialist Workers party is mistreated and its news vendors arrested, once brought to the Komiteh, they often perform minor miracles of conversion there, using it as a forum to talk to the workers at headquarters. "The Komitehs are still, after all, very full of contradictions and diversity. It's very fluid, this situation. At the same time, Savaki have also infiltrated the Komitehs, or managed to get themselves into new ones set up since the insurrection. It's hard to say what they want in the long run, one wouldn't even rule out the Shah, with them, but they do want to be in there manipulating, dissembling, their old way. Everything in fact goes on at once. The CIA are still around too. The big problem with this government of Bazargan's is that it's not decisive. This revolution is very crazy," he laughs—it's evident he believes it can be pulled out of the fire too.

We pass a school and huge placards of guerrillas mounted on the walls and over the doors. "Pictures of their martyrs," Siamak says. Pictures of Khomeini abound too, everywhere, from every conceivable lamppost, shop front, vendor's booth. Almost a dialogue of pictures.

Khomeini, Siamak says, is preventing elections by trying to appoint the members of the workers' councils. "They won't stand for it, they're striking all over again now. They will not give up control."

Siamak isn't afraid to go into the streets at night. Guns in the streets don't bother him as they do us. "Arms," he laughs, "arms are no problem. In Kurdistan everyone's armed, all the young men, the sheepherders, even old grandfathers." "Women too?" "Of course you don't see women armed, it's very backward there." The ease of it, the serenity, even the smugness rather surprise me. "Everybody's armed, it's okay," he explains again. "Everybody's armed and the women are not armed, so the women aren't anybody?" I ask, annoyed at the confident tribal vision in this. "No, no," he assures me, "it's not a question of repressive force, people control their own space." Are women people? I wonder. "My friends who go there say it's like another country over there, very open, very hospitable."

I also have great expectations of Kurdistan and the courage that is holding out there against Khomeini, but I am startled too by the difference in perception between male and female. A band of swaggering machine guns represents freedom to Siamak, provided the politics of those who carry them agree with his own, whereas my group is completely forbidden access to guns, that dubious privilege is entirely denied women. More to the point, women and children make up the civilian population upon whom the guns are trained. Women are to obey those who hold the guns, however close to them they may be. Lovers, brothers, cousins, husbands. They were always to obey, and now those who command them are armed. And refusal would meet with reprisal of some sort. We are, in fact, more circumscribed, more suborned under these circumstances than under ordinary civilian conditions. In the thrill of revolutionary esprit, and his masculine identification with force, which is a large part of what revolution means to Siamak, he has failed to perceive how inherently oppressive machine guns really are. How rule by arms is rule by force and intimidation. Identifying with the holder of the gun, whom he clearly admires and approves of, he is quite unable to understand the feelings of those who are unarmed, never will be armed, women between one gang of armed males and another, Shah, Savak, militia, or Kurd—hostages always—and in a state of continual threat against which they must pit their wits, rely upon the gestures of submission everywhere required of them, and their own wisdom in backing what they judge to be progressive. Having cooperated in ousting the Shah, they now find themselves in the sights of a newer, more enthusiastic gun. Vibrating with machismo self-importance and potency, even more eagerly ready to fuck, to kill. Bizarre.

Kurdistan, Siamak goes on, is tribal life sifted through centuries of trade and trade-route mercantilism, with Western aspects of city life, the cities not yet industrial but old centers of commerce. In fact, one of the great issues is a demand for the industrialization of that part of the country. They are teaching their own language at last too. Like all the minorities here, they were forbidden their language by the Shah, a cause of much illiteracy. "Imagine all those people sitting around learning how to read. That's the atmosphere—I don't worry about arms," he laughs. "If the arms are in the hands of the Shah and Savak, then I worry."

"What do you do on a day-to-day basis?" Sophie asks him. Like the others in Caifi, he is giving much time right now to help with International Women's Day, to establish the right of women to observe it. Women workers are also much concerned, we are glad to hear. "The question of women is a very big question now," he assures us. "There have been restrictions, on women judges for example; Khomeini has issued an order that women may not be judges under the new Islamic republic. Women judges and attorneys are up in arms. And the problem is, there still aren't any real independent women's groups—this is crucial." Sophie agrees, and points out that it is much the same way in the PLO, drawing on her years of observing it; "Women are permitted to carry arms, but in the hierarchy itself they are never in power." "During the insurrection, women came to the demonstrations by hundreds of thousands, women who had been sitting around for years and years," Siamak exults. "Religious groups tried to separate the men and women, not because the women were coming out politically as women, but to separate the sexes for puritanical reasons, like in the mosque. There was no issue yet that women would walk under their own banner." Yet I wonder if it had an effect never intended, that women faced danger together, roamed the dangerous streets in the safety of their chadors, in bands, bands of women.

"Khosrow told us that women had lately tried to hold meetings and were harassed." "By whom?" "Maoists." "Or maybe Savaki disguised as Maoists. Mixed with Maoists. But you know, these disruptions they make, it's not like the States, where people get confused and then bored and then just start leaving. Here everybody stayed, they didn't get confused or misled—they got pissed off. I mean it—they stayed there till eight and nine at night discussing and debating with those Maoists and took a vote and won. At first the Maoists started chaining the gates of the university and not letting anybody in. So the others started shouting slogans saying that the university belonged to everybody and chains belonged to Savak. Then the Komiteh had to open the doors immediately."

Siamak's enthusiasm, telling this story, a victory. "It's wonderful to be home." He chuckles. "When I came to the airport, it was early, the Shah was still here. I didn't know if they were going to take me in the back room and shoot me or not." His parents are still abroad, his father taken ill on the way home. This very night his sister finally arrives: she couldn't wait any longer by a sickbed. "She's impatient to see the revolution": his laughter affectionate, conspiratorial.

We are near Tehran University, the crossing of Shah Reza with Pahlavi Avenue. Traffic crawls. Surreal traffic, you lose all sense of time and place in it; three hours we have been trapped now—an entire afternoon wasted in going partway across town. The time involved in short distances is enormous; people read magazines, books; newspapers are sold to drivers by vendors going amid the stalled cars. Little boys sell cigarettes. I have never seen traffic like this—what it must do to the stomach, the nerves, punctuality. "If you want to know the real reason we had to have a revolution—it was because of the traffic. Just because of the traffic." Like a burly-chested gangster Siamak exults over this and then gets back to business: "A lot of people are out of work. Just about nothing here is running or in production. We are headed for a major economic crisis because of this. But the new government, Bazargan and the rest, they want to run on the same old track, same old deals, same old big companies. Trying to bend the revolution to the wealthier strata, a group a bit disadvantaged under the Shah perhaps, 'cause he and his family had such a monopoly on everything, every project ever undertaken—but the revolution was made by the poor and workers and women. So they want their share. And it's not settled yet. Nothing's really shaken down. It's not even a government yet. See those little boys selling cigarettes to the cars as they go by—Khomeini is cracking down on these kids. Just urchins. He never attacks the big black marketeers. It's like the executions. Criminals and Savaki, sure. They got to get it. But I say, have an open trial, put it all out front, don't do this secret business. What you're doing then is executing the truth along with them. Due process would really show what these guys have done, it would show that the revolution is justified."

I know that Siamak would never agree with me in opposing capital punishment, I also know the hatred felt for those being executed now, the years of Savak terrorism justifying that hatred. But I suspect that when he agrees with me that to lose due processes of justice in revolutionary circumstances is to permit a dangerous precedent, he would give it a lot more latitude than I do, finally I know he would probably never agree with my conviction that the first revolutionary crime is the existential moment when revolution becomes counter-revolution.

We pass a concert hall, "Farah's favorite," he comments, "Farah bought up intellectuals and artists." The embassy section, we are going there, to France Street. "What is the United States embassy used for now?" Sophie asks. "Oh, it's still the embassy," Siamak says, to our surprise. "Of course you knew it was attacked once by guerrillas because Savaki were holding out there—but it's still in business. The big issue now is to open up all the files. Savak files. CIA files. The Maoists here are going around calling the Socialist Workers party CIA agents and that stuff, calling Reza CIA. Reza says, 'Let's open them up.' Of course for more important reasons than that. But the hell of it is, we can't get them opened." We park the car precariously over a trench, the trenches that once brought fresh water and now run with filth and danger. The last words on this tape are my voice saying "Oh my god" as one tire slipped deep into a gutter.

Entering the house on France Street, wondering if it's to be our home. Arrangements all seem so haphazard here, the exhaustion of our friends must contribute, they are so overworked; the traffic too, paranoia as well and some real danger. Yet why does no one ever tell us where we're going till we're halfway there? And why is where we are going never our destination? Forget Khalil's exotic hospitality, side trips to Isfahan and so forth; if we could just snuggle down somewhere so I could work on my speech and read a few books in peace. Maybe when we get with the women, they'll take care of us. One shouldn't overly rely on men in a feminist cause; their concern is new and wonderful, but will it be enough? I hunger for female company as much as for lunch, a place to sleep, to study, to work and prepare my speech. A typewriter is clearly out of the question. But a room of one's own, a safe place to lay out the equipment, load the cameras, unpack . . . just wait till we finally reach the women.

Will Kateh be there? Maybe later. Everything is later. All the women are rushing about today, finding a hall, leafleting. As for Kateh, how busy can this young woman be? She might bother to find us and say hello sometime. Perhaps it is all a test, this waiting. Perhaps I have to establish my credentials all over again. And though Kateh and I know of each other through Caifi, we have not yet come to know each other. That takes time. I'm certainly aware it's her turf, however. In fact I feel I am running after feminism in Iran; despite their invitation, I have yet to meet even one sister.

When we see the house, I imagine it the house we will live in here, a gray building and you walk two flights up. It seems good luck, and a manageable size, a pleasant street near the embassies. Outside it was inviting. Inside it is oppressive in a curious way. Very Iranian middle-class, dull, petty bourgeoisie. Two servants on their knees wiping down a staircase, unctuous, humble. It is cleaning day, yet the sight of them is dismaying. They have telephone messages to give to Siamak; it is clear that neither of them can write. They come from the country, they sit on the floor when they rest. Siamak the socialist goes among them unselfconsciously. I find the situation suffocating. I also under-stand they are old family retainers keeping an eye on things while the owners are out of town, perhaps even a mildly restraining force on their son's political activities which include introducing two very odd foreign women. We salaam a great deal during introductions and gratefully accept some tea. It is as if we were suddenly in Persia after two days of public airports and American hotels. But the servitude of the servants is somehow compromising. I hope I don't stay here; the traditional climate of parents is one thing, that of keeping servants is another, too much. I want to stay with women, feminists, sisters. Where are they?

Suddenly Nemat is in the room. Good strong Nemat in a white sweater, seeming so sane, so reasonable; the man who actually ran Caifi, who ran the office. How fond I am, seeing him here, at this distance from where we met, this old comrade again where everything is strange and unfamiliar. How one trusts Nemat automatically. We report on Khalil and how excited we are to be invited, how we look forward to the rally, to meeting the women. Balancing the teacup on the arm of the frieze chair, the tedious sofa, the factory-made rugs; it seems a funny place to meet again, but this too is Iran. After all the formica tabletops of student cafeterias, the podiums and folding chairs of American universities, we ought to meet finally in Persia sitting on cushions, a good rug. Questions of taste rather than expense, but of intention as well; the place one wanted to see when they said, "Come see our world." Instead it is Bahram's parents' place without either Bahram or his parents present, only two servants who squat, an old man and an old woman, in the corner of a room, just within eyesight, their patient subjection centuries old. Even in Japan such personae would be more assured and homey. This is not at all how I would have it be, to see Nemat after all these years of work. The last time we met at Phoebe's, an art theater bar downtown and three blocks up from me on the Bowery, Nemat squinting in the sunlight of the enclosed sidewalk café while we made up lists of famous women we would enlist, I would write them letters begging their cooperation and concern, Nemat laughing that I didn't have any proper stationery

Nemat

with my name on it, had a box printed up. And I have never used it. Because the Shah fell before we got the letters done and now we wouldn't ever need it. We laugh about it now, I laughing uneasily because for all I did I never felt it was enough, and sometimes Nemat's honest confusion about how to run a benefit or do fund raising would send me into panic—because I knew even less than he did and could never guarantee that the luminaries of my country, still less its literary celebrities, would really read in Town Hall if we got up the nerve to try to rent it. "Try them," I'd say. "Iran is in the news so much now; if Ginsberg's in town, I'll bet he'll do it; Vonnegut has always been good to us. I think it would work. Maybe even Norman Mailer."

And now Nemat will never have to worry about it again. Already he seems less nervous. So much more assured than the anxious young man who visited me in Berkeley the time I lived there with Sita, the winter of seventy-three, Nemat an engineering student then. Asking me to speak against the Shah, the first time it must have been, and primed with pamphlets. The next year I wrote one myself. And could never get it published anywhere except the Berkeley student newspaper. It was Reza who got things published, it was the Iranian students who carried the organization at the risk of their lives and under penalty of *ishteraki* (sedition) laws of three to seven years in solitary confinement. At the end it was a life sentence.

Nemat patiently explaining the danger he was in over coffee at Sita's breakfast table that first morning. This guy has guts; even then one knew it. Nemat all these years quietly explaining to my American frivolity, celebrity status, overextended inefficiency—the realities. Doing it again today in Bahram's family's living room. It seems that Caifi is under some cloud here now; it was not expected that this would be the case when the Shah fell. But the situation is by no means stable, changes every day. The television is on in the foyer, Siamak watches the ceremony at the graveside of Mossadegh and finds it a good sign, vast hordes of people, an accolade for democracy, a portent. Nemat is calm as ever, short strong thick-chested in his good well-worn sweater. Reliable. I like him. He is not going to promise anything about this situation. The Shah is gone. Nemat was there and watched the political prisoners released. Past that, not much positive, though he agrees with Siamak he is far less optimistic. As for the women, there will be a rollback, the culture itself, and the revival of Islamic traditionalism—bound to be very hard on women. In fact it already is. They haven't yet found a place to have the rally; it may have to be canceled.

Very bad news indeed. Sophie and I look at each other helplessly. There is another woman in the apartment, a member of Caifi and a feminist, and she joins us to commiserate. She has been following the struggle to find a hall, following it moment by moment, reels off a formidable list of places that were possibilities, others that were assured, grand things like space at Tehran University. Right now every university, however humble, has turned us down; we now have our eyes on high schools. There is a certain misery in this, even a certain ego deflation—just as well. And by now any space we could get . . .

"We may get nothing and so we might be forced to tail on to a big rally of the Communist party held tomorrow," she says. "That would be terrible," I argue. "It wouldn't even be doing it on the right day, tomorrow's the seventh, International Women's Day is the eighth. Why can't we celebrate our day the right time; why isn't there anything in the whole city for women?"

"Well, Khomeini, of course. Permission is given through the Komiteh. They are under his orders. Several of us have already been arrested and brought before the Komiteh just for trying to give out broadsides announcing our organizing meetings. You see, before we did the big thing on the eighth, we wanted to have preliminary meetings, since our numbers were so small. And involve other women, ask their advice, involve them on how the rally itself should go, don't you know?" "Of course, wonderful idea, necessary too since there are so few of us, feminists hardly constitute a representative group yet." "We do now, though, two hundred women found their way to the first meeting. There was trouble that day too over getting a place. But we found one somehow, the Komiteh was easier then. And all the women were very enthusiastic, signed up, took responsibility, we have a great many names—and the women were really eager to work, distribute leaflets, help with the poster, all that. The next meeting was even bigger. Three hundred women. But there was trouble. There had been at the first one too, but this was more serious. Men came and blocked the doors, threatened us. The women stood right up to them, were even going to defend themselves, plenty of them, you have no idea how mad they got, even women wearing chador. And these guys were going to break up our meeting, calling us all sorts of names: usual thing, you know, 'counterrevolutionary,' 'prostitute,' 'Savaki,' 'friends of the Shah,' 'dancing girls.'" By now we are laughing. "Who are these guys?" "A combination really. Some are the Maoists, or they call themselves that." "They used to break up Caifi meetings too—I never could understand their ideology, can you?" "No. But their violence is clear enough. And the other ones were Islamic, fanatical, you know, Islamic fanatics. The Islamics want us to stay home and the Maoists want us 'not to divide the revolution.' That's what they say. So the women shouted at them, old women even, that we are the revolution, we are the revolution too. 'Who the hell are you, you young . . .' Nemat, how do you say . . . ? I remember. '. . . you young puppies.' It was wonderful. You should have seen it."

It is already wonderful. There are women here—they talk back. Now we will go to lunch, Nemat and Siamak and Sophie and I; the feminist has to run, and so without her, and regretting her, we saunter a block to a restaurant. To eat *chelo kabob* washed down with Seven-Up and Coca-Cola because there is no wine. On the way home, dodging traffic, crossing the road, I was nearly run over.

It is still not decided yet if we will be able to stay in this house or if the rally will even be held, but we have permission to rest in the larger bedroom. I can read, work on my speech, nap with Sophie; it is all up in the air but there is at least some respite.

3 ✳ ✳ ✳

I SEE KATEH FIRST as in a dream. This handsome girl bending over the bed where Sophie and I have fallen asleep; a beautiful face, wonderful, radiant. And most remarkably intelligent. Intelligence and enthusiasm, swimming up from our fatigue and homelessness, this face, this vibrant presence like some reassurance, salvation in our confusion, our growing uncertainty—should we have come? Was it all a mistake, Khalil's innocent miscalculation, our own naive gratitude at an invitation that has merely become a burden on our hosts? And we went to sleep, the way when I was a child people used to say that Arabs slept, merely for the oblivion, the release from our troubles, the nagging intuition that we'd made a mistake in coming.

Not with Kateh, she is delighted, certain, convinced. "It will happen after all. The big rally at the technical university, they have promised us time tomorrow; we may even do better than that still, on our own— anyway we have this." "But the CP here, the Tudeh party, are so reactionary," I say sleepily. "It's something," she says. "Now we have something." We sit up in bed, she gives us each a hug. "They called us so late. They called one hour after you had already arrived at

Mehrobad airport." "We've been so excited to be coming," Sophie tells her. "Thrilled—hell, we were hysterical," I say, stretching, turning on the tape.

"It *is* exciting, things are moving." Kateh begins to glow. "So much is happening. It's not an ordinary situation. It's not that everything goes smoothly. It's that everything we want to do—you see, there is really no government, really, no one you can appeal to—we could get a hall and find the speakers—and somebody will come along and say no, you don't have the permission. This has been going on for day after day. Even the owners of places can't promise anything. It's amazing. It's really unbelievable how we live now—I couldn't understand it at first when I got back." I am struck by the difference in the attitude toward the new authorities between the men and the women I have met here.

"As soon as we arrived we wanted to start something for women, to start by celebrating International Women's Day. It hasn't been celebrated here in fifty years and so we came along and said, let's do that. When we started proposing it to a bunch of women, they were so happy." The way she says "happy" is delight itself. Confirmation.

"Did anyone tell you the story of how we started out?" "Just a bit here and there," Sophie says, "tell us all of it." "First I just said it to friends. Over there, outside the country, we were hearing all this stuff in the papers about women here wanting to go back to the nineteenth century. And we knew it wasn't true. My friends, they were all excited. They said we should go ahead. But we can't do it ourselves, I thought, it has to be the Iranian women. So we wrote up the eighth of March, all the history of it, and we said, because of the revolution, we have to start this new thing. There's a lot of pressure on women now, you know, everywhere it's said that the insurrection was men and women together—they've achieved this. And that's true. But we also have to help our own cause."

She strikes her hands together for emphasis. "At first anything that women do separately was regarded as against the revolution. We could explain it wasn't. We held a meeting to propose that everybody—anyone—who wants to *build* this thing, should come to this meeting. We had a room at the library. Two hundred and fifty women came. It was the most beautiful meeting I've ever seen. Proposals—ah, but at first, they were confused at first, people said 'Who are you? What is behind this? What are you doing?'" Her voice conveys all the snarling paranoia of politics, factions, grass-roots indignation—it must have been grueling for her. "But then I just stood up and told them the truth, that it came to my mind and I told a few women and we got this room to discuss . . . 'It's you who will decide what we should do. No one's going to decide for you.' This is very explosive . . . that it's *us* who decide."

"Some people said there should be persons *elected*. But nobody knew each other." We share our amusement over this political dilemma, and the awkward fact that election presumes an organized body and persons known to each other. "So we all said, okay, forget elections, propose something, some people who can do something, who know the city, who can go after the speakers. So twelve people and I myself started this. Volunteered. We had three weeks. Next week the meeting would be again on Saturday. Women wrote their names down and started doing things. It was very good. Everybody's helping. It was both sides of Islamic women, left women, women in the middle."

She is irresistible in her happiness at how things went, the pride in her phrase—"Twelve people and I myself started this." She is carrying us along. "You know people here are sort of afraid of ideology; but at the same time, they think because it's a revolution, they have to *belong* to something. But we say no, you don't have to belong to anything. We will start from the questions that have been posed in Iran for women in the last year. One thing is nurseries, free nurseries, also free abortion, equal payment. Abortion went under the rug after Khomeini came, so nobody talks about it. But nurseries still, and equal pay.

"Then these things were going well. Till the next week's meeting. We went to the library, that same place. Two hours before the meeting—they suddenly say we can't come in. That was really frightening. We started looking for someplace close by because people were coming already. We got a boys' school. We had no choice. We got that and about three hundred women. They were really fighting mad; they were beautiful. They were angry first of all, they said we shouldn't have come out of the library. 'Why did you give in?' I said, 'Well, we didn't want any confrontation because the schools have started now and it's not the students' fault—it's the head of the library who promised us.' They were very angry but the meeting got started and about ten minutes later a bunch of hooligans came. Women started screaming and running away. We cooled it out. A man said you can't hold your meeting here. Boys from the school and some men, we didn't know who they were—a sign, often, of the Komiteh. It took two or three hours. Women arguing with these men—explaining over and over—we want to get together, we want to organize.

"I was so frightened because I felt so much responsibility. So I said, 'Let's leave and we will get together sometime later.' They said, 'No, we're going to stay.'" How clearly she is proud of these women. "They said, 'We can get a gun if you want to. We can do this; we can do that.' They were jumping up and down. It was a scene really. They got into arguments with the men, of course. Two women were arrested. Actually it wasn't quite like getting arrested; they were taken to the

Komiteh. And they wrote a statement of what happened and demands that they wanted this looked into.

"So since then, they have taken away from us the hall that they had promised us, the place where we were to have our big meeting, at the Polytechnic University on Thursday, March 8. The speakers are frightened. So everything fell apart. Although the sentiment was strong. But they've said all kinds of slanders, like 'They're right-wingers, they're prostitutes, they're left, they're CP-ers, they're Trotskyites, this, that.'" Her voice imitating the various flavors of contempt in every epithet. "I ask them, 'Why do you attack us?' And everybody gives me different reasons; but it shows there is something behind it which I am going to find out one day.

"Since Saturday, till now—twenty-four hours a day we've been looking for a place to hold our meeting. And it has been *impossible*." The exhaustion in her voice, the hurt, the having to compromise now. "Different groups were in our meetings. It wasn't only that it was just individual women. You see, women's organizations have started. But they're very small. You find ten members here, twenty there. They think they must be the only ones who want to build a women's movement so they organized themselves; they want to know each other." Isolated women in knots, and the women in the left. "But because we've been abroad, we have a concept of how to build a women's organization and can bring this to them, to help, to help them get together. Now these organizations have been very helpful, they've been looking for places for us. And they've been proposing speakers from their own . . . well, not really organizations—group-ings.

"Just a few hours ago we achieved it. At one o'clock we met with two, three groupings and we have a huge place for the speeches. But it's tomorrow."

"That's the seventh, not the eighth." She's settled for the CP rally.

"Because all the places are taken Thursday the eighth. And to show these women that we have not *lost* this fight, we're going through with it, we will hold it tomorrow. We have no choice." Kateh has made up her mind. "I can tell you who the speakers are—but there's also another thing—we told them that international supporters are com-ing. It was to be Bernadette Devlin and you and de Beauvoir and a woman lawyer from Algiers. But they didn't come. You're the only one who showed up. Another thing you should realize; there's very much anti-American sentiment. There's really a great deal. So I said to them, 'There's some little lack of understanding here, that there could be people in the United States who could be with us.' I think that's why it's so important for us to have you here. To show the solidarity."

Kateh

This is graceful and diplomatic, but in coming to terms with all the groups of the left who comprise the CP monster rally, Kateh has come upon the embarrassment of my nationality. "Well, they proposed, these groups, that we shouldn't say 'American,' we should say 'foreign.' And I accepted. They know you, lots of them know you. There've been things in the women's magazines, for example, but, you see, all those belonged to the government. And anything that had to do with the Shah they hate." I find it odd I should ever have been mentioned in women's magazines under the Shah, having once refused Farah's invitation to a feminist meeting which others accepted. I should be known in Iranian circles only as a resolute opponent of the last regime. "Well, what we've written is that you've been fighting against the Shah and for the political prisoners. And that is very popular. But what we've agreed on is that we won't say 'American,' we'll say 'foreign.'"

Poor Kateh. Poor America too, that its foreign policy is so rotten, bloody, and corrupt that an American feminist who had nothing to do with that policy and has spent six years of her life opposing it is asked to hide behind the chador of "foreign." "I have messages from France too, and Italy. On tape. There was so little time that they were done by phone—we bugged the telephone": an idea we all enjoy. "Robin Morgan and Gloria Steinem also sent greetings."

This makes Kateh a bit nervous. "We now have a lot of speakers, I don't know when the solidarities will be. It's a big hall, a very big hall, it may be full and the program is long." Sophie inquires about our other speakers. "There's a mother who lost four sons. A woman whose husband was lost in the last coup in Mossadegh's time." Kateh emphasizes "husband," aware herself that the speakers are all women whose thing to say derives from their relation to a man, a typical left requirement, tactic even. "A woman whose husband is a worker in the car industry, he was killed. A nurse, a housewife and a teacher. A woman poet. And also a man poet. A woman from the paper associated with the Socialist Workers party." The man poet, as she calls him, clearly gives Kateh a lot of trouble at a women's rally—yet he seems to be a key figure in the event. "This man poet—it was very difficult—I said it should be all women. But these groups, they don't have this concept. This man is a supporter of the CP. But people also know him as a very good poet. A lot of people will come because of him." We tease her that she ought to keep him to one poem. "Sylvashroe Khasroe. He's very popular. Even people who are against the CP respect him. So we said okay, to give his support to women, that's good. So this is it."

"How did you get the hall?" I ask, expecting to hear that the CP could get what it wanted. "This group had some base in the university." "Which group?" "There's no group, it's some students in the university, who actually . . ." Kateh flounders. "Because this man poet, because he has some sympathy, and because we said he was coming. But the question of eighth of March, it's something they don't seem to understand. You know at our first meeting, someone proposed him and I didn't know what was going on—I said, 'Don't we have women poets?—let them speak.' They said, 'If this man speaks, no matter if it's the eighth of March or not, thousands of people will come. I said, 'Let's have our own thing,' and nobody liked it, nobody could understand.

"But I did see, during these two or three weeks working with these little groups, that I could discuss things more openly as we went along. There is a change in them. They have the feeling—but in their mouth is always that line that if men and women have different things, it's separating the mass, dividing the revolution."

"Congratulations," Sophie says, "you've been working very hard." For myself I wonder what it will cost us, this compromise. I have my misgivings, but it is impossible to blight her victory. She's been negotiating all day. First there were objections, but she has overridden them; she has spent six hours in debate with the bosses. Women will be rewarded some time. And the meeting is promised to be nonsectarian. I bet it won't be. She knows what I think, thinks so herself, wrinkling her fine nose and grinning. It is somehow a warrior's grin. There is a Persian lord in her as well as a lady; she is one of the most perfect androgynes I have ever seen. She is also utterly determined; not only quick but patient and indomitable. And her optimism is infectious. I find myself persuaded as well as charmed. Part of me also thinks she's daft to trust the deals she's made; I smell betrayal already, they will say yes and then say no. But how can you resist her rejoicing? Or frown on her achievement, for that matter? This has been a heroic struggle. She sits cross-legged on the floor, her head just below ours as we lie on our stomachs on the bed, watching her. There is something about this young woman that is heroic, that commands respect. Something commanding in her, even; you know she's a leader. She carries that when she speaks to you, a certain authority she's won, worked for, suffered for during years of apprenticeship in Caifi. Now here, among women, she wears her years in the other cause with modesty, but also with a certain assurance; she is a foundress. Years abroad in exile, in danger and under threat of solitary confinement should she return. *Ishteraki*, the Shah's thought-crime. And now she has nearly alone, with only ten or eleven comrades, dared to establish a women's liberation movement. The first meetings to discuss the rally were splendidly attended; in fact the numbers still enchant her and sparkle in her eyes. Just a leaflet, and two hundred and fifty came. The next time three hundred. "So these guys threaten us, 'Break it up, cut it out,' they tell us. 'No!' You should have seen the women. Old women in chador even and they were calling out, 'Get out of here, thugs'— that's what they were mostly, street men with not much to do and anyone tells them, the mullah maybe or some little official, 'Go break up that bunch of women,' and they come along to do it." "Did the Maoists give you trouble too?" "As always, but we are talking to the women in the Maoists. They don't hear much yet, they are controlled, but we are making a beginning there. Especially at the university. There are days I think: Just forget it, they will go on sabotaging you forever. Then I get through to one. At least to the point of coexistence. Agreement on a few points. It is absolutely essential we have the recognition of the left."

"They will recognize you when you have power. At least that is how it went with us; when there are thousands of women in the movement, it becomes respectable among socialists." "But they can still call you bourgeois feminists whenever they feel the need"—she grins back at me from where she is crouched at the foot of the bed. We find an ashtray. Sophie asks lucid questions, but I am taken by a phenomenon—Kateh. A really perfect young leader. Remembering our own inexperience at her age, twenty-five; we were still full of rhetoric and the Columbia strike and the peace movement and egotism at that age. She has already faced Savak and the possibility of torture, years of putting together a small, never popular organization in a foreign and frequently hostile environment, using an alien language. She has years of organizing, setting up offices, carrying through on details, analyzing, reacting, speaking, representing, listening and publishing. And now it is women; she has found her way there. I wonder idly how long her new politics will coexist with her husband Babak's. Or her life. People seem uncertain about whether she and Babak will be living together when they move from her mother's.

The very way she stubs out a cigarette is decision raised to elegance. She will arrange a place for us to stay, a vacant apartment, Bahram and his friend need this one; his parents' nuptial bed, its chenille bedspread, his own resting place now with whatever lady. A vacant apartment sounds wonderful. And there is Asad, who lives nearby and can drop in and show us how things work, groceries, that sort of thing. We won't be entirely alone, but we'll have privacy and a place of our own. Perfect. Where is it? No one seems to know, but they'll be getting the address; a car will come soon. And tomorrow Resvan will come and help with the translation. Since there is French, the French message to translate, Mimi will come too; she's proficient in Italian as well. We'll have the morning to prepare, the Communist meeting is at the technical university and it begins around three in the afternoon. We have only to gather up all our stuff; the car will be here soon.

And then she is gone. Everyone else is pale beside this force, or slow and indecisive. The car takes longer, getting the address still longer. We hang about watching an Ayatollah on the television. He's from today's rites by Mossadegh's graveside. Tolerani, he's a good one relatively speaking, we in Caifi spent years getting him out of the Shah's prisons.

And then finally it is arranged. We say good-bye to Bahram's apartment without ever meeting Bahram. And with a car trunk full of posters announcing a rally we are still unsure we can ever hold, the substitution of a few moments of CP time our only consolation. Yet somehow Kateh's appearance has put it all right, made us all comfortable and the entire project credible.

Closing the trunk, Resvan and Asad let me have a look at the posters. They are marvelous, a good design, and wonderfully, lovingly printed. Silk screens, the black laid on like velvet. Each one hand-pulled. We hardly ever come across a political poster this well done at home. How sad if a place can never be found for the eighth. Kateh ruled out an outdoor rally when I suggested it. Too dangerous altogether. There are already men who have attacked the first gatherings; the speakers at this rally would be unsafe. One in particular, a socialist, a Trotskyite; there is particular concern for her. And the foreigners.

4 ❋ ❋ ❋

WE RIDE through the night, the house on France Street disappearing, the place we had thought of as home when we first saw the road, the houses, our nest. Our first house. There being a number of others to come, a thing we never suspected on entering the next, the place we thereafter always referred to as the unknown apartment. First of all, no one ever knew quite where it was, address and phone number were rationed out and quickly forgotten. Then, too, no one ever—in the full course of our time there—had even the vaguest idea whose apartment it was. It was thought to be some comrade's, a student, maybe a student and a wife and child. The owner even had a relative quartered there, unknown to us at first, a young girl from the country who rigorously wore her kerchief even indoors, but she was never able to enlighten us. Or perhaps it was too embarrassing for Resvan and Asad, our occasional caretakers, to bring up the problem of being quite in the dark as to just whose house this was. Occasionally I'd ask Nemat or Bahram, administrators, and they would take a guess as to whose house I inhabited, but they were never certain either.

We are getting to know them. Though we don't know where we are, we are getting to know the Iranians. Knowing them in Iran, rather than as foreign students, the way I knew Caifi people. Majid is from Caifi; it is his car that's bringing us to the unknown apartment. No one ever speaks of secrecy, they simply practice it. From habit, I feel at times. From years of it. And perhaps because the minutiae hardly translate into English, though of course it is just the details of our lives that interest us most. In what part of the city is this place? I ask, still harboring a few art tourist fancies. "It's near a big hospital, isn't it just across from one of the hospitals?" Majid asks Resvan, who's riding with us. "Around there someplace." I abandon the quaint and historic, settle for an apartment complex, and turn to my companions. I knew Resvan at Southern Methodist in Texas, watched her speak, the first woman I had heard speak out for the cause of the prisoners. She was competent, utterly trustworthy. Sensible. She is a chemist who came home to help the revolution in the area of public water, pollution, purification. The new government could find nothing for her to do, because of her disability in being a female. We found her a rock of reliability and kindness.

Only now do we seem to be in Iran. Going through the night streets with them, the closeness of the car, four of us in it; Majid, driving, Resvan in the front with him. The translators arrive at noon, Resvan says. "We'll have lunch together before the rally, it's not till three—there's plenty of time." It is the kind of amiable prediction that we were to hear hundreds of times: an ease and precision that never took place. We do not suspect—and neither does she—that they wouldn't be able to arrive until one, that the translation would be difficult and time-consuming, that we would nearly be late for the meeting then, that there would never be time for lunch. There would never be time to do it as we wanted to. Always this gracious, hopeful air before circumstances: the circumstances of general poverty, without trans-

portation among the women and having to travel by taxi in parts of
the city where taxis are scarce, snow, rain, curfew. It is a pioneering
hardly aware of itself, assuming that life is always this difficult, that all
progress was necessarily heroic. And highly improbable, complicated,
barricaded off. "The big news of the day," Resvan laughs, "is that we
still can't get a meeting place of our own." And yet there persists this
desire to entertain (on their part, and on ours), a desire to enjoy the
place, act as though life here were not war, as though women could go
about living and doing and building this shadowy edifice of our
future, undisturbed.

Among us there are no cars; only the men have cars. Mimi was the
only woman with one. And Nelufar. But with both of them the car was
part of a family, a child waited at the other end of the road or a
husband. No women lived alone whom we met here. Unmarried
women lived with families, so a father waited and worried, for Asad,
for Resvan. Nasrin's mother and their poverty. There was never the
autonomy that at home we were accustomed to in this work, the
autonomy all Caifi members enjoyed abroad. Coming home for them
was not only coming home to the absence of the Shah, it was also
coming home to an uncertain new regime—and back to family life,
dependency, pinched economies, narrow circumstances. And everywhere the hostility of the authorities, the certain knowledge that what
you are embarking upon would bring greater pressures, repression.

But tonight we are hopeful, Sophie will begin filming tomorrow
with the Bolex. "Let me know if there's something I can do to keep out
of everyone's way," she says. "Do you come from the States too?"
Majid asks her. "No, Canada." Sophie is always delighted to disassoci-
ate herself from America. We ask him about himself. "I was down in
Texas, at Houston. I did Anthropology for a while. But they hassled
me a lot. We're supervised abroad. I had to leave the country. So I
went to England." Caifi in England, different acronym, but the same
work. "I switched subjects a lot. Finally I had to drop out."

It is something I hear a lot, the gradual commitment to politics
preventing the completion of one's studies. The "hassling" by governments, the student visa in danger by Savak or by the Americans, even
the academic authorities who often cooperated assiduously with
Savaki spies and agents. And then politics takes over completely.
Kateh once told me that she had done her undergraduate work in
math. "Then I started out in graduate school. Math again, of course,
but it began to drop away from me. Slowly it fell by the wayside.
Politics took over. I majored in Caifi." It is not a bad course of study,
one learns a great deal of the world: whatever skills and proficiencies
one acquires become far more a life-and-death affair than in the usual

curriculum. But you have sacrificed your "chances" by being "unqualified" as well, at the end of it. And having helped to rid your country of its tyrant, still outsiders, you regroup again around the dangers to civil rights that remain or spring up anew.

We drive along quietly, making small talk; the posters, how we must remember to get some, collect them, how curious the kind and variety of thing that comes out of a revolution, Sophie muses. We are trying to find a restaurant. That one was closed. The car hums on. Sophie asks about tomorrow's Communist party meeting—will it be mainly members of the Tudeh party? Resvan thinks not, most of those who come will be independents, teachers and students and working people. Street after street goes by, gray beyond the car windows. We appear to be lost. I wonder if we are still looking for a restaurant or going directly to the apartment. It is late by the new standards here now; it is ten at least. Resvan tells us that the women who work for the airlines are becoming restive over the question of equal pay. Majid explains how women are generally contained in certain job categories so that the question of equal pay doesn't even come up. Back and forth from Farsi to English. Farsi dealing with the restaurant or directions to the apartment. The lull of the car. "We're trying to take you to a place that serves beer, but we can't find it." The car seeming to go in circles through the same neighborhood. The destruction of political tension, that particular inability to concentrate on even ordinary detail I saw in the young supporters of the FLQ once in Montreal during the troubles. A tiredness we all feel. Farsi in the front seat, Sophie and I in the back, the backseat having access to doors so my claustrophobia is at peace. It is pleasant driving along with them, getting to know them, like them, growing closer in the time and motion of the car. The lull of the driving. The interest of the streets.

Resvan discusses her parents with Sophie who asks, "They don't agree with what you do?" "They agree with everything, but just over my safety they worry. Worry too much." At night, particularly I think, the checkpoints. We have seen a few in the wider streets wave us on harmlessly. One slows down, says good evening. Majid is very friendly with them, we women seem a bit less so. And we have our contraband alcohol in the ubiquitous duffel bag in the trunk, the precious bottle of French brandy for whoever eventually becomes our host. Khalil said it would be good for morale, much appreciated. It was still legal for air passengers to bring it in. Traveling around with it now is another matter.

"My family, they just don't like my ideas," Majid says with great charm and a gentle bemused irony. We all laugh, conspirators. Revolutionaries riding the city in search of the general radical goal—a late-night restaurant. Where we can talk politics in greater comfort. "They know that I've been active. But when I sit down to argue it out with them, it's impossible."

"Who are those men over there by the fire, are they militia?" Sophie asks, thinking the figures by a roadside fire have guns. "No, they probably sleep in the streets, so many do now," Resvan says. Reassuring, bringing home the realities to us. "Maybe they're street vendors." "Are they armed?" Sophie wants to know. Still curious, or insecure. "No, the religious hierarchy okays it or you don't carry arms," Majid instructs us. "Every neighborhood has a mosque. That used to be the place where they rallied, planned demonstrations and decided what to do. Right after the uprising the religious leaders issued proclamations ordering people to return the guns." The guns of the Air Force, the guns distributed to the crowds on 21 Bahman (February), the turning point, the moment the people were armed. "Most of them did give them back. Just a small number who were controlled by the religious hierarchy were then still permitted to have guns."

We roll along through the night, the quiet engine, the rhythm of stoplights. "What have you seen of Tehran?" "Just Bahram's house and one American hotel." Amusing them. "Aha, so what do you think of how people drive?" "Even the sidewalks are dangerous," Sophie says, "because the motorcycles use them." "But so do the cars." Resvan chuckles. Desultory, comfortable talk, corny jokes. At ease with each other. Sophie and I relaxed by the music of their Farsi. Back into English Sophie asks about Caifi. There are two, three, even four groups joined together now since people have come home. Perhaps as many as three hundred Caifi workers in Tehran. Farsi again from the front seat. I am about to suggest we drop the restaurant, since it's getting so late, so hard to find. Yet a part of me is delighted to go on driving around Tehran's night forever. Majid turns on the radio. Music. American jazz. "Isn't that decadent?" Sophie smiles, and we all enjoy the stolen quality of it, siphoned through the censorship of foreign disease and imperialist corruption, a black man's voice innocently claiming "I love you just the way you are." Strange little moment in time, somehow precious, our collective enjoyment of this tune, our place heard from in their place, the affection we all feel for this kind of music, tradition of bar and saloon and smoke and the secular, the downtown call of it. The mood it creates, nights and cities and being with friends, restaurants, streetlights, all of us humming along with the horn section.

Still with the radio on we inquire of a militiaman directions to a restaurant, his enormous gun leaning into a car, our request its own alibi, harmless. The place is very near here, but we just keep missing it, our friends explaining all this to the enormous gun while Sophie and I chat in a relaxed manner in the backseat. As we drive off Sophie teases, "Did the man with the gun know of a place that sells whiskey?" Majid is amused and then serious. "You really must never let them know you've been drinking." "How about this flogging people for drinking?" I ask. "Is it just in outlying regions, is it merely an abuse of power, or is it more widespread?" "It's almost like a law." Majid sounds frightened as he says it. "In Tehran?" "I know only what the newspapers say, they say nothing about Tehran. Tabriz, though. Mostly there. And a few other places." "What do they use to flog people?" "It's leather, a whip. Eighty lashes." It must come near to killing you. For a drink, for drinking. The maddest thing I have ever heard, the most absurdly fascistic. "Is there a tribunal?" "They just do it in the streets. Right then and there. But they never mention in the papers about people's response to that kind of thing." "What have you heard?" "Nothing yet."

We have come again into a cul-de-sac by a large building. I recognize it. We have been lost here before. If we keep going in circles, we will cause suspicion. "If we're still looking for a restaurant, it's terribly kind of you, but why don't we give up. We have to do the translation tomorrow, it might be better just to get some sleep." "We were looking for a special one, we just can't seem to remember where it is. We could still go to an ordinary place." So eager to please us, so patient. The radio plays, we're indecisive. Then I see him. Out of the corner of my eye. A man crouching behind a car. A machine gun pointing at my face. "Let's get going," I say even before I think. If it were my foot on the gas, we might all be dead.

Fortunately Majid sees him too. *"Bali,"* the word that saved our lives. "Hello," the word for answering the telephone, the word for "yes," the word you say to the rifle so it won't shoot. All four of them, in fact, for we are surrounded. I die a little death just wondering what is in store. "Could you come out?" Majid's voice polite, calm, "They just want to check us. It seems we didn't hear them call us to halt; they became upset."

And at this point the tape recorder, which had been playing in the car, recording our talk, recording the recorded music, now registers our exit, a great scrunch of coats and bodies getting out from the car. And then registers hardly anything. While I, the rest of its intelligence, its powers of memory, wait to be shot. A search of the car, the guard disturbing the machine at one point, but not shutting it off. Our voices recorded still at a great distance outside the closed doors of the car, four guards demanding explanations, our friends' easy laconic stuff about restaurants, and being famished, Sophie and I of course silent as the tomb, lest we expose our accents and descend into the mouth of the Komiteh or an instant tribunal. We are a photo from a war movie, four silhouettes leaned against a wall for body search, the terrible outlines of the machine guns—two pointed at us the entire time as two men feel us up for weapons. No problem there, but wait till they go through that trunk and find the damn booze—will we be shot for a bottle of Teacher's, Sophie's favorite, and one good quart of brandy? Do I offer my life to alcohol? I wonder, the question forming just over my heart as the man prods the duffel. And the gun looks me in the eye. It is too absurd a circumstance even to laugh about, and were I to burst out in the hysterical humor I feel, they'd probably shoot me for being strange. I am also too scared to laugh. And far too frightened to die.

The cassette picks up Sophie as we pile back into the car, a very cool Sophie. "You must remember they are scared out of their minds." "Lucky they didn't kill us out of sheer fright." I grumble. "They said they shot at three cars tonight." Resvan laughs cheerfully. "We really are lucky." "Let's just go home. All this homicide exhausts me." I am not cheerful. Sophie is as always exquisitely polite. "You realize this is all new to us. Thank you for taking so much trouble." "But we're sorry for the trouble you have had here." General apologies, gestures of courtesy that are both lovely and ridiculous.

"There are still a lot of Savak agents running around with guns," Majid explains. It is the official explanation, but I have never been impressed by it. Curfews are to control the populace, and guns are to intimidate them. And seeing we were four women and one man, any guard could conclude we were not heavily armed Savaki. We are ordered now to drive without our lights on. "They can see you better with your lights out, they can see the passengers better. And the headlights freak them out. They are scared youngsters anyway, for the most part."

So many guns in the hands of simple guys, I think. I hate guns. Realizing in a settled fury how much I hate them—how unfair they are, how oppressive that one human being should ever dare to point a means of instant death at another and order him like a slave. That so and so daring to threaten our lives like that. Harmless people out trying to find a damn restaurant and eat some food. And that object in his hands mastering us. What if you refuse to get out? Does he shoot you and say you resisted—but who ever refuses a gun? And the thing so blatant, it is not in a holster and part of his office—it is his whole office—all he is is that organ of death. Humiliating, infuriating circumstances; the more I think of it, now that I am over being frightened, the more angry I become.

"Glad he didn't find the whiskey, anyway." "Oh my god, another militia." Same business, gun pointing right into the car, are we going to have to get out or will he shoot us right here? Majid beguiles him with his restaurant, a thing we no longer desire but still cling to as the perfect asinine reason to be out at this hour, posing as silly young people, need a bite and so forth. There are commands and instructions. It begins to dawn on me that one could be killed here, in this country, for holding a bottle of Scotch or wanting to eat past ten at night or just arriving at the wrong moment and colliding with the wrong guard or playing a car radio loud enough to fail to hear an order. *"A l'est"*—"Halt." And then the machine gun. So masculine, so oppressive. A rage grows in me against violence. Military rule. The figure of a man with a gun. Because of course no one else ever carries them, and the man carrying the gun is in such a frenzy of idiot manhood he is a dangerous person. Armed.

We arrive finally. The neighbors find us highly suspicious, as probably they should. We are in the embarrassing position of not knowing even whose apartment we enter, though our friends finally win the day with being polite and respectful to the elderly couple from across the hall, who could, in fact really feel they should, call the police and straighten it out. Finally our key works, and this is some proof, the tide turns against the police; it would be the Komiteh, actually, and that could become very interesting—the door opens. We are safe in the unknown apartment. Where we can all drink Scotch and talk politics as late as we want.

5 ✳ ✳ ✳

I WANDER AROUND the unknown apartment, a dull gray morning, it is even beginning to snow, an unseasonable snow, because this is already March 7. It should be the last snow of the season here probably, though we get them as late as May at the farm. A wince of memory for the farm—it's just as dreary there now too, forget it. In this peculiar apartment, watching the snow out the big sealed plate-glass windows; they call it the crow's snow here, after this last snowfall, the crow appears, they say, and that's the sign it's finally spring. Today is murky, blue-gray, desolate—and already that tension building in my stomach, the knowledge that I will have to make a speech today. It's written now, ready for the translators. Who are late. Everyone must be late today with the snow. The apartment itself is so desolate you wonder if anyone will ever find their way here. Our good times here last night now seem a hundred years ago.

We woke to discover the unknown apartment, the place itself a thing we hadn't really taken account of at first, so glad for shelter, for the company of friends, refuge from the guns on the streets. But in the morning light the unknown apartment is pretty awful: by daylight you notice the fact that it's filthy, that the urinal stinks, that the shower is cold water, that the whole place has no heat except a portable electric contraption we are almost afraid to use. There's a water heater in the kitchen, but it is out of kerosene. There's no coffee, no soap to clean up the kitchen, a very dirty broken glass table its only ornament, but still a center where we tend to gravitate, hoping to figure out the samovar. Last night the country cousin, whose name is Fatimah, cooked some delicious eggs served with a bread very new to us, but now the cupboard is bare. This morning she came through with tea, a little shade functioning like a servant, afraid of us, cowering in the little room she had chosen for herself, the children's room it would seem to be. Our friendliness is only a further burden on her; her hospitality is mixed with a vaguely hostile servility that makes us uncomfortable, compromised. Even though she is attending a college here she wears Muslim headgear at all times; we are probably anathema to her. We have broken in on her solitude, her possession of the place; her prior presence here, of which our friends knew nothing, nor presumably did the unknown owners of the unknown apartment. And from our point of view, her presence rather dampens our hopes of privacy and a place to work. Fatimah copes with the samovar and our smiles and thank-yous. "Thank you" is easy— everyone says *merci*—the word grabbed whole out of French. We cope. Sophie copes through cheerfulness, sign language; I cope by grinning a great deal and then by writing out my speech at the dining room table in the big cold lounge while Sophie loads all the cameras and catalogs the film.

We wait for the translators. Maybe Resvan will bring coffee, she promised to stop off and buy some last night. We have no food, and since there has been no opportunity to exchange money, no rials either. We don't quite know where we are. To go out and buy anything would be an overwhelming undertaking if we did have money, and our friends have asked us not to go about by ourselves in any case. All this in addition to our ignorance of the language. We have reached a state of dependence neither of us has experienced since childhood. And we wait. It goes on snowing. I watch the figures crawling about outside the windows on the pavement, the cars running by in the snow. Across the street is a huge building which could be a penitentiary, but I'm told it's a hospital. More of the Shah's soulless modern. The apartment itself is the grimmest instance of how a bastardized misrepresentation of "Western" architecture can imprison inhabitants in any part of the planet. In the West, no one would rent a room in it, here it passes for chic and new and wonderful and foreign and—without care or attention to the fact that human beings would live here—expensive, either to the inhabitant or to the community having to subsidize it.

One large room: dining room on the right, a living room on the left, good proportions. But the floors are actually made of cement. So are the walls. I have never observed such naked rigidity anywhere. A central hall then leads to two bedrooms, one small, one very small, to the left, and a good-sized kitchen to the right. Even if this were lit (there are no windows except in the living room), even if it were clean, there would be no possibility of ever making it habitable. Because of the surfaces; everything is so hard, so adamantine, so fast, cheap, crummy. The cement floor tires one even to look at; two bad rugs do not improve it. Nor does the remnant of Western carpet that covers the floor of our bedroom; bright red, dirty; dirty pink walls. It is sordid sleeping there on a questionable mattress directly on the floor. Obviously whoever lived here would be unable to keep the place up, would surrender, would let it go to hell and then leave. Probably they have.

If there were soap we'd be faced with the possibility of washing the whole place down, the least we could do to repay hospitality, but even clean, the glass table in the kitchen, part of a wrought iron "outdoor" breed of furniture fashionable in the suburbs of the West, the glass broken in so many places you have to put your tea down very carefully not to start an avalanche on the other side of the table where you have balanced a book—even clean it is broken beyond hope—and with no hope of getting another, since we cannot forage nor shop nor go out on our own. Enough. I can't go on refurbishing the place.

In fact, one's impulse is to demolish. To wish places like this were never built nor people ever forced to inhabit them. Still more, to have relinquished whatever excellent provisions they already had—the beautiful tradition of sitting on the floor, a good floor with a good rug and some lovely cushions. That is Persia. This is the Shah. For he destroyed nearly every older house in Tehran. Not that old a city either. Talking about it with Majid last night, Sophie said this culture, which was once so magnificent and precious, the art, the poetry, the artifacts, has now devolved into something worse than ersatz Americana. Listening, I thought of Japan and how hard you had to look for its culture even fifteen years ago when I lived there.

"Deep down, it's different, a different world," Majid said. "Go out of Tehran. In the villages, the provinces, vast areas in fact. Tehran is not the norm, only the Shah. All these damn buildings of his. Other places people still sit on the floor on cushions." "The schizophrenia, though," Sophie said—"knowing the other way is so delightful, so aesthetic, and having to put up with this invasion of bad taste; it's not only Westernized, it's bastardized, an inferior form that is neither Eastern nor Western but nothing at all." "Yes," Majid is tired. "I was brought up here, I've been away from it, been around the world, seen a contrast. I knew before, but seeing again with your own eyes is different. Now coming back here, it's like seeing it for the first time." It seems to him now that Iran's old ways of living crumbled too fast; whatever new has taken their place is ugly. "It's not that people wouldn't like to have what's good in the West or in the old ways—they just *can't*, I mean they weren't permitted to have anything decent in the new, nor the old to console them either. It's a cultural limbo, a social and economic one too. It came to a point when it exploded." The revolution had its cultural and therefore its aesthetic aspect too. That is why the skyscrapers rot outside every window—unfinished, perhaps now never to be finished. The Shah has destroyed the very quality of life—not only does your soul live and thrive in your freedom from a secret police, but in your very buildings, flooring materials, floor coverings, design, plumbing. Persian plumbing may be very simple in places, but a well-conducted privy like the ones I knew in Japan can have a flower arrangement, a pleasant odor, a good view, and in country settings even a communion with nature, immaculate but also useful and fertile ecological appointments; the honey bucket enriches the fields.

There is no reason why this amount of space set up for shelter should be so uncomfortable, so corrupt in its use of material, so confining and penurious, so full of repellent corny touches like the American dimestore lamps. Imagine a child trying to play on the cement floors, lovers trying to enjoy the six-inch balcony, any reasonable sensualist trying to cook good food here—the kitchen full of appliances that no longer work and perhaps never did. If the Shah succeeded in making Tehran look like Cleveland, his domestic architects have managed to make this flat look like industrial space. Or perhaps a small jail converted to the appearance of family quarters.

Painting cement walls with nauseous institutional colors does not change their substance and feel, and the cement floor obtrudes everywhere, hard, indomitable. The windows, like those of modern motel chains, do not open, were made never to open. Outside, the snow comes down and women go about in chador. Pairings of them or trios. This is the Iran the Shah built and Khomeini inherits. The veil never left, yet all else seems to be stripped bare, to combine with the most hideous jerry-built, misunderstood, half-satirized versions of America. Not only as bad as America—worse. And that's hard to do.

The snow comes and we wait for our friends. Like females, contingent beings. When they do come, we will turn my rather spirited exhortations to rebellion into whatever Persian they find acceptable for the group addressed—because I have come all the way to Iran in order to make a brief address at a meeting overseen by the Communist party where I am to be passed off as a foreigner rather than an American. Only the cognoscenti will have an inkling of my true identity, and only because they read foreign books, but even they may fail to make the connection if my name is said rapidly and my nationality adequately obscured.

Good, as an anonymous foreigner I will read off my little speech, get it over with as promptly as the organizers wish, the program being overcrowded already, squeeze my messages of solidarity in and then become a private citizen trying to explore Persia. I may even leave Iran for Persia, exit right out of Iran, the political entity, and enter right into antiquity. Pictures. Rugs. Museums. Isfahan. Perhaps in Isfahan Khalil's folks won't find themselves so pushed for time and energy as the people in the capital. And if we're very careful, Sophie and I can find some cheap pension to live in. Maybe when it all quiets down, someone will just let us crash at their place or even be talked into driving us around. I am in a typical fugitive mood, wondering why I came, what I'm doing here—and rather inclined to chuck it all. Of course there's that damn film, my dread of film returning, the technical difficulties, the cost, the burn of past fiascos, but with almost three weeks before us we can shoot interviews after we do the CP thing today—we'll stay and get to know the women. I guess that's it— why we came. For the women. Will they ever get here? And will they be even a presence today in the masses of men of the Tudeh party who have come to hear their man poet, while we get, at the outrageous most, one hour for our eleven speakers? There are so many things wrong with this. There are so many things utterly crazy about it, disappointments, false expectations. If I'd known it would be like this when the phone call came to California as my fat lady baked in the sun under a tree—would I have come? Probably, just because there still might be a chance to do something, see something happen for women here. You have to hang on to that, the point. Even as the snow falls outside these grim windows on the figures of chador going about the mean streets. A noise in the hall, the door, they've come.

6 ❋ ❋ ❋

RESVAN'S BROUGHT COFFEE, all will be well. How quickly one revives when they are there, the Iranians—and particularly the women—as if we wilted or grew faint from lack of oxygen in their country without their presence. In a few moments all the paraphernalia of composition are with us: coffee, cigarettes, a dining-room table, its flowered plastic cover rolled back to put us in contact with the wood. Asad and Resvan puzzle through my English at one end while at the other Mimi does the French. Mimi, Asad and Resvan. Asad from Portland, Resvan from Texas Caifi. But Mimi is new to us. There is something wonderful about Mimi, a passion in her very carriage, a sensuality, stature; a worn and beautiful face, fierce, southern, woman. While the others studied in America, she lived in Italy, laughs and calls herself an Italian—why not, fourteen years? That's half a lifetime. She was married to one of them, divorced, came home to endure the life of a divorcée here. She is the only woman we are ever to meet who can look forward to the prospect of her own independent home, an apartment she has rented and is now fixing up for herself and her daughter. Something about her is adult rather than student rebel like the rest. She has lived, traveled, borne a child, been a long time in politics—she was here during the insurrection. And bears its exhaustion, its struggle. Most of our friends, because proscribed for their political activities, were unable to return until the old order had been overturned; they laugh and boast over how early they got under the wire; Kateh herself came when Bakhtiar was in power, terrified in customs, passport and at the barrier. But Mimi was here during the entire series of events that led to the overthrow: clashes in the street, demonstrations where the Shah's army fired into the crowds, the moment when the guns were handed out to the people—all of it. Day after day of disruptions, civil insanity, the nervous breakdown of a social order.

A breakthrough too, of course, but you see its toll in her face, the fatigue of her shoulders even early in an afternoon, the way she pulls her coat around herself, the concentration with which she smokes, the intensity of her writing, working, translating, transcribing the words from Antoinette's voice on the tape. The message from Des Femmes—both the informal conversation which she chuckles over, the rap between the two voices, Antoinette's idiosyncratic French and my American—and the text itself. And how beautifully Mimi writes, the signs of the Farsi script in her proficient hand, better drawn in her broad-tipped felt pen than the ball-point scratchings of Asad and Resvan. Who trouble over every word, consult with each other, with me, with Mimi. It is not only the difficulties they encounter with terms so long forbidden. Farsi has very few feminist terms, and no feminist literature has been permitted into the country; all these years since International Women's Day was celebrated here by the first wave of feminists long ago crushed by Reza Shah, the father of Muhammad Shah, late of Iran and presently living in splendor in Marakesh—we have just been merry over the fact that his face is still on the money. But there is another problem as well: adapting my speech to the audience at the Communist-party rally today, hardly the audience it was written for. But since there will be no International Women's Day this year after all, since we have been totally unable to get any hall to hold it in, we are forced to accept this second best and are being stoic about it. There are, however, plenty of "difficulties" in what I have written.

Beginning with the messages from America, greetings from Gloria, Robin, Angela Davis. I left messages and never got a call back so can only assume Angela would send greetings and solidarity to the women in Iran. Gloria, whom I never was able to trace from one airplane to another in her peregrinations over three days, left me a message with carte blanche. Robin has her message all written out to be translated—but they are all Americans. A giveaway. Sure to be unpopular. There's a preference for emphasizing the French. All right. And now Robin's message is to be severed from mine—reasons of time. Different reader will read it, if there's time. One compromise. There are further problems: my entire speech, references to religion, to patriarchy, to matriarchy, to male and female as classes, as castes, as political entities. We plow on. I stand by to explain the English in varied terms, they natter through the Persian equivalents, with sharp corrections from Mimi. And then return to a political correctness test, one that will not have us thrown out of the meeting.

I get the impression that Mimi will take a stronger line than they. Which would appear strange because she is closer to communism than they are. Caifi is not aligned to any party. But Mimi is Trotskyite. Just as some members of Caifi are socialist workers. Mimi, on the other hand, is a lifelong "Trot," as she assures us, enjoying the irreverence of the term, yet utterly serious in her commitment. There is also a miserable sinking suspicion, borne out by a number of discreet phone calls in the hall from time to time that none of us will be able to talk today. Because another of our speakers is a Trotskyite. Mimi is enraged by this, "Always they push us around, always we are discriminated against." I remember the ax that split the master's skull and remember that Tudeh is Stalinist. We may all be disqualified. Hard trucking for a bunch of feminists who'd merely like to say a word on the occasion of International Women's Day. The rally this afternoon is nominally in honor of this occasion too, but one already suspects we will be shunted to the end and perhaps left off the program altogether. We, the feminists. At a woman's feast. How manipulated we are by the left, how bitter it is at moments around this table.

But the other moments are quite unlike this, the moments we are working, using language, turning its phrases from one thing to another, translating culture, history. Antoinette's comparisons to the French Revolution—the ideas of freedom glowing like a little bonfire between us, the two at the end, Mimi at the other, I rushing back and forth between them. We are making something. Together. Some corner of trust. Some agreed-upon theory, analysis, declaration, challenge. I have asked Mimi to be my interpreter at the moment I speak. When we are done we are ready to race against the world together. Resvan and Asad have prepared my words in Persian, I am repeated in this strange and beautiful language of mysterious symbols; even to see it is a pleasure. Mimi will read the translation, phrase after phrase, quick, simultaneous, her passion filling out what I say, her obvious ability to project, to act, to be the words she speaks. It is perfect. We are all delighted, we go forth laughing and hugging each other, late as always but not seriously late—there's enough time to stop off and eat pizza.

"Pizza, Mimi, for god's sake you've got pizza?" "Yes and it's some of the best in the world, naturally we do it differently, but we do it well, and this is my favorite spot." We all scramble out of her car and into a curious shop, Khomeini in full color gravure presiding over hippies and workers and the kind of kids who hang out and listen to music, eating junk food and drinking coffee, all over the world. It is curious to see someone of Mimi's great sophistication enjoying a place like this,

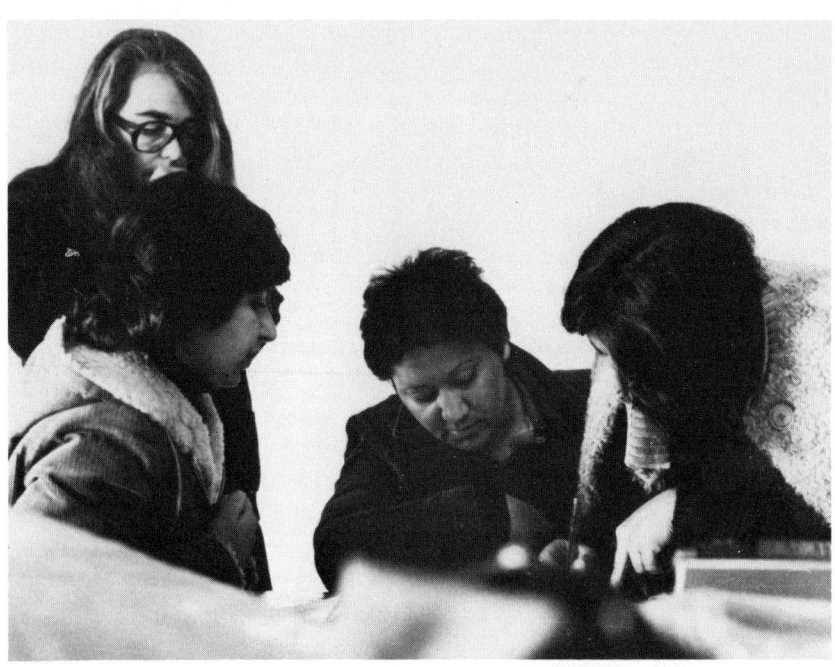

Translating: Asad, Rezvan, Mimi and the author.

so much is she the European in addition to her own Persian elegance. We munch our pizza at a table by the wall and talk with everyone in the shop. Or our friends do. As for us, we are safe within the people. They are carrying on and showing off for us too, a real Iranian pizza stand complete with scruffy young men and revolutionary music. It is another step in being in Persia. Mimi explains the songs—several by a woman with a good chanson voice, throaty, desolate—songs of just before the uprising, songs of despair and fury, a terrible sadness. Then songs of men, marching songs, songs sung at the demonstrations, songs now recorded in male army chorus voices, still stirring if you know their past, but already a bit prescribed, imposed upon one. Mimi is less happy with them. I would hear from her the insurrection, but now in this place: "All I feel is exhaustion—the noise, the hurry, the need to wolf down our food and run—I'll tell you later."

Back to the car, still carrying of all things a tin of Coca-Cola. "Imperialist garbage." I smile at them. "What else, with pizza?" they laugh back. We are friends now.

Then at the rally, the distance opens again. First of all it is immense, the biggest room I have ever seen. Used for indoor sports or something. From the time we drove up, the others have been tense, Mimi parking the car while Resvan and Asad hustle Sophie and me through the crowd. We are not to speak in English, therefore we are not to speak; we could hardly converse in French even if Sophie were up to it. And she has plenty of problems of her own, the movie camera, the film, a vast bag of stuff weighing maybe forty pounds. Many days later I tried carrying it across a street for her and could hardly lift it, have never understood how she could bear up the long way through the technical-university campus in the snow. Carrying it miles that day and for days to come, through the marches even. Today it is only a rally. None of what was to come, the miracle of the demonstrations has not yet happened, is still unguessed-at, undreamt-of. Today is only a CP rally we probably won't be able to speak at. Already it looks bad by the gates, there is hostility: to the camera, to us, to things in general—thousands of young men looking menacing. We must not speak in the crowd. Our friends close in around us like a phalanx; then at other times they inexplicably disappear, leaving us forlorn and nervous. They stay with us a moment and then vanish on an errand, running back and forth to Kateh—she's still arguing for feminist speakers on the program.

But I knew as soon as I entered the mammoth arena—we would never speak here. A sinking feeling. Futile. There are thousands and thousands of people, too many. My terror before speaking is appeased—to address this many people would kill me; it was only once I can remember I did it—August 26, 1970, the great march to commemorate the fiftieth anniversary of woman suffrage in America. But it was a fete, a true celebration, eighteen thousand people in a good mood sitting on the grass as the dusk came over Bryant Park behind the public library. You never see the millions on television. But I saw all those people, and trembling in my habitual and deplorable manner—rallied the rally, rallied the movement—scared and shaking in the usual way, I crowed and cheered us on.

This is no festival, no celebration. This is an unpleasant paranoid mass, and I am a foreigner whom they would hardly enjoy in a good mood, or with good feeling between nations. But translated, female, inferior to them—male, overwhelmingly male, and what women there are are attached to a male as by a cord. What we have to say is not important, this scene proclaims. Worse, it's dangerous, seditious. Resvan and Asad hurry us to a spot on the floor, we should keep our heads down, not be seen. A chador would be useful on this occasion. Many women here wear them, the chador having, under these circumstances, transformed itself from the costume one wore during the insurrection out of defiance of the Shah and the West into a sign of obedience to the stand-by-your-man line, the endorsement of Khomeini, who has been endorsed by the Tudeh. Students. Young men and women, workers, intellectuals. Some older persons. Maybe even some poetry lovers wanting to hear Sylvashroe Khasroe.

He doesn't seem much in evidence. A woman speaks first, assuring us that this is an open meeting, not one governed by any party or group. A statement invalidated by every message Resvan and Asad return with from Kateh. It is certain now, we will not be allowed to speak, any of us. The fatal blow was the Trotskyite. Earlier, back at the apartment, Mimi's anger over this—the years of persecution of her comrades, the despised righteous who preserved the truth of the revolution despite Stalin and his crimes—was wonderful, terrifying, tragic.

I have read enough Trotsky to admire him, particularly *The Revolution Betrayed*—and I admire just as much her life's dedication to his politics. How dare they forbid this woman? She is also, I am told, the first woman in Iran to have written a book of feminist analysis. I long for it to be translated as I listen to the approved speaker praise the martyrs, praise the role of women in other revolutions, fighting beside their men; and then on to introduce a string of party speakers, mostly men. We understand only scraps, our friends come and go to Kateh and the other feminists behind the scenes, still exhorting, then consulting, finally arriving at a plan of protest. We will walk out. In fifteen moments. When the signal is given. Sophie and I try to be as small as we can, an unchaperoned puddle on the floor, Sophie shooting the camera when she dares, taking stills when she can. Of course we draw attention, trying to turn it into goodwill with smiles, lights for a cigarette, gentleness with curious children.

Far from being a speaker, I am now in hope I won't be beaten up. And yet the people are wonderful to look at, even in this dark mood—the Turkoman mustaches of the men, their great eyebrows, and the drama of the chador coming through even its servitude here. But the women so ruled, even as they sit and listen; next to the man, leaning to instruct now and again. How all the language of their women's bodies is deference; the very headscarf, nunlike, modern—worse than a chador, updated and without the ancient beauty. These are women closed to us. To see them is to feel defeated. Hard to believe this is a mass of persons pertaining to the left. Hard to believe that this patriarchal bullying atmosphere could even associate with revolutionary, socialist ideas. In fact, it doesn't. The "revolution," in this place, is only a word for tribal patriotism, tribal patriarchy. Revived in the fierce arrogance of the men, the frightened docility of the women. Khomeini is everywhere. Even in the shouted salutes to the guerrillas. The guns throughout the hall.

I am glad when the order comes to stand and leave, our numbers so small I wonder if we even register as an exit—but Kateh has made it known in a statement. Near the door, we dare to chant our objections. But it was not our intention to disrupt or call down hostility. A moment or two, and we have finished, are outside in the snow again. And yet we seem to have awakened something. Others follow to dispute with us, argue, contradict. Still others, women now rather than the men who harass us with argument, have come to join us. Newcomers beyond the numbers who may have attended Kateh's organizing meetings.

These women want to start right at the beginning: "Why'd you leave?" "A women's meeting about women?" "I see." "Why not?" "Yes, sure." Sophie and I stand a bit apart, unable to help with the proceedings, wishing we could, wishing we could turn our anger and outrage into something useful—but this is for the Iranian women to do. Our job is to keep the record, attend to the archives. And we do. The tape recorder. The movie camera. The stills. This is the moment when Iranian feminism declares its autonomy from the left, its independence—something it must do if it is to live, if it is even to influence the left in any significant way. If the left is ever to develop a feminist perspective, it will do so only in reaction to the pressure of a large and powerful independent feminist movement.

"Our Nasrin"

And we are only a couple hundred people blathering away at each other on a wet strip of sidewalk, while indoors the monster rally of entrenched leftism goes on serenely. Well, it's a beginning. And there is also this figure disputing in a circle—I push forward to catch sight of her, my god, she has guts—furious and solitary in a ring of men, shouting, witty, a street kid, an urchin, I would guess at times obscene as well, bawdy. A Turk, the green eyes of a Turk, and will not be put down. She is funny too, she wins points, she sasses one back and the others laugh, their contempt for a moment lifted in admiration at the sheer "balls" of her, the effrontery, the fearless salt of her tongue, slangy, tough as the road she stands on, refusing to move for a car illegally making use of the campus roadway, finally stopping all traffic, the crowd around her growing.

"If we could get her," I say to Sophie. "Looks like someone already has," as this phenomenon tells the mob of what now appear to be her admirers, what appears to be the Persian equivalent of "Fuck off, go to hell, the bunch of you," and someone leads her toward us. "You may not have met Nasrin, but she was in Caifi too . . ." I'm sorry I never saw her in action till now, she's dynamite. We like her at once. Sophie particularly likes her proletarian tone. Her English is good, she could write things. "Wouldn't it be wonderful if she had the time to hang out with us while we're here?" "Someone like that could teach us everything. She's not only got all the theory, she's a doer, street-smart."

But she's off already, scrawling messages along with the others on the back of their poster, the silk screen poster that was to advertise International Women's Day, but never could. Now it does—but how? I ask; you still haven't got a place. Kateh appears, the posters are being held up, the back side, the blank side now covered with a scrawl proclaiming we will rally anyhow on International Women's Day. Where? I wonder. "We got a place, we just got it." It's Kateh. "Just a few moments ago. It's a miracle." All the bitterness of this afternoon, the humiliation of that mob, the bosses who refused us, all drain away from Kateh—it will happen, her dream. "Where?" "It's a school." "Where?" "Near Bahram's." "France Street?" "Right. Just there. The corner." I remember noticing that school as a motorist casually tried to run me over. "That's the sort of thing that happens to women a lot here, no chador, you look a little too free—they try it on me all the time," Nasrin laughs. We are all hugging and pounding backs and grabbing, squeezing each others' arms—we have a place. Laughter, the camera, the faces of all our friends smiling, the smile of having just pulled it off, a hairbreadth from defeat.

Nemat is there too now, Bahram, all the men in Caifi who support

The rally announced

us. A delightful young man named Hamid whom I met once in America at some meeting or other, Bloomington smudging into Austin, into Dallas—neither one of us can remember just which. His sister works for the television here, a producer, the only woman they still haven't fired from a key position though she is not permitted to appear on the screen—no woman is now. Would I like to talk to her? Sure, I guess so. We have still not gotten around to telling "the media" we are here, an early notion of Sophie's, contemplated in prudence, the idea being that we might thereby be safer as foreigners. Since the consulate would probably not be interested in our welfare, journalists might fill in, something like that. But I was not enthusiastic and we have been busy; I am in no position to pronounce on the situation of women here—could only refer someone who asked to my friends. Knowing, at that point, Western racism and the media hounding of "celebrities," they might thereupon cease to be interested. "Really, before I talk to press, I would rather check it out with Kateh and the women here." But for Hamid's sister, it hardly seems to be that great an event; she probably can't televise me anyway, but she might teach me something, be a good source of information on the situation here. Kateh thinks it's fine—we could do something together, a few of us.

Another woman, someone who has recognized me, asks if I'd speak at Damovar, the English-speaking university, something on the history of feminism. Sure. Wondering the next moment if I brought material on that, a speech, a file—out of instinct maybe this might come in handy. But the texts I should quote from, probably unobtainable. Yet if I have a few days I can remember them. Let's put it off till after the rally—I should be perfectly free after tomorrow.

All of us euphoric standing in the snow, evening coming. Let's go get something to eat, better yet, let's go get something to drink. There's only one place in Tehran where you can get a drink. The Hotel Intercontinental. Well, let's go there. Everyone makes a face, the Hotel Intercontinental—bastion of foreign imperialism; noses wrinkle, our friends are uncomfortable, the cold is impressive. "Okay." They have made this concession for us; I am touched.

Leaving, we pass a man selling posters from the insurrectionary days, a strange and hideous poster of people tied alive to posts, then executed by gunfire, the figures slumped in a heap at the moment of execution, a series of photographs. It sobers one. We do not know if they are the victims of the Shah or Khomeini, because we cannot read. Our friends tell us the Shah. But the victims in today's newspapers, Khomeini's victims, look just alike, the method is the same; the hooded face alone is different; today's victims face their gun, and the dead face is photographed so that the masses shall be edified and rejoice. Somehow both photographs sicken me. Despite my hatred of the Shah, I do not want to choose between styles of execution and call it a revolution. This place deserves better. Persia deserves better. And my friends, the vibrant loving women I am becoming close to. How unlike such horrors they are, how long they have all labored to put a stop to them. And now that the perpetrator of them is gone, there comes another. And an atmosphere where whatever they may do to stir their fellow women is done at enormous risk. So much remains the same for women; the issues clouded by a specious revolution. Our own yet to come. If it could.

7 ✳ ✳ ✳

MIMI'S TIRED. More than our tiredness with the cold and the tension of the rally, our rebuff. Two hours of debate and proselytizing on the pavements in a hostile atmosphere, one super-left young man even deciding Sophie and I, Westerners, had to be CIA agents, our friends very speedily tucking us under their arms and marshaling us out of there. It is almost agreeable to be in an international hotel, it is almost homey, the West, service with a smile, bourgeois appointments, the familiarity of being agreeable to the waiter, walking on carpet, drinking coffee. We have put off the heresy of a drink for a while, and it looks like the bar downstairs is closed in accordance with the new rules. There is rumor they still serve on the roof. We'll start with a coffee, the ladylikeness of sitting in our big rattan chairs, the service of coffee raised to a mystique here. That and fancy pastry, Persian, French. Lady food, gluttony food, idle food. Luxury. After seven hours of snow and clamor and fracas—it seems both funny and necessary that female revolutionaries partake of pastry, tea, chocolate, antithetical comforts. We amuse ourselves, observing ourselves in this light. But you can talk and be warm and be comfortable. It is a permitted way for women to be together, like the chicken-salad lunch, the Women's Exchange in New York, Ivy's in St. Paul. Ivy's being the archetypal ice-cream parlor for female consumption: homemade chocolates, a private booth wherein to discuss a separation, complain of a husband, brag over children, discover other women share whatever predicament you imagined you were alone in. I grew up there at my mother's side during shopping expeditions, the great visits to downtown St. Paul, our four blocks of business district and department stores. Days like this had to be relieved, tired feet, aching legs. Sit you upon the perfect walnut hand-carved bench of your own booth—it was always quiet, only the hum of ladytalk, the silent devouring of exquisite calories prepared as if forbidden food were also art. I have always wanted to sculpt it, the whole place with one hundred and forty women eating ice cream in their best clothes, a soundtrack of St. Paul ladytalk in the nineteen fifties murmuring from every booth.

But the Intercontinental Hotel, Tehran, is rather a different story. It is Millett, rather than Feely, my father's side, not my mother's; my aunts would be at home here, probably have been many times. Mother stayed here, but she probably worried about the food. And was not that comfortable with its seedy sophistication. The overpriced rug boutique. The souvenir shop was not to her taste, mine either. But the bathroom is divine relief after the unknown apartment—this must be a notable record for constipation, I muse. Traveling unsettles one.

But offers novelty as well; when I return, I see the man at the next table smoking a huge hookah—for all the world as if it were opium in public. It is only some exotic tobacco with which the management accommodates its guests—for what whopping fee? Otherwise I might have a go at it, pretend I'm in Persia, play. It is probably interdict for women, the ostentatious pleasure of it. We are conspicuous enough. Though for once, our race or nationality or the simple crime of being foreign, outsiders, not born here, is permitted. This in itself is a relief. Xenophobia too is tiring, tiresome. Two years in Japan left me exhausted with insult at the end of certain days and made me need an international population for the rest of my life.

Crossing the vast red carpet of the hotel on my way from having changed some of our money—we are no longer paupers and can even treat our friends tonight—feeling glad that we can show a bit of good manners of our own, approaching the table where my friends sit primly chatting, I think about women and class. Curious how women can sometimes enjoy bourgeois culture, often feel safe in it. Perhaps because it is older, has in its smug and easy security made a nominal place for women. Whereas the proletarian revolutionary tradition, being new, and yet still part of the patriarchy, is, like all young patriarchal creations, fiercely male, fiercely arrogant of its prerogative. The revolutionary male is more contemptuous of women than a "gentleman," and in joining their fortunes to the former, women lose all their concessions from the latter. The revolution has made no place for them, sees them as mascots, kid sisters, demanding absolute obedience and loyalty, but conceding them nothing, not even lip service to their claims. Yet in the old order there were comforts; all decadent institutions have their little pockets of joy.

As every village has a well where women gather. So that all women seem to enjoy getting dressed up and going downtown sometimes, playing lady, matron. Of course it's appreciably harder if you're poor; because clothing is precisely what creates your security, your position; downtown, any saleslady can knock you dead, the ultimate snobs of the world, the wardens of class.

But almost every woman is a proletarian in her own house: the housecoat, the housedress, a purely proletarian garment. Cleaning, scrubbing, the work of a maid whether she has a maid to help her or not. Maids were common still when my mother was an engineer's wife twenty years ago, working side by side with "our Celia," the same clothes, the same tasks, two housedresses cleaning. Maids have since become extinct in our part of the world. But take any wife, her own situation only a variation on a servant's. Because, of course, she is her husband's servant. Her children's servant. And by dressing up and going downtown, like a maid on her day off, she becomes no longer a servant but someone giving instructions to a waitress in a tearoom.

And in these solemn observances class gives us an illusion of freedom through mimicry; we ape power and status and hierarchy and imagine them ours. Class, our falling for class, the pitfall of gentility always exhorted upon women, the trifling assurances we are brought up with, the little comforts.

The clerks in the department store, of course, are fierce judges of ladylike pretension, but by a careful diplomacy you can persuade them to deliver your packages, the things they have permitted you to buy, thanks to your husband's position (nobody in the world would give you credit; you, yourself), charge everything, and having divested yourself of your burdens, amble across to Ivy's or the bar at the Plaza. And sin in perfect composure until it's time to run home and serve your boss's dinner. But there is still the lovely afternoon at Ivy's or the Plaza or the Rainbow Lunchroom or wherever you light upon to impersonate a free person, a paying customer, a lady behaving herself. You can also, with a certain discretion, mimic in a diminished way your husband's business lunches, the carefree way your engineer husband stands drinks in roadhouses for his crew till all hours of the night, the wonderful liberating world of male persons, who, whether they dress up or not to go out into the world, will do so every day, spending money they do not account for, drinking potions you are not to know of, saying things you never imagined are said.

With us, the bourgeois decor of the Intercontinental covers rather heady political conversation—for a group of ladies; we are fairly incendiary and it is a good thing we speak in French and in English and even keep our voices down, remembering from time to time, noticing that we are noticed.

I am noticed by a young foreigner going by, odd little Vandyke beard, it has the air of being glued onto his face. But his smile is very winning, something of the elf in his short stature and amused eyes. He's Ralph Schoenman, he says, he's heard I was here in Tehran, but wasn't sure of it, what a pleasure, he "admires my work." Very flattering indeed. Usual fluster remembering where we have met, always my weak point. But of course, he was Bertrand Russell's secretary years ago when Russell was doing the international tribunal on the crimes against the Vietnamese people committed by the American armed services, America in general; rather a fine idea in peace-movement practice and in pacifist tactic as well. We feminists copied it with the international tribunal of crimes against women. Schoenman also reminds me, as we pass by him on our way out, that he was a sponsor of Caifi in the United States, so as Caifi members we chat over the times and the troubles. This very morning Ralph has given a press conference here at the hotel; logical, it's full of journalists, practically an extension of the media. Sophie is carrying a long list of resident reporters provided by the front desk, we have gone through them over our coffee, hoping to check off just the key figures (we scarcely recognize a soul among them, only the high-sounding names of the corporate information monopolies they represent). We have neither much time nor ability to do well on the phone. But we have offered to round up a few journalists and point out on behalf of our group that we are in fact having a rally tomorrow to celebrate International Women's Day. Something we already know they could care less about—the real news is masculine revolution, guerrillas, who got shot last night, Khomeini's pronouncements, Bazargan's policies. Women, though they are half the population, are hardly about to compete, and not reported on beyond the jokes about chador, or a very occasional quizzical item "Will this new Islamic regime be a step backward for women who received so much education and Western privilege under the Shah?" A *New York Times*-type question. There is, of course, innuendo in the way the question is asked—as if women were on their own never entitled to education in third-world countries, but taken for granted as an undeserving backward people who never got anywhere unless compromised by imperialism, bourgeois collaboration with dictators and Uncle Sam's CIA. As if it were a tradeoff—everyone's wretched in your country, but look, five women got to go to college and one even became a judge, surely that's progress.

How the capitalists manipulate the position of women, how the bourgeoisie trumpet their handful of career ladies of good family, how the oppressor sets one oppressed group, the proletariat, against another oppressed group, women in general. As if the proletariat comprised no women at all, and the single female pointed out is regularly a member of the middle or moneyed classes. Lady Chatterley again, Lawrentian revenge posing as class hatred, but being in truth only male chauvinism and patriarchal privilege insisting on its rights despite its class origin.

Ralph's telling us amazing things, his press conference (how does one manage to hold a press conference on one's own, I wonder, what nerve it must take, what organization, what busywork and telephoning and secretarial assistance and organization). "Nonsense," he says, "you just call the three Persian papers and then put up a sign in the lobby, every reporter in the town shows up, the foreigners are all living right here anyway, and have very damn little to do." And at his press conference, he denounced this morning a member of the new government, a Bazargan appointment, who had been, Ralph has evidence he says, actually a big shot in Savak. He is exposing corruption in the provisional government. Good for him. Troubleshooter, gadfly, freedom fighter, all on his own taking on the government, the country. Hardly the sort of thing we have in mind, but if he can do that, perhaps we dare to offer a polite invitation to pressmen (there seem to be no women on the list—Tehran in revolution is not regarded as an appropriate female assignment) to attend our rally and listen to Iranian women announce the beginning of a women's liberation movement in Iran. Ought to be good for a line or two. Sophie's optimistic.

I'm not, really. I know the press and its treatment of the women's movement—some hundred years of it—have even read old newspapers ridiculing suffrage. It helps. It takes away some of the sting of personal attack, alleviates the personal hurt of this general contempt. Anyway, it's our responsibility to try—it is the only way we have been able to think of to be of assistance. Kateh and the others have been and will continue doing what phoning they can to their own press and their own contacts. Mimi will spend the night at it. But places like this present a bit of a problem to them, and they do not like nor do they come often to the hotel. We can rendezvous, glad we're even now on our way up to dinner. The rials are hot in my pocket. I'm hungry and I'd like that drink at last—but Ralph has another thing to say.

Leaning close, conspiratorial, this is very hot stuff. He knows, he says, just who are the members of the secret court—their names. A thing very few people know beyond the court itself and Khomeini, who has convened it. Every night this court condemns men to die. Ralph has worked a long time against capital punishment, and he is also dubious if every single one of those dead faces in the papers—he has a copy in his hand—is really a known Savak, a guilty party of the first rank, even deserving to die by the standards of an understandably vengeful people. There might be some innocent, some merely dissident, or some little apolitical folk in those ten or eleven corpses every day. "I recognize most of them as true war criminals, though I would never execute them, and I would certainly try them openly, but several others I'm not sure about, you see." And the power of the court derives from its secrecy, which makes it indomitable, answerable to no one; expose the identity of its members and it might slow down, act with greater attendance to the rules of justice. "They don't even believe in the idea of defense counsel, for godssake." And we both see that everything the people struggled for in the insurrection is destroyed, morally annulled, by this perversion of justice.

I begin to think of the executed on the way to the elevator, an appropriate place for a claustrophobe to think of death. State murder, the violence of that official homicide who pins a note on your front and shoots your staring photographed face. Trial, sentence, and all, often a matter of moments. As for the homosexuals, they were shot right in the road, judgment took seconds. They have begun to haunt me. How it must feel to die that way. The kind of terror. Heart attack is often what kills those tortured. Perhaps here as well. Fear itself coming to rescue the body from intolerable pain, from unchangeable fate. The fatality one must feel when the knock comes on the door, when the car comes in the night, when you find yourself thrown handcuffed into some basement room and you see the looks on their faces. A popular member of the parliament was arrested and held in a room so small he couldn't lie down for eight days. They never fed him. A police chief discovered him and apologized one day—the newspaper account said he only smiled in answer.

Mimi's smile when we ask her of the insurrection, her tiredness, which does not go away. "I sleep now at night, I have got my child; it's over, we're safe, we lived through it—but the exhaustion stays on. Even doing this work with the women. You see, so many of them have just come back from abroad, and they are full of hope and energy. They even have illusions about what we have now. Not me. And I can hardly go on living, sometimes I wonder if I really want to." Even thin Persian wine (the better sort has been sold out since the prohibition, and the best was actually destroyed) does not seem to revive her

Mimi

Italian self, though it is reconciled to the hotel dining room with a worldly shrug. This is a terrible restaurant, but the only one we can afford. The one across the hall is "French" but prohibitive; this one is ersatz "Polynesian," a tutti-frutti tourist trap, a buffet of misunderstood Chinese, Western, and island food—one is never sure what each pot of stuff commits one to, since ingredients are indistinguishable, might feasibly even be leftovers—we make the best of it. We're sitting down before food and something like wine, the circumstances of all civilization. How well Mimi seems to represent that.

Even her existential fatigue. She has looked on weeks of shootings, been present when the troops slaughtered demonstrators standing near her, come out alive but without rejoicing. "Too much violence makes you sick someplace. And now what have we? To have gone through all that." "Would you do it again?" "I'd have to—anything to get rid of him, the Shah was like nothing that can be imagined, what life was like under him. I mean everyday life, I mean the Savak, the spying everywhere, the whole population cowed." The informers, the spite, the pettiness of police state, a whole nation made to truckle, collaborate, connive. Made cowards of. "Until then, until then . . ." She looks away—we are not likely to understand what she still sees. Living with ghosts.

The first ones who went forward into the streets wore white, to signify their willingness to die. Accepting the cost. I know of no parallel. "Until then . . . And I could never understand just what made them." Nor can I. That they couldn't stand it anymore, that the moral nerve was pinched until it sprang back to life and insisted? At what risk, at what cost. The blood still in her eyes as she sits here with us, the almost defeated shoulders. If there were not what the women are doing now, I doubt she would want to go on living. But there is also a child. . . . "Sometimes I think we could go to the country a little while, it might help."

One speaks of the country as if going there were nearly sin. Frivolity. Really, it is sanity. Murder is sin. Does politics alienate one from nature? I wonder, the farm looming a second. It will be spring here next week. "Being outside the city, those places it happened." Because when you drive in Tehran with Mimi, every corner was where there was a pitched battle, a car or a statue overturned, where there was firing, where someone was hit. But the countryside is always itself. "I have a villa there," she says, using the Italian word. My eyes light up at the word "villa," conjuring Persian gardens. "It's a little place in the country, actually it belongs to my family, it's not being used right now and it's probably a mess. Nothing very grand, just a little place, I think I could fit you both for a few days if you'd like to come. We could take my car." We'd adore it and we think we'd be free for a few days, after tomorrow. I could put the university talk off till later, they'd want time to put out a notice. Sophie'd love it. After hauling that camera all day, any comfort is welcome; she's just remembered the unknown apartment's cold shower.

If Mimi can get free of her job a few days—she teaches at the television school, and since Khomeini has his people in charge of all media, it has ceased to be much of anything but censorship and agitprop and all the women are being chucked out at a great rate—she would love to be able to quit it, or at least have some time off. Like the others there, she is now virtually on strike anyway.

We all wax enthusiastic at the idea. We could film an interview out there, I think, watching Mimi, wonderful face to film, get to know her better, she is one of the most interesting women I have met here. The maturity, the mellowness, the passion, the tragedy somehow inherent in her. To be able to film her talking, telling us again and in greater detail the story of the uprising, to have that kind of account. For you never hear what real people experience in revolution, only those dreary manifestos of the leaders. I would like to film her, I would like to be her friend. We must film Mimi, really record the women here as we get to meet them, we must do this sort of thing. It's just as well that tomorrow will be our last overt and public political manifestation here—a thing that has worried me a great deal—because secretly I had hoped the thing might keep going, other rallies or something. But maybe it's just as well. Return to civil life as much as possible; in a time of peace one can do the inner history of women here. We are finding them now. The women who are our Persia.

PART III

1 ✳ ✳ ✳

THE HALL is filling up. There were moments when you wondered
. . . but not after this morning. Something has happened. Something
has started here. We first got wind of it when we heard there would be
a Maoist meeting for women at Tehran University this morning.
Depending on our friends, we arrived dangerously late, trooping
through the snow and the hordes of malign young men who keep the
gates there, their Muslim hostility bristling as we enter, two independent Persian women without veils, and two foreign females. Nemat's
presence with us doesn't do us much good either in their eyes; they
revile him for being with spies, prostitutes, whatever else we represent: we are grateful for his company. There is a feeling of danger
here now. The men who stop to stare at you, the taunts and
comments, the occasional groups of fanatics in march. It is odd to look
at men in open fear. Complete strangers. And in daylight. Crowds of
men. Marching. Shouting. To see them coming in formation. Or
merely standing around staring you down. To be in fear that they will
strike you for being a female and a stranger. It is odd to go about with
one's head down, silent, to pass through this force field of masculine
violence. Directed not at each other for once, but at us.

Naked—whatever contempt, guilt or ambivalence men harbor
toward their female subjects everywhere—it is here undisguised
hatred, direct malevolence. Like every woman, I have grown up being

113

afraid of men, conditioned by society and education, by the facts and experience, but in the daytime, peacefully entering a university, we do not usually expect to be set upon. The university to which we have so recently been admitted and which is still so precious to us. Perhaps it is symbolic that women are most threatened here now. That we gather here, are attacked here.

Otherwise the campus is thrilling, full of people arguing, disputing, endlessly haggling over points—of law, of political theory, of practical life, of social benefit, of economics, of history. It is how one imagines a revolution should enliven sensibility, should enliven that vast communal discussion which is to end in a new social order. People are here who would never have entered a university campus under the old order: the poor, the uneducated; suddenly the university belongs to them, becomes the collective property it should have been from inception. The groves are full of snow, the landscape is transformed, still that familiar feeling of campuses, yet changed, changed utterly by the wheel of history, the force of insurrection.

We wander about looking for the women, the meeting of women, which must be much further into the campus, we are not that sure which building, threading our way through mad, often funny disputations, Sophie and I rigorously keeping our mouths shut as we are supposed to do for safety. There was a hairy moment just beyond the gate when we were all pushed off the path by a phalanx of men. But most of the groups we come across now are peaceful, if emotional in their confrontation; a woman or two surrounded by men and talking back to them, five men lecturing a woman, two women taking on two men. Everywhere it is woman, woman, woman which is the issue of the altercation.

The new order, Resvan whispers to me, this morning it came over the radio; Khomeini has ordered women back into the veil. "But *Hejab* . . ." one woman contests to the men who hem her in, fierce, cruel in their laughter. *"Hejab"*—the word itself being debated, what it consists of, the old prescribed costume and demeanor ("modest dress," our friends translate the term)—clearly it can mean many things, caste, status, a way of life. The order refers only to women employed by the ministry, one older woman argues. Another, younger one, concurs, goes further. "Naked into the ministries"—she spits the words out and signals her contempt at the phrasing of the order "Women shall not go naked into the ministries"—the men edge in aggressively, berating her, contradicting her. The older woman reasons. Another young man has a different point of view. The women are joined by another pair, who are for or against. Often

Dispute

women debating the men will look up and smile at us—we are, I suppose, transparently, allies.

Women in chador eye us differently, are likely to be suspicious at first, shy in registering a glance, long in answering a smile. But something has taken hold of all of them, men as well as women; it is as if what we used to call "consciousness raising," that vast communal discussion between the parties at issue politically, men and women, were being played out here on this ground between men so bullying their very physical attitude and body set is violent, frightening, and women so outraged they almost seem to make a point by spitting on the ground for emphasis. A fury—in some cases—and in other knots of women, those in chador, a bewilderment between the ancient servility and submission, the distance and obedience, the blocking of vision and engagement that chador stands for, and a thrilling new siren call that permits them to speak up occasionally, take issue, refine a point, address their wisdom not only to women they disagree with but cannot entirely resist, but even to the young men whose outrageous arrogance keeps on lecturing at them.

Perhaps it is the arrogance after all that gets to them; this boy telling a woman his mother's age her place has transgressed the bounds of her patience. She disagrees with him, corrects him. His cohorts swarm about her, jeering, contending. Another woman, one of the new ones, the ones without chador who say they oppose it, wore it in demonstrations but now will not be told what to do—"No, not by you!" she harangues a pushy male body back as he surges toward her, his movements, like the others', a rhetoric in itself, a threat, a refusal of words or whatever points the speaker may make in debate; he is the stronger, his fist shaking in her face. "I was there twenty-first Bahman!" she shouts at him, her passion coming back, the masses surging against the soldiers, the danger of the guns. And now this; her indignation is wonderful.

We look on. Another group just ahead are discussing the class struggle and women, leftist women with and without chador, even the middle ground of headscarf. Men monitoring, giving out the line, women confined to responding, the ways dividing and coming together as two women differ and then agree and differ, the men still insisting on their original theoretical premise. Obey the revolution. Lenin has little to say about veils. Trotsky. Mao. But the nationalist line, Fanon. Woman must subordinate herself. All sources quoted are really only counters, whatever the text appealed to, the Koran throughout most of the campus, the bibles of the left elsewhere in pockets such as here. It would make the old masters of the left smile perhaps; surely their line on women should be sufficient to rule out the veil. But one hears distorted echoes of their doctrine in the endless reiteration that the revolution must not be divided and that the class war preempts female emancipation in importance and priority. Therefore it is unwise to recognize male and female as political classes with inherently different aims, women must adhere to the class and economic line only—"But women are workers too," a woman argues. "No, no, you cannot pit the women against the men; they must stay together. These new ideas are dangerous; they are against us, counterrevolutionary." If women will only do as they're told, show their solidarity, the class war can continue, the female loyally by the side of the male, who alone represents the interests, class and identity of them both in the manner of *femme couverte* (the concept in Continental law, and carried in Common law as well, that upon marriage man and wife become one person and that person is the husband), the assumption automatic and unconscious as well as unacknowledged.

Patriarchal assumption: the chief source of its power being its ease, its automatic and unexamined quality. And the leftist man offers himself as a model of fairness; the others are not comrades perhaps, the orthodox Muslims, but he is, his tradition is a more optimistic one for her. That he cooperates blandly with the orthodox, the mullahs, is of no real concern, nor to party leadership either. That she be denied her rights—over which he will not raise his voice, has not so far, nor does he plan to—is something she hardly dares upbraid him with. He is a kindly refuge among so many harsher masters, and he plays at being her comrade. She prides herself on speaking the party line to other females, especially the bourgeois feminists, as she has been taught to call them, though many have credentials as impeccably socialist as her own, and even longer years in the service of her ideology. Ah, but they cooperate with others who are not socialist, women who are barely political at all, plain housewives, fashionable women, careerists who study the professions and have no thought of the masses. "We cannot just see ourselves as women," she calls out to them insistently. "We must take into account the distribution of wealth, property, the economic conditions." "And do you think the Ayatollah is going to rearrange all that? Or that a religious government which ignores domocratic rights will give a thought to economic reform?" they toss back to her. "Follow them and you will not even have your own rights. For one thing, socialist revolution requires secular leadership." "But nationalist feeling dictates the endorsement of Islam, the repudiation of the Western imperialists . . ."

The argument goes round and round, but the issue of women is lost in it. We meander through it all in the snow, often without understanding a word, or only the few words our friends whisper to us in translation, usually too entranced themselves to remember us—but there is so much you understand anyway: gesture, circumstance, the courage of the women who dare to talk out, admiring the pith of one speaker or another, their guts and ingenuity in causing a man to be laughed at by the other men in a circle, the shocking, outrageous daring to speak up at all in these circumstances.

Perhaps we have missed the big meeting after all, perhaps it is over. Someone directs us to the Faculty of Arts and Letters, the statue of Ferdosi the poet perched on a plinth before it, covered peacefully in snow. I love coming upon him this way, having waited so long to meet him, lonely for sculpture and poets, bewildered with quarreling and ill will. How sane he seems, how literary, how unmoved by time; even the snow does not disturb him. Courtier poet of a past distant enough to be myth, culture, treasure, its own inequities now beyond contention; I frame him in my camera, evoking him, imagining him regarding today's proceedings. But the hall behind him is packed to capacity when we finally approach it; they will not let anyone else enter. We are sent away. Wandering disconsolately back past Ferdosi, enthroned in snow and height, his turban floating above events. Turning up a pair of stairs, debating if we ought to give up and go home. We missed it. Through our own fault we have missed whatever it was.

And then we see Claudine. Or rather a voice calls my name. To hear your name called out in the falling snow at Tehran University . . . I turn and see someone familiar. So surprised to see her, realizing slowly that she is from France, one of Des Femmes; I am not even sure which one, is it Sylvina or Claudine? Claudine. She even forgives my confusion. Because, just as I am astonished to meet her here, she is relieved to be no longer alone. Surreal snowscape punctuated by a voice, by Claudine's bizarre summer outfit, a French voice.

I begin to remember that Antoinette had said maybe one of them might come, a thing forgotten for days now; I never heard from them again and of course it would be impossible to get a ticket on this short notice, a visa. I gave them up. And now to find an old friend, a Westerner, a feminist from France, like a comrade from home. We are no longer alone here either, of course, we already have Iranian feminist friends, so perhaps it's simply that the "internationalist" feminists—Sophie and I struggling along under this term—are no longer alone. The whole thing seems easier now: France, or a French women's group, is sharing whatever curious responsibility we imagine we hold today. March 8.

Arriving only an hour ago, Claudine went forth out of her hotel, launched herself on the unknown, stepped into a cab, and guessing at

The poet Ferdosi

a university and the hope of some meeting or other, some action, has gotten herself here. Where we come upon her in the snow, wearing white trousers and a thin pink sweater, open-toed shoes. She is profoundly embarrassed over her clothing, so we can't tease her much about it: "I thought it was nearly tropical in Tehran, I looked it up in a book, it said it would be terribly hot in summer and this is spring, how would I expect snow?"

"You're just in time. The rally is this afternoon; the women here have had a terrible time even getting a place to hold it and have despaired time and again. But it's on."

And now the crowd files in. Claudine has found a French speaker in one of the rows below us, they are busily translating further French messages of solidarity. The woman who befriended Claudine tells us that many workers are on strike because Khomeini has decided to appoint what were to have been the elected representatives in the industrial Komiteh. Next to her is a German reporter. He will be the solitary representative of the world press here today and keeps exclaiming his surprise that no others have come. "We tried to notify them." "It's the strangest thing." I thank him and climb up to the platform. "Curious," he keeps muttering.

News is brought in every few moments. Because within the university today the women had begun to rise. Everything is strange today, like the snow. As if all speeded up. We have already begun to hear in corners of the hall about what happened today after we left the university, the miracle. Five thousand women marched out the gates of Tehran University and downtown to the offices of the government. They were met with guns. But they had begun the revolution.

Our rally will be bigger than we ever anticipated it to be. Because, quite independently, a vast number of women—just women, non-aligned, not leftist, not feminist, just women—have taken to the streets. Who would ever have imagined it? We were there and missed it—the last thing we saw at the university today was a terrifying march of men, followers of Khomeini, Islamic fanatics, storming out the gates, coming on very fast; we had to be pulled out of the way or they would have attacked us. Young men responding to Khomeini's order by taking to the streets in bands to terrorize women. Running and trudging in the tired snow, we took refuge in a coffeehouse. And missed everything.

Within this morning's meeting, women had agitated for protest, for demonstrations. Women reacting to Khomeini's order to go back to the veil. Furious women from all over the city. No, said the leftists who had called the meeting, intending it as a public education forum for women; demonstration is unproductive, shows dissent from the new order and divides the revolution. Wait and see how the order for chador is qualified. "No, we won't," many women called out. "We are going into the streets. Now." Long arguments. Some stayed. But a great number left the hall.

Would that we could ever have known this and followed them, these leaders and makers. And coming on these same paths we had just walked in search of them, arriving at the gates, they found them locked. Locked with chains. By fanatic Islamic youths. And so they climbed the great iron fences of Tehran University—if we could have seen that, photographed it. For a shot of that! That is the photograph that *defines* an uprising of women, I nudge Sophie, if we could have made that image. I bet nobody got it; there were no press there today either. From the walls the women called down to the crowd, "Is this our freedom?" and shamed the militia into having the chains unlocked. "Chains belong to Savak," the women went on shouting, boldly reasserting the insurrection, bringing it back. And then, as they must have been so many times those harrowing days that taught them how, they were back in the streets and in danger, in revolt.

That electricity is here in the hall as it begins to fill. The spontaneous march in the snow. The guns downtown. The wandering bands of young men sent out to terrorize. The Caifi men are here, guarding the doors, much talk of security. That this building is secure relieves them, going over the system of doors, the big doors in front leading to the street, the little side passage that comes up to the speakers' platform. Caifi men bounding in and out with a gallant rather delighted sense of danger, mission and adventure. It may be rather gently paranoid, of course; this sort of thing usually tends to be inflated. But while I wait in my corner at the back of the stage as the final touches are put on our translation, I begin to wonder: who are these strange men hanging out at the university and in the streets, ready to pounce on us, how did they marshal themselves into a force the moment the order for chador was given, how did they arrive at the marching, shouting bands who take over the streets and become the formation we barely escaped today?

And when the women marched in the streets, these men were there already, stoning them, spitting insults, carrying knives. The women's demonstration has already been threatened by counterdemonstration from these fearsome men; one really wouldn't want them storming our building here on France Street. This gray formal street in the early evening. This street where we first began. I wondered that first day what it would bring us, and here we are in a girls' school, the institutional space of our childhood finally serving us. A high school it

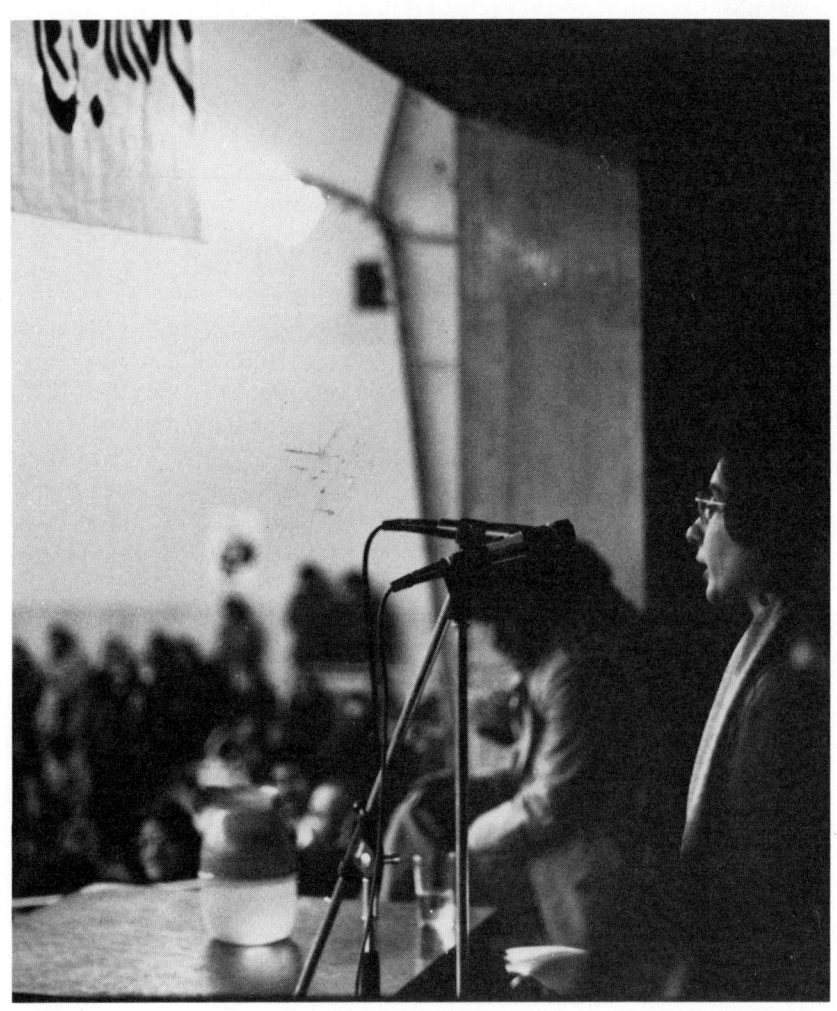

March 8 Women's Rally

seems, by the size of the indoor playing-field-cum-auditorium. One that seems to expect an enormous crowd to supervise its intramural sports and award days. Nothing like so big a hall as the Tudeh party enjoyed (a university space for men's sports), but still it may be too big for us; embarrassing if we can't fill it.

Usual thoughts of a nervous speaker, eyeing the translators as they embark on one more version of my poor speech; adjusted, I suspect, for today's different circumstances. Perhaps a certain militancy has returned. They are also pursuing the last graces of Persian expression. Mimi is assisted this time by a student of literature: English, French, Persian. Across the stage, in another corner, Sophie adeptly loads all her cameras, the Nikon, the Zeiss, the movie camera, reads her meters, prepares her perch to catch the speakers' faces. Speakers are everywhere. I pace. I try to be businesslike with my tape recorder. But something ominous is with me. I remember the wrong things. Today's march of women excites me even more than our rally. And the rally itself, now that we have it, are in the heart of it, fills me with dread. The dread of having to "go on," the dread of politics altogether. The hall filling, the excitement of bodies, the electricity on the platform— not only all the microphones and lights, but the electric energy coming through the crowd—I hover in a corner of the stone enclosure at the back of the platform, recalling apparently without reason, or at least any reason beyond a vague existential chill, certain passages in Sartre's political short stories, read in college and never adequately under- stood, remembered now only as a blur, a fear, an impression of the cruelty of politics, the irrational danger, the loss of nuance under the cold fanaticism of ideas, the kind of thing Sartre's ambivalent prisoners feel before they are to be shot.

The first woman to speak had four of her sons shot down in the insurrection; she is the mother of four martyrs whom we were to have heard yesterday. A great cry goes up for her as she comes into the hall. A wonderful entrance in full chador, the beautiful garment truly costume here, the cloak of mourning and drama. The crowd roars for her. *"Garout, Garout,"* a chant of salute very much in use nowadays. Called for, she comes slowly. With dignity and eminence. An elderly woman but a firebrand speaker. We are started.

Socialist women. Women of many groups and persuasions, teachers, nurses, professional women, women in unions, a woman from the Palestine Liberation Front whom we ran into this morning at the university, her greetings from the PLO, messages from France, from feminists abroad, women from one field of study, work or industry, political group or another, the Trotskyite, Kateh. Figures of women seen from behind as they attack the microphone, the crowd's exuber-

The Palestinian

ance, the chanting. The spirit of the revolution reaffirmed, then directed toward the new energy and passion of women. Today's march was the first protest against the new order settling in, the first reminder of the insurrection. The tendency of the people to prolong revolution, to keep it going on, reach change, now in conflict with the forces of stasis, of stop here and no further—you feel them at play out there, you feel the tug of further insurrection like a siren's call. The people hesitating, afraid, then slipping into courage, the temptations of logic, of their own ancient hope, their fugitive desires—although all that is being urged is human rights—it has the air of treason, the thrill of insubordination. The crowd feels like it must have felt in the uprising: a wonderful feel. New to me.

Much of what follows is lost to me through language, though saved on tapes I can spend time later to unravel, yet even at that moment much is clear. I feel the crowd deciding, a mixed crowd of men and women, but deciding for women. With an excitement rarely seen. I feel women becoming the revolution here, the revolutionary force. And when the awful moment to speak comes, I am carried away with that. The crowd before me reminding me how women are beginning a rebellion here, how powerful that rebellion. And in this place and with its peculiar history. General as patriarchy is, it has its own flavor and experience everywhere, but how keen and jagged, how bitterly continuous, how ancient and recent the long history that women here know of our universal enslavement, a knowledge eaten in the mouth, the experience of male dictatorship over us. A kingdom reasserted again now after a glimpse of insurrection. So that the struggle has a monumental, immemorial quality, almost eternal. Yet everywhere we were held down. In all recorded time. And everywhere now we are rising. Our slavery becoming freedom. Place after place, the world changed and all lives in it. A movement of vast proportions, historical, enormous. A world liberation. Transforming human ways beyond old recognitions, overturning millennia of the ancient order. Illuminating.

Seeing this, the way one does see at times, the clarity of certain occasions. Venturing to name patriarchy, patriarchal religions. Here. A different and dangerous rhetoric. The most fundamental sedition. The crowd listens, permitting me these few high moments. As if to be able to say these words were to declare it over, to end an era. To begin another one. Feeling, almost like a chill, that we have, here today in this rather silly stadium of adolescent sports, announced something vast. Something already begun, but announced now. We have announced the birth of a revolution among women here—with Home Team and Visitors marked at either end of the hall.

The speakers' platform, raised up above bleachers and at the center of this huge room. From the microphone I have the awesome honor of addressing several thousand persons whose language I cannot even speak. My own words in English and then the translator, enabling me. Mimi has disappeared, defected at the last moment in favor of the literature student. Who hurls my phrases out, swift and adroit after each is announced in my useless English. The humbling privilege of taking part in this. The cause of women, ancient and eternal. These few high moments.

2

FINALLY WE'RE ON OUR WAY out of the unknown apartment and into a real home. We've been all day about it. Kateh and the others had heard we were cold, that the place was dirty. Now we're to be moved. It is as if the days in the unknown apartment were a kind of testing zone, a hazing period. And we have passed. Asad and Resvan were to pick us up early in the morning. When they were not there by two in the afternoon, I gave up reading my *Modern History of Iran,* on the broken glass tabletop by the heat of the one electric grill, and gave in to Sophie's objections. I called Nemat. He arrived within the hour with Nasrin, the firebrand we had so admired before. I would like to go over to Tehran University to see what's going on, if there are more demonstrations planned, if the impetus of yesterday will continue. Sophie would like to have her coffee at least. And we had promised to pick up Claudine at the Intercontinental hours ago, so, since it's Friday, the Muslim equivalent of Sunday, and probably fairly quiet politically, we feel safe stopping off there first for coffee.

And a deal of talk, now that we have Nemat, we can quiz him about the regional, ethnic, and linguistic minorities. And the Jews, does he foresee persecution there? A thing many people had asked us to look into. In view of the Ayatollah's promises, he doesn't. Though it could happen. The Ba'hai are already threatened. And homosexuals, what of this minority? My own, after all; Sophie's and Claudine's. Nemat knew gay liberation in America, by now an accepted political group on the left, like any other, respected, taken into account. But here everything is different. Here homosexuality is something persons can be executed for under certain very cloudy circumstances. I find myself diffident before his unease. And he really doesn't know, he says, aside from the news articles of executions and the charges of homosexual rape. The paper says they are first accused of rape. Another report says the rape victim was lashed too. What victim? I wonder. Possibly there was no victim, no rape either. It is even possible they are not homosexuals, just undesirable to whoever is interpreting holy Islam in that village at that moment. To call someone a homosexual is probably a very likely kind of slander just now.

Having seen Iranian men chatting, their virility, a man with his arm around another man, the two relaxed, at ease in a public affection forbidden in my own country. Because it would be taken to imply homosexuality, whereas these men are confident it will not. And can therefore express a fondness everywhere condemned if it is sexual, whereas the world permits and even promotes a sexuality often with no fondness whatsoever. Watching and enjoying these men, I wonder vaguely why I, a lesbian, was so eager to arrive in Iran, a country where homosexuals are being executed.

But then steady it up again, the perspective. The paper says it was a small village in a remote area. Khalil and Nersi, Kateh and the feminists know very well that I am lesbian; no one regards my going as dangerous. Neither do I. Isolated instances, what we read bears so little relationship to the place as we experience it through Khalil and Nersi, through the years in Caifi, the civility of my friends.

But what is life like here for homosexuals, what has it been in the past? What is the tradition? Having some notion that it would replicate—among men—the younger and poorer, the older and better off, the very hierarchical relation of male and female, dominator and dominated. How much of this is a matter of class? He's a bit confused by this question. There's a good deal of it, I suppose; perhaps you ought to talk to a sociologist or anthropologist from the university. I look at Nasrin and we grin at each other. Nemat does sound a bit outlandish. Nasrin has brought a friend with her—Ferdosheh. They seem absorbed in each other, they seem to give off the frightened ecstasy of two persons falling into a forbidden love. They are very beautiful together and very dangerous.

Perhaps I should look to other informants and return the conversation to safe and approved topics, the Ayatollah versus the progressive forces. Claudine holds out her little tape recorder to catch every word of Nemat's analysis. This good brother. A second cup of coffee, the comfort of the lobby with its big soft chairs and acres of red

Ferdosheh

carpet. We really ought to be on the road, checking out the university, seeing if something is happening.

But not much is. It is much like yesterday. Again we are late, this time altogether too late for the Maoist meeting, broken up after the leaders of the left advised the women not to take any part in tomorrow's demonstration. A demonstration at the Ministry of Justice. Now one must wonder if it will even take place, since the left advises against it. But why persuade an awakening group not to demonstrate? What sort of politics is that? The sidewalks are full of argument, but the women are more definite today, even the women in chador. How moving it is when they speak out, how full of authority and outrage when the words finally issue from beneath a veil. Whereas the women of the left seem even more ambivalent today than yesterday; it is as if an order has come out that yesterday's demonstration was in error, was held without premeditation, permission even, from the male intellectuals who make decisions for these women. That their sisters flatly took to the streets—the very proletarian and working class who are the subject of their theories—is very shocking.

Sophie is in the clutches of another sort of theorist, a violently persuasive young man who is also profoundly religious. We have heard young men all along the sidewalks lecturing women with the news that their hair, if not covered, is radioactive, dangerous in itself, that women have smaller brains and must cover their heads lest they get a chill—but we haven't heard this guy yet; a Koran preceptor, chapter and verse. All passages prove conclusively that men would be the masters of women everywhere, else Allah is disturbed, nature is violated, religion is insulted. I notice in surprise that he wears the ring of the Air Force Academy of the United States. And point out the fact to him. Yes, he was there for training; he's a militiaman on his Friday off. He was there in the Shah's time, now he is here: the same duties. This ring wrapped around the trigger section of an automatic weapon—here? in Arizona? does it matter?—the insignia, the accoutrements of military rank, power: shiny button, epaulet, or ring; all of it is the stuff of his dreams. That together with a religious ideology that makes him right and better. He bores me after a few moments, but will not let us go. He towers over us, he bullies. I wiggle away and fall in with a subtle Frenchman, a reporter from *Figaro;* he'd love to know our opinions and discuss the situation here. Fine. We'll meet you back at the hotel. And he saunters off in his flawless and immaculate gray trousers, a cashmere sweater, the appropriate thing to snuggle under his perfect suede jacket. Leaving us with the hulking Air Force man, his mustache and his wrath.

No one satisfies. There are women from a Maoist group along the

Confrontation at Tehran

sidewalk on the way back; we debate the chances of women after the final proletarian revolution, versus before. We agree and disagree by turns and moment to moment; it is still more interesting. But I liked best a woman before the engineering building who was defending herself to a whole group of men of different persuasions, left, Muslim, just opposed on principle. And she was tireless, to be neither shamed nor silenced.

But it is also oppressive. Equally oppressive in a trivial way is the lunch at the hotel. The lunch arranged with the *Figaro* man, who never shows up. As for our Persians, they hate the place and haven't got enough money. We'll stake them. Nemat and Nasrin do not even want to sit down. If they will do us the favor of putting aside their dislike—but a look at the menu infuriates us too—any place that charges five dollars for a hamburger probably ought to be bombed. The other night after the rally it seemed that it would be; all the lights went out, the militia gathered in the foyer and advised us not to leave until the shooting stopped. Even back at the unknown apartment the guns went on for hours. National Public Radio managed to telephone me from Washington, D.C., in the midst of the firing, because a friend of mine had a friend there and they are checking up to see if I'm all right. Would also like a little radio interview too, now I'm on the line; they've just had a statement from Reza Baraheni and would like one from me as well, a thing impossible with the gunfire just outside, so we hung up and went to sleep. And now Figaro is impossible to find, though we would love to fill his ears with our opinions, or had thought we would; now it just seems better to get through lunch and find a place to stay tonight. No one is quite sure where we ought to be put. Bahram is really in charge of this, but we have rung his house several times without an answer. Nasrin's friend Ferdosheh might have room, but the house has no phone, and a phone would be a convenience in making arrangements. There is one other possibility that Nemat has thought of. We'll check it after lunch.

It did in fact sound perfect, an old house, an extra pair of rooms used by a couple who are out of town, self-enclosed, like an apartment. Now we are finally on our way there. We drive through the city, watching men line up for the movies. Women are not permitted to attend. Movies themselves are rather suspect; one participates in Western decadence in seeing them. We drive along in the early dark, comforted; we will at last have a home, live with people in reach, be closer. The place we are going is to a comrade's, we'll be safe, looked after; in a city full of guns, uncertain taxis, a city where we cannot read and do not know how to speak the language. We will be able at last to hang up our clothes, a thing never done at the unknown, since we were always just staying there a day, then another. I can spread out my books, Sophie can load her cameras in peace. There will be coffee. We won't be cold anymore, we won't camp and wander.

Down a small lane, will it be this house or that one? Good, they are old. Which rooms will be ours? The road narrows, the treacherous gutters on either side. We park, drag our bags around the corner, the ubiquitous duffel. To be able to unpack at last. I am already hanging up the rumpled clothes in my mind. A man answers the door, gruff manner, enormous mustache. No, he says, he has a better plan, he'll guide us.

By now we have no idea where we are going. Why doesn't someone explain, for godssake? Bother to confide in us our own destiny. I am even annoyed at Nemat. It'll be fine, he says, it's not that far. It's better. Why is it better, I haven't even seen this place, I grumble to myself. For the first time, even I have lost patience with my comrades, their elaborate and apparently useless secrecy, their carting us about like children or baggage; why should we have no say at all? The great mustache says his stove smoked. I could care less, I feel I could lie down in the road from sheer homelessness. I have been six days without a bath or what I regard as food, I am tired of rummaging through my rumpled clothes in that duffel bag for thirty minutes just to find one clean sock, my boots leak, have leaked for days of rain and snow—is there no shelter in this whole country? If we went to a hotel our money would be gone in a week but it is apparent we should, we have taxed our friends past their capacity—maybe even Bahram can't find any place to put us up, these are clearly times in which we cannot hold them to their promises—but the excursion ticket will not permit us to leave for over two weeks. The hell with it, I'll just shut up and trust them—it always used to work. In Japan it never failed; people take care of you if you give them your allegiance. And Caifi has never let me down yet.

"It's only that they never bothered to explain anything," Sophie says, looking at the beautiful room—"we don't even know whose house it is." "Have faith, kid, I hear ice cubes." There is a man here who welcomed us. No woman, or at least she hasn't arrived home yet. You met her yesterday at the rally, they keep telling me. I met thirty-five women yesterday. Nelufar, they keep saying. And when I see her I'm delighted. She is a beautiful woman, I do indeed remember her, a face of wonderful sophistication, poised, classic, the line of the cheek, the acumen in the eye. Her husband is also very handsome, the two sitting side by side at a table while he pours out Scotch for us, his treasure. His illegal, probably hugely expensive treasure. I am quick to present the long-traveled French brandy, at last I have a host to present it to.

At Nelufar's

And a hostess. Though it is Hermoz who has done all the work of greeting us before Nelufar's arrival, changing the furniture around, converting what appears to be an upstairs sitting room into a bedroom for us, a few low chairs, a rack of pipes—perhaps it was his study, perhaps he has given up his study for us. Maids run about carrying things, a countrywoman and her daughter; Hermoz introduces them as part of the family, I am still wondering if they are relatives when his daughters are introduced, adolescents who speak to me in French. They go to a French school. Everything is in French, even I am. Hermoz prefers it to English, his children as well, Nelufar vastly prefers it. Poor Sophie, who prefers it not at all. It is I who must perform for our Scotch and for our supper, lovely cutlets that appear magically, perhaps from outside, perhaps from downstairs where the kitchen and living and dining rooms are.

It is a beautiful house; it is, as I suspected when I saw it, an architect's house, and though Hermoz is an architect, it is not a house he has done, but a house done by a friend. But everything in it proclaims this man, his taste in things and colors and shapes. Country rugs, folk-art beds, low chairs and tables from the provinces, a big round table to drink with his friends. And there are a good number of us—Nemat, the mustache, whom it appears very early is a Trotskyite and at once he takes on the table over the issue of revolution, a hilarious discussion in French and Persian, many of whose relevant portions are lost on me. But I adore my new home. Hermoz, Nelufar. The daughters, Bahar and Gouli. Being elbow to elbow between the mustache and Nemat, across from Hermoz and Nelufar, who sit very near together as if the day that separated them were long, their connection full of life. It is a pleasure to watch how much Hermoz loves his wife, with what vibrancy he smiles at her, courtliness honed into intimacy. This is a good place to live. We have finally found a home. In a way, we have at last penetrated Persia, a household, a family; how satisfactory.

We go off to our room. Outside it at the big table everyone is doing the revolution in Persian. The mustache is far too opinionated. I am glad the others get on his case. The voices go on, friendly and reassuring. I have not been this happy since I came here, as peaceful. Even though we go to sleep in slender single beds, their heads coming together at a corner. We could put them side by side, but that might be construed as rudeness, I apologize to Sophie. Our clothes are on hangers, what more could one want—she smiles and falls asleep.

3 ✳ ✳ ✳

AT THE RATE we're going, we may miss another demonstration. Just
because of traffic. We all started off at the crack of dawn in Nelufar's
car, but at eleven we are still entering the inner city. We are excited,
we anticipate something important; today is expected to be very big,
despite all efforts to quell it. I'm in the front doing the French for both
of us; Sophie in the back, understanding most of what we say, but
preferring to phrase her own comments in English. To her vast
annoyance, people say to her, "But you're a Canadian, you must know
French." Someone said it this morning at breakfast, one of the
children, their bright quick little French putting me off much of the
time too; their shyness saying a word in English, their fear they will
make a mistake in French, my fear that I shall. They are so shy and
gauche and like slim frisky young horses, girls that age, liable to go off
in laughter or in a pout or hurt feelings or delight—at anything.
Sophie tries everywhere to explain she is from Vancouver, way to the
west of Canada, where there are no French, even if long after she
finished school the separatists succeeded in making French an official
language, but she, poor Anglo-Saxon thing, has none. Isolated in
English, Sophie becomes English, which really she is not; she's Scots
and Irish. But with years in England, living with their cold and their
personalities—both of which seem to descend on her in the presence
of our French. Not that my poor French recommends itself at all; but
in Persia many kinds of French are tolerated, and it is always easier to
speak French to anyone but a French speaker—I even survived on it
occasionally in Japan.

I am presently surviving for both of us, a taxing job since Nelufar's
French is, by comparison with mine, quite perfect and very rapid. I
ride along arranging my replies, questions and expressions with the
nervous flurry of one taking examinations. To be with Nelufar is to be
near France, or France as it has mixed and been absorbed by Persia.
She holds a doctorate in sociology from the Sorbonne, my own student
days hanging out there coinciding; Oxford vacations spent in Paris;

Rue de Seine, Odéon. But it did not make me ever so French as she, its very rigor in thought, even its very chic somehow blend with her fine Iranian face, her quickness. Her polish like old onyx polished long and deep into the vein. Even the way she smokes is to be with a European. I light cigarette after cigarette for the two of us, the traffic crawling, infuriating; the morning wasting away from us in memories of France or the prospects for women here, the repression of feminism we fear coming. The sight of a Ba'hai center out the corner of an eye passing over a bridge, the one moment we were free to move quickly, then another traffic jam. Our haggard suspicion we will get there too late.

The traffic may indeed have precipitated a revolution, but it is now endangering all our chances of participating. And today is expected to be a very big gathering. We have already passed throngs of schoolgirls marching and singing along the way, holding hands or carrying banners proclaiming women's rights. The sight is beautiful, their hopefulness, their courage. Later we will hear that several were stabbed, and one child, a thirteen-year-old girl in her school middy, was smashed in the mouth with brass knuckles. Which here are called American knuckles.

Watching the young assemble, I remember that we never marched this way in my childhood, convent school, uniforms, ranks, this age— when I was this age no one marched yet. Nelufar's daughters will be marching too; girls are skipping school all over Tehran today. Many girl students are marching with the women who teach them. We are not sure how this demonstration was called, the word was already being circulated at our own rally—that the women who had gone to see the government that morning in the snow, the great spontaneous march of them, had set the Ministry of Justice as their next target. Getting no justice that first day, going to "Justice" itself next had seemed to be making a good point. And since the order to wear chador was officially directed toward ministry employees, women with secretarial jobs in the government, the role of feminists and women demonstrators is to support them. We converge from everywhere toward one idea, the Hall of Justice. Slowly, slowly, winding through the south part of Tehran, penetrating the older section of the city, the place of the poor, a place of terrible stares, of men in the streets who bristle at the sight of women alone and unveiled in a car, neighbor- hood of bazaar and mosque, thousands of men in the streets and only a few women, all veiled.

Although nothing ever does seem to begin on time, we are still not sure if we are too late as we park. And indeed, being two hours late, we are almost early. The place has not even begun to fill up yet but friends are already here: Kateh, Nasrin, Resa, Asad. Even a "team" from an American network, the woman with the mike spotting me in some disbelief and dragging me off in a corner with her two-man crew to ask me questions. All the other press is European, but there is very little of it. We could use a great deal more; the place is full of guns. Militia are everywhere, one is surrounded with machine guns. And it is like a trap—the huge main hall surrounded by tier upon tier of onlookers—many of them armed. Shooting fish in a barrel, I realize. Only one gun need go off, only one incident, only one person lose his cool, and we are all massacred. The front section near the door is full of men who have come to revile us, the militia holding them back, but not that strenuously and one wonders for how long.

Steadily now, women trooping in, filling the entire floor of this vast building, groups filing in cheered, phalanx after phalanx; here now is Tehran University, a great cheer for them. Signs along the wall, along the first tier looking down upon us, proclaiming that these are the women workers of one ministry or another, the nurses of this or that hospital, secretaries of businesses, teachers of schools, and the schools named. We are safer already, the men of the first tier are either with us or outnumbered now by women. It is so crowded that the newcomers go up to the balconies. We are shoulder to shoulder. And the chants roar out, banging from wall to wall, the great stone walls of this curious building, part palace architecture, part penitentiary tier. And guns looking down from the upper tiers, men, more guns on every plinth, staircase, behind us and at all doors. And we roar like no chanting I have ever heard. It makes the skin prickle, it makes one proud. I have never heard women make this much uproar, a fury contained always with cool appreciation of those guns surrounding us. All work must have ceased for the day in the ministry, most of its employees, men and women, look on; the latter coming obediently this morning (lose your job or obey) in chador, but loose now, they too join the numbers looking down on us, until you hardly see any guns above now, perhaps they have come down to stand guard over the demonstrators on the floor, tighter and sharper. Yet each time the chants crescendo, and the guns move forward, we develop a peaceful stance, sit down, are quiet for a moment; it is always just short of violence.

I find myself thinking that men probably could never tread this fine line between great anger and great peacefulness. There will be much congratulations of the militia today for not killing us, absurd when you consider that we are unarmed and peaceful demonstrators, their very weapons upon us are an insult, an imposition utterly unnecessary. Yet how long before a group of men would lose their tempers being herded about this way, ordered, commanded to move here or there or

Sit-in at the Ministry of Justice

forward, how long before you cuss them? And there would always be one fool who would "mix it up" with one of these nervous young soldiers; an insult, a shot. It is very difficult to abstain, particularly if you also see yourself as a fighter, a wrestler, a gunman. But then of course we don't. We have never been provided with these fantasies in childhood, and even should we adapt them, reality here and now would disabuse us. It has been a long time since women bore arms in the revolution, and then very few of them. We are another sort of fighter, our courage is in the spirit that got us here against odds and even danger, attack. One group of men guard us like felons, another, the fanatics, surge against them to reach us and tear us apart, calling insults, invocations of shame and inferiority heaped on the female since childhood. We never came here to hurt anyone. We are after something different and better than arms. Justice. The cry ringing over and over through the perfect acoustics of stone walls, before tier on tier of onlookers; like a theater we are now, not a place of assassination. "In the dawn of Freedom we have no freedom," the voices surge, time and again. *"Azadi, Azadi, Azadi."*

Sophie goes above to shoot film. I am in the sea of women, we are packed so tight as it is hard to stand, still harder to sit down when the speakers begin. And yet claustrophobia never comes. Nor the fear of being lost here, nor even the fear of being shot; the chants, the surge of upraised arms, the power of the crowd sustains me entirely. They are women, how safe one feels with women, that many women about one, how odd that one never fears physical harm from women, only from men, and there are now so many women we could overpower anyone, anything, the entire government—or so it feels. The Ayatollah clinging in ubiquitous photo to the wall, and his minions, the tough young men with guns, behind them the robes of clergy, bureaucrats, the laws, the lies, the edicts—we are a greater force. Greater than I have ever felt in America in our demonstrations. Even the mammoth demos of the peace movement, we are a wild force with unknown power, fresh tapped, springing, yet careful, controlled for all its passion. And the chants are passion itself. *Azadi, Azadi, Azadi.*

Azadi, the easy one, the word for freedom repeated three times, tape-recording the rest, adding translations as someone tosses them at me, Bahram at one point, because the Caifi men are here too, faithful to all our events; Bahram has excited the curiosity of a militiaman who cannot understand that he is demonstrating with the women, a friend of theirs, finds him suspicious until we vouch for him. Nasrin is right here too, and Nelufar smiles between chants, all of us standing up to chant for one very hard-hitting speech, sitting down again, almost delirious with the power of our voices, bringing down the temple of justice with the rhythm of Samson, the pillars vibrate to our force, the glory of us this strong, united, unmovable. We have occupied the place.

Sophie joins me again, the movie camera high over her head, our fear of its being broken; its weight by now is great. And finally out of film. Militia helped her through the crowds, she says, probably thought she was a reporter. We de-escalate to still film, little cameras, both of us shooting. A light floods the speakers, some Italians shooting sixteen-millimeter film with a big movie camera, sound sync. We envy them a second, I remember the Eclair we had to leave at home for lack of crew to handle and carry; all the privileged opportunity we have here, our closeness to the principals—if only. There is but one roll of black-and-white movie stock left in our knapsack, today's ration, we'll save it for later. Meanwhile we have lots of thirty-five-millimeter and each a still camera to shoot with, shooting like maniacs, loading for each other, Sophie often loading for both of us since I take longer; but loading and shooting continuously, the frenzy of the chants making us high, the fierceness, the valor of the women shouting down Islamic prejudice, the mullahs' repression. Beginning the revolution again. This is how it must have been during the uprising, this the fury, the fearlessness. And the guns surrounding us, an army undecided, never protective but at this moment neutral or almost, their own notions of what we are put aside, yet the finger still holds the trigger.

The light the Italian filmmakers carry has appeared at another portion of the room now, silhouetting a soldier standing on a column by a staircase, women in a sea below him, women thronging the tier above him. And he stands there like a bully and a fool yet even, one is sure in his case, proud of himself, superior to all the numbers about him by virtue of his self-importance and his gun, though probably the first makes him far more secure than the latter might guarantee against such numbers. The rule of men over women that he declares with his stance and his posture is as old as a spear, as a swagger, as a headman. He is having his picture taken and instead of feeling silly or an oaf, he is posturing absurdly. The light is on him, towering over the masses of women and now illuminated, the arc light, light grace or irony, a comment; I see it through his shadow on the wall behind him, the huge light and the monstrous shadow, bigger than he is, big as the media, big as movies, big as fantasy, the shadow of a gunman. I want this photograph. And I take his picture.

Now the militia have decided to evacuate us; our speeches are over, but the chants continue. The doors are locked, those right behind us, for example; if they were opened, we could disperse in a moment. But no, we will have to exit by the path of their choosing. This exercise of

Shadow of a gunman

Guard, Ministry of Justice

Militia outside the ministry

their power and guns. It will cause us to surge in line some thirty moments through narrow corridors and tight places, whereas the doors right at hand would admit us at once to the street, the cool air of freedom—but no, they have guns, we must do as they say, they must show us their power, must cow us, must order us, must be authority. Authoritarian. The stance, the pose, the gesture moving us along, the finger on the trigger and the gun pointing.

We continue to photograph them with the little gun of art, shooting their pleased vanity, putting them into an agreeable mood. They are reclaiming their building for men, for male government which employs women only in secretarial capacities (and in the Komiteh not even in that capacity; women circulate jokes about the unused typewriters in the Komiteh, no man has ever learned to use them), and we, using still another copying device, reclaim the reclaimers, their faces and stances, their humorless self-importance: the self-absorption of one posed with his rifle against a sunny wall, another trigger-ready as he walks the street when we emerge. They are the new order, smug, young, well-fed and cocky. But the first guard we captured back in the hall was an older type in the Near East, a permanent fixture, a small man with baggy pants who guarded against our just walking out the nearest door and saving ourselves the trouble of meeting the others. He is young, but he is old, looks like a Turkish soldier in the thirties; you could print him in sepia. Behind him is the sleeker, fatter figure of the Komiteh and the official, the bureaucrat, a knot of men in the distance and behind them a corridor leading to the power, offices, ministers, male power in a male state. The new breed of gunmen are loutish but fierce as desert warriors, the old faded little guard still breathes the air of civil service, long waits, bureaucratic tedium. To that obscurantism is now added the fascist force of the new militia outdoors. While within, the vast hall emptying now, the rule of petty tyranny is reasserted. Tier upon tier, Kafka's ghost floating upward in the hall of state. Past the sad little guys, the sepia types, the small men who guard the entrance and protect it from people, people as small as women, so small as to be hardly visible. And above, huge upon the wall as he is everywhere, the Ayatollah, high up, the voice of God, direct intercourse with heaven; patriarchal religion ruling here without the usual pretense that it is not, ostentatiously supporting the state, the rule of men everywhere.

It is time for fresh air, for something good to eat. Nelufar knows an excellent *chelo kebab*. It's not that nearby, but it's worth it. How wonderful to escape the mobs of hostile men lying in wait to attack the demonstrators, to go from that peril to the urbanity of going out to lunch. And into this very civilized old restaurant, public, even common, but uncommonly good in its adherence to tradition, to the best ingredients, to the only dish it serves, the lovely fillets of beef over buttered rice, the yoghurt, the sturdy bread, and probably loved by hundreds of thousands for being the real thing—yet still there comes the thundering voice of the Ayatollah. On radio, like some totalitarian big brother interrupting everyone's meal to pontificate upon the veil— first the edict read by a mullah, then the interpretation of it by a female voice (radio is permitted women, television is not; radio is invisibility), both voices prevaricate, put off, claim and disclaim and then claim again, stuff about dignity, a code word for subjugation here, then the bitter pill—it will be required.

We have gone and shown our power and our anger and our temperate demands for justice. We have been answered. In words of impossible pomposity, rigmarole, repressive authority. There is no escaping. Even in a public restaurant; the diners resentful of the new loudspeakers, then hearing the subject, curious, then indifferent—for this being a public place and a pleasant one, they are nearly all men. Whatever else they feel, they do not show it. We have heard. We know we will demonstrate again tomorrow. This is only the beginning. This is a force roused from millennia of slumber, there is no stopping it now.

4 ✿ ✿ ✿

 NELUFAR STRETCHES OUT on the sofa and puts her stocking feet up on the armrest. Sophie and I take turns luxuriating in Claudine's hotel bathtub. Living it up. The contradiction between this moment's comfort and the dangers that preceded, will follow; how precious and exotic hot water becomes, scented soap, a cup of coffee. Our comradeship ripens around them in the little islands of rest and safety. The demonstration still resounding in our blood, the din of triumphant voices still reverberating in our heads; the women, the chants, the cries, the fists raised, the wonder of our power. There is another demonstration tomorrow and a major one planned for

Monday, March 12, a great march beginning at Tehran University and proceeding all the way through the city to Freedom Square, the Shah's vast monument to himself now reclaimed by the people; we have passed it in cabs, a handsome sculpture that will do far better with its new name.

Something has got to be done to publicize all this. Tell the rest of the world what women are doing here. There were very few media there today, hardly better than the rally with its single foreign correspondent. It remains to be seen if Iranian television, so heavily censored that nothing appears right now on Claudine's set but a test pattern, will broadcast anything on today's enormous demonstration. We can expect a few articles in *Kayhan* and *Etela'at* and *Ayandegan,* perhaps, but television is the book of most people here; with illiteracy so high among women, television is crucial. There are the women in the countryside, housewives; today's secretaries and nurses and teachers are an elite, oddly but logically enough, where so few women work outside their homes and where so many do not read or write. The chador—reaching the women still within it. There were chadori there with us today, more than the handful who came to the rally; but to break across that line—between women without chador and women still within it and the bounds it represents—that's the struggle, for of course they will divide us right there.

If there is censorship here, why not try another tack, the world press? "What do you think of talking to some foreign reporters, Nelufar, you and Nasrin?" Another Nasrin, not our fighting Turk with the green eyes, but a humorous lady who wears her bourgeois costume like some sort of joke. She has just made it up to the room through a lobby of spies, the desk clerks who watch and then seem to report on visitors. Coming here is a risk. "This could get me through army lines," she laughs, pointing to her chic. An interior decorator with her own business and some French. "Of course it's better if I can talk French," Nelufar stipulates, Nasrin too. "Well, we've run into some reporters here from time to time."

"It's hard to avoid them, they're all over this hotel like fruit flies," Claudine laughs coming out of the bathroom. "They keep telephoning my room late at night, asking about the women, about Kate, where she is, if she's in Iran, what's going on—two, three in the morning—I feel like the resident call girl." "And there we are, safe at Nelufar's," Sophie laughs. But the time to use some of this, maybe, is now, if we could announce the big march for Monday the twelfth, if we could get a lot of international media at that event. "If we could get these demonstrations shown—think—women everywhere would see it.

Imagine what it would mean to them, fire their imagination . . .
Claudine, wasn't today like hardly anything you've ever seen in
feminist demonstrations?" The possibility of course seems remote, but
that ardor, if women at home could see it—if my own mother in St.
Paul, women like that, if they had access to our history as it's being
made, think—what communication could do if it really were that.
Claudine holds her hand on her chin and then begins making lists.
She has already been reporting nightly to France, located her telex
and begun the dispatches to Des Femmes which will later be available
to all French media with the sense to use it.

"We do have to talk to some reporters." Sophie was a reporter, she's
for it. And we have simply been too busy to contact each one
laboriously. A few reporters have begun recognizing me in the lobby, I
can hear their minds wondering, sometimes they even say hello, as if I
had some kind of yearbook notoriety in the vast high-school of
American popular life, to wave at or shake hands, to spot with a little
rise of self-congratulation on the recognition, to address by first name
with a curious mixture of familiarity and contempt; a libber after all,
something vaguely silly they can condescend to. But a "household
word." Right now we could use that. Politically. And more pressing
than that, safety; the demonstrations are already dangerous. We have
heard reports of women injured today, stabbings, we are not sure how
serious or how many. There was talk in the lobby that an American
reporter had photographed a schoolgirl being hit in the face with
brass knuckles; his name was John Snow. Follow that up too. We do
know that many women and girls were waylaid en route to the
ministry and beaten by gangs of fanatic Islamic men. There are
already theories about whether they are organized. I wonder if Ralph
has any ideas.

"It comes down to this, that we need the media as a kind of
protective force. We can't count on the militia; they were there today
to defend a government building, not us. And the fanatics were there
today too. Getting out of there was sheer hell, walking along the
streets of the south city to our car, the militia as threatening as the
guys who ganged up to harass us—there were many times I expected
us to get rushed." "There is no doubt that they're dangerous, and they
will only get more so. Who knows what orders they're under," Nelufar
says, rubbing her tired feet on the sofa arm next to where I sit, a
friendly arrangement, oddly reminiscent of college house parties.
"They can go out and clout a woman over the head and then feel
they've performed a religious duty." Nasrin shrugs and smiles. "Do
you know what it is they scream at us—'Cover your head or we'll break

it'—that's their position on the chador." We had never understood this slogan and are shocked. "That's how they are, crazy. We've had all this to put up with for centuries." She shrugs again.

"But it's coming out now as a new viciousness—I have never seen this in Iran," Nelufar emphasizes. "This—how do you say—this completely open hatred. It's a revelation." "There are parts of Tehran we could take them . . ." Nasrin begins. "Of course, but that's the poor, class resentment—this is different, though the other's being used too." She turns toward us: "You can see these men are from the people." Yes, the faces even more than the clothing, faces that are closed, with little schooling, little literacy beyond the mosque Koran, no opportunity, much resentment. "So," Nelufar goes on, "they take that and use it." "Who does?" "Who knows exactly? The Komiteh, the far right wing in the Komiteh, the hierarchy, the religious bigots, even some of the old right—they can use shock troops like this."

I consider it, and measure it against what we have in the Catholic world I come from, twenty years of church culture growing up in St. Paul making Italy and France and Ireland closer than Washington in some ways. Would reactionary forces use such proletariat piety for their ends, even goon squads? Sure. Remember *Studs Lonigan,* and we have had Irish race riots in Boston as recently as a year ago. Suppose Italy or France were to be overrun by pope and bishop again, you would have the same interdictions on abortion, persecution of prostitution, return to male authority under godhead—the prospect is dizzying. And pious old money would love it, would operate with a proletarian following who would do their will on promises (they are right now giving out food in the south of Tehran) and nationalistic or church pride, tribal insignia mesmerizing the poor, leading them away from their own class interests into the service of their old oppressors with the euphoria of thinking they were all one grand clan on its way to the renewal of ancient majesty. Italian fascists are devout Catholics, black- and brownshirts received communion with closed eyes. Clan over class. National unity. One hears it everywhere. Studs's Irish brutes went to mass before and after rape and only needed a "nigger" or a "kike" on whom to blame their poverty. They are the poor too, the dispossessed, the discontented. Satisfied with a scapegoat. With the impression of superiority over the appointed victim. Though it's strange, in view of the ethic most religions develop and sometimes maintain, to see men pressing to attack with the name of Allah on their lips, imagining themselves devout; it is surely a tradition with the holy war in Islam. Bigotry under cover of religion, bullying cloaked in supernal rhetoric.

It makes sense. One has seen it before. But not the war of men on women. Not as open fighting in the street. The thugs, as Nelufar calls them, a doctor of sociology who can give you their class experience to a hairbreadth, has studied it here in the city as well as the peasant populations in the countryside, has taught among them there too, lived, researched, and has great sympathy, forgives a great deal, sees them as manipulated men who would have nothing to do, are angry, vacant, frustrated—but that these men, part of the people, exploited themselves, would be sent out against the women, while the other men, clerics, laymen, the righteous, comfortable men maintained their guiltlessness, men who smile and shake their heads about it all—this infuriates her. The hypocrisy. There are already statements from Khomeini that we must not be attacked. And yet a throng came against us who are only expected to increase. A hypocrisy reminiscent of the Bourbon in the South, who always blame the "cracker" for lynchings; "rednecks," their social inferiors. Set up to do the job for them. How much are these men set up?

Who would protect us, stand on our side? The left? The Fedayeen? "We are asking them now, Kateh and the others are in conference with them, we may have them tomorrow, we may have them Monday." "If we could make that alliance . . . the women and the left . . ." "Exactly the point." Nasrin's shoulders signal agreement. Nelufar only raises an eyebrow in a more skeptic Gallic accord, set off by a still more subtle Persian irony. I am American go-gettedness—I will step out and find a paper in the lobby and think it all over.

The media, what can we do with the media? *Time* magazine spread out in several months of colored issues on Iran. Been in the news. If one had nothing else to do, it would be fun to compare the "versions" of things; I used to do that with the artists, the turnabout between the year De Kooning was a faker and Pollock a fraud until they were the master and the late lamented genius. Khomeini and the Shah must have gone through some interesting evolutions between January and this tenth day of March. But *Kayhan*'s afternoon edition in English does not seem to be out yet.

There is another American lady in the newsstand. Being nearly the only two of the species in all of Iran, of course we physically collide. Which affords us the opportunity to speak, in apology. She is even a reporter, her name is Elaine Scholino. And she seems to be a sister—in a moment we are past reporter and the object thereof and on our way to being friends—I can invite her to meet the others. She'll be up as soon as she meets her deadline. Her room is only one floor away. Josef Ibraham of the *Times* is just down the hall from Claudine. Since our own batteries are running down, she thinks he might even loan us some so we can tape our own copy of what transpires. "We'll get you plenty of reporters: Jon Randall's upstairs—he's Washington *Post;* there's the fellow from the Los Angeles *Times*—the place is packed with reporters, the networks stay here too. Everyone except UPI and Reuters." As I come down the hall I hear—it must be Ibraham—bellowing his report to *The New York Times* through an open door. For a lark, I leave my tape recorder outside his room for a moment. A preview of the news. I can't resist telling Claudine this escapade of media on media; it is all so unreal, cinematic. A moment later I decide it's impolite and plagiaristic and collect it for replay. When he's done, Ibraham kindly steps over in response to Elaine's call and loans us batteries. He'll come back in a while for our statements.

"Nelufar and Nasrin may have to leave . . ." I say, trying to make contact between Iranian women and the *Times*—these are surely the first Iranian feminists he's met and his story tonight was full of news on the condition of women here, but only hinted at the demonstrations today—which he did not attend. No, he's too busy now; he'll come back. So much for the *Times*. There is still Jon Randall of the Washington *Post*. I met him late one night in the lobby here, a rash of shooting outside the hotel, the lights put out, everyone ordered to crouch on the floor; a big business or espionage type with a German accent asked in the dark what we were doing in Iran, foreign ladies. And this man Randall somehow part of that same surreal evening. Because before the blackout happened and just as we were leaving the Persian restaurant, the best in the hotel and the least expensive, Sophie, Claudine and I rather intoxicated by conversation and one really good meal, walked through the lobby where at desk after desk reporters typed up the news of the world. We rejoiced in the sight. Thank god we don't have to do this. "I do," Claudine said, "I have to go up now and start—but not with this panache, of course." Past a man feverish on a portable, a pendant dangling from his neck. An American for sure, Sophie indicates with her Canadian radar. "Are you Kate Millett?" Interrogative force. Oh no, it's happened.

He's wonderfully familiar, but not that interested in whatever I might have to say—he has his deadline; I should call him up sometime and make an appointment. The idea seems ludicrous; I live in an unknown apartment and can hardly operate its telephone, have no transportation, cannot go anywhere alone and am involved all day long in being at other people's disposal doing what political work they assign me, a great deal of the time just waiting around. I am not likely to make appointments of my own. But at this moment it has all changed. The women we are with have a message to the press: Sophie,

Claudine, and I can help convey it. If we use me as Jon Randall's bait, we get him to talk to Nelufar and Nasrin.

And indeed, to my delight he does know French and we leave him to rattle away with them in it in one corner of the room while I answer questions for the man from the Los Angeles *Times*. He is gentlemanly and a pleasure to speak with. He would like a figure on the number of working women in Iran. Nelufar will get it. But in all the press of things to do, this sort of thing becomes rather a nuisance; there are still leaflets to compose with Nasrin, "our" Nasrin, preparations for the big march on Monday, distribution at every school, the thousand posting places at the universities, offices; the press of their own work leaving them harassed and exhausted, a permanent condition of our friends here, the feminists even more than Caifi. In a few moments they must leave, leaving us to field the media, a thing we hardly feel well equipped to do. But obviously it's to be our job, the one way we can be of help right now.

Each time they go out, they are in danger of arrest while distributing leaflets, arrest while driving at night through checkpoints with political literature in the car; arrest before the Komiteh, which is not jail, or not quite, just detainment for most of an afternoon, the hard bench, the tedious questioning, the fear that it will go further. And the streets and the fanatics still in the streets. We should stay here to wait for them, they say; we cannot help write the leaflet for Monday, but we can do something with the reporters.

Of all the reporters who tromped through our bordello, as Claudine referred to her room, my favorite of all was the man from the *Daily Telegraph,* our first visitant. He came at Claudine's request after she had encountered him somewhere in the hotel in the course of a breakfast. He heard there was something about women going on—the "chador story." "Now just what is this, ladies, let's have an explanation." He is several different kinds of checkered trousers, tie and coat, British to the point of satire, and jolly past all speaking of it. He interrogates us like schoolgirls, it's our first interview—we sit up primly and give our names, permitting him out of amusement as well as a sense of dutifulness. He writes down my name without recognizing it and decides as I'm an American he needn't bother much with me, lots of anti-Americanism right now, Sophie's better, she's Canadian. "And the other ladies?" Nelufar's name, Nasrin's—both of them enduring English for the sake of the struggle. I am delighted to discover that I won't have to answer any questions and settle back to enjoy the spectacle of my friends patiently responding to schoolmaster Smith. The interview as pure aesthetics, live comedy. And yet, when we did give a press conference, Smith was the only foreign reporter who bothered to come up and ascertain the real spelling of Kateh's last name.

Because of course it came to that, a press conference, we had thought of it even before Elaine came up to the room, the men gone now and a sister in the media put it on the line—the need for one—and offered to do the arrangements for us. "Around evening, when they're all back in the hotel just before deadline—they can get it on that day's report that way. Say three, four, five—somewhere in there. Remember the delay in television and everything else coming out of here—it's eight hours later in Iran than in New York so you're losing a whole working day—the news is already a day behind. And if you want to be sure that they come on Monday to the big march—if you want to be sure no one gets hurt and everybody knows—well . . ." Claudine is dubious. "The media—we deal with them all the time in Paris, but they hardly deal with us at all, or they deal unfairly." "Name of the game," Elaine nods. "We have to do what we can, Claudine, this is to help the women here," Sophie urges. "But how will *they* feel about it?" "Nelufar and Nasrin were perfectly willing to talk to the reporters once they came," I urge. "But a press conference is formal, official." "We'll ask them then, we can't go ahead till then, anyway." It's out of our hands. And we won't know till tonight, when they call or when they come to pick us up. We can however find out how to do it. "Just a sign in the lobby, you could put it up as early as that same day, the room can be arranged very quickly too. I'll be here to help you."

I think she's super. Claudine has doubts, is not sure Des Femmes should participate; she must call France. And there is news that a delegation of Frenchwomen are coming; she is not pleased. They could confuse things, make themselves unwelcome with uninformed statements; are they fool enough to think they can "organize" these women? I wouldn't worry about that—the Iranian feminists are the coolest and most self-possessed, seasoned and sophisticated political females I've ever run across—you don't "organize" them. Sophie and I have been days just following around, learning the ropes, probably being tested by them, being patient, waiting outside their circles. Realizing finally, as I say it, the purpose of our period of trial. A period that seemed to end with the rally, the speeches made in public together, with being accepted into Nelufar's house and family, and demonstrating side by side in the feverish crowd in the Hall of Justice.

Kateh is not that enthusiastic about the delegation either. What impression will it make among people here? Simone de Beauvoir is president of the delegation, but unwell and unable to come herself. The delegates themselves are mainly French, but also German, Scandinavian: European feminists, writers, journalists. There is the question that some members of the delegation may not be acceptable. Especially filtered through Claudine's dislike of Claude Servan-Schreiber, editor of *Effe*—a slick magazine, chic—this is not women's liberation, it's fashionable people, to Claudine. To Kateh, it's insufficiently political. They might just come for a story, as reporters, or as superfeminists, to colonize. I argue uselessly for sisterhood. Sophie joins in—on the other side. I am alone, pumping away for international feminism, an idea which has brought us all together and whose full ramifications I still hardly grasp. It seems to point toward the press conference, protection through world coverage, communication with women everywhere—which Kateh does endorse. She will talk to her comrades and see who wants to do it. But she will do it herself in any case, so that is one speaker for Iranian women. There should be three or four others, so there is a balance of Iranian and international feminists directing the attention of the press—the international press, the foreign press our target even more than the Iranian one, for the world press has so far neglected the demonstrations—announcing the great march on Monday and introducing Iranian feminists to the reporters and the people they report to throughout the world.

"Let's see how that goes—and just mull over the delegation awhile—they aren't coming for at least a week. I think they mean well, and surely sympathy from abroad is very important," I plead. Sophie disagrees bitterly, even after Kateh leaves, even when we are alone. Has she caught Claudine's dislike of Claude, a woman she's never met, one whom I liked upon our acquaintance, though our points of view are as different as uptown and downtown. Kateh distrusts the foreigners, Sophie claims, that's enough. If it's an unfounded suspicion, why reinforce it? We still disagree back at Nelufar's. I am exhausted with being the peacemaker, holding the factions together against their imperious will to divide. Smooth and certain on the outside, the vision you advocate becomes privately an ambivalence within you, doubts descend from both the sides you try aloud to neutralize, harmonize; you advocate goodwill and become a vessel of others' hostility, a sponge for ambient ill nature, suspicion. While you go on leaping in faith, an idiot optimism. And you end up feeling lonely, feeling disliked, weakened. How do you know you're doing the right thing, anyway? Their arguments have merit. Yet it makes so much more sense to cooperate, take help where you can get it, trust women, build support throughout the world.

The thing we saw today was history: raw, unorganized, vulnerable, miraculous. When I am most vexed by the arguing, I summon the demonstration to mind—the roar of voices—that's the reality we must pursue, the naked manifestation of political energy—the test is to put it to use. There is another demonstration tomorrow—ride them, see them, watch to see what happens here, record it, participate in whatever feeble way you can. A demonstrator who can't pronounce the chants right and is gun-shy with the militia, in dread of the attackers, the Islamic fanatics who hang around waiting for our numbers to dwindle in order to beat us up.

Falling asleep with all these figures around me and the walls of the Hall of Justice stretching up, reverberating still as you fall into unconsciousness. A single bed at Nelufar's, her family asleep around you, Sophie asleep in her bed, all the house quiet. Even the cats asleep, who seem to have shit in your two long dresses as they lay on the floor of the closet, not yet hung up. In a revolution of course there is cat shit.

5

WE HAVE ALWAYS BEEN under the guardianship of Iranian women; this is the first demonstration we attend alone, all Westerners. And we stand out. Objects of instant recognition and attack. When we get there we are appalled at how small it is. Even given our habitual lateness. Hermoz drove off early, taking the girls to school today, we had to wait for a cab, picking up Claudine and her friend Sylvina, who has just arrived from France. We are now four international feminists threading shakily through the crowded streets of Tehran toward the south where the poor live, where the government offices are. I ride in front to substitute various charming smiles and transparent gestures for a knowledge of Farsi, and to insist on the address. The driver slows and points his finger, good soul, when we reach the first cross street we search for, and we believe all the way to the second. Then courtyards, then buses, then the very small crowd. What a pity. Has it all lost momentum? Has there been dissension, rebuke from official sources, has the left put an interdict on demonstrations, has religion, has the government itself forbidden women to support its female employees? Do things peter out this way?

Of course many have left already, the remainder tell us; it wasn't planned to be a big demonstration—Monday the twelfth of March is the real effort. Today is only meant to be a minor affair in support of another branch of government workers, the secretaries in the Ministry of Foreign Affairs. Many of them are present now, milling around in front of their work place during their lunch hour. There are still several hundred other women of varied but increasing feminist perception, ourselves, and the press. Plenty of press, rather more than needed in such a crowd. Even the networks are here today: ABC, NBC, CBS—my confusion distinguishing among the three will continue from this moment on. Also Canadians, Reuters; French and Italians for Claudine and Sylvina.

I am assailed by Americans who have begun recognizing me. Every time I try to draw their attention to whatever Iranian woman I have been talking with, recording her often on my own little machine, the whisper box, they intrude, ignoring her, to ply me with repetitious, loaded questions. "Isn't this just a matter of chador? Just what are these women demonstrating about?" "These women"—the casual racism with which the big American pressmen ignore and disregard the Iranian women, who are perfectly capable of speaking for themselves. Many speak English and have plenty to say.

I find myself nearly incredulous watching it. And while I may have a word or two to put in—to lionize me this way and pay no heed to the participants . . . who, after all, *are* this phenomenon. And what better spokespersons, who more eloquent? What better reporting both as to art and message—than Iranian woman in Iranian accents, their own lovely voices: moving, genuine, authentic.

"Isn't it possible that you and other women from the West, coming here, are trying to impose a Western style?" This from American television. Now it is an accusation. The press that glamorized the Shah is now taking an Iranian nationalist line. I answer that feminism is an international struggle, the fact that this is an Islamic country makes no great difference, we have to fight in Christian countries too; this is an ancient, even universal system, patriarchy. "Have you had any complaints from the government about supposed agitating?" "None whatsoever." What are they up to? "May I have a word with you?"—a Persian woman trying to be heard. "I really would urge you to interview as many Persian women as possible." He pays no attention to her, she gives up on him, would rather speak to me. "Excuse me, we would like to ask you, with the apparatus you have, to support our movement." "We do, this is why we are here." Her face in smiles, the words translated to the women around her. And to him: "We want it to be really reflected all over the world." "We're from CBS." "Why don't you put that on tape—what she has just said?" "We have. We've already interviewed women." "We ask your women to protect our movement, because we are alone here," the woman goes on, pleading. "And in danger, there were women stabbed yesterday . . ." I join her, counting on coverage as defense. He turns and goes off, having thanked us for our "cooperation."

We talk then to each other. They are waiting for the group from Tehran University to arrive. Their importance in all the demonstrations. "Because they are younger, students, free to be activists. They are not employed. The rest of us are always wondering what they are deciding down there in those meetings of theirs." "You are employed by government?" "Yes. So it's our jobs that are at stake. You see, they are thinking of throwing the women out and bringing men in at this point. It's this way: the nurses and teachers are indispensable, but not the rest of us. Their training can't be replaced—ours can, or nearly." Another woman joins the circle. "Are you a journalist?" she asks. "No, I'm an American feminist here to support you." "Thank you."

"Thank you too." This welcome to Persia like warm food in my stomach. The smiles, the dark eyes, the circle of different faces. "If you write down anything—please write down that we women want to be free. We don't want to wear chador, we don't want even to wear these scarves. We want to be free. Freedom is the only thing that we want." "Maybe when we go downtown to bazaar," one ventures. "No, it's not chador, it's civil rights." "Actually Khomeini is a secret agent organizing for the women's movement," I joke. The more this is translated, the more it entertains. The media head for us, another crew.

There is a woman just at my left; she is middle-aged, a secretary, trying to speak to me as the man from the network, a big man and rough, who tends to shove the microphone at me and push me into place before the camera, takes over. His question tedious, the same question as the last man's—and I hear the woman's voice over his—she is trying to speak to him, trying to tell him. Then trying to tell me something, since he will not listen. Will listen only to me, and only if I answer his insulting question about what am I doing here, a foreigner and so forth. Then the jovial, even mocking familiarity: "Well, Kate, what do you think the outcome of all this ruckus will be?" I turn toward the woman, trying to hear her: "Tell your people about this, tell them about us, tell them about the women in Iran, tell everyone in the world," she is saying. "Would you please record what this woman is saying?" I beg him. He turns, he has no interest. I ask him again. He claims he's out of tape. "Would you merely listen to her, then?" He turns and leaves. I am furious.

And she keeps on telling me, that everyone must know, that the women are denied their rights, that at the very moment when they had won their freedom, it is being taken from them. That American women, that women in every country of the world must hear this, must see it on television. "Tell all the women for us. Keep telling it." "I will."

Her words stay on with me. To the press conference, dispelling some of my nervousness, my dread of this pompous rite, the absurd banquet tables with their silk hangings, the raft of microphones—it intimidates me merely to look into the room. The full panoply of diplomats and dictators; this could be a set for the announcement of a war, the pronouncements of government. The government probably uses it too. Or big business; multinational folly and size. It is crazy that a few feminists should be set forth in this bizarre and alien atmosphere. So many microphones, so much tension in the room. Grand baize table. And far too many chairs. This inflated scene of our discomfiture; even water glasses.

I have always found press conferences silly, an embarrassment because so overblown—what do they expect you will say? I do not intend to announce a war or anything that important, I always start off—in Topeka, or at whatever university whose lecture official has been ambitious to haul the three town reporters and the local television station together, to hear me answer the old questions about when or why is the ERA to pass or not to pass. All the things women have to say about their predicament, and for once, the males in authority, have given us the trappings of power. Never meaning to make fools of us thereby. Or not till the questions begin, which are designed to humiliate. The trappings, however, were intended to be honorific. Alas, they are merely ridiculous, a thing we perceive at once, the moment we find ourselves in them. Perhaps, believing in them, they haven't noticed this. Whereas we feel thrust onto the stage of a rather corny play.

And this one is even starting late. Of course. But a good deal of it is our fault. We all feel foolish beginning, so we stall, and we can't begin without Kateh. Who, even when she finally does arrive, cannot produce her sworn comrades. They promised her. She is torn between being angry and being scared. She is afraid for the others, she says, any Iranian woman participating in this essentially foreign press conference risks a good deal of home-government wrath. They may even have been detained en route. She covers for them, nervously copying out a translation of the statement sent by her group. We are looking a bit stupid now; the purpose of this farce was to introduce the world press to Iranian feminists, a few international feminists being done the honor of acting as go-between—and we can only produce one Iranian feminist. The whole table is off balance; there are three empty chairs. We had meant to be a coalition in equal numbers: three Iranians, three internationalists. Two French, one American. Sophie, as usual, will have nothing to do with this stuff, and anyway, she's filming it. So is Sylviane from Des Femmes, who arrived this morning from Paris, a little figure with a big video camera. The enormous cameras of the networks, the wire services, the papers, the video and cinema lenses, lights, pencils poised.

We are taking our places—Kateh nearly frantic with worry for her friends—there is the possibility they may be arrested; they were out at the campuses today delivering leaflets for the march on Monday. The march we are to announce, among other things. We want every media glance throughout the world to focus on this protest. And we want, finally, for the world to hear Iranian women describe their situation in their own words. Till now it has been a matter of male reporters: Elaine and the one network crew woman are the only women here, and Elaine is not assigned to this—*Newsweek* is after the oil story and will give no space to women at all this issue—a piece of misjudgment that piques her. So far, the whole "story" on the Iranian women's protests which is "shaping up" to date, is entirely reported by men. Unless the "story holds," the powers that be will probably not condescend to allow women to cover it. Except for the press women of the French delegation; we are announcing their arrival as well. A thing that annoys Claudine and Sylvina sufficiently to have kept them on the fence all morning over whether they should even take part in this. And the Iranian women we hoped for, "our" Nasrin, and Nelufar, will evidently not be coming. A great deal is falling apart; holding it together is exhausting us all.

Kateh is actually the coolest, also the youngest, and, with reason, the one with the most consequence to fear. Having overcome the others' skepticism of the foreign press, hammered out an agreed-upon statement, taken the risks of appearing in public, a thing they have hitherto shunned (not that the media have put them in demand—a thing they also have given consideration; the star system which the media impose on spokespersons as a way of controlling them and their group, turning them into pawns, personalities), having taken on all this—she will be left, in her handsome and courageous youth, to bear the blinding lights and the brunt alone. In a foreign language.

Sylvina begins. Announcing that we will be an international press conference, using three languages, French, English, and Farsi. Thereby annoying the American chauvinists, who want only English and cannot bear the way she repeats every phrase in French, there

Press Conference, March 11, 1979: Sylvina, Claudine, Kateh, the author

being only a few French reporters, who speak English as well. The Americans don't want to hear her anyway—they want to get at me, which is why she begins. We have arranged it thus: if the Frenchwomen, whom the press don't know and whose organization they haven't heard of and in their arrogance disregard—if they do not begin, they will not be heard at all. I'm the bait in the middle, but my purpose is only to introduce Kateh, which means I must answer almost no questions; a little statement and on to Kateh, the cheese. We are all nervous, we hate this, the first moments are pure hatred; by the end we will be fascinated and fatigued.

For words and argument get to you, and the issues are ones we have given our lives to. There is no way once we begin that we can disengage ourselves; we have put ourselves on the spot and can be seen looking foolish or in error by many millions of human beings simultaneously. Never able to correct an error, an impression, a rash word. This is a firing line before us.

I look down the line at Sylvina, Claudine, Sylviane behind her video camera, out in the audience, Sophie behind her movie camera; at least we have our own media on media, are making records that will last as long as we do. The official version will be aired, if we're lucky, once and once only, reduced to a few seconds between two advertisements for products. Perhaps even erased and the tape used again, if video; if film, they will be shelved and lost and gather dust, if not actually thrown away. It is a difference between a moment and forever—our history and their conversion of it into something to entertain, comedy. Our two tape recorders are at the ready. We are making both the event and the long-aspired-to account of the event—finally independent, self-enclosed.

"Who's doin' the talking here—you doin' the talkin'?" A man's voice shouting at me, another man stands up to move the public-address microphone, with his own microphone copulating upon it like a grasshopper attached with gaffer tape, shoving it closer to me. They have decided how they want this to run, they are running it. We're not going to let them. They order me to move. Claudine, in the center, almost forgets and rises to change places, the conditioning to obey them is so great. No, I whisper, don't move, we'll do it our way. Sylvina tells them the order we have chosen. They have to rearrange everything, all their machinery. We wait.

Firmly and quietly Sylvina begins. "We are both from the women's liberation group in France called Politique and Psychoanalysis and we make the magazine called *Femmes en Movement.*" "Your names?" "Claudine and Sylvina." "Claudine what?" "We think it is not important, the last name." This is a pretty new idea to them. "We can't write

Ralph Schoenman at the conference

a story without a last name." Sylvina shifts to French. "The most important thing for us to say is why we came to Tehran. The struggle of women is international: since the first day. When Iranian women break their chains, women of the whole world can advance. We are here to give strength to the women of Iran, but we are also here for them to give us strength. We are here concretely—with our voices, our ears, our bodies—given to the Iranian women. We arrived for the eighth of March, International Women's Day, and we gave a message that day at the rally." Claudine joins in: "Because we heard that on that day, for the first time in fifty years, Iranian women were celebrating the eighth of March, which they had never had an opportunity to do during the Shah's regime."

Her voice is pretty in English as well as in French; because she is sitting beside me, I know her anxiety, but it does not carry in her voice. How lovely accents are, how lovely English or any other language spoken on another tongue, something to cherish rather than condemn or be impatient with as people often are; the French perhaps most of all. "And the women said it was the first day of the women's movement in Iran," Sylvina resumes, referring to our rally. "We should like to say that in our experience, there is a great movement for international solidarity. For example, in freeing Eva Forrest, who was imprisoned in Spain under Franco; she was in great danger, she was to have been executed. We would like her to come here." Being outrageous. We begin to enjoy ourselves.

Working in an old comradeship, members of a collective group for many years, Sylvina and Claudine take turns, almost like a dialogue. Claudine resumes: "Since we've been here, we've found out from the Iranian women that if the local press and the international press report their struggle, then every day they go out into the streets—the less in danger they will be. Because as you've heard, every time they've been marching in the streets, they've been attacked. And the danger is real." A man begins to ask a question: we must explain again the purpose of the press conference—to introduce the Iranian women's movement to them—so we will not take questions till after Kateh speaks.

I go next: "From the coverage I've read, you have not yet met the Iranian women's movement, you have not interviewed them, you have observed them only from a distance and in the streets. Only in the last few days have you really been there during demonstrations." I recall the woman from the Ministry of Foreign Affairs, evoking her again before the very man who turned away from her today—he sits just in front of me. "The government is one of the few employers of women, clerical and secretarial workers now fear for their jobs, have reason to suspect that their positions may be abolished on the pattern of the new Komitehs who do not employ women in their offices. These demonstrations are a question of survival. One such worker approached a member of one of the powerful American television networks and she pleaded with him to record what she said: 'Tell the women in the world that we are struggling, tell them of our danger, tell them that our story must make its way through the world.' I said to him, one American to another"—watching his face—"'be a good guy, put it on your tape recorder.' His cameraman was there too. Neither one of them would record what she said." He watches me, I watch him. I have not said his name or his network.

"It is perhaps to remedy that situation that we meet today. We are an international movement, the women's movement; the present xenophobia here or elsewhere does not concern us." An American already protecting her flank from the attack on her nationality which will be made by other Americans, media who did condone the Shah all the years I fought him. "As women, we really don't feel that much that we 'belong' to governments. As civil-rights activists, we see the encroachment upon human freedoms by many governments. Certainly the last one here.

"Since many of you may wonder why I am here, may I explain? I have worked against the Shah for years in the United States with the Committee for Artistic and Intellectual Freedom in Iran, changing the public image of the Shah by exposing his treatment of political prisoners, particularly the system of torture." I mention Reza Baraheni and see his round bearded face in the crowd. "Appealing to a free press to spread the truth, we changed the notion of the Shah which the public held and thereby helped to remove him from power. This use of world opinion is a pacifist tactic, perhaps the best weapon we have against tyranny."

And on to my invitation through Caifi and the Ad Hoc Committee and International Women's Day. "I had no idea I would arrive in the middle of an avalanche, I had understood there to be a few struggling feminists in Tehran—a few weeks ago that was the situation—now there are thousands and thousands in the street. And it's our purpose to introduce you to some"—(I'm keeping the door open for Nasrin, Nelufar and Persian time)—"some of the women who've participated in this uprising of women and who hope to build a movement here. Women in Iran are now the center of our struggle in the world. The eyes of the world should be turned upon them. Let it not happen again that the women pleading today at the Foreign Ministry should go unheard. World opinion is enormously important in this uprising of women. Not only to ensure human rights, but because what is happening in Iran may herald the rise of woman throughout Islam and the Near and Middle East. So that we will not only have an international women's movement but a global one. A great deal depends on how you report this.

"There is also enormous danger in the streets. Women were stabbed several times yesterday; we are threatened over and over again. Not only should the eyes of the world be turned on Iran—but there should be a camera behind that eye. A picture was taken yesterday of a thirteen-year-old girl from a high school being hit in the face with brass knuckles—that picture is extremely valuable. Let the world know we are rising in great numbers, but also let us make this a peaceful and bloodless revolution. It will accomplish finally the revolution which has been promised in Iran but has not yet taken place. I also believe that it is the women who will lead the protest of all the people in Iran against a curtailment of democracy and constitutional freedom, will insist upon a system of justice with appeals, open courtrooms, defense counsel, and fair trials.

"I would also like to remind you of the role which the international and especially the American press has played during the reign of the Shah. This is a chance to redeem the mission of journalism." A pacifist eye on this morning's reporter. "I urge you to cover everything. There is an enormous demonstration tomorrow, the twelfth, from Tehran University—which has been over and over the center of this protest—to Freedom Square."

I begin to introduce Kateh—am interrupted. "We're half the game down here," he objects. Of course, we'll answer you all later, after our next speaker, urging him out of his habitual practice of speaking only to white women, Americans, French; the narrowness, the racism in this avoidance of the Iranian woman, the darker, Semitic face I have seen them pass over and ignore so many times since I've been here. "I will be very brief because I know you are all full of questions to ask," a nice irony watching these squirming Americans who want to pin their countrywoman on a frivolous quote. Kateh has a statement, and is very serious. I hope we can force them to question her first, not me, keep her before them till it finally takes, penetrates their bigotry. We have changed places, putting Kateh in the center.

"The question which has come about for the Iranian women . . ." A reporter wants her name repeated, spelled. It is. By the end they will all have it wrong, only the comic Englishman will check and get it correctly. "The question today is—do women have the right to decide what they want to wear, do women have the right to decide whether they want to cover themselves or not? This is the question which all the women today are asking and discussing. Majority of the women today in Iran, starting from schoolchildren, office workers, students, home-makers, workers—they all say yes. Yes, we have the right to decide if we want to cover ourselves or not. But a handful of governmental and religious leaders who are leaning on power are trying to take this right away from the women. Under these attacks on the democratic rights of half the population are the hooligans, become once more lively, to start attacking the women; the ones who were put off by the revolution, the ones who were afraid to come out into the streets by the massive revolution we had—have come out once more with their chains and their knives to attack the Iranian women. That's why the Iranian women are coming out tomorrow to say what they want to do. They are the ones who want to decide what to wear and what to do."

Her hands tremble, she goes on with bravery and with polish; one sees only the courage and beauty, the ardor, the youth. "We are calling on all women, all Iranian women, and on our brothers who are in support of our democratic rights, to come out tomorrow in the streets of Tehran." I remember her forbearance when she told me late last night by the hotel desk that the Fedayeen did not see their way to protect our demonstrations. Nor the Muhajadeen. "But we need this coalition of leftists and women." "Of course, but we will also go it alone when we have to." Kateh determined. Kateh intoning now the translation, the official statement. "We all want to unite, with veil or without veil. They are trying to separate us; they are trying to put us against each other.

"We all fought together, all the men and the women with all different ideas, all different beliefs—against the tyranny. *We* threw out the Shah. Today we don't want anybody to separate us. There is freedom if all the Iranians are free, both men and women. Our demonstrations tomorrow will be peaceful. We want it to be peaceful. And for this, we want the world press to be there, we want to ask you all to be there tomorrow, to see if the Bazargan government will protect us from the hooligans who have come out in the last few days attacking us and injuring women." On less sure ground now: "There are lots of other Iranian sisters who were supposed to come here today, but unfortunately they have not arrived. There have been demonstrations and sit-ins, from moment to moment, decided on the spot; women, because of the attacks on them, declaring they should do something, some action should be taken—against these first attacks upon them. That's why unfortunately our sisters are not here yet." Covering as best she can her embarrassment and confusion that they haven't arrived, her fears at what may have happened to them.

A question—Josef Ibraham of *The New York Times*—to Kateh: "Has your movement made any contact with Bazargan government officials yet?" "At four o'clock a group of women are going to meet with them." "Do you have an appointment or are you just going?" "An appointment was made yesterday when we all went to the Ministry of Justice, about seven thousand women sat in at the Ministry of Justice. From that emerged an appointment for four this afternoon. Probably by Tuesday, after the demonstration, all such answers will be given." Josef Ibraham pushes further: "Question: Vice Premier Entezam made a statement this morning about the women, do you have a comment on that?" "The statements they have made in the last week have been contradictory"—stumbling a bit on the English word—"they have come out with one statement and they have changed it to another. We want them to come out with one statement and say what they mean to our questions of equality for men and women." "Khomeini or Bazargan or both?" "The Bazargan government," her tone firmly denying that the Ayatollah has any right to run the country, since he is not even in office. It is clarified that the appointment this afternoon is with members of the Ministry of Justice, not Bazargan himself.

"Excuse me"—a hostile female voice—"I'd like to know what women's group or groups you are representing right now. I would also like to challenge your statements that the women's movement is emerging only now. We have been fighting since the time of our constitution." That would be 1906—though she has the air of contradicting us, we happen to agree. She goes on to mention groups arising and being oppressed—real feminism has been suppressed here since the Shah's father took office in 1921, she says. We nod. Now she takes another tack. Kateh diplomatically letting her run—"The question of women now is not simply a question of government, and women do not regard the question as one of women only, but of being of the whole society." I wait for the stand-by-your-man line which Kateh has already guarded against in her statement. "Men and women are now being separated and I would like to know who you represent." The question is delivered in English but it is hardly accented at all. Exquisite British, very educated. Who is she—has she been sent to make trouble? The cameras, now as she attacks, are flaring upon her—just what they want—any woman who will contradict us, make it a dogfight—discredit us.

"There are women who are active in political life and their statements are very different from yours." Kateh answers gently: "But what you say of history, I agree with. The rally the eighth of March which some two thousand people attended came out of the Committee to Defend Women's Rights." The Ad Hoc Committee of March 8 having since that day renamed itself and moved on to this title, the only autonomous and purely feminist group in Iran yet so far. "There are lots of women's groups which are forming now," Kateh goes on, the woman's voice interrupting, querulous: Does Kateh represent only her own group? "Yes. But since the eighth of March, when two thousand women met, there are lots of other women's groupings which are being formed, and our purpose is to unite all these groupings which are being formed everywhere." The architect of coalition, a grand job indeed. It is increasingly obvious that the questioner is privy to some other group who have very specific attitudes, generally unfriendly. A man wants Kateh to list each group. "I cannot tell you all of them. I can tell you some: Women Fighters— The Committee of Women Fighters, and the Organization of Women Fighters, two groups—another called Women's Awakening." The names of the Maoists we meet at the university and with whom Kateh deals and dickers. I prompt her with the English versions of their names as I remember having them translated—this to answer a question of a woman we presume to be Iranian, yet her voice is England's. Another woman standing next to her questions—she does have an accent—"The names of the organizers of these committees— what are they?" I wonder if they are spies in addition to being agents of dissension. Kateh eschews this sort of quarreling and concentrates on the size and spontaneity of the demonstration yesterday at the Hall of Justice. Because indeed this is the point of that demonstration—its spontaneity—just as with the first one through the snowy streets the morning of March 8: no "group" has *precipitated* these uprisings of women. Feminists and leftists attend them as well as the masses of women workers and students—but no one, certainly no group trying to incite or regiment, appoints them.

"It's just after the revolution, it's spontaneous," Kateh explains. "At the same time there are women's organizations which try—" The woman interrupts: "Someone must be organizing this, someone should be, there should be somebody." "Is there a central committee, in other words?" the young male reporter who is with the woman inquires. The idea is bizarre. How little the events are being under- stood—how conventional such thinking, how impossible for them to imagine that a group of people simply erupt. "How about tomorrow?" he pursues. How peculiar he is, this young man, how he hangs about these two women egging them on against us. An American. Curious kind of colonialism; what sort of hold does he have over them? Does he employ them—are they his translators? Sophie is near them, tape recording: they are indeed under his tutelage; when they challenge us, they are doing it for him. How long will their allegiance hold? Kateh has already invited these women to come tomorrow and see for themselves, even see if anyone is orchestrating the whole thing.

"Yesterday, at the Ministry of Justice, the Committee for Defense of Women's Rights, we called out for tomorrow's march. And thousands and thousands of women agreed. Many women's groups are cooperating." "How do you coordinate your efforts?" "We put up little signs." I laugh, remembering how simple communication is made. One woman holds up a placard: "Tomorrow at the Ministry of Foreign Affairs." The people around her see it and cheer—in two minutes placards are being made by women in all parts of the room, held up and cheered. Beats expensive advertising, mailing, printing costs. "It is just after the revolution, women are under attack, they are already politicized—it's very easy to do things, in a few moments the signs are made, in hours it is put around the country. The whole city is full of the signs for tomorrow's demonstration." "What time?" "Nine o'clock, Tehran University."

Another lady, very British accent, actually English and not Iranian: "What part have the old women's organizations played in this?" I imagine she means Ashraf's crowd. "As far as we know, none whatsoever," Kateh answers firmly. The lady thought they organized the one at the high school, our rally. Heavens no, Kateh's committee did—but if this were not clarified, we could be smeared. Deliberate? Or only misinformed? "The Women's Organization of Iran that was here when the Shah was here is *finished*." Kateh pronouncing the word like a death sentence. Her hatred of the regime is complete and perfect. "I'm not talking about everyone who was in it; I'm talking about the organization itself. It was created by the Shah's sister, Ashraf. It is abolished and there is no voice of it remaining at all."

"Is it true that your meeting yesterday was broken up by women affiliated with the Tudeh party?" Where does this woman get her information? I wonder; she is a mass of error. Odd how aggressive questions are that begin "Is it true that . . . ?" Kateh corrects her carefully; yesterday was a sit-in at the Ministry of Justice; no one broke it up. "There had been an earlier meeting, the second meeting held to coordinate the eighth of March—it was broken into. By men. The doors were opened, men attacked us. There was some provocation which one day I hope to understand." Before this intriguing chimera is cleared up, another voice in the audience, that of the first woman who spoke out. The men of the press just watch this, filming it, as if it were staged for them; this woman certainly appears to be a planned participant.

"As a Persian woman I'm asking you this question . . ." She stands, surrounded by her friends, against a wall; they must be a faction, they must have come here on purpose to challenge us. Well enough, but before all the media, the effect will only be incoherent dissension through which we shall all be discredited. The network mentality could not wish for anything better. She returns once more, as if it were an accusation, to the fact that she has never heard of Kateh's group. We had taken her for a member of some leftist cadre with a grudge, but still we offered to give her the microphone and to share the press conference with us. She was in the Hall of Justice demonstration, she says. "A lot of women there were housewives. Why haven't we heard of your group before? The eighth of March was last week. Or have you been around a long time; what I mean is—we women are trying to get together for our freedom, we should work together and know the existence of each other," she insists. A hunger giving power to her voice. We relax; it had only been eagerness, curiosity. All impressions are reversed: hers, ours, theirs, the onlookers'. A curious turn of events; the tension mounting in the room had been expecting denunciation, a fight. There is instead—peace, a smile, the beginning of friendship.

"I think we give a false impression if we say there are ninety committees organizing this, when the real point is the thousands of women who attend the demonstrations," I say to her. She agrees. She has even pointed out that many who attended yesterday were housewives. "This is beyond organization," I say. "It simply occurs, a spontaneous phenomenon. "Right, and the point is to get together," she urges. "Exactly the point," Kateh agrees. "But without organization, I don't think it's going to get anywhere," the woman points out, as if pointing out the route of the future.

I was to remember it often in the days to come. But just as women are coming together over this issue, the young male reporter calls out over all—he has lost his ladies, they have taken our side. Through Kateh he will attack me, the French. "Foreigners." He, an American from Los Angeles. "I would like to ask the Iranian woman"—he seems unable to locate Kateh's name—"if she believes the women of Iran need the help of Kate Millett and the Frenchwomen?" Laughable idea, but surely a malicious question. "We are very glad to have Kate and our friends from France and others parts of the world here because I don't think women's oppression is just within Iranian boundaries, but all over the world. We have our own problems, so do women in the United States and in France; the only way we can get somewhere is to work together."

Sophie is urging the two Iranian women to join us. They are diffident. "But you have been in the streets these days?" "Yes, we have." "Then it's good to tell that." The reporters go on addressing Kateh. "Do you consider Ayatollah Khomeini an obstacle to a women's movement in Iran?" "I see no obstacle if women get up and fight for it; I see this happening today. Nothing can be an obstacle to the Iranian women if they unite and fight for it." They keep after her. "Is it Khomeini or is it the Bazargan government that is the source of the problem?" Asking her to declare war; she has a better strategy. She fences: Ayatollah Khomeini gives one interpretation, Ayatollah Tolerani gives another; the Bazargan government makes contradictory statements; the continuous problem here of conflicting authorities. The official government, Bazargan, has not made a definitive statement. Tomorrow's demonstration is to insist that that be done. "We want to know exactly where we stand." Does Kateh see any problem with an Islamic republic? This is soon to be declared, soon to be voted upon—but no one knows yet what it means. "It is they who should define what they mean by an Islamic government, so that Iranians know where they stand."

The reporters are impressed by Kateh, they continue to address their questions to her; it has worked. "Have you received any assurances of security from official sources for your march on Monday?" Kateh rises to this beautifully. Using all the platitudes of the daily pronouncements—whoever is responsible for inspiring them, our attackers are endlessly denounced in pious statements— "Ayatollah Khomeini has repeatedly said that any hooligans who attack women are going to be viewed as counterrevolutionary." Her questioner comes back: "It's quite a difference, Khomeini excommunicating them as counterrevolutionaries after they've committed acts of violence against the demonstrators, as opposed to actual security measures to see that doesn't happen." The man is sympathetic, it's a good question—we are very worried about it ourselves. "We have asked for assurances, we have not yet received them," Kateh answers, her voice is very level, conscious: "We have asked for it today—women have gone to the government to ask for defense for our demonstration tomorrow; no one knows yet."

"What are the other issues beyond the chador?" another man calls out. But the line of questions often becomes an "equation" game— weren't women better off under the Shah; or isn't it just as bad now; and so forth—an immoral balancing game. Kateh deals with it very firmly. "We didn't have anything under the Shah, we didn't have the freedom to come here and have a press conference under the old regime; we didn't have any rights." "But you were dressed as you are now. . . ." "So what?" "Well. Now they are trying to tell you what to wear," he concludes unpersuasively. "There was tremendous advance against discrimination under the old regime," the British lady interrupts, still sympathetic to it apparently. "There was desegregation in education, the veil was abolished, universities—I don't think you can make it all negative, I'm sorry," she closes briskly.

Sylvina interjects: "I would like to say that it is a form of rape to be under occidental and American canons, for example, back then when the veil was suddenly forbidden to women dependent on it." "Compare what you had before with what you're going to lose now"—our Englishman, Mr. Smith. "Okay, I will," Kateh begins. "We had four thousand political prisoners before—all of them women, four thousand Iranian woman political prisoners—which we don't have today." "Right on," I growl at her side. "And today we are starting from zero." "But you had any form of dress you liked," he persists. How tedious, this battle over clothes, as if they were clothes and not states of being represented by clothes; clothes forced to represent things as serious as life or liberty. "The Shah's father forced women to take off their chador—that was force. That means anyone who wore a chador, he would beat them up with the police and his guards." This is civil rights. The English lady reactionary is bringing up the Shah's divorce laws, the Family Protection Act, passed in 1974 and revised in 1976. It limited but did not abolish polygamy. "It was nothing compared with what women wanted," Kateh explains, it gave men the right to a second wife if they could force a first wife to give consent. And it gave only slender provisions for the right of divorce on the part of the wife, previously even more difficult to obtain, though easily accorded to men—who had but to repeat "I divorce you" three times and it was done.

"It did nothing for women. The Ayatollah has suspended this law. There is no new law yet. Ayatollah Khomeini has said that women have the right to divorce." Kateh will keep him to his more agreeable promises, though we all know he is now breaking them. "There are no new laws written yet, these are the things being discussed today, before being drawn up." Kateh hews to the revolution, to its promise, to the demands still being made in the streets. "The rights that women are fighting to get: Ayatollah Khomeini and the Bazargan government have not yet codified any new laws for women—that's why we are out there to get these laws for ourselves. We are there to fight for these laws. We are Iranian women who have come out of the revolution and we are not waiting for anybody to give us the laws. We have the freedom now to demonstrate and say what kind of laws we want to have."

"Are you saying that there is nothing so far that Ayatollah Khomeini has said to which you are reacting?" The *Times,* hammering away for a quote it finds acceptable. "Oh, yes, Ayatollah Khomeini has said that in Islamic government women have to cover themselves. This is what is being discussed by the women; they don't want other people to interpret it, because Ayatollah Khomeini has not said what kind of cover he means. Does it mean a chador, or does it mean a little scarf. Or does it mean that women should stay home. We don't know what he means, but we don't want to stay home." Jon Randall of the *Post* comes in, "Even if he were interpreted liberally here, and you only had to wear a scarf, are you also demonstrating against any sort of limitation? For example, we have a statement from Khomeini that women should dress with dignity, very properly in fact. Do you feel that they should have the right to do so?" "As I said at the very beginning of my statement, women should decide what they want to wear. Religion and clothing are something private, it's nobody's business. Iranian women wore the chador—they participated in the insurrection wearing it because that was a kind of reaction to the Shah's government. But today, if they don't want to wear the chador, nobody can force them."

Now a man heads for me. The same man who interrupted my introduction of Kateh, a bit older, "distinguished," an affected voice: "Miss Mill*ett,* given the fact that the revolution was to overthrow the Shah, it was also to repel foreign interests and influences, including American influences and interests; given the *delicate* state of affairs here—do you feel it proper for you to involve yourself in an Iranian issue?" We chuckle along the table—the man himself is an American; the hypocrisy of this question is wonderful. But it is also a loaded gun—all kinds of conservative elements will seize upon nationalism and twist it whatever way it pleases them. Here is the emissary of an American capitalist corporation, a major television network, rebuking me for being in Iran at the moment of its emancipation, though his own employer must have abetted and benefited during the time of its enslavement.

"I think I explained to you my credentials against the Shah. And, as feminists, we are in an international movement; I don't think we can emphasize this to you enough. We live under male governments. But in a large part of our work we do not recognize these nationalist boundaries. There is every reason for Iranians to resent Americans on the account of imperialism, true enough, but if you come to support your sister, that is just what you are doing. Perhaps, too, it might be that even an American could care about democracy and civil rights. I think, too, that the whole world should be concerned with the real achievement of human freedom here, the real achievement of a revolution coming into being. As I said before, I believe women will lead that struggle. To be with my sisters at this glorious moment of human history is a great privilege and one that I am delighted to partake in."

"What we want to do is enroll your concern for democratic freedoms and human rights, believing in your role as honorable people and as humanists. Because this is a dangerous undertaking, the rise of Iranian women. And for the safety of our sisters we appeal to what I'm sure are your very splendid instincts—" He talks right over me, accusatory tone of a CIA agent, "Aren't you as an American involving yourself in what is an Iranian matter?" As if this were a court of law and I found guilty of some mysterious charge. "No, sir, I am not, sir," answering the tone of the charge of international crime: it was an "Iranian matter" too when we worked to free the Shah's prisoners. Involving oneself with the domestic issues of a foreign country is the very stuff of human-rights work. But it is not meddling. "No, sir, I am not, sir," answering the charge of meddling in his tone. On further reflection I think I would have told him yes, that what we do in this line of work is meddling, its very essence, that the very principle of our activity on behalf of any minority abused by its "government"—prisoners, women, blacks, the poor—was simply to make it our business to serve those deprived of rights—in conjunction with their compatriots where protest was possible—alone and from a distance where it was not.

"Do you feel you are not involving yourself—" he repeats. "To the struggle of women my life is—" "Involving yourself with a domestic issue here in Iran—" He is setting me up. "I think I answered your question by saying that I have devoted my life to the struggle of women, that will take place in every country of the world, whoever is the government." "Will international support not have a negative effect?" "No, on the contrary, it is interesting how international the women's movement has always been historically; in the nineteenth century and in this century as well. Then and now we have struggled for two great world issues: internationalism and peace. The kind of xenophobia that we see taking over here, partly a reaction to imperialism, but also partly a shutting down to the idea of democracy, and the introduction of religious fervor—this is something that the Iranian women's movement will be very powerful in resisting—this xenophobia."

"Do you share any of the sentiments which I heard expressed by some of the women at the demonstration at the Ministry of Foreign Affairs, that the provisional government is hedging toward an apparatus of repression similar to that under the Shah?" A woman's voice. The Iranian with the lovely accent. Asking this most interesting question. I am dying to go for it. But Claudine and Sylvina have not spoken for a long time. I would pass the question on knowing how they would enjoy it. Before they get a chance to do so, a woman erupts in the audience: "The lack of your response to that question shows again the difficulty we all face here. We've all got rid of the Shah. But you are representing us with no political ideology whatsoever." She is clearly a leftist, yet I am delighted to see that, unlike most leftists here, she will not ignore repression and endorse the new regime. "Yours is a purely feminist perspective, there are many women in Iran who are socialists." "So are we." "There are many women who are communists, many women who are left—who will not hedge the political questions you are hedging." "I'm sorry, we are not hedging, in fact we would all love to answer that question."

"It seems to me you staged a press non-event, you have no very real connection with actual Iranian women." She's taking over. "You say that they got lost, but there are lots of them, we are expecting a million women on the streets tomorrow. Where are they, why aren't they here?" Our weak spot, the women who didn't come, the small size of organized feminism. "You say you are putting this before the world press; are the world press really that blind that they don't know there's a slight problem about democratic rights in Iran? The world press is on top of it, you're not helping them, you're not adding an analysis, a political ideology to what the press already sees. And you're certainly not involving Iranian women. You may have lots of things to offer, a perspective to offer—but why aren't you talking to Iranian women instead of the foreign press, who know what you're saying anyhow; you're not saying anything new."

The knot of women on the other side of the room erupts as well, the woman Sophie's been taping and her friends around her; perhaps they do represent some faction or another, one of them adding: "This must all be put in terms of some organization, in the context of some organization—so it is not supposed that all Iranian women are saying what you are saying." The cameras, nightmare. I will invite them to share the microphone and the podium. This is an eruption we clearly cannot quell. All the cameras are focused upon this young woman; she has made her stand for freedom by denouncing us in the harshest voice. The media will love it, a cat fight carried out between two stripes of female leftist. Worst of all, I feel her criticism is just: we have pussyfooted around the Ayatollah, being as careful and diplomatic as possible, following Kateh's lead in steering clear of unnecessary rudeness toward Islamic piety. I love the way this woman slams right into it. We invite her to share the microphone and the podium: "If you feel that you can fill that vacuum, we'd be delighted." Sophie urges her on; she has contacts with many groups. But she is not willing to "blow her cover." And since her question still remains to be answered, I jump at it: "Having worked against the Shah, I am horrified now to see executions again, secret trials again. As someone who believes in the Iranian constitution and democracy, I am horrified to see the whole judicial system taken apart. No appeals. Instant justice. To see the smallest, silliest, happiest human rights withdrawn, like the right to drink, to wear what you want, becoming symbols of a narrow fervor now jeopardizing every democratic right. While of course the people who made the uprising are asking not only where are women's rights but where are everyone's rights, where in fact are the economic reforms going to come from? As a socialist I can see that unless there is a very strong push from the left, everything the people rose up in the streets to gain will be lost. As indeed it is eroded daily."

Now a reporter who had originally asked me a question wants me to shut up. He wants Kateh to answer some other question of his. Then another one dictates to me; I should answer his question. Kateh continues, answering still another man who wants me to answer. The young Los Angelean takes the floor. He imagines that the women's movement in the United States operates as a monolith, "gets together and picks their representatives," as he puts it; the Iranians disappoint him in not doing so. Kateh, he says, "means well," but she does not represent the whole of the Iranian women. "Of course," she agrees. "Do you know how these demonstrations happen?" I urge him, "Someone raises a piece of paper, and everyone says, 'Terrific, tomorrow, ten o'clock.' The spontaneity of this movement is what we are trying to convey to you." "It doesn't happen that way, there are people who organize demonstrations." He's sure of it: there are people behind this. "That's politically naive," he informs me. "There are people who organize demonstrations." "There are indeed, but none expected the kind of mass movement that has occurred. There have been Maoist groups that have worked long and hard, they have organized discussions at Tehran University. But the number of women coming from the streets—who are not political in the sense of belonging to political organizations, they don't—but they have been politicized by the experience of the uprising. They ran in the streets, they fought, some even risked getting killed, they accepted that risk and danger. The courage of the Iranian people to rise up against tanks, guns, and army. We have never seen a people yet succeed in doing this; think of Czechoslovakia. The heroism of the Iranians. The masses of women who arrive whenever a demonstration is called—"

Now I am shut up again, they order Kateh to talk. As soon as she begins, they want me again. I defer to her and persist in it. Kateh explains one more time that the committee does not represent every woman, is only trying to organize, that ultimately everything is to be decided by all women in concert. But women must be forceful; she interprets one of yesterday's chants: "We are against any kind of dictatorship." And another: "We Iranian women are not going to be chained anymore." Struggling against their arrogance toward her. "Tomorrow there will be thousands of these kinds of chants, that's why we want you to come there. To hear what Iranian women want." She is interrupted again. The same young man from Los Angeles who has spent the time setting Iranian women in the audience against us, and failed; now he goes for me. "Miss Mill*ett,* there are some comments from Iranian women who have been organizing a women's movement in this country, that possibly your presence in this country hasn't done that much for Iranian women, but your picture on television in America and your name in American newspapers might do something for your career and your feminist reputation in America." Cheap shot. I begin to loathe this young man. "You should say about the eighth of March and how you were invited," Kateh whispers. How unexpected, such a charge; it had never occurred to me I was on television. The march, but not me. "I haven't even heard anything from America for seven days now, I haven't a clue."

"You made *The New York Times* today," Ibraham calls out, conferring something thereby which I fail to appreciate. Do people go to crazy places like Iran for publicity? America sweeps over me in a sickening wave. No one is listening to what we say, the women here—we were talking about them. Focus on them. I go on urging the Iranian women in the audience to join us on the podium so they can take questions with us. All drowned out by other male voices, like dogs going for a kill; the young man from Los Angeles objecting now that my work among Iranian women is "not clear." "Not well documented." Deliberate vitiation of my credibility. Will I have to say all over again that I was invited? This is idiotic. But he is bent on discrediting me.

Then a woman interrupts him. An American woman's voice, our angel—Elaine. "As a woman and a journalist I should like to take some responsibility for this press conference. No one knew Kate Millett was in town, several people wanted to interview her and asked for this press conference. Kate is representing certain feminists in New York, Kateh is representing her own committee, in no way representing every Iranian woman—if you don't want to listen to it, fine." Our press conference is a shambles—we are all under attack, our credentials, our power to "represent," even our integrity.

Kateh rises to the occasion: "I'd like to make a comment on this—

Kate Mill*ett* [even she does it] came here for the eighth of March. And we were glad to have her here. Because, as women were chanting in the streets today: 'The eighth of March is not Eastern, it's not western—it's international.' We were glad to have support from all over the world. Starting with Kate Mill*ett*, who came here herself, and Simone de Beauvoir, the delegation, Italian, French, and women from everywhere. Thousands of women who heard Kate's speech at the eighth of March, they all welcomed her, and we all love her."

I am covered with metaphoric kisses and a little embarrassed, but very happy. The Iranian woman in the audience, our critic a moment ago, and one of the women whom this bumptious young man from Los Angeles is perhaps again riling up against me, now stands up against the wall. In the camera's eye. We're in for it, I think. "It's not a question of loving her; how many people *know* Kate Millett?" Oddly enough she pronounced it correctly. "How many women here know Simone de Beauvoir? We don't." Kateh tries to explain: "Iranian women don't know Kate Millett but she was fighting for the Iranian political prisoners." "Whatever the hell my name is, I'm a sister who has come to give support," I offer. "As a woman sitting here watching . . ." she resumes. We offer again to share the press table with her. "I don't feel I'm ready for that," she admits, "I still have a long way to go to get there—the point is if you want to get freedom for Iranian women, if you're fighting for freedom all over the world, you should let yourself be known, let other women know. I mean, we don't yet know you." "I came to meet you, I'm beginning to now," I say, mystified by her, her asperity seeming to melt, to have arisen out of misunderstandings and suspicions I cannot even fathom. I have not been close to her all this time, as Sophie has, in the audience. "No, really, only a certain percent of us are educated or intellectual; not as many women read here as men, as do women in America." "May I add to what you say, a question we have not even mentioned yet? The question of education, the high illiteracy rate among women here. We've mentioned divorce, even abortion once, but education is passionately important—if women's education is threatened, when there is such high illiteracy among women in Iran; the Shah kept women illiterate—" "The Shah is gone, he is over. Khomeini is here now—" she says. "Will Khomeini permit coeducation, for example?" I ask. "Yes, that's it, that's the new question," she agrees—and then a strange transformation: "As women in Iran we are very happy to have you here. It's very nice of you to want to help us in this situation. But help us in *our* way, not in an American way."

I promise, and we exchange a curious smile. Peace. Not for the men. Another asks all over again was I invited. We assure him I was. The

Ad Hoc Committee for March 8 is dragged out again for his inspection. Kateh again explaining what she must have explained six times now. It is surreal. How was the invitation recorded? It was even published in the papers, Kateh tells him. The Persian papers. Was I here already? No, I was invited from America. Kateh is dragged through her committee's program and the finer points of chador-wearing again and then the man who questioned my interfering in foreign affairs starts on me again. "There's a man who's been standing up trying to ask a question for the longest time, I worry about him," I plead, could he have a turn? Just this question and he'll quit, he promises. And then delivers—clearly it has been written out, planned, a loaded gun. "Do you, Miss Mill*ett,* consider the Ayatollah Khomeini a chauvinist, a male chauvinist?"

It is the sort of drivel one would expect; silly trivializing, what they want. Of course, it would be hard not to apply the term, given what it means and how it implies patriarchal rule—to any authority in the country—even these reporters themselves, clearly relishing it. Of course Khomeini's a male chauvinist—the point is, are you going to say so in public so that he can print this charge in the papers? To provoke hostility toward feminism here and convert it to thoughtless humor at home? The show, the baited crazy libby. Laughter all around. "It's germane," he says. "It is indeed," I say, avoiding the trap, going for better ground. "It seems to me that the civil rights of women in this beginning of a revolution, following upon an uprising, and the fall of the tyrant—at this juncture, I and ever so many people and my sisters in the demonstrations feel that our civil rights are terribly threatened. By what he says and by what he does. Yes, a male chauvinist would be a very simple and a very idiotic way to describe it, but certainly germane."

I have not really said it—and he's going to make me now. 'Cause he knows it isn't enough, he hasn't got me yet, if he had the epithet sworn to, tomorrow his fool paper will print nothing of what I've said but that asinine phrase spit at power—to bring me danger. I am new here, the executions have not yet really come home to me as Khomeini's work, and opposing him on feminist grounds requires as yet no insult, even if outrage; he is still a figure of magic, robes, his religious force still clings to him. The blasphemy of power, the desecration of all freedom is not yet consummated, only foreshadowed. And my friends put their faith in the people. Oddly enough I feel no animosity yet for Khomeini himself, a kind of awe for his terrible charisma, an artist's appreciation of the force created thereby. Total betrayal of the revolution is not yet certain. Nor would it be summoned up by this reporter's low snickering epithet. I am a pacifist; I won't play this game.

"Describing the Ayatollah Khomeini?" Persisting, needing just for me to say yes, and then he can roast me, reduce it all to just one disposable cliché. No, damn you, I will not let all we struggle for be dismissed that way. Nor will I rise to your bait. "Describing the Ayatollah Khomeini?" No way. Instead I'll tell you what it's really about: "Our rights to education, abortion, to child care, to divorce; our rights to employment, to the professions—all the things we have fought for since the commencement of an international women's movement in the 1840s and throughout the world, are in grave jeopardy in this society, where women have fought along with men to gain again a democracy and a constitutional state and every civil freedom. Our freedoms are terribly threatened; the freedoms of many people in Iran are so threatened; indeed the whole notion of a democracy and of constitutional government is in danger. As I said before, I believe that women will lead the protest against such a curtailment."

Sylvina interjects to remind the Western press that there is also monotheism there. "Religion is a supreme form of patriarchy. No one can forget that the Pope is trying to forbid abortion, even contraception; no one can forget that the Pope during the last war signed a pact with Hitler. Even the American President takes his oath of office from God. With monotheism comes all the hierarchy, all the pyramid of power." Then she branches out: "Democrats often doubt that the masses exist and are always looking for a leader, claiming the people cannot be spontaneous."

It's batted back and forth if democracy and theocracy are incompatible. Finally the man who's been standing up all this time, waiting: "Do you agree with the allegations of some of the women at the Foreign Ministry today that the men who disrupted and attacked previous demonstrations were involved with Ayatollah Khomeini's revolutionary committees?" Soft young man, less vicious than the others, good question. For Kateh: "I don't exactly know, since lots of men have come out and said, 'We are with the Komiteh,' but they're not really representing anything. Because if they are really under the order of Ayatollah Khomeini, they should not be attacking women. He has actually said no one should bother us women in the street with veil or without veil." Adroit. But it's evident, more so every moment, that they will goad and harass us to declare war on the Ayatollah and bring down the rage of Muslim fervor on our heads thereby. "Lots of people come out and attack us in the name of the Komiteh, we do not know if they really are or not." She has left room for peace, for the line to change as it must, if it can.

And now the male chauvinist goes at it again: "I'm merely restating a previous question. If I were a reporter—which I am—and wanted to be on the story, I would write something like 'Kate Millett accuses Khomeini of being a chauvinist.'" "Sure you would, that's why I redefined that question at such length." "But in fact you did do it— that's the way it could come out in some quarters." "No, I didn't." A moment ago Sylvina gleefully even called the Pope a chauvinist, but no one has caught me doing it to Khomeini; only an admission it was germane followed by a refusal to talk at that level. "I'll do it again for you"—looking at him—"I said that I found that a silly phrase—what we are discussing are human rights; that's merely a fashionable 'quickie.' When we are discussing something as serious as this, we should really avoid the banal clichés of your journalism, the way in which the women's movement has been treated in United States media—as a form of entertainment. We are discussing people's lives. Women were stabbed yesterday. The people who attack us in the streets, unarmed, a peaceful demonstration, of women—and to be set on by armed men, either with guns or knives, concealed weapons, men who are not ashamed to beat up high-school girls—to be everywhere in their presence, to see them in columns and masses, despite what Khomeini says about protecting us—but the men in the streets, who believe themselves followers of Khomeini, who believe that by hitting us and spitting on us and throwing rocks at us, they show thereby that they are true Islamic patriots. . . . Do you see how complex it is? How in fact you are dealing not only with one man playing pope and issuing directives—while another man ostensibly governs after parliamentary formulae—but also you are dealing with a culture so deeply imbued with hatred of women, with oppression of women—this is what we are rising against too. Take into account the centuries, the millennia of the oppression of women here—as everywhere—why, even the chador, if you think about it, exists everywhere in the world in one form or another and rests on the philosophical or pseudophilosophical premise that we are inherently evil, provocative—what you are up against is almost the character of taboo, a sense of some inherent evil through the sexuality of women. To us as Westerners, this is also very familiar; it is where we began in examining our own traditions."

"Whether you use the term male chauvinist—" He starts off again; I've had it with this guy—"I think my comrades should speak more and I less," I bow off. "My point is, it seems you have made a statement about Khomeini . . ." How he is yearning to pin me to this idiotic phrase, to impale me on it. No soap. "I have made a statement, and it's ten minutes long," I sign off. Sylvina would be happy to give him his quote—but he can't use one from her, he can't "get her" for saying it; no one "knows" her, it wouldn't be "damaging" enough.

"What political or religious leader in the world is not a male chauvinist?" she asks him good-humoredly. We all enjoy it. The young man from Los Angeles claims Indira Gandhi was a female chauvinist; he is not very bright.

Ibraham from *The New York Times* insists: "These whole demonstrations did not start haphazardly. They started because Ayatollah Khomeini pronounced himself on the way women should be dressed, and should behave themselves—I'm still trying to find out, are you taking a position? He has started this whole thing, have you taken a position, yes or no?" Against Khomeini? Kateh handles it: "We want our rights, we are fighting to get our rights. The statements against women, such as that they cannot become judges [under Khomeini's Islamic law] or that they should stay home, or that they should cover themselves—none of these are laws." She will defuse proclamation into opinion. "They are statements by different ayatollahs, or by different government officials. Since there is no new law written yet and since we want our rights, we are coming out to make it clear to everybody tomorrow. We women will say what we want. We say it is us who should decide. Nobody can tell us what to wear. If we want the chador, we will wear it; if we don't, we won't. We are not going to *ask* anybody, we are going to demand it, our democratic right to have our voice in the new government which is coming about."

And we close it with that—urging them to come tomorrow. "You'll probably have to walk for a long way." Kateh smiles. "Thousands of high-school girls, nurses, judges, the employees of different ministries, teachers—all of us. Nine A.M. tomorrow. And we do not know when it will end." "We expect a great deal of male support, and solidarity demonstrations are being held throughout the world," Claudine calls out. I wonder about America.

The rape is over. But perhaps we won the protection we need for tomorrow, if not from the government, then from the press. We know already we will be blacked out of Iranian television—nothing of yesterday's huge demonstration was permitted on the air—and television has so much power in a country with such literacy problems. We have no choice but the foreigners. It may even be possible to force the national media here to begin to cover, if only to follow suit. In any case, the demonstration will now be seen across the world. We have done the job with goodwill, been treated with scorn and suspicion, but now at least it's over. I see Reza in the crowd—an old friend, comrade, a head so much wiser than I in this country—if only I can have a drink with him, a real talk. "It used to be both of us up there together, now it's you," he says, wistful. It has come to women now. But surely the political thing is better in his hands; he was here during much of it, is of this place, understands it all so much better. I wish he could have briefed me; maybe he will now—if he can give me some time. I have heard everywhere that he is nearly in hiding, writing but not speaking in public, living at his brother's, where I reached him on the phone late at night. And then he was amusing, full of insight and irony; his description of mullahs entering politics was a delight to hear: "They are sorcerers, you see, a combination of sorcerer and rabbi; of course nowadays they function as psychologists too. In many places here they are the only people who can read; naturally they give advice about toothache, problems of the heart, domestic squabbles—they solve everything. To see them playing politics as well is an unearthly spectacle, tonic actually." "What is an Islamic republic, Reza?" "I have no idea, I suspect they don't either." It is too crazy to take with entire seriousness; Reza believes his beloved democracy still has a chance.

The big shots have left the room now, the remnant are friendly or becoming friends. People mill about; the energy after confrontation, public spectacle. Women debate each other and find points of agreement, exchange names and numbers; all our challengers are comrades now but still ironing out this point or that; compliments and laughter. Kateh translates a reprise of my notes for a Persian journalist from *Etela'at* as the others still hammer out ideological detail in the background. It is the rushed and tired side of a journalist's life, yet this man copies out phrase after phrase with patience and exquisite courtesy. How beautiful English becomes in Kateh's Persian, listening with one ear while gossiping with Sophie, who is so angry at the reporters she is almost sick. "This is what they do, everywhere we go," Kateh says. "They will not take women seriously—ever." Sophie had been sitting near the young man from Los Angeles, picking up his personal attacks on her tape recorder: "'She's only here to seek out her own publicity,' he says. So I say, 'Would you repeat that into my tape recorder?' No, he won't." "Well, he got up and repeated it to the world a bit later." "They infuriate me." "You were a reporter." "Not like this, I was a good reporter; these are just assassins." "Press conferences—the civil equivalent of a firing squad," and we all laugh.

A message arrives for Kateh that Nasrin and Nelufar, who were to appear at the press conference with her, have been arrested by the Komiteh. Distributing leaflets at the university. Four hours of inter-rogation before they were released.

6

GIVEN THE RULE of discretion under which he must live now, I ought to have known that the Intercontinental was no place to talk with Reza. He exposes himself to criticism even in being here; but there is also no other place in town to have a drink. The project is hopeless from the start, since Reza has brought Gregory Rose along with him, a reporter who had once written a good piece against Savak; Reza is still grateful for it. Then the rude young man from Los Angeles invites himself to sit down at our table, pretending to apologize for his insults; in no time he comes up with some others. One sickens of the place, the imperialist decadence: "A room like the Shah would have made," Reza says, catching sight of the bar, grimacing at the obligatory red brocade wallpaper, the copied furniture, the "American Bar." Even the mountains, looming through the plate-glass "picture windows," fail to comfort.

Yet this almost feels like the first time I have seen them. This city surrounded by mountains. As by a presence. Surely the most spectacular site in the world: Salt Lake, Los Angeles, nothing at home or anyplace else I know can touch it; the way the peaks float above us in a perfect circle. I stare at them, trying to take comfort from the sun at the end of the day merging into mountains, something to heal. And Reza next to me. But unable to talk, circumspect crowded by strangers. If it were only the two of us. And Sophie; he would not be uneasy with her. But not all these people, not these foolish political opinions, not all this pumping. Politics is exactly what I would love to hear him talk. Frankly but privately. Two old friends. Reza always the one I felt closest to in Caifi; our nearness in age, in literary education, humanists rather than political persons. The press conference is over, we should be given some space now, privacy, no longer on display. They should leave us alone now. And so we remain, even in company; talking a peculiar little parody of scholarship; corny, pedantic, defensive. Oblique stilted dialogue, rag-picker bits of literary criticism and history, sly jokes and allusions; grasshopper evasions of bait, a preference for little volleys played with Arab astronomy, Wilhelm Reich, Ferdosi. Through it all Reza keeps repeating that he has taught English literature in Western universities—his English better than that of anyone else at the table—but what a pity it is that Westerners know nothing of the Persian lyric, he laments, explaining imperialism. The young man from Los Angeles claims he couldn't even get his hands on a book of Persian history. Reza does not hear him; a gentlemanly gesture. I sit quietly on my three volumes and volunteer nothing.

But there is such a sadness in Reza; home again and not home either. The Shah gone, the dreamed-of time, and now this new popery and pestilence—how does he see it? Gregory Rose flattering him that he is one of the most powerful men in Persia and his scheduled appointment with Khomeini could have far-reaching effects. "We will probably talk about our uncles," Reza says, that calm mocking voice. "My uncle was in his uncle's mosque when they were boys." His eyes narrowing as he watches the mountains. I sit across from him now, having moved to avoid our intruder from Los Angeles, my back to the mountains. Reza looks at me and the mountains; we cannot speak. How disappointing this meeting, to be in Persia at last, so long talked of, and to be in it only as far as a Western hotel which serves alcohol through a special dispensation of the new regime. Uneasy marriage of imperialism with puritanism. And silence.

Then a plethora of American talk. Nighttime. With Elaine among the pressmen. Opinions. Before dinner, during, after. What Randall thinks of Ghotbzadeh, chief of media in the new regime, therefore head of censorship. Gregory Rose had called him the most dangerous person in Iran, an intellectual thug. Ghotbzadeh was in charge of Khomeini's "security" in France. Others say that there he became a Savak hunter, one who went out to locate and murder Savak agents and became much like one in the process. Tales of foreign intrigue; reporter talk has a trace of movie script. Elaine and Randall furnish the "human" side: Ghotbzadeh hankers for France, his mistress there. One hears so many versions of a man, all possible, possibly even true simultaneously. It is certainly true that he keeps our demonstrations off television, and the women are talking more and more of a demonstration against the television itself. Maybe the next demonstration after the march. The television workers are out on strike, the women at the station particularly angry at their new Islamic exclusion from the screen. The single exception so far is children's programs. There, suitably garbed. And there are kerchiefs at the entrance to the station now; wear one or you don't enter.

The intrigue unfolding as you listen to reporters, sometimes even recording them—reversing the process. Hearing, learning, being informed, misinformed, gleaning bits of the world as they see it here; the government. Iran has its two governments to them, the religious and the secular; the personalities who govern; Ghotbzadeh, Yazdi, Entezam, Bazargan. Portraits and cameos of people in power, press conferences—Entezam gives two a week—I sometimes get the impression that these are the only times the press emerge from the hotel. Until our demonstrations disturbed their peace, their coffee in bed, their secretaries and translators and loathing of the place. Their homesickness. They are prisoners of a hotel, fancy but tedious electrical glass box. Some have been here a very long time. Elaine is leaving tomorrow after six weeks; celebrating, ecstatic. None of them can bear it for more than a few weeks; the worst dangers of the insurrection are over, but the ennui remains. The asperity, the alienation.

They don't live in private houses or miss their surrogate families tonight as we do: Gouli and Bahar's arrival from school. Hermoz and his bottle of Scotch and the cut-glass bowl of ice. Calmly cleaning his revolver last night in the upstairs room, cleaning it meticulously before giving it to the maid to give to her son in the Kurdish guerrillas, and having cleaned it, pointing it at the evening news while we photographed his surreal playfulness—"You musn't show this, you know," the revolver in silhouette against the tiny image of the Ayatollah televised: a Persian comment on things. From one who lives there, can joke about it, meaning and not meaning the joke. Whereas in these hotel rooms, all is official, international earnestness, posture— the quasi-governmental stance of media, knowing itself to be an extension of government, even a kind of government on its own. Propaganda fancying it is truth. Put in power, therefore finding reason to exist.

How different, even splendid is Elaine in the midst of this masculine seriousness. Holding her own. But going home to Paris exhausted, not staying to do the women's story, not assigned. It will be lonelier without her. She has given Sophie and me each a chador, for protection. She has also given us her space to rest in, hospitality, friendship, even her twin beds for the night.

Somewhere in the middle of that night Robin Morgan and Gloria Steinem are on the phone from the offices of *Ms.*, heralding not only Claude Servan-Schreiber and the delegation from France, but a possible landing of their own. "How do the women there feel? Just tell me frankly," Gloria says. A good honest question. "Well, it's a bit dubious at the moment, touchy you know, the paranoia about foreigners, everyone's paranoia about America . . ." "Justified, of course," she interjects. "Well, there's even a feminist paranoia about foreigners at this juncture. There's very little organization here, there hasn't been time—they went from a dozen to a few hundred in a few weeks and then overnight to thousands. There's no structure yet, no name of anything even, except the Ad Hoc Committee for March 8, and that was two days ago—since then it's changed into something called the Committee in Defense of Women's Rights. But really, it's the women who flock to the streets. We had a knockout thing at the Ministry of Justice, watch for it, there was at least one American television crew." "I've heard from the wire services already."

Of course, Gloria is a reporter, organized; with a magazine at her disposal. "What can we do to help? Just tell me." "Well, rather than coming over"—this will break Robin's heart, she has already applied for a visa—"if you could get up some bread for offices, a publication. They could start, you know." "Is there anything you need, don't hesitate." "Maybe some film, cassette tape—Claude could bring them." "What else for the women there; how can we help from here?" "Virtually everything is needed here—there is no feminist literature even at hand; it was censored out in the old days. There's a good number of women who could write stuff we could help place. And support—solidarity. They need to know you're with them." "We'll get going on that; we're organizing demonstrations here."

"In front of Rockefeller Center and St. Pat, the old corner, you know," Robin chimes in, chuckling from her end of the extension phone. "And then on down to the Iranian embassy to give 'em hell— like we used to do to the Shah." The New York battle cry; how odd it seems at this distance, a hotel room in Tehran with gunfire intermittently in the road outside. How miraculously you can be called from New York, how difficult it is to call them. But how still more complicated to explain without seeming to be smug—the thousands of differences that separate our experience, friends that we are, have been so long. Not just Uptown and Downtown differences, but differences of half a world away in an armed camp that has swiftly replaced an uprising—all the nuances of left and nationality and religion. Positions of Iranian women, of international feminists, forming every moment, shifting, coming into focus. How do you help—how in the hell do you help? Goodwill, common sense, sensitivity. And yet how eager we have been throughout these days to discredit, argue, distrust. Claudine's reaction to the French delegation. Sophie's reaction. Kateh's skepticism.

I am bewildered with trying to figure it out, keep peace, bring factions and foreigners together—yet if the thing could work, if we could see this impetus and keep it moving, maintained and supported everywhere . . . the Iranian women might not only be safe, they'd have a real chance of winning. And already they are making the rest of us feel alive as we have not in years.

The adventure again. The excitement. Even after a day of press conferences, reporters; their arrogance in public, their cynicism in private. Their study, their knowledge of maps and trips to the north, the finer points of Islamic schism—much knowledge put to little use due to the confines of their assignments. Tony, for example, has done graduate work on Islamic architecture, reads Farsi, has been all over the country, but is kept to the oil story. An evening full of the "lowdown." Often they seem so much better than what they write, surely than what they write for. How do you separate the person from the office? Feeling rather like a reporter myself hunting and pecking on Elaine's little portable—does she really use this thing, against deadlines? The first typewriter put into my service since I've been here, so as to explain, still later into the night, for the perusal of the press at breakfast—the absence of the two other Iranian women from our press conference.

They were arrested. If we went outside tonight, we might be. The reporters and the revolutionaries and the difference between. The island of the Intercontinental, still serving French wine, phones that reach all over the world, room service in a country running out of food. It's said that large shipments of frozen meat have been left to thaw and rot because they were not butchered under religiously correct conditions. The Shah had let agriculture deteriorate perilously, had begun importing food, creating a dependency on foodstuffs brought in from abroad, into this rich and fertile country, squandering oil money to do it. There will soon be no more French wine, only Persian, and the commonest bottle will be sold for thirty dollars. The Intercontinental is a den of thieves and spies and pirates—you can get a drink there and a bath and talk American.

7

MARCH 12. The day of the great march. Tehran University to Freedom Square. Though it looks like we may never get there, never even leave the university. Already ringed with thugs, the men one must first pass through, the crowds of them hanging about in the entry road before the great gates, the bunches of them milling around on the walkways if you get through those gates. Wearing your foreign clothes and your foreign face; rumpled slacks and a further rumpled sweater—we haven't been home to Nelufar's to change clothes in a while. But a march is not a press conference, and these are marcher's clothes. There would be no chador, no kerchief either today. Nor is my face that foreign; my hair is dark, I'm short. Still it's felt, smelled out, and endangering. By now a photograph in the local papers could get me in trouble; if that foreign face—there being so few foreign females pictured there—if it were seen by this lot, picked out . . . then. We move fast and without speaking. I have sometimes been a little embarrassed, shy, silly-feeling in places where I might be "recognized"—I have never had to be afraid.

And the place breathes tension. You don't play your tape recorder here, you don't show your cameras, still or moving. You just put your head down and get past the danger. Further up the walk there will be the disputants, further still the women massing, hoping to march out of here and through the streets. But already you wonder if they'll make it, if they'll even try. And there are so few, compared with what we had hoped for. A woman explains that last night Iranian television warned women against coming: their rights would be respected, it was promised—there was no need to come to this demonstration, no need to protest. Everything was already taken care of.

"It's defused already, it seems," Ralph Schoenman muses. He too has a camera, a tape recorder. The media are here in droves. The irony of it—all of us recording what may be a non-event. But Iranian women, censored by their own television, unaware of the enormous coverage available in the world press, Iranian women, each woman in her home this morning deciding whether to come or not, must feel terribly isolated. The wavering of action, the push or the falling away. I had such hopes for this march. A man tells me my picture was in *Kayhan* yesterday; I have become "recognizable," or possibly so. There are men everywhere, disputing, obstructing, trying to take precedence. Somehow we women seem to lack the force we had at the Ministry of Justice. The chador is no longer obligatory—"but it was never the chador," the women reason—the national broadcast has been "unfaithful," the women say gently.

Are they marching today? Sophie asks. Of course, I say. No, I don't think so, the women say. It is already almost half-past nine, and there are so few people here. They must be up ahead, near the cluster of buildings, I go on hoping. All because of last night's program on

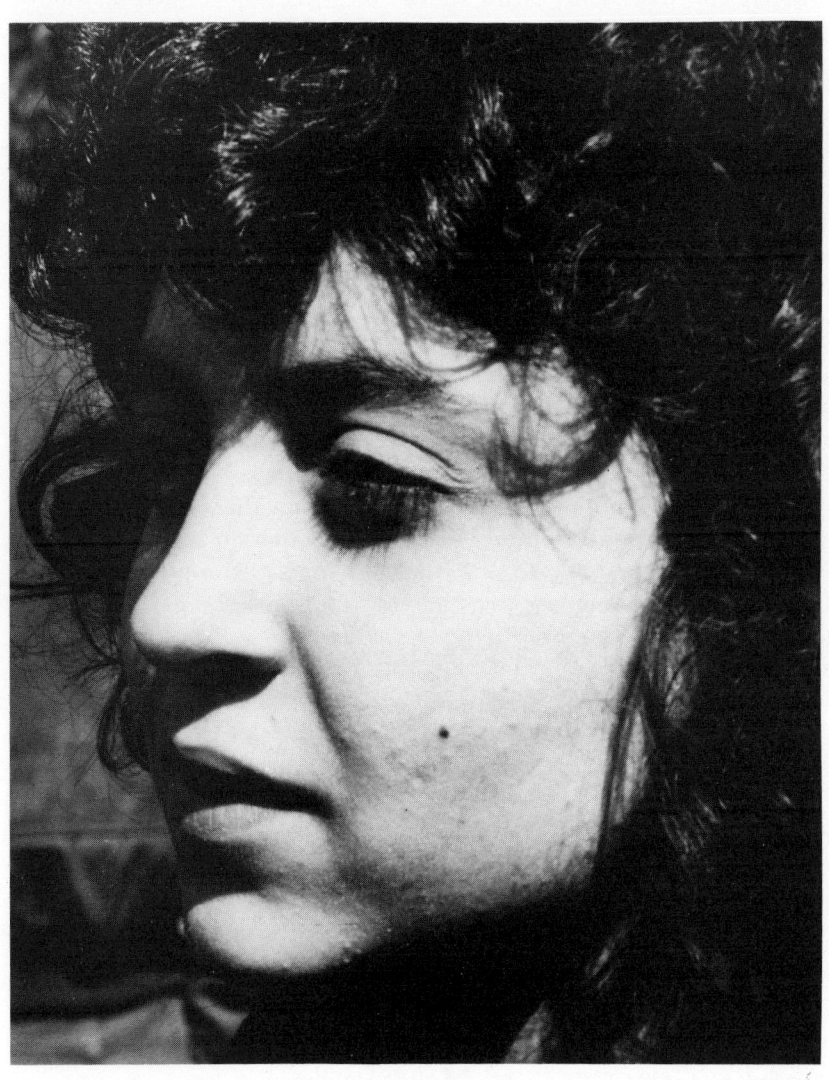

Terranie

television. Everyone talks of it. "But it's everything, not chador," the women keep reminding each other. We must stay with Terranie, a young woman who has been given to us today by our friends as our protector; cool, street-smart. Look, up ahead, a whole playing field of women, surging. Plenty of them. But not what we had hoped. Still—if they kept it up, if they started to march. I see Hámid and inquire about his sister, the last woman producer left in television. "But she can do nothing," he says, "the censorship." Hamid is discouraged. "There was another announcement this morning, telling the women not to come. The propaganda reduces it to chador." "But so does ABC"—a young Iranian woman here is furious about it, threatens to boycott the foreign journalists here. Iranian government television has cautioned its people that the imperialist American media are covering the demonstrations only for counterrevolutionary purposes. And everywhere the real demands: education, employment, civil rights, are buried under the chador. Endlessly substituted for the substantive by official Iranian statements, governmental and religious; trivialized by the Westerners into fashion, exoticism, or entertainment.

Today has an air of demoralization. But maybe not; it's still early. The crowd in the playing field is growing larger, louder. We come upon friends; Claudine arrives to tell us that the women gathered already on the field are now discussing whether to march or not. A march or a sit-in? My own savvy wants a march—announce a march, you better have one. It was planned and is expected. But only a minority are for the march. The government has done its work. So has the threat of danger. By staying within the university we remain safe. But silent, ineffective, or not the effect we would have with the promised thousands in the street. The smaller we are, the greater the danger of attack. A chant is translated for us. "The problem is not the veil." Men around us argue so loudly we cannot hear the women speakers. In the distance women's voices haranguing, women cheering; how sorry I am not to understand, to hear only the odd phrase, hardly able to see the platform, a man blocking my view and separating me from Terranie and my translations. "Down with censorship." I see Nelufar through the crowd, apologizing, quietly explaining in French her absence at the press conference. Sophie is afraid for her movie camera, we must move to a safer place. Men, men, everywhere men, I grumble into my tape recorder, small and not as risky as a camera. "One of the main demands of this demonstration is equal pay for equal work," Terranie translates; then, "We are here not only to fight for our rights, but for a real democracy. Men and women together, against imperialism." I spot Kateh. The woman from the Foreign Ministry inquires if we have sent her message. "Front page, *New York Times*," I grin at her. "We are really waiting to receive another answer; the American women, what will they do for us?" she goes on. "We are organizing committees of support, demonstrating with you today, and more American feminists may be coming." "We appreciate it. If you leave us there will be less; then you should expect victims." The prediction haunts me long afterwards.

The debate goes on, to march or not. If they knew how many eyes in the world were watching. If I could speak Farsi I might be able to say that. The speaker now is for the march, the crowd roars. The world expects this march. If I had the right to speak, I would. If I even had the ability, how much I would like to speak out. I urge Terranie to start talking up the march—talk to the people around you, that's how you do it, I proselytize. Talk it up. Terranie is unmoved; the group will decide it by democratic vote. If we don't march, we look like we caved in, I urge. "But we don't have safety yet, we need guards," they reason. "But if we go into the streets, the other women will see it, take heart and join us." Safety in numbers, I'm thinking. "The trouble is they aren't organized," one woman says, "there is another group already waiting in Freedom Square, for this one to join them."

Perhaps if we're patient, they'll vote to march. Terranie's right. I respect her integrity before my well-meaning pressure; utterly ineffective even if one interpreted it as fair persuasion. It is the only time I was ever tempted to interfere or have any effect whatsoever upon the events I observed in support and sympathy. The temptation passes; I accede to the wisdom of the women themselves. I have never seen it fail. Women themselves, this simple democracy. Unorganized, fresh, authentic. The Maoists have had control of the microphones for long stretches, urging the women not to march, to wait, to see what the government decides; to obey authority. A most unrevolutionary position. Waiting for bureaucrats. Some statement due to come out on Thursday. Why Thursday, when we are here and ready today, the crowd growing every moment, many thousands of marchers now. People coming to a march should get one; they shouldn't be sent home. No leftist worth the name dissipates popular energy; it's too precious, too hard to generate. How curious to hear the speakers of certain Maoist factions and their male supporters, everywhere around the area behind the platform where we stand, exhorting the eager women who have risked much to come here today to do nothing, to wait for officials.

If we're patient they'll vote the right way, I have a secret assurance of it. No one else thinks it will turn out well: Terranie, Kateh, in touch with our own speakers, who are urging a vote for the march, are quite pessimistic. Other women around us wish there were organization, a base of opinion, coherent and understood ideology, a general consciousness, less possibility of erosion from each new wind.

The new worry, the new scare tactic, is that if we march, the attackers will say that we are demanding the return of the Shah, that we are counterrevolutionaries. This is the strongest form of intimidation—these women would rather die than be taken for supporters of the old regime. No accusation could be more hurtful. We can't be intimidated, I say, my own hope insisting.

Great banners have been unfurled over to our left. "Freedom is our culture," Terranie translates; "Silence is our shame," a new twist on an old admonition. And a funny one, "Don't leave us alone with the mullahs." The crowd has spilled over out from the field, even off to the side, where we stand, bodies are packed tight now. The crowd roars, its energy rises, you can hear it moment to moment transform itself for action. The fear seems to float away over the field and toward the woods, the uncertainty. It was printed in this morning's paper that the punishment for attacking the women demonstrators had been increased. There are a lot more of us now, I tell myself, if we stick together . . .

Because of course I don't know what to expect either, once we are in the streets. The crowd of women roars, the men among us are restless. People around us are arguing their heads off. It occurs to me that I am a participant in these demonstrations by now, but crippled; without the resources of the simplest high-school girl, without Farsi, without a voice. And yet I hear or imagine the word for "march," echoing from the field. I check again with Kateh; the word for march is *Rahpaymai*. What if we chanted it? "They are chanting it down there," she says. Sophie changes film, losing patience with me as her camera assistant; I am too excited, too involved, too busy wishing myself closer to the action. *Rahpaymai*, the chant rises from the field. The very word. A group of men explode through us chanting, "Cover your head or we'll smash it." Islamic fanatics.

Many of the women are physically afraid. This is the unexpressed problem; mentioned, but not confronted. The Fedayeen have found they are under "too much pressure" to help us today. The women are protective of them, respectful. "They fought a revolution, they could come to a demonstration," Ralph Schoenman says laconically. The militia are completely absent here. Women have made signs by now, even a huge one in English and Farsi, "We want equal rights." Men are holding signs in sympathy. All our male comrades from Caifi are here. A great many men who are friends of the demonstrators, sympathizers. We have men on our side; we can trust in their protection, or if that is putting too large a burden on them, at least their solidarity.

The women with the signs begin singing. Everyone chats happily, excitedly; political excitement, speculation, the big talk of history perceived on the spot, participated in, moments of freedom, glimpses; one remembers the sixties. An Englishwoman married to an Iranian, runs a little paper; we ought to get together, interview, have a drink: people who were unfriendly now being friendly. Two older Iranian women beaming at us. An eight-point set of demands, including child-care centers, has emerged from the platform; a meeting has been appointed for Friday to create a democratic structure of organization among women. One of the older Iranian women, a chemist in the Ministry of Agriculture, where they have defied the order to wear chador: "This is the twentieth century; it is no moment for ladies to go back to the chador." I love her indignation. "Imagine a chador when working in a laboratory. I am a chemist; women here have fought a long time to go this far. I am ready to die in this struggle." The cries for a march grow louder; the word spreads that some women will march in any case.

We move nearer to the speakers' platform, we're at the back of it, a parapet that rears up at the end of the field. The field full of women. A Maoist orating against marching. Everyone around us agrees they will never march. We start chanting the word *Rahpaymai*: Terranie, Claudine, Resvan and I. The committee ought to speak out over the microphone, I urge. Otherwise male-dominated groups like this are permitted to manipulate women. "Two of us have talked." "Fifteen of them have." "Let's go back up," they say. As we reach the top, a big man in a navy coat intercepts us, rerouting us roughly.

"I'm trying to get this damn thing organized," he says in English, by way of explanation. "Are you in charge?" I ask. "Yes." "This is the women's movement; what's your role?" "Women's movement is not for women, it's for everybody, you feminist!" He spits the word like an outrageous insult. The media turn their lenses. Violence excites them—they have been raptly filming the fanatics, now they come running. There she is, get a picture of this guy shoving her around. "Tell us, what do you think of all this?" the interviewer demands. "We're going to march," I say stoutly, having no assurance beyond my hope. "And the whole world will be watching women in Iran today."

When this little exchange is over, the man in the blue coat closes in again, yelling at us to leave. "I am trying to save people's lives," he claims. Odd megalomania. A leftist out of bounds? I wonder. A fanatic? He reaches inside his coat near the shoulder where it bulges. Sophie says he has a gun. "We don't talk with Trotskyites," he bellows. "Get the hell back." A woman asks me if I'll be speaking today; I assure her I'm unable. "We don't want agents of imperialism." He goes on shoving me. "This is a women's meeting, who are you?" I ask him as he shoves me closer to the parapet. Deciding it's time to avoid this guy. It is a gun; we stop arguing and retreat. The way he looks me in the eye, the fury—this is someone who would enjoy hurting me. Using common sense finally; having been afraid and then angry and unafraid, and now past belligerence. The television whirls away.

And then the miracle, the women have begun to stand and move down the bleacher steps in the playing field. Are they marching? My god, they are. Let's go. Let's join them. As we reach the top and look down on the walkway, hoping for a march—there are marchers. Even then we're not sure. Terranie reports that some of the marchers say they're bound for Freedom Square; but some say they are only going to walk within the university walls, they are not going out anywhere.

They begin to chant, marching chants; wonderful hypnotic chants— you hear them less than a moment and your legs move, your feet beat in time, your heart breathes a new intoxicating air. This is how the insurrection felt. They sweep past, smiling, inviting us to join. The march is only a few hundred feet long, the march that has passed already, but looking back, it goes all the way to where the women spill out of the playing field, the vast field of women slowly emptying now. It is the moment we have been waiting for. They invite us, they call upon everyone to join. It has happened; they will keep their word, they will not be intimidated. The wonderful chants, the courage and hope. How happy I am to join this march, the little moment of catching step, linking arms, smiling at your neighbors, swinging into their new élan. They sweep past like a cool brook the first hot day when you want to go swimming; the exquisite plunge of it. We smile and enter.

In the march, in the flow of the march, the high of it, the complicated rhythms of the chants, the laughter, the smiles all around us. We find the French again, everything's working out. The lines growing, as we pass the very spot where Claudine appeared in the snow, days that seem years ago. "Repression in any form is condemned." We are winning as we come around the great circle of the campus and past the playing field where women are still lining up to join the tail of the march—which is as far as the eye can see, the march which is everywhere, endless. There are now more than ten thousand, we guess fifteen; more will join us in the streets, the long way to the square. Because we are going now, all the way. We will not just march around safely within the university, we will go out the big iron gates into we know not what danger, the thought of it a little thrilling, a little sickening. But the men who are with us are making a chain around us, our comrades, protectors, friends. They are leftists, many of them;

young, students, intellectuals, but also friends, husbands, lovers, cousins, brothers, in the chain—when they pass they say hello, or just grin between chants. One lovely mustache after another. How fine these men look, how one likes and admires them. As we near the gates they become very organized, the tension mouts, we are glad to have them. They are all we will have today against dangers we cannot estimate yet.

"*Azadi! Azadi! Azadi!*" The word for freedom, a word Sophie and I can now rap out with the best of them. I am not really much at chanting; it embarrasses me a little. I never wear buttons either. But today one is swept away. To chant "*Azadi!*" and to fumble through the more complicated chants is a delight. My pacifism balks before certain "Death to . . ." types of chant—"Death to the Pahlavi Dynasty," "Death to the Censors." Sophie suggests one translate it as "Down with . . ." which is rather more comfortable and perhaps more accurate. She is with me from time to time and always in sight, but busy shooting movie film, doing her thing. Whereas I am only being. Because this is one of the rare demonstrations of my life and I feel it with every step. On a par with that afternoon in United Nations Plaza when Martin Luther King spoke out against the war in Vietnam; the night we stood in the rain before the president's house at Smith, my outside agitator days, bringing that college out on strike against Nixon's invasion of Cambodia, or the great march on the fiftieth anniversary of the suffrage, the crowds along Fifth Avenue and we filmed it as we marched, and then speaking, that mass before me as I spoke across Bryant Park that evening, the soft August twilight, twenty thousand real, not televised, real bodies sitting on the grass. And today you don't even need to talk; you can just be a part of it, one of thousands, chanting, marching along with your little tape recorder, moving with them all, part of it, part of them, one of them. Chanting. In order that I can remember later. When I write. Because I know now that I will write. I will even write it for Claudine and Des Femmes, the book an account of our adventure together and therefore fitting they should publish it, the agreement reached without agents or commercial publishers at all. Just women. And we will do it in French and Farsi and English, the Farsi paid for by our royalties and contributions, smuggling it in if we have to. Somehow. Designing it ourselves, a book of pictures, Sophie's stills and my prose. Certain things demand they be written about, remembered with that labor, that love.

The gates now. Beyond them the danger. The streets. The long way to the square. Some say it's five or six miles. Through the attackers. "I'm sure that this will be peaceful; I have instincts about this stuff," I say to Sophie. Nevertheless we find Terranie and ask her to stay right by us. Over and over I am placed in the middle of the line—"You'd be the first to go if they spotted you," Sophie says, a cool Saxon appraisal covering her affection. *"Engelab,"* the chant goes on—"Revolution." It is important to generate a peaceful feeling, I tell myself, playing the pacifist. Sophie is out of film and cannot change rolls, on the go. The movie camera is also too dangerous to display at this juncture. She argues that it is some form of protection too, imagining her little Bolex could resemble the corporate safety of the networks. "With and without chador we brought down the Shah," the chant goes on as we rocket through the gates.

The women's movement has just passed its first great test. The march goes on and on, past our vision in every direction, twenty thousand people now. Women in chador, women in headscarves, children, men. Many men, friendly men, the men encircling us with their arms, a great chain of them all along the march. Past the iron fences of the university, like the iron fences of Columbia—it has been years since I have seen a university alive like this; since I have been so happy within its walls, the walls that the women climbed over only a few days ago—four days—it is only four days since the start of the demonstrations, March 8. In the snow of that morning women were locked inside by the fanatics as they first took to the streets. So they climbed the iron fences—that photograph we never took, the symbolic moment when a movement of women was born here. No one has it; we lament its absence on our cover.

The chant calls out to the men around the gates, "Brothers, where is your fighting spirit." Fanatic Muslims, they look on sourly. You wonder what their lives are like with the women they are close to. The place of privilege, the university, is behind us now. We are in the big world; the chain of men around us is broken over and over. "It will become disorganized now," Terranie warns. We have been going too fast and stop now to regroup. The chain reformed, the chants going up strong and clear. A wonderful big truck goes by full of foam rubber; surreal tangential grace note to the entire proceedings. Many of the men protecting us look poor, they even look like Muslim fanatics, it is a class look, a matter of education or opportunity, but they are protecting us—one gives up ideas every moment here. The chant now is a salute to the men who protect us. They chant back a salute to their sisters. It is an odd feeling, a happy one, being on a women's march with men. Men who are endangering themselves, subject to merciless insult for being with us; men who have risked their safety—for they will be the first attacked when it comes. I have never been in this situation, never marched for women's rights—or anyone else's—under the certain circumstances of being attacked, under circumstances where the enemy lines the street not merely to jeer but to invade and assault. And secretly armed. Knives, bottles, chains, blackjacks. And the men around us, the other men, our comrades and protectors, how new to feel this great affection for men. Men as strangers yet friends. No man in America has ever risked life or limb to affirm his belief in women's freedom, no man in the West, no man in my world before. And seeing them, one has to love them. The smiles go back and forth between the marchers, the protectors in their chain, the women in their ranks; it is an altogether new relationship. Men fighting, albeit peacefully, in our behalf, for our cause. For once. The lovely novelty of it.

The heat and the long way ahead of us. But happy, peaceful, a holiday mood, the chants consistently spirited. The chain around us just at this juncture is composed of high-school girls, absolutely delighted with themselves. They are the heroines of these demonstrations; for their youth and promise, for the casualties they have endured. Women in chador stand on the roofs of low buildings along the way, the mountains behind them. Some wave, some stare in whatever complex ambivalence. All the people are at their windows as we march by, a whole apartment building on its verandas; offices empty to see us. A woman waves, then others. We are festive, peaceful, militantly nonviolent. The wonderful picture of a woman alone on a rooftop in chador, beautiful garment.

The men who protect us now are not only young leftists but poor men as well, older men. Even little boys. Feeling important, grinning. The avenue is called the 24th of March, Terranie explains, the Shah having named this main street in honor of his own birthday. It is a real Near Eastern day, everyone jammed together and sweating. Asad, our comrade from the old days in the unknown apartment, surfaces to march with us awhile. Women wave from apartment buildings. The men lining the streets grow in numbers, are more menacing, shout insults. Our own protectors bring water in buckets, the tin cup going the rounds in the heat and thirst—how one loves to see them coming. And buns are passed round, strange sweet breads we have never tasted before. The men sweating as they hold the chain together, their arms straining as they march, man holding hands with man. Their backs straight, their arms bared in their sleeves, heads erect, glorious mustaches. They are proud of what they do today. The attackers call them faggots, pederasts. I wonder if indeed there are gay brothers among these to endure this further insult. But how the manliness of them all makes one love the very word. How handsome they seem, the faces busy with their fatigue and the heat and the awkwardness of marching six miles sideways, actually sideways and through heat and the delays of traffic; how beautiful their arms, the arms straining to give us safety. They have walked it all, this distance which is already fatiguing me—they have walked it all sideways. And with the restriction of holding each other's hands. Nor can they break the chain to drink water. Or even to smoke, though I observe one fellow, bearded and Jesus-hippie-like, who has managed to hang a cigarette from the side of his mouth and smoke it the whole length without touching it, his hands engaged in maintaining the chain. Because once it's broken we will be attacked and they may never restore it. Our protectors wear a look of concentration as well as their good spirits.

The press of the world are here too to protect us. "The enemies of women are the enemies of the revolution," the chant proclaims. The faces of the marchers are beautiful, Sophie takes still pictures of women's faces, the women of Iran, type upon type, rapt in their march, the ecstasy of their chants. I am subsumed in them, merge, and become one. The fanatics chant against us: "Talking about the veil is a Savak plot." An older woman near me comments, Terranie translating, "We did the fighting, and now they lie to us. We brought back Khomeini, and now we regret it." She has a wicked humor in her eye and is also furious: "Khomeini is merely deceiving us." A great many women speak to me, recognize me, are familiar with me; others see me as a foreigner and stranger and ask me what I think of the march, always pleased when I say I am a feminist here in support. Anyone with enough English to risk it speaks to us, is friendly, offers to explain things, proffers opinions, extends a welcome. "Freedom is neither East nor West, it's international," the chant goes up; Terranie says this one's her favorite.

We catch sight of the French shooting a great big beautiful Beaulieu from the top of a car, the sight of women making movies, Michèle holding the big camera, Sylviane turning the zoom lens. The batteries go in my tape recorder and when they return our march has been cut in half by a band of attackers; being such slow walkers and burdened with machinery, Sophie and I are now at the tail of the first segment. Only a few yards and a few protectors separate us from the attackers now following hot behind. We scramble further up in the march for safety. At a factory the workers cheer us; how different from the Islamic proletariat they are, far more politicized, far less pious. They salute us as we pass. Chants in praise of nurses as we pass a hospital, the white figures of women on balconies waving to us. One nurse blows kisses. Their splendid blue capes; the style nurses have, the kindness of that calling. All the feminists of the first wave who followed Nightingale in one of our chosen professions.

The word goes down the line to keep silence out of respect for the sick. Thereafter we applaud each other quietly. An old woman on the hospital balcony, a babushka, not a nurse, more likely a domestic, her wave to us more like a blessing than all the others'. Sophie and I keep sliding back in to the march, losing Terranie, slipping into danger, having to scramble forward along the perilous corridor, the edge of the march, near the attackers, and back to the security of the center in the line of marchers. There are now two rings around us, an inner one of women, an outer one of men. The attackers pursue. "Iranian women will not remain in bondage," the chant goes up. A woman in chador marches alongside us, her fist raised. Sophie photographs her; it is a picture most on our minds thereafter; the old and the new together, the risk of being here even in the safety of that garment, worn as protection or perhaps deliberately insisted on for its ambiguity, beauty, Paradox of the hand clenched and raised in feminist gesture; revolution and tradition together—somehow the chador makes her more a rebel than all the others—because there was more to rebel against. An icon graphically representing all that we see and experience here among women.

We chant our praises again to our protectors. An elderly gentleman bows his thanks in antique Persian gallantry. And a portly bourgeois holds hands with a leftist and a little boy, a street urchin. "Please tell our message to all over the world; we want only our rights," a woman speaks into my tape recorder. "This demonstration is a message from Iranian women to the whole world."

We are hot and tired, near exhaustion, especially Sophie, under the forty pounds of her equipment. And the square seems forever away but at least we see it now, looming before us, the enormous and actually rather handsome sculptures commissioned by the Shah at the end of the avenue commemorating his birthday. Shayot, now called Freedom Square. Beckoning like rest and liquid. I experience a temptation to sit down in the street at every pause, but I would never drop out. I will make it there if it kills me. And the danger by the side of the road induces one too. The attackers are now not only behind us, dividing our march in half, they are also all around us to each side. The pillars of sculpture loom. Block after block away, growing slowly bigger but apparently no closer. It is still a mile or two. The fatigue. The heat. Putting one foot before the other. The chants go on without remission, for this is a people schooled in street demonstrations. Even in the tactics of keeping the peace, being silent while abused, being determined and in unison in chant, confident, overwhelming. Without marshals each marcher understands she is responsible for herself and those around her, watches out. Keeps the peace in sentiment and yet never slackens her rightful anger.

The mountains bear over us to the right above the buildings and down the side streets and the monument far in the future. "Even under torture I chose death or freedom," a chant calls out, a memory of the insurrection, the fury of this march carrying that moment still. It is not only the rights of women we carry with us, the men enrolled along with us, but the whole cause of democratic rights here, the hope still alive in us, the hope for which the uprising was undertaken. The rapture of the marchers assures one, the ardor of the chanting, the tireless fists in the air, this is a people only a few weeks after a revolution. Centuries of outrage and oppression. Shahs since Cyrus, only a few moments of freedom under Mossadegh.

We have seen only two militiamen in miles. Usually they are everywhere, officious, annoying, stopping cars both day and night, directing traffic with machine guns. And now invisible. The attackers mass more thickly on either side of us. The square is only a few blocks away, a little boy has chosen to protect me, bobbing along at my side, a grin covering the entire lower portion of his face from one overgrown ear to the other. Nine years old. Khomeini's face is on every building, stenciled even on buildings under construction, perhaps it will wash off, someday, we speculate; the attackers follow behind and we keep lagging at the end of the march in our exhaustion. But we will win the square, the march which almost didn't happen is arriving at its goal in triumph now.

"Repression in any form is condemned," we chant, the square full ahead of us. "Do you know about tomorrow? At nine o'clock at the television, we demonstrate," a woman tells me. The next demonstration is already announced. She is on strike, we will be supporting her. I am also asking Iranian women to talk to *The New York Times* at the hotel this afternoon. The coverage is with us, we have only to keep on. "Our rights are your rights, join us," we chant to the onlookers in the streets. A pewter pitcher is passed around, we all drink from the same cup. Gratitude for the men who bring it to us. A man tells us Iranian television would like to interview me. For all my suspicion, I agree. He disappears to find his colleague and finally reappears to say that if I go to the demonstration against the television tomorrow, they will interview me there. I make a note to stipulate that some five of my Iranian sisters talk too. Women on strike at the station gather around, giving messages for the television and the chief of it, Ghotbzadeh. My favorite was simply, "Go to hell."

The militia appear at last, now at the moment we begin to enter the square. Many wear handkerchiefs over their mouths. "Tear gas," Sophie says. Our dread mounts, there is no guarantee they will be protecting us. We are passing a mosque, guns mounted on its walls;

once a center of organization against the Shah, now an arsenal. Mortars, sandbags. Behind it a clinic with white-uniformed nurses waving to us. Men and women, their different purposes. The militia of Khomeini are now on either side in great number, mixed with the attackers—who are also behind us, staging a march in support of Khomeini. How long will the prophet's order not to attack us prevent them today? Already our progress is blocked, we seem to be prevented from entering the great open area surrounding the monument.

The mountains. My feet. Thirst. Impatience at being trapped when the square lies ahead, grass to sit on. "Remember Khalil telling us how we would have time to see Isfahan?" Sophie says. "We sure didn't know what we were getting into." But this is better then museums; "We're in history," I smile at her. If only history served cold drinks, we muse. The waiting to enter our Eden. The park just ahead, to sit down. An agony, the open space ahead, the grass of the park. So near and still so far. Guns, lines, orders now, the press of bodies, the chain of our own protectors holding us back, held back in turn by the militia; the mass of us stalled, prevented. The attackers swarming at the outer edge, engaging the militia who stand between us now. But treating us as the culprits, rather than those who come against us in violence. We the peaceful are curtailed. Perhaps they will never let us reach the place, perhaps we will be turned away in defeat.

The attackers have climbed on top of cars and are haranguing us, exhibiting a page of what looks like *Time* magazine bearing a picture of the Shah, and another picture of what appears to be his sister, Princess Ashraf, dancing with someone indecipherable, probably one of the big parties of the Shah's ambassador, grand affairs attended by luminaries like Andy Warhol and Elizabeth Taylor. This decadence, they accuse us, is ours; we are in sympathy with the Shah; Ashraf called herself a feminist. Taunting us with the very thing to make us angry, a charge so transparently false yet an affront to our honor. "Death to the Pahlavi dynasty," we chant back.

Claudine and Sylvina borrow my tape recorder to record a woman making a statement. The woman has said to them that she and others are ready to fight for their freedom, ready to die for it: "For the first time in my life I have something to fight for. I'm going to do it and I'm not afraid to fight, even to die—I have a little baby, it doesn't matter; my baby can grow up and I can die for her freedom. I will do anything for her to live in a free society and have a free life. I want her to grow up in Iran, in this country, but free, not to have to leave and live abroad as I had to. But I came back even when the Shah was still here—we could not live all our lives in another country far from home, so we came back to Iran to do something about it. Why should we live in another country when we have everything here? Everything but freedom. I have talked to the women here, they say they are willing to die. For their kids. They want them to live in a free place. I have lived my life, I am thirty years old. Now I am fighting for my baby. I have been fired for going to the demonstrations. An American company. I told them, look, I've got to go to fight for my freedom, nobody is going to fight for us. But us." Another woman speaks then: "I am living in this country, my own country, we don't have anything left in Iran. All we had was our little freedom—what to wear and what to do. And now they are taking that. After the government was overthrown I woke up. I told my husband, I feel free. Now I'm very sorry, it's all a trick, just religious people, who don't care about democratic people at all, just to go ahead with their religious rules. I am a religious person, inside myself, but I don't want to be ruled by religious law." Another joins in, "I don't want anyone to take my freedom. We are not fighting only for chador, far more than that. They will start with the chador and in a few months they will say women are not allowed to go out of the house, to have jobs at all. We will not wait for that. We'll fight it. Because this is my country, I love it, I just want to stay here, I don't want to go anywhere else. I was born here, I will die here. I said I would die for this and I would."

It is strange to hear. At home or anywhere in the West I've never heard feminists speak of dying for their cause; women in demonstrations, mothers of small children. Still we don't move and the danger builds around us, more and more, as if we were being made to wait for our enemy's arrival. The word comes that they are arriving in busloads, green buses, the color of Islam, also the color of government buses. Ralph Schoenman has made inquiries and believes the fanatics have actual representation and sanction through right-wing elements within the Komiteh. But condoning acts officially condemned, furthering them with transport? When we examine the faces of the attackers, we almost have the impression we have seen them before, yesterday, the demonstration at the Hall of Justice. Certain ones emerge as leaders, marshaling and massing the others, directing them. The assumption that these are spontaneous demonstrators such as our own was perhaps an illusion. Buses mean organization, a place to meet, a time to assemble. Even we have that. But the bus is a connection with authority. They crowd round us now shouting, chanting, for they have chants. One begins to fear we are being held back while they gather to attack us.

A large number of attackers have been with us all along, growing in numbers since we passed the technical university, our march a war of chants. The attackers accuse us of being counterrevolutionaries, we accuse them of the same—a torrent of chanting, shouting, the attackers running along beside our ranks, menacing us, their fists waving, the placards of Khomeini held up. "This is our freedom; behold it and judge for yourselves," the women chant to the onlookers, their chant when locked inside the walls of Tehran University that first snowy morning. A woman in chador with three small children stands beside us. You look at the faces of the attackers and wonder.

They run alongside us, so that we never pass them, they never go away. Now we are stalled as they gather about us, screaming, jeering, threatening; the square just in view, the rest, the end of the journey, the grass to lie on. I throw myself on it in my mind, willing to listen to speeches, to be orated to, anything, as long as there is a cold drink at the end of it. When we reach there we can disband, relax, congratulate ourselves. A few hundred yards if we make it.

If they let us, the militia everywhere holding us back now. The heat, the tiredness. And then we are pushed into a tight file and we do move. Guns all around us, the militia. Our own protectors straining to keep their chain, smashed against us. Even this way, we'll get there; we won't have to give up before we reach the grass. And once there, past the plaza and the stalled traffic, it will be easy, disperse on the grass, speeches, the chance to organize —we will have achieved it all.

But as we enter the square we are still more corralled. The militia who have waited for us here and whose protection we could have used along the way have waited as if for an enemy. And behind them swarm the attackers. A whole square of them. For it is the attackers who hold the square. And we, tight frightened files of us, are funneled along sunken pathways; how strange they are for a park, I think, more like fortifications for war, our protectors guarding us from above, walking the trenches and looking down on us, their feet along the fieldstones set in the cement that line the tops of the trenches. We are huddled, crushed. The press of tired people in the narrow defile, so close to the luxury of merely resting on the grass, throwing one-self down and taking off these tired boots—how unreasonable this is. And in the cramped trench, no room to stand or sit in the multitude of bodies, my claustrophobia takes over. We cannot move. The militia over us with guns. Ahead of us and around us. I become terrified of the guns, impatient even of the protectors asking more patience of us—why the hell can't we proceed, emerge peacefully from the end of this idiot trench and onto the open grass? Are we waiting for the militia to clear the park of attackers? There is a battle proceeding in the square, much of it out of sight above the top of the trench, the legs of the protectors shield it, but you can see the smoke of tear-gas canisters. The attackers are being routed; we are a peaceful demonstration, we will get through. Then why are they so long about it—the militia are armed and are everywhere conceded authority. Hurry up, we are fainting with the heat, exhaustion, the confinement of the trench. Sophie too feels claustrophobia. We are no longer free to leave the march as we had been at any moment along the route, no longer free to do anything at all, and we are surrounded by guns. Is it a trap? Hurry up, let us through. "Calm yourself with a little nicotine; this is a very unlikely place to lose your temper." I do so, aware that if I were at home, I would behave very differently, agitate we go forward. I'd talk it up that we should be allowed through. And resist. But when the order comes to retreat, to turn around, leave, I am too stunned to grumble. It is also too fast, the protectors, straining and sweating, are running us back. Through the trenches and toward the plaza, our ranks once twenty abreast are now only three or four, then the tense arms of our defenders, arm locked in arm, the veins bulging with the effort to hold the line—for the attackers are right behind each tired arm.

Somehow, they have moved right through the militia and from the far side of the square, the grassy area they had covered before, and now surround us. We are driven into their net by having been balked in the other direction. Or perhaps they are a new force, waiting all the time—because the militia have melted away, utterly disappeared. The attackers have us now. And we flee from them. Right and left they surge against the line of arms. "This is the way it is," Terranie says, "they will wait till the end, they wait till the ranks thin. And then they get you."

The screaming is hideous. Chant against chant, our side and theirs, the arms straining. Looking up from a strong young arm, I see Khalil's younger brother Saïd. And reach out and touch his arm in thanks. We smile into each other's eyes like love. The purest gratitude, the warm flesh, the strong skin, bone and muscle. One group of men is terrorizing us, another risking their lives in our defense. Civilization and barbarism. Both of them men. We would need neither group if left alone. Patriarchy at its fall divides those dedicated to the old ways from those amenable to the new, which are also older still, and the oldest, the time that preceded the war of men and women.

The hatred in the attackers' faces, the folly of their insults, ignorance only: misunderstanding, propaganda, arrogance nourished on poverty. Looking at one, a fat one, I have intimations of that form and variety as a pug Irishman—my own people, growing up—and remember he could be grand with a beer and an undershirt and a joke or he could be the devil. The rage in his eyes is real and personal.

Though when I look at him, straining to break the chain and reach me, he sees only an abstraction, a label he would kill, there, then, with his bare hands. Scared enough to experience fright as sickness, the motor running its panic in my stomach. Keep running. Still, looking at them as their faces rush past, hating them, fearing them, still you know they could be something far different from what they are, their sneers turned to smiles, nice guys—or they could be this: half-mad, thirsting for blood and yelling obscenities.

Run, keep running. Stumbling as you are hurried. Your eyes still looking for militia and finding only the assailants, their numbers growing behind the single line of our protectors. They too, afraid by now, their backs to the attackers, the knives they may carry. We are moving in silence now, only our fists raised in protest, further chanting only arouses further attack. We have done this before, today, but then our enormous numbers only bespoke confidence in this as pacifist technique. Now it feels almost like surrender. Because for the first time today, we are outnumbered. Every moment more so. And as they crowd us from both right and left side into a tiny file of two marchers, we are moving through a sea of violence that has been in search of us all day and now in our flight has found its quarry. For we are a rout. My mind keeps calculating that if we held our ground a bit and regrouped we would not look so vulnerable and inviting: but the balance is lost now, we seem only to be scuttling for safety. If we had only not been turned back. If we had not been betrayed by "Authority," the militia—how manipulated we are between one group of men and another. And the militia have abandoned us, were in what collusion of sentiment to begin with? It is only the protectors now. Finally, it is only ourselves. Which it should have been in the beginning—if it were not for the others, the ones who now hang about like wolves beyond the line. And the line is broken now, over and over again. A panic each time this happens and the attackers surge toward us. We are blocks from the square and then a mile, and things get no better. They show no signs of leaving, their masses grow larger and larger; we are, the long stream of us, running their gauntlet, but a handful to their hundreds at any given point. We who were twenty thousand strong an hour ago, a triumphant march. Till halted and demoralized. Sadly, for I think all of us had put faith in the militia, expected the troop of the revolution to have some traces of insurrectionary solidarity with unarmed women, peaceful petitioners. Put to flight and then preyed upon. Now seeking only to get out of this nightmare alive.

Sophie wants out right now. It's far too dangerous, I argue. We'd have only to cross the line of our protectors toward the avenue, full of fanatics, to be spotted instantly as having just left the march. "We have to keep going, the marshals want us to; I think we must do it their way." "No. I can't stand it anymore, we're run like cattle, we have to get out." I explain to Terranie, she remonstrates, but Sophie is adamant—no matter what danger she faces, outside, she must get there. I look at the masses of men come against us and dream of being on the other side, a cab could get us out. Here's Hamid. He will try to get us out on the right side. But Terranie heads for the left side, the boulevard of the 24th of March. We are in tight defile in the service road to the side. But a few hundred yards away runs the broad avenue, the city, civil behavior, taxicabs, shoppers, any Monday afternoon.

We make a break for it. But they see us at once. Even though we got as far as the traffic island in the middle of the first lanes of traffic. And then they close in. It is so quiet, the way they come toward us. From several sides until I guess that some fifteen men are making a circle around the three of us. You think of funny things, like the camera; that you borrowed it from a friend. Or that no one can do this to you in broad daylight. Whatever it is. A beating. A knife. Or being thrown in front of the cars. For the cars keep right on coming at a wonderful clip. And the figures closing in on us, in deliberate speed, avoiding a car, waiting till it passes, threading their ways. A good number already on the narrow island, slowly advancing.

"Stop a car—it's the only thing left now." I am not sure whether Terranie decided this in Farsi or English, but I know what it meant—having to flag one, jump out in front and force it to stop. But of course the men surrounding us will crowd in too, follow, prevent it, talk the driver out of it. Just what happens when a blue car miraculously draws up, as if ordered. Though unsteadily, the driver slows to look at us, then the men denouncing us, the driver starting up again; we are pleading, he slows once more, the men threaten him. He wavers and he accelerates again. Just as I reach in the window and pull up the button of the car lock on the back door and pull it open. A most superb thank-you and a smile and we have everyone inside, showering the man and his companion, another man, businessmen they are, with lavish compliments and gratitude. He has indeed saved our lives, watching the square fall away beyond the windows as we glide suddenly out of danger. Miraculously, the miracle of a car. The strong body, the quiet rubber wheels—that it has wheels after being so long on foot. The speed, how quickly it crosses the square. The faces of our assailants are only things beyond glass. Everything is transformed.

He had recognized me from the photograph in yesterday afternoon's *Kayhan*, he says, Terranie translating for Sophie, and he slowed out of curiosity, but then . . . My friends both gracefully pass over the unexpressed willingness to leave us in the road to our fate and inquire after his own life; he's a Jew, he has worries of his own here. And business has just plain gone to hell. Business was ladies' dresses. Outdone by the chador that hides all defects in dress and is often a godsend to the poor or the blue-jeaned. We all find a certain amusement in this, our driver included, a gratitude and ease coming over us. He will even drive to the hotel, he wouldn't think of accepting money.

I hear the others talking happily, laughing, the humor that follows on danger, an edge of hysteria in it. My own leaves me slowly as I lean my head on the backseat and watch the city go by, quite alone. Thinking I may just have nearly been killed, a bad way to die. And when I close my eyes they see the farm, entering at the back, the door to the yard, the tulip lamp over the back dining table. The living room, a splash of color in the rug, the ledge of hearthstone where I make my little gin and literary declamations to cronies before the big fireplace—a million years ago when I was young. It hurts to think how young that was, last summer, for example; and the front hall, the farmer's desk and the telephone, the big farmhouse double doors open to the lawn and the road and you talk to New York and thank god you're not down there in the heat, or the sunrise over the cornfield out those doors, a golden mist, the time of Michael X and my loony-bin persecutions, I used to watch the sun rise from the tail end of the night, Judy Collins doing "Amazing Grace" a cappella, the tears fighting now between my closed eyes. So there is hardly time to see the other dining room, where I wrote *Basement* the first fall with Skippy and where Millie and I filled one wall with bookcases and the leather books from Oxford. On through the kitchen, the hub of the house, past the round table and out the door—because I must see if the trees are where they should be, if each one stands, the maples around the farmhouse, so old and huge they don't even look like maples, the bark is more like oak, and the birches I planted because Fumio loves white birch, the red pines, one thousand in their rows like fluffy soldiers, the white pines we're clearing out—how the lawn runs into them, almost mysteriously, alleyways then, even secret places, a little protected circle for bedding down new seedlings, maybe a bench on that big wild cherry—no, don't worry about details, hurry to the woods, over by the western boundary of the new land, the elusive part, still not really explored. And see the brook where the first house in the colony will be built. Then come back and check out the barns, the studios; okay now, have your martini by your sacred pond.

Because you have survived to see all this again. Tears like benediction, the farm as dear as life itself; no, not quite—but a further grace, being alive, seeing it one more time.

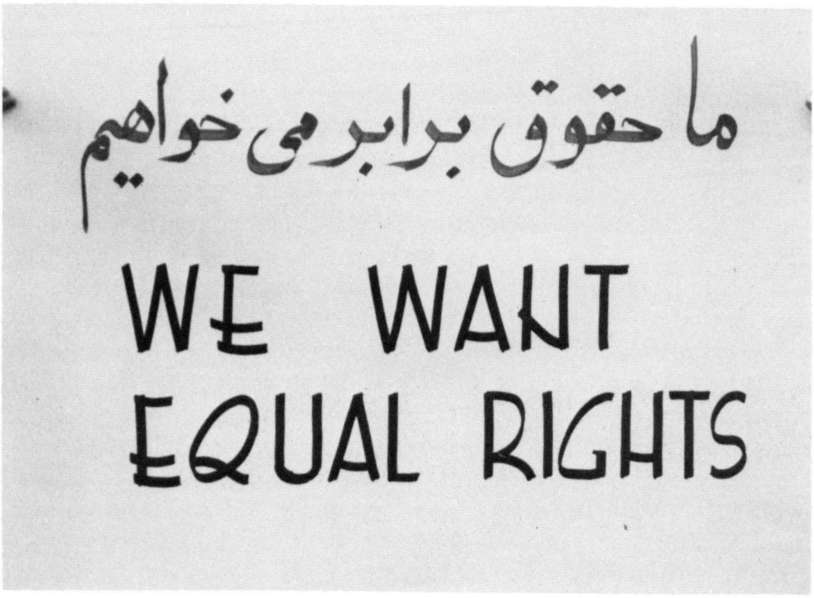
ما حقوق برابر می خواهیم
WE WANT
EQUAL RIGHTS

March 12, Tehran University

Woman demonstrator

Militiaman

Islamic fanatics heckling the demonstrators

Volunteers protecting the demonstrators

Islamic fanatics

Volunteer waterman

Sylviane and Michèle film the march for Des Femmes.

Islamic fanatics

A woman chemist in the demonstration

Approaching Freedom Square

Islamic fanatics

A demonstrator shouting *Azadi* (freedom)

Penned in by fanatics at Freedom Square

The fanatics attack

8 ✳ ✳ ✳

IT DOESN'T LOOK GOOD today. Very few people. Many reporters. Many attackers. But a small demonstration, and more men than women. We take all that in with a glance, getting out of the car, a cab because we stayed at the hotel last night through the hospitality of the Frenchwomen; there is too much to do right now to go back to Nelufar's house in the suburbs at night. But I look forward to returning there, and this is the last scheduled demonstration. From now on we concentrate on organization, the Iranian feminists have decided, and for this reason they are not attending today. It is also expected to be very violent, particularly in view of the fact—but is it a fact?—that Ghotbzadeh, the head of Iranian national television and radio broadcasting, was attacked last evening, shot and wounded—by a woman. The story swept the hotel, that the woman was one of the demonstrators, had gone off the rails, Valerie Solanis-style, and surprised Ghotbzadeh in his office with a gun. It sounded familiar, logical. Assuming of course that the woman was a loner, representing no one but her own fury. And after the reports came in of all the women wounded at the close of the great march yesterday, and the private news of friends being cornered, chased, narrowly escaping a beating—the rage of it even made sense.

Again we had been ignored by Iranian television, a bizarre thing in view of our numbers. It is inevitable by now that we direct ourselves against censorship. Ralph had been at the rump of the march as it was terrorized through the streets, had done duty as a protector, had very nearly been beaten by the fanatics and then nearly shot in the confusion by a Fedayeen, one of the few who came out to protect the women at the end, when the government finally sent a few buses to help them escape. The bus was loaded and off, and Ralph surrounded by attackers and shoved against a car, was then held under a guerrilla rifle until he could explain himself in his beginning Farsi and get his position as a defender of the demonstrators sorted out with the Fedayeen. He described the aftermath of the march as hideous, a rout, a defeat, full of screaming marchers surrounded by attackers and at the mercy of their stones, insults and fists. And again we had not been covered by television, a perverse thing in view of the size of the march, its danger, the fact that the government had had time to warn women away from it—by voice, but without pictures—and thereby endanger its success and attendance. If there is any man in Iran who exasperates women now, it is Ghotbzadeh; today's demonstration is in support of striking television personnel including women whose jobs are now in jeopardy, but it is also a protest against this man's censorship. One of our favorite slogans is "Down with the censors." The news blackout on Iranian television is the only thing that prevents the women's demonstrations from becoming massive and massively powerful and spreading all through the country. There were parallel marches in Tabriz and Isfahan yesterday—we hear—though censorship prevents us from knowing anything more.

Small notices in the newspapers are our only coverage. The journals are not entirely controlled yet; broadcasting is. The women who work for television are furious; I met many of them yesterday. They have been taken off the air entirely, in any capacity: newscaster, interviewer, personality, actress—except for one children's program—no woman's face will be permitted to appear on Iranian television. Under the guise of religion, half the population will be erased, vanish and become invisible: the perfect means of repression, how better could the state deny the rights and presence and claims of a minority than to deny them even public existence?

Women have every reason to be angry. And the anger to focus at this moment upon Ghotbzadeh. An intellectual thug, Gregory Rose of *New York* magazine called him; a fascist, one hears many other reporters say. The most dangerous man in Iran, I've heard him called many times; if he should take over—and there's always the chance of a coup—Ghotbzadeh, Yazdi, Entezam—I listen to the masculine talk, reporters playing politics as if it were a game of Monopoly. Speculating on how they themselves will fare; would the press be evacuated, as was the case in this place or that?

But Ghotbzadeh is still remote to me, to most of the women I know. An attack on him is the personal adventure of some unfortunate woman, probably now being interrogated—let us hope not tortured or beaten or roughed up; but she probably needs a lawyer. Sophie has obtained Martin Daftari's telephone number from Elaine Scholino and will see that he is consulted. As a leading civil libertarian and the only person in Iran trying to organize a democratic opposition party, he may be sympathetic or able to advise. We see this only as civil-rights procedure; endorsement of her act could not be further from our minds. The feminists here are nonviolent in principle as well as tactic.

There is government rumor that the woman was of the left, one of a Maoist group. I find this unlikely, so does Ralph. In fact, as time went by last evening in the hotel, the woman's very existence became moot, her crime, her whereabouts, her name even—were never attested to. Lacking a name, she could not even be helped to a lawyer—I begin to wonder if she is not a convenient invention to discredit the demonstrations. At first it seemed only a sort of tragic excess that could achieve this, endanger our movement's chance of persuasion, its moral leverage with the people at large—since if you promise to bring reform or even revolution, you cannot, must not lose your position of probity in the minds of the mass. And now it appears the government may have arranged our "error" for us; set it up so that we are not without blame. Which could make our case far harder.

This morning it is obviously already harder. Thousands of women who would have come have heard instead about the very well-publicized attack upon the chief of broadcasting, and have chosen to make clear that they are not lawbreakers, assassins. The march has been answered by the criminalization of our activities. And the thing we feared in any case, after yesterday's violence, the growth and entrenchment of the attackers, has also taken place. They now have greater numbers than we have. They are massed to the right of the long road that leads into the broadcasting station, garrisoned like an arsenal (which it is—Ralph has told me they have a stockpile of machine guns there and Ghotbzadeh commands something like a private army), the Air Force holding them back from outright attack upon the peaceful demonstrations to the left. The road in between.

I take it all in, getting out of the cab—but the cabdriver does too. He strides right over and joins the attackers, chanting most enthusiastically and straining against the not-so-enthusiastic blockade of the blue uniformed Air Force. It is disconcerting: we asked this man to stay with the car in case we were in danger and needed to leave quickly. Now, to see him with the men who would attack us. "On our time," Sophie laughs, since we are paying him to wait. At first we stay near the cab and the street and some memory of egress and safety, but the demonstration draws us in. We are here as observers more than participants, since our own comrades are boycotting this event. Yet, as we explained to them, we could hardly miss a women's demonstration in these times, and they understood. They feel that demonstrations have become too dangerous for the moment, the attackers escalating each event into a war of their own. It is better not to demonstrate for a

while and not until there is better security and organization, organization of women on all lines being the main priority now: to reap the
benefits of the hours in the streets by setting up a series of meetings to
establish structure. We have been invited to attend and to document
them and this is how we plan to spend our next ten days in Iran, our
final ten days, the excursion ticket permitting us to remain only until
the twenty-fourth of March. The Shah's birthday. So this is our last
demonstration before the quiet time, the time of solidification.

In quiet then, we can interview women for our film, perfect our
friendships, visit in their homes, perhaps even get out of the city and
into the countryside. I am invited to speak at Damovar University on
feminist history. The feminists here, the Committee for the Defense
of Women's Rights are arranging seminars between Iranian and
Western feminist organizers: we will exchange, analyze, contemplate.
A quiet, thoughtful time lies ahead.

But this last demonstration is a tacky affair, a disappointment.
Demonstrations themselves seem coopted now: there is a demonstration of "Chadori" on Friday by the government, "Antis" who will
demonstrate the willingness of Iranian womanhood to wear chador
and keep their place. Already one hears that this demonstration will
now also be a march in honor of Ghotbzadeh the "patriot censor";
government buses will be provided. The personnel is expected to be
made up of attackers and whatever women they induce to follow
them, obediently wearing chador. The lines are drawn now.

Apparent here too the moment you arrive to see all access to the
station blocked with soldiery and guns. Even a trench has been dug.
Forget about being interviewed, you can't get near the place. A forlorn
number of leftists, mostly men. This is not really even a women's
demonstration. Men, and male oratory, the strident swinging arm of
the followers of what passes for Marxism. On the other side, our taxi
man and the fanatics shout well-rehearsed slogans. The attackers are
already like an army, you see them marshaled, orchestrated, ordered
from position to position by their leaders, conducting like musicians.
Sophie worries for her borrowed movie camera and rehearses the
Farsi term for "journalist." The attackers wave their fists. The male
Marxists orate from a platform. The fanatics laugh and shout
obscenities at us, some of the Air Force join our taxi man, all shouting
"Praise to Ghotbzadeh." A pleasant young English journalist remarks
to me on the sadistic character of the few entertainment programs
permitted on television here; one wonders how anyone could praise
Ghotbzadeh for censoring and perverting this precious form of
communication as he has; television is one of the few pleasures still
permitted the masses. Perhaps today's attackers, so well organized,

such a step beyond previous turnouts in size and enthusiastic discipline, come from those elements in the Komiteh who back Ghotbzadeh; is it possible the whole thing is engineered by or for this man himself and his ambitions?

Tiring of the speeches of the men of the left, annoyed that no women are permitted to address the group at what is supposed to be a women's meeting, and finding the phrases translated for us—"women's strength," "solidarity with the revolution"—rather flat and self-serving, we begin to watch the faces of the attackers. How closed most of them, how unfortunately deprived, illiterate, unemployed—but you also see the brute face of Savak, familiar after all these years, all those meetings against the Shah where faces like this would make their way to obscure Midwestern universities. There seemed actually to be a Savak face, a Savak type. The "interrogator," someone you knew would beat you up if you were in his power. So would these other men; it's why they came today. But the Savak man is professional, a government employee, he beats you up at so many rials per hour and by a method and an ideology not merely religious but bureaucratized, protected by the state as well as the deity. It's the surer thing. And a few of these men stand out as undeniably bourgeois. Well-dressed, even. One man in particular, we have our eye on him from before, other occasions where he has always directed the others. We begin to concentrate on this man, to follow and photograph him and certain other ringleaders. Especially this one we call the "boss."

"Every place we go, they go there with a knife," a woman alongside us says. "Who brings them?" "The government. They don't want us to get together, they don't want the television to say we get together, if they did there would be a lot of us here today, a lot. We are women and we love our country, but we won't wear chador. We can't. Can't. I like to die before I live that way again." This woman has a daughter she is hugely proud of, a doctor. "She wants to kill herself now." The attackers shout on. "Write about this," she tells me. A woman recognizes me and says I am freedom to her: "How on earth did they let you come here?" "Well, anyhow they gave a visa," I laugh. "I bet they didn't know you." The idea amuses her immensely, this "subversive" being issued a visa in pure naiveté. "Tell everyone what you see here." I promise her I will. Without news here, she is cheered to learn of the international delegation coming from France next Monday, the nineteenth, Simone de Beauvoir its president.

Another woman describes the attack last evening at the end of the march when many buses of women were stoned by Muslim fanatics: "We were all crowded into a bus. And not all of us could fit. Two of us were left outside when the bus pulled out. The men who were supporting us tried to take us out of the crowd of attackers who still crowded around hitting us as we went along. Then they started beating up the men protecting us. We were finally given refuge in a school building—but just shoved in and the doors closed; it was horrible. These attackers are the same, the same men who were chanting for the Shah a few months ago. It is my conviction they are Savak out of work and needing to justify themselves with Khomeini and Islam."

Our eyes keep scanning the attackers. Sophie has picked one man to study, shooting picture after picture. The "boss." If we can get this still film developed quickly we can give it to Ralph and he can check it with his connections in the Fedayeen and elsewhere. If it's a Savak face in fact, we may be able to document it. As Sophie changes a roll of movie film back in the taxi a strangely appealing man comes up to assure me that he too is a Muslim, but no fanatic. "These men"—a disgusted glance over the savage faces of the attackers—"do not represent my religion, or my country." We're busy, yet I like this man. He's from the country, a farmer. "Why go back a thousand years to Muhammad? Why? Why can't we be free? Why not live? We have enough money, we have enough petrol. Six million barrels in a day. We could have a beautiful country. If it goes on like this we won't." We talk about the Shah, how hateful, how wasteful. How cruel. "But they killed eleven, just this morning," he says, "they kill every day." He has a newspaper in his hand, the dead faces of those executed last night; the victims of the new regime look so much like those of the past—he glances around us. "Everyone is afraid now. Look at the people, nobody is happy in this country now. Now no one smiles anymore. Even the people in the revolution—they were so happy when Khomeini came, even they don't smile anymore. They didn't think it would be like this. Look at them shouting there, if this government falls, they will shout against it and for another—always without civilization." His despair is ancient.

We pass through the crowd after Sophie has reloaded, the fanatics snarling at us, yowling like cats, making vulgar and derisive noises, the kind of mocking insult they specialize in, just behind it violence. Bumping against us, threatening, it is almost too dangerous to film but Sophie is intrepid. I'm her assistant, and a rather inadequate guard. She is sharp with me today, the pressure is getting to us. This demonstration, its complete co-optation by men, men of the left, and men of the right, demoralizes us. Everything is so clearly outlined, right and left, but the men of the left have now given up the role of supporter where they were so admirable, and taken on the role of boss. They do all the talking now. A Fedayeen in his kaffiyeh emerges

Two women protestors

among the young men on the platform. How elegant he looks. And how aware of it he is. The peacockery of uniforms, guns, leather gloves, a bandolier of gold and silver bullets, the cachet of revolutionary. A high-ranking Air Force officer comes on to the platform. Watching him, I remember that a field marshal of his Air Force was executed just this morning. Our Fedayeen struts in his bandolier, his leather clothes, caressing his gun, pointing it absentmindedly at the crowd. A woman tries to speak, she is not permitted.

Now we are being motioned toward the television station, through the grounds and toward the station itself, the fanatics are being held back. Perhaps we have permission? The Air Force officer. Or perhaps it is a trap? The television station is set still further back, maybe a block from us, we are not even sure what it looks like. The fanatics stand now to the left, and the leftists stand now to the right, in an area something like a parking lot, the demonstrators standing on a slope, the attackers below them, the groups divided by Air Force men who fill a trenchlike roadway. Set for battle, we appear.

Should we just play it safe and stay out of this? "I want a meeting of women," Sophie insists. "But any demonstration against censorship is a good idea," I say. The number of women has increased and the men are no longer making speeches; it seems promising. A newsman wants to know if I don't think the attackers are really just uneducated men whose religion has persuaded them that women who don't veil themselves are prostitutes. Sure. Fascists, even Nazis often religiously believe what they have been taught; it makes them no less dangerous. These men are also manipulated, brought in by buses, led and managed, organized by signs and placards.

They surge forward and are held back. The women, for we are mostly women now, sit silently and peacefully on the grass, the picture of nonviolent response. Then a cheer: the women who work for national television have come out, at whatever risk, to join us. A woman who has just resigned from television recognizes me from the picture in *Kayhan* and thanks me for being there. "Television here's a terrible place, right now, the whole country's a terrible place. They are ruining the revolution. This is not what we fought for. This is the same sort of censorship and dictatorship that we fought against. Just different clothes. The executions this morning—one of them was a terrible Savak, but we don't even know who's putting them on trial, making all these decisions. The thing we fought for is not respected. They are putting on this ridiculous referendum. Where there is no choice. The Shah or an Islamic republic. Of course, no one will vote for the Shah; but no one knows what an Islamic republic is either. Worse than that, the constitution will not be revealed to us until after

we vote for it. Whoever heard of such a thing?" This woman talked to
Paris last night. French television is reporting that four women
demonstrators have died. Stab wounds. Here we have heard nothing.
Another woman interrupts to claim that the feminist demonstrators
are paid and that the government has guaranteed all "real women"
their rights. "But do you *have* them yet?" Sophie challenges. "I have
been promised them." She must represent millions.

And below us, the attackers, who represent the worst of more
millions, surge back and forth, laconically held in check by the blue-
uniformed Air Force. On the hill, a young Marxist in a beard rather
pedantically explains class system to me and then cannily refuses to
name his group; he has studied here and in Paris, tasting various
ideologies, and has not yet committed himself. He is on the side of
liberty. So are his brothers here.

Sighting the attackers across the way in her camera, Sophie has
again located the ringleader. The "boss." A man in a three-piece suit
and a styled haircut, clearly a person of means, seemingly accorded
every class privilege over his followers, his dupes. "See? In his light
brown suit? He gets them down there, then he works them back up
toward the soldiers, then he calls out the chant." A woman standing
beside her claims the attackers are paid to come here. Sophie has
studied the attacker we call the "boss" as if he were a rare species, she
has not taken her eye or her lens off him in thirty moments. Round,
fleshy face, tinted glasses. Striped tie. Prosperous among the poor.
He'd be fascinating to know more about. If we could locate the leaders
and publish their faces, we could find out who they are. If they are
Savaki—or whatever form of professional provocateur: Savak, CIA,
Islamic. He consults with one or two others and then issues his orders,
deploys the mass of his troops, calls the slogan. He begins to resemble
a cheerleader—so staged it is. "Why would he be so stupid as to wear a
suit?" "It sets him apart from the others, it gives him authority." The
Air Force are not actually protecting us, Sophie points out, it is simply
that the attackers are not yet ready to go after us. "When they are
ready to strike, they'll let them go; they'll break ranks." The attackers
call out that we are communists. There are plenty of Air Force troops,
I reason, unable to believe Sophie's cynical assumptions—and yet how
is it that we were suddenly left undefended yesterday? The militia
simply melted away. A young man near me points out that the
attackers are not only lumpen proletariat, but that section of the
working class who are now chronically unemployed—they gather daily
in front of the Ministry of Labor to protest. "The kind of man who is
in the street at this hour of the day, who can be organized to come and

Sit-in at Iranian Television, March 13, 1979

Fanatics mass for attack

attack women, is the kind of man who has nothing to do, he has no choice but hang around the streets."

"Khomeini promised us every freedom, but when he came to power he didn't want to give us anything at all," an Iranian boy with a cockney accent tells me, sitting on the grass. I'm having a lovely time gathering opinions, Sophie gathering views of her "boss," the attackers swarming about harmlessly below us as we sit comfortably on the bank, shielded from their fury by the blue coats of the Air Force. We denounce censorship and smoke cigarettes. I am given the leftist line on President Carter, together with instructions to relay certain messages to him. Notions such as that the chador is a CIA plot, or that Khomeini is a CIA plot. A bouquet of opinions. "The Americans endorse Khomeini because his reactionary foolishness brings things back to the Middle Ages, permits the imperialists to go on laughing at the new regime and praising the old." "They would support any anticommunist, and a dictator always seems to please them best," I say. We gossip, sitting in the sun peaceful and at rest. The fanatics chant against us, we chant back, but without their animosity. The attackers sing a song accusing us of being prostitutes—odd the contempt for prostitutes, the outright hatred. A hatred of sex itself. At Khomeini's arrival, the entire prostitution quarter was burned to the ground and the inhabitants left homeless throughout the city.

Now the attackers surge forward, the Air Force seeming unable to corral them. One's impulse is to run, but it also seems possible that if we go right on sitting quietly, affirming our peaceful nature, we will prevail—and the Air Force will be compelled to protect us, so clearly will the lines of aggressor and nonviolent object of aggression be drawn for the world to see. When we sit we feel stronger; the sun on our skin, the breeze. Standing, we are packed together and tend to panic. But how much longer will the Air Force lines hold? Will they be treasonous? The Air Force are the crack troops, the heroes of the revolution. I doubt if they will be overpowered. Is there some sly collusion in the back of the soldier's mind that will turn him away from us at the last push?

Attackers now fill the defile before us, they have jumped their bound. Yesterday we were ten to one, today we are equal in numbers. Two opposing groups shouting across a defile; silly really. More sensible to sit in the sun. Sophie has discovered the "boss" and his friends use walkie-talkies to coordinate. A man comes through our group and takes my picture, one wonders why. He then joins the attackers. "They're bound to take your picture," Sophie says. "It's even routine." "I doubt I'd be that fatalistic about it," I protest. But it feels sinister. No wonder people call it the magic eye: Muslim fanatics now have my image. The major networks are also here—probably as much protection as the Air Force, so long as they stay. Like the Air Force, you only have to worry about it when they leave. The NBC sound person is a woman, wearing a scarf for "religious reasons": I wonder if it helps or hinders, filters out or adds static. Michele, one of the Frenchwomen, has taken off her cardigan and her arms are bare since she has a short-sleeved blouse. I realize suddenly that this is the first time in ten days I have seen a woman's arms in public. And it has been hot. *Hejab* (modest covering) is not only head covering, it is covering of the arms and legs as well, the neck and of course the shoulders. *Tale of a Tub:* clothing is symbol and substance. Of course uniforms always are. But here street clothing is a uniform. A country where a woman's arms are taboo—ordure of the flesh.

Signs are being made and held up, I regret that none announces a next demonstration. Demonstrations themselves seem hopeless now, attendance off because of danger, the clear-cut lines of war which the attackers have created, each occasion better organized, more a conspiracy against free peoplehood. And the left now, the men who control it, its policy, rhetoric, ideology—controlling their women as well—they too have taken over. As the women sit peacefully on the bank, the men cannot refrain from standing and yelling back at the attackers, taking up the challenge we so grandly and wisely ignore.

A group of old women in chador are chanting slogans; seeing I am a foreigner, they wave to me and say *"Azadi,"* freedom. And now the attackers surge again—I must run back and guard the equipment. "It's all a stage, they run them up, draw them back and run them up again." Sophie is content, amused. We sit and stare at them, sunning ourselves, while the men, left and right, bellow at each other; we are like ladies watching the lists, a performance. The attackers have found one woman in chador to be at the front of their line, she's the only woman they've got. They are performing now for CBS, tonight the world will see this artificial image and believe it. This one woman in chador among the attackers is photographed at wonderful length, how she must love it, a cipher all her life and today for an hour a star. The Fedayeen, his lovely kaffiyeh cloth looped around his neck, struts on the ledge of the wall in full camera. We have converted politics into something beyond theater (which it perhaps always was)—into walk on costume cinema.

The attackers, cooperating in the creation of an "action shot," have flooded forward toward us. Our protectors run to man the wall with arms joined. Men and men. How easily we could simply sit on the grass, if we were confident. We urge women to sit down, not to be intimidated. A man of the left urges them to stand up, mill about, be ready to run. Finally even he is persuaded to sit, yet how much he prefers to stand, a martial figure with the rest of his kind. A pacifist's reaction to violence: sit in the sun and force the Air Force to perform its duty in controlling the violent.

A leftist man orates, the women go on sitting in the sun, sure of themselves at last. We come in peace, the others in hatred; the tactic of sitting only clarifies this. We will leave when we want to, not when we are routed. Even the men are catching on; they are now ordering us, *"Beshinin"*—"Sit down"—through megaphones. How tedious their repetitious magnified voices, the place suddenly flooded with men giving orders and, having a seated audience, unable to resist the impulse to orate. How endlessly we are manipulated, coopted. We become a field for masculine argument, factions disputing whether to stay, to leave, to sit, to stand.

Sophie and I have had enough, prefer to leave while things are still peaceful, while it is a choice; but it will not be one for long, I fear, the men being in charge. We made it out safely, but a few moments later there was chaos. The Frenchwomen who remained behind were attacked and chased down a street along with other terrified women, pummeled, pushed up against cars, spit on. The dream is over now.

"Khomeini, good, good," the cabdriver laughs all the way to the hotel, his colored photograph of the prophet Muhammad done up in a halo dangling from the rearview mirror. We never saw the television station; I am reminded of the promised interview as if it were a fairy tale.

PART IV

1 ✳ ✳ ✳

WE ARE GOING HOME today, back to Nelufar's: Gouli and Bahar, Hermoz; the comfort of a house. No more hotel life; no more journalists—from now on we will live with Persians. With the feminists here. Study, get to know them, do our work as documentarians. We are out of the streets and into the period of organization, solidification, beginning, suitably, by drinking tea, enjoying the rich fall of late-afternoon light on objects, examining pictures. What a good feeling to run up the stairs again, see our room, change clothes, have a shower. Sophie and I join Nelufar downstairs in a room never visited before, all other times we have been at the round table upstairs, conspirators theorizing on revolution or political impatience trying to reach Paris late at night. And now we sit clean and rested in the great armchairs of this formal room, or to go about and get to know the script in so many old paintings framed on the wall, calligraphy of a new kind. Nelufar and I drink our tea and enjoy the light, talking of plants, tucking our feet up, acting as if we were laypersons, mere civilians, women visiting.

We talk of how rugs are made, the long ill-paid labor of women and children, the inflation of dealers, the artisans robbed of their handicraft and paid starvation wages. "If it were to change, if the makers of the art themselves were paid accordingly, it could be reformed—otherwise rugs are made through more or less criminal means." "But how tragic if rugs were to cease being made, or made through a mechanization which trivialized the pattern, cheapened it, which is usually the case," I say. "If that were the only alternative—yes—but they could, the women could, because they do the work and many have a very high consciousness now—they could reform the economics of production without spoiling the product or the traditional way it is made. It is art, it should be made slowly and carefully. But the artist should come to own the artifact and be given a commensurate price. Without middlemen, the people who do nothing."

Hermoz joins us and we talk of rugs, how the symbolism of the tree remains in a stylized motif even long after the Islamic interdict against representation. He shows me a tree woven into a rug by the entranceway. We bend down over it; yes, of course it is a tree. I may have something like that myself. I have seen it a hundred times and never seen it. A cyprus. And the trees in the miniatures, their blossoms. What if one could grow a Persian tree at home, the farm? A glade, a garden, to keep Persia with us. "And here are patterns that look like your American Indians'"; he has a book. The great ruby rugs in the colored plates, like Velázquez masterpieces. Will the museums ever open again? Charming, handsome, serious man, his kindness and patience teaching us the simplest things, basic motifs, differences between schools.

Tree farmers in another life, Sophie and I begin dreaming of trees, what kind of tree is Persia, its essence? Is there a tree we could bring back? Could we get it through customs? Nasrin has an uncle who's an arborist. Maybe, if there's time. We have never even been to the bazaar. Sprawling on a rug amidst birds and flowers—there will be time for everything now; our public life is over, we will be subsumed into the privacy of small groups, political seminars, friendships, the women. We are accepted now, everyone will show us around in their spare time, for there finally will be time; the demonstrations and their fourteen-hour days of danger and exhaustion are over. Someone will know the bazaars, someone will know the museums. Nelufar knows the city, its slums, old quarters, architecture. Today we may even be permitted to sit in on a crucial meeting where the charter and policy of the women's movement here will be decided. We are chosen now, accepted.

There is a kind of peace in the room, the light from two long windows, the green of plants, the comfort of old things and pictures, a nineteenth-century Persian bureau where Hermoz's family pictures are kept: his father looking like a Turkish revolutionary or a grand old man, the charm of period in the clothes and mustache, mothers and aunts and cousins and family outings, Hermoz's sophistication softening to family pride as he exhibits them; how good he is to us, how we seem at last to become part of the family, communicating even with the Irish setter through a window, then letting her back in at the door, careful to wipe her paws. How sane we can be today after the barbarism of the streets and the shouting mobs of attackers; there is civilization itself in a handspan of Farsi script painted by someone who studied a lifetime for this grace, the keen edge of it, the sureness. Peace itself in the sunlight, the pictures and rugs and furniture, things people have made who had time and leisure to do them well, things saved and cared for.

It carries over as the women begin to arrive: Mimi with her hair tied back, looking different, a sharper outline to her face, and Kateh; drinking tea in the little prelude before politics, the greetings and funny stories, the news and anecdotes, the sentence or two that sum up situations with an urbanity which later discussion will only prolong through abstraction before reaching the same conclusion. Like the answers in the back of an arithmetic text. Sophie and I watch our friends sitting on the couch, enjoying without understanding, without needing to. Hermoz still with the women till the others come and we divide into those artificial categories circumstances now impose upon us.

And when they are all in the room, the amenities satisfied and Hermoz departed back to his office after the lunch break, then there is another hesitation as they prepare to mount the stairs to their meeting—will we be permitted to come? If we pushed it, we could go with them. I will never do that, much as I want to attend. I hang back, making it easy, in a moment I can drift off unseen. But they stop to consult, Kateh checking the eyes of her comrades in a glance. It is a delicate moment. And then I am firmly invited; the agreement is genuine. One of the dearest moments I will have here; even at the time I recognize it. And Sophie. But not the camera.

And so we have pictures of the room only. Empty of persons. A strange emptiness, but safer. The room where we met is Gouli's room, a child's room covered with drawings in crayon, the room of an adolescent permitted her own art and opinions. A charming creation, though a surreal setting for such a grave meeting as this, and yet the crayon pictures give the proceedings a flavor, a lightness across generations of women, Gouli's bold stroke a language holding its own, reminding us we decide for the young as well, the high-school girls who have been the backbone of the demonstrations. A room we could photograph only without its people, without the presence of the women who still inhabit it for us as ghosts when we go over the prints, their faces too dangerous to be shown together in such collaboration. Nearly everyone here has Savak records against them from the days

The room at Nelufar's

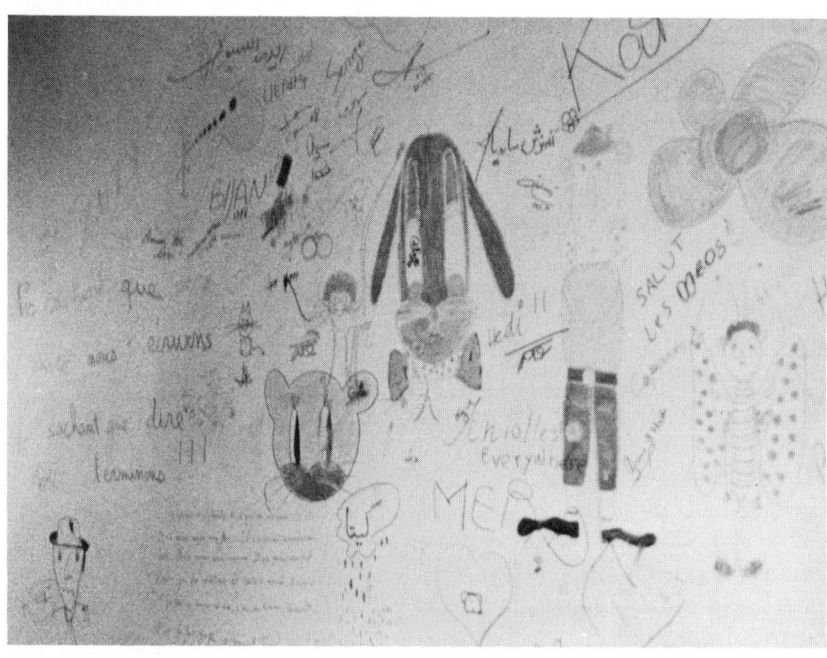

against the Shah; the same records are used now by the new regime, which has refused to make them public, and which is operating therefore by the old "intelligence" and its point of view. We meet in a small room in secret. Sophie and I are privileged to be there but we may take no pictures. Nor would we want to; we have requested and obtained permission for every photograph we have used, and at times are so chary of endangering our friends that we reject many authorized pictures out of the merest possibility of danger. What then of a tape recorder? Further consultation. The tape will be in my hands and they trust me. If I leave it, I leave it with them; it is after all their document. And of considerable historical value, but more for them than for me; a tape generally in Farsi, with only a few scattered quick translations into English by a serious woman with glasses to my left, a Trotskyite, rigorous, precise.

I can only watch and keep the record. As I did once for the first *conferencia* of Latinas and Chicanas that Sita organized back in Sacramento. It was a fascinating exercise and a pleasure then as it is now, to watch and listen and interpret by indices of one's own, given the subject only now and again. One studies the faces and hears the tones, my eyes carried often to the walls, their strange and delightful combinations of child wisdom in Farsi, French and English, the cartoons, the favorite sayings, the slogans of youth culture, a mock newspaper headline announcing that "The Son of King Creon Has Been Executed in Crete," the exhortations to peace and love. I am taking notes as well, notes on how a teacup looks on a rug as you hear policy hammered out, notes on shoes and cigarettes, the borrowing of matches in moments of greatest intensity, the way a hand stubs out a butt in an ashtray in the midst of debate, how an argument is settled in friendship, how the purpose is held to as a car backfires in the distance, and Nelufar, always near the window, adjusts the curtains, concealing us again, reflex of how much experience?

There are eight points. Equal education, to which much attention is paid, the situation with regard to literacy being of emergency proportion. Equal pay and equal opportunity, and of course this is tricky since there are so many ways this principle can be frustrated by employers. Abortion—a difficult issue in view of Khomeini's rigid new pronouncements—but there is no wavering. All this is finally agreed on. Child care, easier, this has been a demand ever since the uprising. We return to the abortion paragraph and expand it to contraception and sexual education, statements in support of these issues. The select committee who will write the actual draft make careful notes. But everyone is taking notes, one almost hears the concentration. Even as the eye roves the zany colored pictures, studies a face in the circle of women, watches Mimi dispute with Kateh. Agreement excellent and differences friendly among them.

How well they all know how to work with each other, how refreshing the absence of ego trips, leaders, stars, rhetoricians, tangents, pointless digressions, enmities. How sophisticated they are, these women trained in long hard schools such as we have never seen, clandestine work in foreign countries, being spied on, knowing the certainty of prison terms, the possibility of torture. "If it gets worse we will simply have to leave again; there is still France," Nelufar said the other day. "And Hermoz?" "He can't get work over there. We will have to be apart again. But I can bring the children, their French is good enough so they can go on in school." "It is so much to lose," I say. She only nods her head; you see the sadness, the years of exile beneath her beauty; one perceives its source, like music in a minor key.

After all these things they are close, these women, as we will never be at home, even with years behind us and between us. They are better too at being friends: kindnesses, courtesies in debate, a holding back of anger or contempt, the poison of opinionated position. But between Kateh and Mimi there is a sharp difference now, which proliferates from the immediate issue to larger divergencies, even theoretical stance: the appeal to the mass which is Marxist dogma as seen through Trotskyite practice, versus the more pragmatic feminist strategy of pursuing any woman's objective, no matter how unpopular with male opinion of any of the various political stripes or classes. This is the first lengthy dispute we have witnessed, expert each parry and thrust. Kateh holding back her power, the easy and natural acknowledgment she has from every woman in the room. Even though she is among the youngest here, no point is settled without reference to her, even if it be the flicker of an eye. And Mimi, older, member of a group and party, dedicated, seasoned in many countries, here with us against the approval of certain of her comrades probably, increasingly intense in her protestations, even Mimi respects her young opponent entirely. It is edifying to watch women differ with great heat but without rancor; moving to see Mimi's passion flash out of her exhaustion, her tragic alienation. And sad to see her defer at last, as much out of sorrow as through persuasion. Kateh has never bullied her once. Has never used youth or arrogance, scorn, derision; has actually deferred to age. Oddly enough, both have deferred—though Kateh has won her point by winning over the others, the majority. Without denying Mimi her minority position—which she maintains, somehow concurring and not conceding—her right to air it, counsel, persuade, and if not to sweep the others to where she is, to remind them, and influence them as well. Her arguments and presentations have made a difference, one feels it as they go on. Confrontation has become influence; there is no win or lose, but a swaying, a balance.

There is also the usual boredom of meetings, even ones as crucial and full of energy as this one: there is a foot to scratch, ashtrays to pass, the sound of the telephone ringing outside the room. Marriage and family law. Should the professions be listed under "Employment"? The time of meetings, the endless time of talk relieved by the pictures on the wall, the pictures Sophie and I make in our minds, arriving at notions of how to film this room devoid of persons, this crayoned chamber, an interesting problem in itself. Yet we are, even in the sea of incomprehensible Farsi, aware of the privilege of being here; the moment when a women's movement is founded in a country, if you could pinpoint it, it might be this moment, the drawing up of a charter, a statement of purpose, the founding document. The rebellion in the streets is given over now for deliberation and principle; the women who will make this take place in time, many if not all of them are here in one room; it will probably never be this simple again. Factions will come, friendships may fade, the government may strangle the new birth still.

When they have done it, when it is written and we are standing to leave, someone asks me if I have anything to add, a thought or an impression. I am flattered; in fact I did have something to suggest but did not speak, out of courtesy. Now I can: "You know that paragraph on reproductive freedom, where you discuss abortion and contraception, why not expand it to a statement on sexual freedom itself, and make it a means of offering protection to two groups much persecuted here: prostitutes and homosexuals."

A little ripple of astonished mirth. "I know, they burned out the prostitutes and they are executing homosexuals—but . . ." "You must realize how dangerous such a statement would be here now?" someone points out. "Yes, but if I may offer advice from our experience—the dangers of not following principle from the first must also be weighed. Because we were timid and intimidated with regard to lesbianism, for example, there was bad faith and resentment which took a long time to dispel once the women's movement did belatedly acknowledge lesbians. There is also the sheer morality of it—no human rights should be denied." Some nod. From the corner of my eye I watch Nasrin, our Nasrin, and Ferdosheh, whom Sophie and I have begun to notice are growing a shy new flower between them, making them tender and awkward and preoccupied. They are especially so today. Nasrin has a cold and claims that as the cause of her alienation during the meeting; the original distance of her class added now to the hidden one of her kind. It is the very thing I had tried to warn the others of. She is too afraid to meet my eye.

Drinking coffee with Nasrin and Ferdosheh one morning at the hotel, I began to imagine they were lovers, or were becoming lovers. Ferdosheh's lovely long hair is now cropped short in a familiar, if regrettable, symptom of conversion. As we drank our coffee in the hotel with Nemat I pressed for information on homosexual life here; he could offer only the expertise of sociologists, anthropologists; three days later Sophie and I sensed the expertise newly among us. But didn't dare speak. Nor did they. There is something vaguely absurd about all this. And now everyone in the room hesitates; the pariahs wait for acknowledgment. I had deliberately phrased this issue theoretically, to make it easier. But it is real and personal finally. Still more so for the lesbians who will remain among them.

It will be taken into consideration. Well enough, things are learned in time.

2 ✳ ✳ ✳

A LOVELY DAY. There is even time for breakfast. I come back into our hotel room to find Sophie. Let's order eggs, the works. We stayed over at the Intercontinental last night because of an early-morning interview with *Kayhan*. The last thing of that sort I'll have to do, just a wrap-up. Now my private life begins here; or rather what few public things I'll do will be as a scholar, a more comfortable self. In addition to speaking at Damovar University, Reza wants me to address the faculty of arts and letters at his own Tehran University on the luminous subject of narrative form in autobiography: it tickles me, I'm flattered. How agreeable this return to civil life again, how civil. There are seminars with the feminists ahead, some gentle tourism; eight days until our excursion ticket takes us home. We will find and enjoy Persia. Indeed, pouring my coffee, I already am. This morning's interview was certainly pleasant, the interviewer a charming woman, her husband along with her to take the photgraphs. "Come for dinner at our house, we have so many friends, teachers and writers who'd like to meet you." I accepted. The interview itself candid and relaxed; I even permitted myself to deviate from the "tactful" approach to Khomeini which Kateh usually takes: the demonstrations are over, I may speak for myself. And the abuses are mounting: there were more executions last night. We hear them from the hotel, they haunt us. A shot, then twenty minutes, fifteen, sometimes only ten, the length of a "trial" or a sentence, and then the next victim. At first we assured ourselves it was merely the militia firing to stop cars somewhere, but by now the timing convinces us. The papers print the dead faces every morning; the press here confirm it, we cannot pretend anymore. It makes staying here in the center at the hotel an unpleasant and exposed feeling.

But now we can move back to Nelufar's again for good, probably this afternoon when we check out. All our public things are over: interviews with the press, marches, sit-ins. Now we will give ourselves to documenting the women here and their push for organization. An office is being searched out today. We should all have an answer on a lease this evening. Last night Gloria telephoned that money was being collected from American feminists to fund some sort of printing arrangement. Nasrin, our Nasrin, will be writing a whole series of pamphlets here; she can also do things in English for women at home. It is all in train now. And the international delegation arrives the nineteenth, just a few days away. My old friend Carole Rousopolis has flown in from Paris on her own like a happy surprise and as much fun as ever—Carole learned her English from sixties radicals and even refers to her apartment as her "pad"—and her good humor and tolerance and her sense of adventure are superb. Also her native Swiss tolerance and goodwill. And since Claudine and Sylvina have objections to a few of the French members of the international delegation and may have even left before they arrive, Carole and I, over a good dinner, have outlined a course of diplomacy to ensure that the international feminists meet and become as close and helpful to the Iranian feminists as possible during their short stay. This in addition to their formal duties of interviewing government officials and investigating the present threats to women's rights here. Things should go smoothly now. The pleasant part is ahead.

The telephone. I answer it lying on the bed fully dressed, comfortable, relaxed. All the midnight calls from New York and Paris: Servan-Schreiber announcing de Beauvoir's press conference in Paris, Robin and Gloria reporting on demonstrations of support in America—telephone calls always at midnight, the nervous excitement of it;

reporters from far corners of the world infallibly getting our number at three in the morning to ask silly questions and pretend innocence of the hour. But all good news, necessary publicity for the women's struggle here, the push of the world press, the eye of television sent through the globe telling of the struggle here, the stand the women are making. History.

This is a man from Reuters. He calls himself "Dicky," the boy's name pronounced in a British accent makes it impossible not to grin. The voice, however, is tense. He has just been to Vice Premier Entezam's press conference. Entezam is the official spokesman of the Bazargan government. He holds press conferences every Tuesday and Thursday. "I see," I mumble, expecting that Dicky will now announce some new wrinkle in the chador policy and ask me to comment.

"Did you know that you are going to be expelled from Iran?" Like being hit with a crowbar. The thunderous surprise and then the chilling fear. I feel cold. And sick. The news of a death. A catastrophe. Fatality of a divorce, a lover's betrayal. But more; that falls upon one and settles, this comes running. They are coming to "get" you. You are caught. They got you. The doors of Napa, of Herrick Hospital, locked psychiatric wards. I was already free, saved by a good civil-rights lawyer and celebrating our victory in court (you don't often get to win your own insanity trial) with a little dinner on his boat, the lamp low, the talk of writers and America, Fitzgerald and St. Paul, Berryman's suicide from a bridge in Minneapolis, and Donald Heffernan's wife Mary Ann looked up from chopping vegetables . . . "And your mother committing you" . . . the news mercifully after the fact. Because I hadn't known it was that bad. Examination maybe, her naive mis-placed faith in some doctor's theories—but not commitment. Not that, not the whole way. I was free already, free to weep and curse and drink bourbon on the deck a while in the wind, alone. I was already safe.

Now there is no safety. It's coming toward you. Not past, but future. The fantasy of every guilt, every random daydream of being thief or murderer, the participation in fiction, in movies; you are Joseph Cotten or somebody and the indictment is handed down, the detective proceeds toward you through traffic. Raskolnikov knowing the jig is up. Wait—this is real. A government is against me. As if I were a thief or a criminal. Shame. I am unwelcome. But I love Persia. Dicky wants a comment. Would it sound silly to say I love Persia? Is Entezam Persia? Or only its government? Is Entezam Persia or its government? But everyone else in Persia is governed. When condemned by government I am unwelcome to all. A public figure of dislike, opprobrium. Shame. Singled out, a pariah. Disgraced. St. Paul comes back, good manners, the dishonor of disgrace. How still more disgraceful "in a woman."

Try to see it as the immigration department; not the secret police, not the knock of Savak. Numbers of my friends have always lived under threat of deportation; it got me to the altar. But expulsion is immediate, terrible, irreversible. Why on earth would Vice Premier Entezam, whom I have heard of only vaguely, and who surely can never have heard of me—a mere writer, a female at that, a women's-libber trailing along at the end of the march, and one quite incapable, for linguistic among a thousand other reasons, of ever being accused of outside agitation (whatever that means, particularly in civil rights, where agitation is the job itself and a moral duty), why has Vice Premier Entezam looked up from his grave matters of state, the oil crisis and the executions—to expel me from his country? Where I have friends and purposes, responsibilities and obligations, university lecture engagements and work to achieve: my little historical films and tapes and archival tasks, things far beneath his purview? I have also, crude matter of necessity, an excursion ticket that isn't good until eight days from now. Premature use carried a penalty of four hundred dollars per person—my god, there's Sophie—will they throw her out? Is she safe? Could she stay on and finish the work? Will she leave with me, keep me company?—I'm scared. I haven't got that much money. I can't afford to be expelled. Perhaps he could expel me just as I'm leaving, when my ticket could be honored; perhaps you can negotiate an expulsion. I laugh inside, predictable hysteria in the face of such illogical terrorization.

"So, have you any comment?" Merciless Dicky. I could cry, perhaps? I could surely huddle in terror. My mind could snap. Easily. What comment is appropriate? Dicky wants his comment. Good manners, the habits of a lifetime, the political reflex, responsibility to a cause, demand one as well. Maybe I'll throw up. Have I a comment? "Well, not really. But as a pacifist. Invited here, and I came in peace. I must say I find this incomprehensible. So I think I'll look into it a bit further. Thank you very much."

"Be sure to call me back if you have any further comment." Comment . . . cormorant, I mumble, turning to tell Sophie, who is answering the door. My god, Sophie, I got her into this, ashamed at the danger she shares now. Needing her and ashamed, telling her is an apology. For bad news. And another for my groveling fear. Hearing the words again from someone in the doorway of the room: Entezam, press conference, expulsion. Today, this morning. Already I see the police. Sophie's calm, reasonable voice, efficient if surprised.

Even able to laugh with a slightly nervous British aplomb. Must be a reporter there. Tony from *Newsweek*. Wondered if we'd heard yet. For a moment I am sorry I could not tell her myself: she too must hear it as "news." Do we have a comment? I explain it to Sophie, Tony explains it. All three of us try to explain it. Tony tries to remember how it happened, to repeat Entezam's words as his interpreter, who was present, had copied them; he himself had been in the countryside. Tony can't explain—but this is how it went: it seems there was a question from the floor, a reporter's question to Entezam: "Is it true that you have expelled the free-lance journalist Ralph Schoenman?" "Yes, at nine o'clock this morning."

Sophie and I look at each other: our friend Ralph, all the times we came across him in the lobby, his sympathy, his interest, his tidbits of news, his presence at the demonstrations—he was in so many ways our comrade. And now he's in trouble. Already slandered in the Iranian press to such a degree that some of our other friends, Nelufar, for example, actually profess to believe he was an "agent," as the papers called him. And it is under such a rubric that his summary expulsion was explained this morning. "He has already left the country," Entezam says, following this up with a series of spy-heretic accusations. Ralph was a provocateur, an enemy of the revolution, a foreign agent and so forth.

All this because Ralph has been fearless in criticism and beautifully nervy in exposing certain generals of past Savak ill repute now restored again to power. And also in saying he knew the names of the members of the secret court and would divulge them so they might be publicly responsible for their actions against international law. The executions. In the past week he has put this government on the carpet: challenging it through the Iranian press to prove his allegations were false. The very first question asked of Entezam was in fact in this vein—would certain allegations about recent military appointments be answered that morning?

Entezam replies smugly that Ralph's expelled, a spy and all that. And the next question's: "And do you also plan to expel the American feminist Kate Millett?" "Yes, we will be taking further action against her and others," as Tony has it. "But what the hell for?" I ask. "Same sort of stuff as with Ralph—counter this or that, enemy whatever— blah blah—we'll get someone to check the exact wording."

"But on what grounds? What charges?" Tony can't really say exactly how it went, just that Entezam, having denounced Ralph as some sort of agent or something, the next questioner demanded if Kate Millett would be expelled and Entezam says she and other provocateurs will go too. "Something like that." The mysterious business of being an agent, a provocateur. The magic words of thought crime. I am not too sure what these words mean. An agent of what? Another government? If so, which one? Ideological plots and invasions? Does international feminism have agents? How do you get appointed? What is a provocateur? French, rather nasty sound, a sly word. Conrad's *Secret Agent*? Emma Goldman's anarchist assassin friends: sepia prints, old books. *The First Circle*.

How do you prove you are not an agent if someone "important" says you are? It is rather like proving your sanity. Totalitarianism works like that, I know it from books, from reports on political prisoners. But never me. Not me. I help persons in this situation; I have never been one. Not till the booby hatch, when the family gave me over to the state, turned me in, as unsatisfactory relatives can be turned in, as rejects. But not the state itself coming after me. Not governments and arrest, expulsion, deportation, political seizure and imprisonment. I help people because books have taught me to believe that these things happen to people as innocent as I. But they must still happen only to others. Not to me.

Something breaks in me as it did when I was imprisoned before. The loony-bin trip. Hope fumbles, optimism, the expectation that one will be treated fairly: something breaks in fear, the nightmare known about but never expected, what happens to other people, the unlucky ones. You become an unlucky one, marked. It happened once, but I have since lived with such care it could never happen again. And always so scrupulous before the law. And still . . . Because I am already imprisoned now, by words; it is only a matter of hours before they come, maybe minutes—and they will have me in custody. The fear of custody in a claustrophobe.

Of course you hope you will only be expelled. Seized and then let go. "A free ride to the airport, it will save taxi fare," Sophie and I joke in our panic. But arrested, held, deprived of everything—at their mercy. For long? Will they ever expel us? Or will they take us into custody and say here that we were expelled? While we languish in prison. How long before it's noticed that we never came home? Rely on the media? Can a newspaper article get you out of jail in another country? People in my line of work have never found that very rapid. Would there perhaps be a blackout? Some convenience to Iranian or even American departments of state? Would there be a hue and cry? What good could that do if they had our persons?—the networks would still have their news.

At their mercy. The body imprisoned. How big they are, governments, their places of detention, their buildings, doors, locks. Power. The power of the state. The loony-bin trip—now, there was a learning experience. There were no lawyers in that case till the end. But there probably won't be any here, the same stripping of self. Murder thirty people and you have rights—as indeed you should. But be called crazy by a few zealous relatives who have no notion of what they are about. And you have none. I could have told them—I'd even worked as an aide in a snakepit one utopian college summer job, could deplore conditions firsthand. But wore the keys and was not a prisoner. Had not yet the holy wisdom of one who has lived behind a lock.

Still it was not full prison, prison on the initiative of the state. An enemy of the state, one searched out, sought, hunted, captured. As before, I didn't want it. Didn't feel I needed to know captivity that well to do my job—intellectual understanding was enough. "Crazy" and "agent provocateur" are analogous terms: mystic, existential states of being, effective as heresy, religion, ideology. Annihilation.

Call for help. The French. Claudine and Sylvina are in their rooms. Run through the corridors. Tremble in the elevator, the elevator powered by electricity and controlled by the hotel management, shut off during every blackout and exchange of gunfire. To a claustrophobe always a hellish experience and now the perfect trap: controlled by the hotel management—who are of course controlled by the government. The Bazargan government of Entezam, the Komiteh, Khomeini, the guards slouching in the lobby. The surly hotel officials themselves who listen to every phone call and must have already heard the news—from Dicky if no other messenger has yet arrived to put a police hold on my registration form, my passport number, room number, whereabouts. Of course they know this room number too.

Sophie and I tell our story in our friends' adjoining hotel rooms, telling ourselves, retelling in our stunned disbelief. Our French friends decide "That must mean us as well." Thereafter one or another is on the phone to Paris while two or three others begin shredding notes, papers, the harmless reportage they have sent every day through the hotel telex, a machine as public as if it were government-owned. Certainly government-controlled; copies of what is transmitted are surely made. I watch them, their paranoia, throwing clothes into bags. One is leaving this moment. We watch her go. The rest will leave tomorrow, they think, having already missed today's plane. In the next room, the phone to Paris; they take turns on it, consulting with Antoinette: sybil, mother, political strategist.

My superior in these things, I feel, taking my turn, trying to present our alternatives, the possibility of hanging on to exercise whatever civil rights we may still have, gambling to stay in order to finish our work, the long shot of exposing this as harassment, further evidence of how women are treated here, the chances to demonstrate this before world opinion. Antoinette prefers they leave and advises me to do the same. It is her experience that still further repression follows swiftly on this sort of event. And time in jail is wasted time: they can do better by returning.

Exemplary logic. But I do not want to leave. I want to stay as long as I can. Sophie and I begin phoning America, messages on the answering machine for Ruth to act on. We are being expelled. Tell Gloria, tell the media. We may need money. Will someone reassure my mother? We have already phoned Kateh. She is sending someone to be with us. Someone special. We must be careful not to use her real name, she is hunted by the police still from the old days against the Shah. We must remember to call her Mina. She is remarkable, quiet, contained. So very ladylike. Cool. Sleek brown hair, brown clothes. It is awesome, almost funny that this calm young lady could be wanted. But then, here we are ourselves—the lot of us sipping tea, as if deriving some intangible strength from decorum. My American side would rant, has just barked at Sophie who has got Ruth on the phone at last, insisting I give Ruth the instructions myself. But I am conquered now by this other manner of dealing with emergencies. I am in the presence of experience.

We recount our tale to Mina. With a new bit of information supplied by one of the Persian translators for the press: the man who raised the question of Kate Millett—the man whose question seemed to have baited Entezam to reply—seems to be a plant. "Most of the reporters at those press conferences are foreigners. They all know each other, foreigner and Iranian. And none of them had ever laid eyes on this man before." His affiliation was so unfamiliar that she had even asked for his phone number. We try it. Wrong number. There is also a rumor that Agence France, their top man, called Entezam an hour before the conference and inquired if Kate Millett would be expelled. Entezam appeared to have no idea who that was. When pushed in public an hour later, he was ready. "We seem to be harassed," I say to Mina. A smile of lovely subtlety crosses her face. "Mina, what if we were to prepare a statement?" "Of course," she says over her teacup. I love her cool. We women can draft something. Would Caifi like to join us? "Naturally." "Then we must consult with Bahram and Nemat and the others." "Yes. But wait till later in the afternoon. And do a really good job of it. When you are composed."

Mina herself is entirely composed in her armchair; feminine, as if femininity were a resource in itself. Paris calls again. Sophie's voice goes on saying hello as the connection fails. "The real truth, Mina, the real truth is that we are terrified." "You must stay in the hotel, not at Nelufar's." I was afraid of that, but of course it is how it must be. The hotel is tension itself: reporters, police, the spies on the phone—I hate it. But we must stay here. And never mind the expense: if we run out of money, Gloria or Des Femmes will help us; our bills can be paid in New York or Paris where the Intercontinental also has branches. We must stay here; any friend who took us in would be under suspicion. Nelufar has a husband and children, a house, an entire life to lose. No one can give us shelter now—even the unknown apartment is risky—it looks like hiding. And we must never appear to hide: on the contrary, here—the hotel—is perfect, a fishbowl, a branch of the government.

And what of the media—one of the few defenses we have now is publicity. The old pacifist tactic; shame the authorities into treating you, if not well, at least with less barbarism than if they were not being watched. Since my own government, though unrepentant over its opprobrious relationship with the Shah, is nevertheless very unctuous toward the new regime out of its continual need for oil, it will probably be willing to do nothing to defend my rights. The press is the only chance I have left.

Paris calls again and I tell Claude Servan-Schreiber we are being expelled. Should they consider postponing their arrival? No, by all means come if they'll still let you. Feminists must come and keep coming. All the more so if they kick us out. "Claude, put on all the pressure you can over there, that we not be expelled, we still have so much to do. And we regard this as governmental harassment of international feminism." She wants a statement for today's press conference in Paris. I comply and then tell her our own truth: "Claude, we're all frightened to death." "May we say here that the women there support you?" "Yes, I feel that they do—but let me check with . . . Mina, may I say that the Iranian feminists support us?" "Of course you should."

But there is still one ticklish problem for the international delegation—will the Iranian women make a statement welcoming them that they can read today in Paris? Mina and I hammer out a wording: the foreign women are coming in solidarity with Iranian feminists and with the other international feminists here—keeping back the name of the Iranian committee, since it is so newly formed and in danger of being persecuted. Claude promises to arrive Monday morning.

United Press International is sending the news throughout the world that Entezam has called me a counterrevolutionary. Having checked with the translators that this term was not in fact used, we can now insist on a retraction. "In a situation of this 'delicacy,' one ought to be able to insist that the government at least be quoted accurately," I laugh. But the term is so unsavory, I must shed it. Sophie wheedles and argues with the UPI in a dozen phone calls retrieving what honor is left. The translator's story haunts me; how Entezam seemed still unsure just who I was. The question itself seemed a provocation he could not resist. Knowing and hating Ralph, when some unknown woman is linked to Ralph in a question, pushed under his nose as it were, he may, in sheer bravado, macho compulsion, authoritarian transport, have said, sure, we're expelling her too. Why not, he has the authority of a god, can expel or imprison anyone he likes without cause. Sophie reports that UPI will now retract my counterrevolutionary label. A good thing for feminism here. We've been called everything in the streets; we hardly need more abuse from the government diffused through the press. One wire report has Ralph and me expelled together, winging through the air to London, side by side.

Yet here I am, expelled and not expelled. Or under threat of expulsion but not yet expelled. I confer with Mina and it is decided I should politely inform the government of my whereabouts. Further, that if they should wish to expel me, I am happy to comply. Yet not that eager to leave, having another week's work to do. As a pacifist I will do everything correctly, keep right in sight, await their disposition. While maintaining that the thing must be some misunderstanding, some error they are welcome to back out of. We agree exactly on tactics: exemplary civil behavior, reliance on civil-liberties assumptions; our own correctness of deportment setting an example to them. Not merely a strategy, a way of life, a moral philosophy.

But how odd the whole thing is, the very manner of my being informed is marginal, accidental. I am expelled but never even informed of it myself. Directly. I don't go to Entezam's press conferences, how on earth should I know I am to be expelled unless a friendly reporter tips me off? I don't read Farsi and am just as likely to miss an issue of the English-language newspaper. How odd they don't send round a public servant with a decent piece of paper in his hand, someone in a suit with bureaucratic forms. Surely that must be the practice, surely in being expelled from a country one is entitled to be informed of the fact? In return for the insult and inconvenience, surely a messenger is not too much to ask, a document. How was I expected to discover my condition? And how oppressive and ridiculous that we should now have to call them—the powers that be— to find out when, the day, the hour, they dispose of us. Never knowing from moment to moment our fate, or even if a man with a gun is now on his way to get us.

A battle of nerves. We have only the journalists on our side, very uncertain support—if the man with the gun hits us over the head, they will delight in photographing the event, merely to have obtained "news." Nearly every reporter in the hotel has called, many have asked specifically to be notified as we are dragged away, so they can be right on the spot; petitioning this ghoulish scoop in perfect good nature.

3 ✳ ✳ ✳

AT NASRIN'S, not "our Nasrin," the other Nasrin. The way the women spoke of it, the way we headed for it, as a safe place, a "safe" telephone—I had expected intrigue nearly. And there has been some. After those bleak moments in the hotel room, realizing that the Frenchwomen from Des Femmes could not get our materials out of the country now: the movie film, my tapes, my notebooks, Sophie's thousand still photographs. Everything may be seized now, we are told, even the networks are not safe, even their private planes cannot protect their news photos and footage, anything and everything is put under scrutiny at the airport. Videotape is put through a monitor. Exposed sixteen- and thirty-five-millimeter film which has not yet been processed would be ruined if opened: reports are contradictory as to whether it will soon be torn open, confiscated, or permitted to pass uninspected. Anything coming out of Iran now may contain scenes of the women's demonstrations and they are embarrassing and infuriating to the government.

If we are going to save our work, the record we have made of women here—for women everywhere—we are going to have to entrust it to someone else to protect. Found with us when we are found, it will certainly be taken into custody as well, impounded, probably destroyed. Nothing of our film has been processed, if opened it would all be lost. My notebooks? And the tapes? They too are really manuscript to me, my method of remembering, later when I compose, and I will surely compose now. If we can save our sources. Which means risking them, surrendering them, entrusting them to someone else. Conferences. Frantic packing, finding, searching out every tape, cataloging the stills. The work of quiet hours and quietude must be done now in haste, fear, unbearable anxiety. A Mack Sennett movie. Like bank robbers scattering the loot. Part of me would really prefer to be arrested still clutching my crummy thirty-nine-cent notebook and daring the tyrant to wrest it out of my hands. Fortunately there are adults around me: Sophie, Carole, "our Nasrin"; they know nothing's safe with us now.

But where is safe? Any stuff of ours is too hot for the women here, as feminists they are already watched, or rather, still watched, the Savak apparatus of the Shah never having been dismantled, only converted by the next regime, every day more repressive. So it must be a foreigner. The women from Des Femmes are leaving, but they are suspect, so it's too dangerous for them. And they are certain to be searched.

"I'm the only one who isn't hot," Carole laughs. She is full of Mata Hari schemes: "The French diplomatic pouch," she snaps her fingers. "I'm having lunch with a lady who might go for it and has access." This seems harebrained. The French diplomats better not be taking any chances on us. And it would be unfair to sneak it through them, the French are in an awkward situation here now anyway and even their pouch is no longer sacrosanct. "I used to know Ghotbzadeh—can you believe it—I actually knew that guy? In Paris, the old days, when he was over there with Khomeini—I was doing stuff with the Panthers, fund-raising, that kind of stuff. Ghotbzadeh was a big deal in Paris then, radical in exile, you know? And I met him . . . I wonder." "Carole, don't be crazy, be practical." We are laughing; a spy movie.

"Listen—I'll get it out—everybody here knows somebody in Paris. All the women here. Everybody travels. Everybody can bring a little something and drop it off." But, Carole, there's so much of it—the cans of film are big—there are even a lot of tapes, boxes of them. Be sure it goes in little bunches, so we don't lose it all in one basket. And so no one gets caught." "It will take a while. Sure. Don't worry. And I'll do it cool, man. Trust me. I'm good at this sort of thing."

She probably is, I think, watching her about to take off with my favorite Italian leather bag; how long I paused before I bought that bag in Milan airport to console myself for losing Colette. And there it goes. To the Park Hotel. Where they must search your rooms just as diligently as they do here. Where the phone is probably bugged just as regularly. "Ah, but it's French, so it must be better—wouldn't you say, Kate?" "Undoubtedly. But they have no alcohol." "Which is why I come over here to have dinner with you," she laughs. "Wait for my signal. I'll phone you in some interesting code when I'm safe in my room."

The next bag, Sophie's movie film, still being meticulously cataloged by its stoic photographer, is to go with "our Nasrin." The moment we hear from Carole. An hour goes by. What's happened? We can't wait any longer; the other women are here to take us to where there's a safe telephone and another plan to carry out. Must we risk Nasrin's going to the Park Hotel where they are already waiting for her, the Italian bag and Carole in custody? Nasrin's undaunted, the green Turkish eyes of a cat: "I'll go and not get caught. If Carole's there and it's okay, I'll drop it with her. If not, I'll go on. To Nasrin's if it's safe; otherwise to someplace that is. I'll keep in touch by telephone. I'll talk slang."

Shall we risk it? Sophie and I look at each other. What choice have we? We can't leave the stuff in our room now. It could be searched even if there are none of the bugging devices Claudine is so sure of. And we can't take it with us to Nasrin's—if we were busted they would nab everybody on the idiot evidence of photographs of demonstrations in public places. We can't incriminate our friends. But can we watch Nasrin take this risk like a fish rising for bait? "But I'm a smart fish, an old fish, I know what I'm doing. I've done these things all over America when I was with Caifi; we had our immigration problems too. Don't you worry." The green eyes of a tiger, a street kid, a woman so generous and full of courage it has taken the form of a crust. "Okay."

And so we made the drop. We're clean. When they come there will be one harmless roll of movie film we forgot: street scenes on the way to Nelufar's: a donkey, a woman washing clothes in a canal, a flower seller, children of poverty, middle-class apartments, a man washing his car. And only one notebook, the one I carry with me today, fresh. Anything I write down or tape from now on will be for the eyes of my accusers, the ears of the prosecution. There are nice humorous possibilities in that. Beyond the surreal fears. Because the two are always together, in paranoia, in totalitarian states. Reza does that beautifully in his writing. I wonder if he's safe. And the Caifi guys. Intrigue and more intrigue.

There is also the sheer ordinariness of apartment house life, the concierge when we arrive at the other Nasrin's place, the teenage offspring, the din of rock music in another room behind a closed door which the sociable among us open occasionally for a shot of this universal opiate, even a little studio with an oil on an easel, and Nasrin's drawing board. But the rest of the place is a thing in itself, a creation, Nasrin's fantasy: chic illusion, futuristic lamps, elegant chairs and sofas, mirrors, pictures, even a Warhol of Marilyn.

First the intrigue of calling Paris, a more polished and political statement has been prepared and is to be phoned directly to the big press conference there where de Beauvoir is announcing the departure of the international delegation. The call is scheduled, parties wait

"The other Nasrin"

at the other end to receive it, the timing is precise. All the frustrations of governmental interference on calls made outside the country will be bypassed. And this achieved, our next problem, the more dangerous and immediate one will be addressed—expulsion.

The war council has been going on since the Iranian women arrived at the hotel to pick us up, the bunch of them: Kateh, both Nasrins, Nelufar, Ferdosheh, Resvan and Asad, all of them striding into the Intercontinental, braving the certain attention their presence will invite, the consequences, the risk. They have all come to be at our side. And to solve this thing. First of all, a petition will be brought to government by a delegation, protesting this unheard-of attack upon a feminist their group had invited to the country, a writer of international reputation, a great humanist—all the splendors of formal statement. That's the long-range plan. Today being Thursday, the delegation must wait until Saturday, after the government offices open again, after the Islamic Friday holiday tomorrow.

But an immediate strategy is necessary as well. The ministry, we must address ourselves directly to the ministry. Also indirectly. Someone knows someone. I smile, remembering the East, remembering Japan, the cousins and saké bottles that bought extensions on a visa. But this is earnest. There is call after call to be made. The minister himself bearded perhaps. After inquiries. After oblique means have pointed the way. There are also law and civil-rights champions to consult. There is a lot to do; we must do it at Nasrin's. "It's safe." Not at "our Nasrin's" who is young and poor and lives with her mother when she is not shunted about at night, in hiding in one house or another. The other Nasrin's is different, is safe; she has her own place, the offices of her decorating firm; she lives there as well. It's her own.

On the way there, racketing along in a car, we read the telegrams of support sent from women everywhere during the demonstrations. Even the United Nations. "We can use that one now," Kateh says. "We'll bring it with us to the ministry Saturday." How it all matters, receiving these pieces of paper. That first telegram of all, the one from UCLA, made Kateh's eyes fill up. Probably she was as unprepared as I—it seemed so random, such unexpected goodwill, the gesture of some undergraduates half a world away, the gratitude caught her by surprise. It was just as unlooked-for and eerie to find a telegram from Jacqui Ceballos coming from New Orleans. I knew her in the New York movement in the old days. And Bookie, wiring me here from Florida, an old friend and lover who has just reached me with a mischievous telegram: "Congratulations, you are scaring your mother even more than usual." I lean back laughing, fighting the sting in my

Nelufar pleading with ministers

eyes. . . . Bookie, if you only knew. Putting myself for a moment in a private and separate place, balancing the terror and the sweetness: hers, that of the women around me, Sophie's, even my worried mother's. Who could hardly—even if she's heard by now—be as worried as I. And yet we are rescued: all our friends are around us. Trust them. This is their place, they will know what to do. We are on our way to do it.

Looking around the room, it is pictures. Not paintings, not even the wonderful ubiquitous Marilyn presiding like a goddess, but photos, Sophie's flurry of photographing, seeing the shots as she makes them, for it is photography, this room, the present. If not the future. Modernistic, mirrored, prisms of light refracted. Its opulence, its possibility, its hedonism. Perhaps the very sheen of it accelerates my fright; shall we be punished the more for this? an ancient voice announces in my gut. That the room was beautiful, that the women were beautiful, intelligent, elegant. The voice of blood and poverty and hatred, the crone hidden in her veil, the pious, the barbarian past will loathe us the more that these few hours we were in Nasrin's illusionistic hideaway, time out of time.

The calls to Paris continue, are cut off and placed again, the waiting, the frustration, the women taking turns at the desk, the mirrors behind the desk, the curious lamp, the lights reflecting in mirrors that go on forever, more lights that reflect in the glass of the desk itself, the faces seen over and over, Sophie delighting in her effects. I would enjoy this another time, now all its aesthetic enticement is only more worrisome, more of a risk. The calls to the ministry are beginning. We sit now, the photographs are taken, Paris is as far away as ever, we are here. A different mood settles. The glamour and euphoria of the past hour, when we were the women of some time to come. Henceforward we are women of today forced to live in what is already our past. Controlling us still. The voices of my friends assuming the polite tones of wives dealing with relatives or acquaintances of husbands and uncles and classmates, wheedling a favor, a straw of information. Fumio getting me off the hook in Japan when I stupidly told the truth and admitted I had a job at the university, quite unaware I had no visa permit to work there. The smiles in the voices of my friends, the burdened courtesy, the social unction. The mouth going down as they lower the receiver: the tired look, the grimaces exchanged with one another. This is how one helps a friend against the powers that be, all over the world. And here they are helping us, my gratitude commensurate with my utter helplessness.

And it isn't going well. A lot of that is tactfully concealed, making me still more anxious; but what one sees emerge is not encouraging. It becomes clear that the order for expulsion has indeed been given. Several of our connections were still unaware of it—we began to get hopeful—it could be passed off as a press leak, a press error, mistaken identity, something that was said for effect but is not expected to be acted upon. Leeway. But Nelufar has come upon someone who finally confirms it. . . . "She will be expelled." He will say no more. When? Further calls to ascertain this. If we could know our schedule, the amount of time allotted to wheel, deal, change it, petition, protest, whatever. She calls another source. But there is no information on this point. Try another, a referral. He is near the government but not quite the government, or he is in the office, but not high up enough—it is very hard to follow—but in most conversations the ladylike behavior ends now in long impassioned arguments; all over again, they can't do this, it is unjust, philistine, uncivil. I love them for this, that they cannot control their final outrage.

Our Nasrin sits through the whole thing with something like a sneer: this is not her class, not her way to deal. Bourgeois garbage, the smoke says, breathing through her nostrils. Sure, I answer her with a look, a shrug, a mere echo of feeling that is without even gesture, still less words. It is like that in this room of mirrors and telephones. Like dope, the danger, like a rapport so perfect that the same existential fatigue is shared by all around the table. While the ladylike warriors continue on the phone: Kateh, Nelufar, the other Nasrin, still bravely trying their luck. Around our table that malaise of waiting for the end. The spirit sinks. In each of us. Looks are longer, embarrassed with impotence. The cigarette that awaits the inevitable knock, search, arrest. Ferdosheh listens to a little transistor radio, waiting till the expulsion is confirmed on the government's own station. Someone has already gone for the afternoon edition, the papers should be out by now.

These things are happening to me, I think; I am waiting to see my name printed as a kind of criminal, scandal, dishonor, danger. Finally. All the books. But we aren't a book. Crazy as this room is, we are women, ordinary persons, citizens law-abiding to a fault; the paradox of course, that our allegiance to the law as constitutional right has put us on the other side of the law—when government disregards law itself. As it becomes lawless, we are called lawbreakers. And we haven't a chance. They run it, they are the police and the court and the propaganda that deceives the masses. How long has this been going on? From the Inquisition to the Gestapo. The witch trials to Stalin. From the czar to Chile's junta. Has it always been thus? Or is it only getting worse? As our perception of it intensifies.

I am sick and would escape, the claustral panic big enough to

The radio confirms our explusion.

encompass a whole country. The mirrors constricting. No, comforting, a hideout, a safe place. But only for a few moments. Soon they will have to take me back to the hotel; I cannot be gone long. The hotel is where I should be at all times, in view. It is something we all agree on. When I left today, I gave careful instructions to the front desk that I would be visiting with friends for the afternoon only and would return exactly at five o'clock. No address. Driving here we took the most circuitous routes and for once can be sure we were not followed. All hotel cabs report their fares' destinations. The knowledge that our time is running out fills the room. Calls are still made but it is clear there are really no more to make. Kateh is getting legal advice, our last resort.

And the papers have come. "It's there." Kateh says it with the determined courage that makes her Kateh. The others groan and curse and we try to laugh. I look at the page, being unable to read my own name or know my sentence. "Interesting where they've placed us," Sophie says. Kateh grins, being unable to help it: in the adjoining columns are the faces of those executed today, the dead white faces photographed after being shot. I wince, being unable not to wince. "Still, some of them are Savak," Kateh says. "Some. But nobody got a trial." Like Nemat and Reza and the rest of us, she deplores the executions, the sham trials. Her eyes put out their amusement, their bloodlust after the hatred, the torturers, the ones covered with anathema. We exchange a glance. I know that whoever reads this paper will be as certain that I am an enemy of the people as are these dead, these terrible pale faces, the rows of them. Kateh has just discovered it. The adjustment between our different selves, ages, cultures, experiences shifts to a deeper level. Around us, the circle of women bending over the page: the dead, and next to them this news. I ask for a copy of the paper; Kateh hasn't read it yet, she'll bring it to me at the hotel next time. Something forms around us all these moments we stare at the page.

It is still there in the hall as we prepare to leave, to take a pee, to find a pair of gloves, to have another look at Nasrin's oil painting. A rather saccharine rendition of a flower. She is enormously pleased with it, one cannot say anything unkind. Or even unjust, since one picture never really predicts another; one could do schlock for years and then suddenly make something good. This is her first oil, encourage her. Then play with her drafting board while you wait for Sophie to emerge from the toilet, decide to buy one for the farm, to draw plans for the artist's shacks at the colony there; you imitate your father in many things, why not this too, he was an engineer. Odd fond thought of a father and his board and his angles of lovely clear plastic, a triangular ruler, a T square. Odd fond thought when you remember he is dead and you are a wanted person about to get arrested, expelled and yet staying on in a strange place. Yet what's strange about it? women standing in a hall all talking at once: if anyone else wants to go, you better do it now, it's a long drive back. The familiarity of all this.

"By the way, we are going to the country tomorrow. Would you like to come?" "Sure—could I leave the hotel?" "Why not? It's Friday, the ministry isn't even open. They can't arrest you"—our Nasrin grins—"it's their day off." "Great, I'd love to go." Sophie too. "Where will you go?" "There's a place. It's our practice to go into the country together. To spend the day. To recreate ourselves, you see. After our work, just to be together. Simply to enjoy." How civilized, I think, how wise. "It helps us to go on; it's actually a necessity," they laugh. "And our countryside is beautiful, you'll love it."

They are Persia and the government is merely something else. And their country is Persia seen at last. The mountains. The flowering trees. "It's spring now." A garden. Women in a garden with blossoms and small new flowers. Yes. Yes. Yes. Sanity. All the way back in the car I am warm with their love. Safe in it. We make jokes about our situation. We are sane.

4 ✳ ✳ ✳

THE BATHROOM, a hotel bathroom, its light a curious modern fixture, the fluorescent radiance it gives off vibrating somehow, the artifice of artificial light still more suspect, nervous, claustral, a room without a window. As the room beyond, the hotel room itself, the bedroom/sitting-room seems sealed too, despite one large window onto the guns of the road, the night shots, the militia stopping cars, the executions. If we open the window, a vast sliding thing never really meant to be opened since the place is both heated and air conditioned with processed air controlled by the powers downstairs, a blast greets us reminding us we are not to take these liberties with our environment. At night we are afraid to open the windows lest we call attention to ourselves, paranoia imagining the guards outside know our floor since all the staff do now.

When Mina checked us into the room we will keep for the duration—whatever that will be—the clerk, "knowing all about us," chose to remark that I had come here "to seduce Persian women." Then some smut that infuriated Mina. The sting of insult. The moment when you must cover yourself, show no anger, appear to be amused. Or nonchalant. Or unable to comprehend the nastiness practiced upon you. The invasion of privacy by a stranger, a hostile and judgmental stranger for whom your way of life is koranic anathema. I've faced bigots, religious and otherwise, through some ten years of gay polemic, but how will Mina take this? As further unnecessary trouble, a side issue, a special and further complication in an already awkward case? She takes it very well. Considering that we are putting our last money in this part of the world into a hotel room for which they are charging us seventy dollars a day, it does seem outrageous that this bully can object to our choice of a bed. Sophie looks uncertain. Dammit, I think, I am being robbed, I might as well be comfortable.

Lined up before the counter, the three of us look at each other in exasperated mirth, I explain all over again that the rooms with the double bed have more sitting-room space, and a nice large sofa. Their color arrangement is also less offensive than the bilious yellow in the cramped twin bedrooms. That seemed a good enough reason to ask for a double room. The "political significance" of the entire exchange cannot make an impression on me. Not yet. Charges of "perversion" and the like seemed out of place in this transaction, absurd. This is neither a time nor place where one feels like making love. Though the comfort of sleeping near each other is precious now, we have only felt free enough to make love once since our arrival, and a twin bed worked nicely. I have forgotten sex, we think now only of survival.

Brushing my teeth now, thinking of survival. Fighting nausea. In the privacy of the bathroom, remembering how I blew up last evening, how I need, really need the comfort of a daily martini. As Claudine needs baths. As Sophie finds she needs coffee now, is constantly annoyed if without it. As we fight tears now. Many forms of hysteria. Quarreling, for one. I shudder at how we are ragged with each other now. The obstacle of the brush in my mouth, choking me. You lose your temper; you need booze. Interesting to do a little study on booze and totalitarian life. Is that what pressure does to people, to relationships? What about the entire civilian population outside the Intercontinental who are forbidden booze? Does the black market save them? And you quarrel. We are quarreling, who have lived together nearly three years now in perfect harmony and even with great politeness, without quarreling. It shames me that I lose my temper, am short, petulant about little things. Scared.

And the egotism, the megalomania this situation brings with it. Reporters after us continually as the subjects of scandal and punishment, we are the center of interest, even as suckers, victims; the "Gary Gilmore" syndrome of the press. But what illusions it precipitates, what meanness of mind, what specious self-importance. At the very moment one would like to be good, gallant, gutsy, fine—in fact really needs to be good, has to be—this corruption sapping one's slender courage, tearing our purpose out of our hands and converting it to other purposes. News. Entertainment. Comedy.

The interesting parallel between brushing one's teeth and examining one's conscience. Logically I think of my mother. "Mother Millett," her daughters call her archly, my sainted Irish mother in St. Paul, I say to my friends, camping the provinces, the Catholicism, the sod. And suddenly I'm weeping. Realizing with a terrible force how much I love her, how fine she is, how real in the midst of this unreality, cops and media freaks. Consulting her instinctively, as the faucet splashes and swirls carrying the toothpaste away, consulting her like an oracle. Staring at the mirror, the flickering lamp, the fan whirling its artificial air—what would she think, what would she have me do?

Get the hell out of here, of course; my mother is a discreet soul, fond of respectability, timid before authority. She was opposed to my coming here at all, wept on the phone, keened her terror and disapproval. She is American, Midwestern, peasant become middle class, she is convention itself. But that's not all of it. She is also a woman who followed every step of Gandhi's marches through India to the sea and even to independence. Followed him with the obsessive interest you would need to keep track of such events from St. Paul, its press and radio. And every day she would discuss him with me. Probably no one else to talk to. I fell for it. In fact I was the advocate on days she doubted him, wondered if this guy was just the nut everyone said he was, this fasting business, for example, the whole big gamble he was making against an empire. Because the guy was a gambler. Not Daddy's kind, the kind that would blow a month's salary on a horse race, but another kind, worlds away, who could gamble as if morality were money and you bet your integrity against the other guy's shoddy bullying and spread the two before the world and waited for a verdict. Being little and poor. Even making yourself poorer, on behalf of the poorest—we loved the spectacle. We were a woman and a girl, a housewife and a schoolkid thousands of miles away, following this man as if he had invented an entirely different form of statecraft. Because of course he had.

And all these years since I have aspired to satyagraha I have her to thank for it. Because she is a woman in love with morality. Moralistic at times, and we quarrel over that, but it's the lesser part, merely the world she inherited. For the rest, it was a world she helped to give me, this reverence, this passion for Gandhi. And King. A young sculptor just home from two years in Japan, I watched the great march on Washington on the television with her, the two of us sitting on the floor, crying into our tomato sandwiches, unashamed at grandeur. Sorry as I was that I couldn't be in Washington to see it, hadn't come east yet to be there with my friends. I was still very glad it was mother I saw it with. No one better to share that moment with. Odd our political rapport, the way we call each other at every turn of national event: nomination, war-mongering, Kennedy assassination, the long distance we consume in our curious confabulations. So I can summon her now, hearing the scold and worry in her voice, the rebuke and the pride and the consternation: "You had better get yourself together, Katie Millett, you are going to have to be pretty brave from now on. And sensible, for God's sake be sensible."

Then the dim figure of Gandhi, filtered through books, biographies, definitions of nonviolence, his own and others', Bookie's psycho-literary sermons, old photographs. Surely he was up against something bigger than this, he was imprisoned innumerable times, long terrible stretches. And the hunger strike, the tactic of the suffragists. Get ready: a little guts and diplomacy and some largeness of spirit are going to be required now. This is not ordinary life where the stakes are books and pictures; this is tougher, and you didn't need it, are not really made for it, would never have sought it, but somewhere you had all these dreams too. There's a price, a risk, playing this high; having stumbled into this game, you could leave, there's a plane leaving every morning, you were expected to be on the one taking off right now. But having elected to stay, having bet on staying, play well. This is not a card game, drop that metaphor, this is for women. Here and everywhere. And for any noddy of a citizen to whom the worst befalls and it does, daily. And for peace, the idea of peacefulness. Nonviolent satyagraha. It is silly that someone like me is supposed to shoulder all that, but then it's silly of them to put me in this position. I have the feeling this is all some comedy of errors, theirs, mine, fate's own.

Remembering Elaine's simple formula for holding a full-fledged international press conference—just Scotch-tape a note to the pillar by the front door announcing a time convenient for the press corps, an hour or two before the event, and presto; I have betimes scrawled my message and approach the desk for the rental of a conference room. I am giving my own press conference. In response to all the requests for a statement on my expulsion, I will make one now finally and take any questions. This is necessary simply to stop the hounding, the sixty-two daily calls to our room. And to reply to the expulsion itself. Peacefully, reasonably, civilly, gently. To question why it should ever have been issued, even to open the door for it to be withdrawn. But, also, if it will not be, to assure the authorities I am ready to comply, would like only for a date to be given me. And if possible, a reason.

If the government corresponded with me through the media, I can do the same. Having no alternative; the offices we called yesterday never replying, never returning calls, are closed now today due to the holiday. This being the case, the hotel will not be busy either, all the meeting rooms will be free, the press corps will also be at leisure and even bored. They profess themselves delighted to come, and the lobby is abuzz with them. The manager, or rather the undermanager's assistant, is happy to book a room, he will just have a word with his supervisor as to the choice of room and the price. Very well. The undermanager himself, a very hotelier type, swallowtails and all, is not nearly as willing; he must consult the manager himself. Who will not be in for an hour. This is awkward, much time has been wasted already. The conference is due to begin in forty-five minutes. There are rules, I am told. One must apply the day before. This is not what I was told. I was misinformed. Could an exception be made because of my error and on the precedent of all the other press conferences which are held here at a moment's notice? Several a day, at times. And also because it is the holiday and the rooms—I have seen them—are self-evidently free and therefore for rent. Undermanager is becoming pasty-faced, angry, rude. We must wait for the manager, in any case.

Very well, I will give the conference in my room. That is forbidden. Why? No reason. Then I will give it in the suite of one of the American networks, they have offered it to me. That is also forbidden. Why? Because it is.

As we argue this back and forth like terriers, the annoyance rising, a presence bursts upon us, someone pushes me hard from behind, then a man nearly crazy with rage is standing before me shouting me down, shaking his fist in my face. He is presented as the manager. A goon, a soldier or thug in fatigues who would have difficulty getting a room in this kind of hotel. A brute posing as an innkeeper. He is the Komiteh boss. The journalists ready their cameras, a television crew moves in. I am too frightened to remember to turn on my idiot tape recorder. In a moment he will knock me out and it will be a terrific story. I am petrified. He is screaming for my key. He is going to throw me out of the hotel. Why? What have I done? My room is paid through tomorrow. Mad thoughts, I don't even ask for extra towels, I make my own bed, never play the television because I hate it and it never has anything on it except mullahs and giraffes.

Why? I ask again, the effort of reason, calm. He can't kick us out; we have no other place to stay and the government must know where we are. "You will not speak in this hotel," he shrieks. Curious price to put on a room, free speech itself. "You will not speak in your room or in any other room, you will not say a word in this hotel." I almost laugh. The journalists do. Apoplectic irrational fool, who the hell do you think you are? He's God, that's who, and seven times more wrathful—so shut up. We are all silent. Only Sophie persists. "I demand to know the meaning of this"—praise be, for British interrogative hauteur. "You come inside," he bellows at her, pushing her into his office. They won't let me follow. "Don't worry, I'll handle this." She disappears into the office behind the desk. The big door closes on her.

Now I really have to worry. But I will appear not to. If it costs me my life I will not be bullied this way, forced to surrender even dignity and calm. My legs rattle. I'll hold my ground the only way I can—sitting down. I order coffee. Gandhi would have done this, a mad twinkle in the eye of the mind, surely Gandhi would have outraged them further with the quiet urbanity of ordering a little something since this is a place of comfort, an inn. Even a swank hotel. And I must not turn into a puddle on the carpet or cringe while waiting for Sophie's fate and my own. Instead I will play the traveler, the lady ordering a coffee, the civilian, the well-mannered provincial, the peaceful one. To my astonishment the waiter brings it. With a sneer. Never mind, I smile sweetly and tip him. And the press keep their distance, knowing that I am really in danger if I speak to them now.

Behind my newspaper I try to think. Abandoning the irritation of print, I try even harder to think. Stared at but making myself alone, calm, the hand controlling the cup, the coffee, refreshment: the ethos of a cup and saucer, contemplate that; the rugs and the service, the spoon, the lovely sugar pot: hotels should be places of refuge, inns, they should never be part of the government, dens of thieves and spies, functionaries of the police. Here in a cup and saucer, here in a spoon and a silver-plated service, here in sugar and cream, things that have withstood time and become order; think of the teacups in Persian miniatures, see them. Hold on. A plan had formed behind the newspaper. I test it now, sitting up, being seen, the brazen looks of waiters and reporters, the bloody technological eye of the lens. It sees everything—it could see you leave. You know, you could do it in the road. "Do it in the road," the Janis Joplin of that.

They don't own the road. Or they haven't claimed it yet. If you do, if you go there, they may bust you. You could get arrested for real.

Still, the hotel, forbidding you to speak under its roof, cannot forbid you to speak in the roadway outside. Though the government sure as hell can, they own the road and the grass and the land, they have expropriated the earth and the sky. That's the chance you take. But the gamble is that they wouldn't dare, not yet, not on international television, where the very manner of your being taken would be open and seen, not the knock unheard in the empty corridor, the early-morning bust they gave to Ralph. So play it? You get to show up the hotel—pacifist strategy of demonstrating its discourtesy, sheer unfair-ness, arbitrary behavior—it has branches all over the world—and you get to say what you want in addition. Because by now I have plenty I'd like to say. I undertook this thing first because I was asked, the press wanted to question me and I could do it in one go, instead of twenty interviews. But now, prevented from speech, I find I am burning for it.

I also realize at last its danger. Free speech. Run your mouth, it had always seemed so easy: press releases nobody ever read, Caifi's little effort here, all the Xerox copies run off at home and disregarded. They ignore you. That's censorship too. But when they tie a gag around you, threaten to toss you into the road houseless—then? The hotel may really expel you now, never mind how dare they. See what Sophie says; if we act very quietly, and if they'll let us stay—then I'll do it. Hell, do it anyway, do it on your way to the airport or to some other hotel; you might try the Park Hotel. See what Sophie says, see what she thinks.

Our French sisters wanted no part of this press conference, preferring to lie low; will Sophie have had enough of my defiance, this holy rolling of our dice? I sit like an imitation Gandhi, sipping coffee with aplomb, an epicurean on the plush sofa with the plush red rug, wondering if they'll beat me as they take me away. I believe I have never been this frightened in my life; I am positive I have never contemplated such a gamble, done anything this rash (but I will do it with infinite gentleness, calm, quietude), been in a place so dangerous and had to be so brave, find this much courage for the sake of a principle. Because they must not be allowed to shut me up. Me or anybody else. One thing to expel and persecute a traveler, but to forbid one a voice is still worse. I am entitled to my opinions, particularly when it appears I may be permitted nothing else. And at this moment I am feminism in a fight they are calling espionage, imperialist provocation or whatever craziness they can get by with —if I can tell my side, the truth has a chance. I have a chance. The women here will have a chance to go on. Rather than be silenced. Because that's how it might go. Throwing out the foreign females could be the prelude. If I can stay till the next lot comes. If I can go on telling it like it is.

Sophie says it's bad. They have been watching us since we came. Have tuned in on every phone call. "He tells me so himself—'we have followed you, listened to you, watched you each moment'—he was screaming." "Who in hell is he?" "He's the government." "He says he's the hotel." "Same thing." "What does he say—can we stay?" "Only if we shut up." "Where?" "Here." "What if I talked out in the road?" A slow smile; she can't help it. The naughtiness, but the risk, "You want to?" "Yes. You know, Sophie, if we went out very slowly and quietly, if we play it cool. There's some grass over to the left-hand side, past that fence. I expect their land ends with the fence. Wouldn't it be nice to be outside?" Already the sun and the cool air. "Okay."

We were to have gone to the country today, but it has been decided it's too risky. Even a few moments in the real air, the real light. I go through the door, smiling at a doorman, gathering magic where I can. This man knows me for a Savak spy or something, thinks I'm a witch. But he's still capable of humor and a grin. The media really are not, they march as gravely as I do down the stairs and across the drive. "Kate, look this way," directed as in a B movie. I walk along, alone now, Sophie is shooting, she too is a reporter this moment, I am on my own. This enormous task. "We are leaving the Hotel Intercontinental with Kate Millett, who has been forbidden to hold a press conference here . . ." Take that, reputation for hospitality, I grin inside. Before I recover my awe at what I must say, how well I must say it; the whole matter of expulsion, how reasonable, how full of peace it must be. The struggle of women here. Gentleness. Gentleness the most important thing, not to draw the violence in this situation, to neutralize it with goodwill, a little humor, a large compassion, logic, care for principle. But gentleness, that most of all.

5

I PACE AND THEN STARE out the window. And then pace again. Throw myself in a chair and then pace some more. The mountain is right there. Just beyond the glass it seems. You could touch it. Walk there. Can't afford to order from room service anymore, can't afford the restaurants, can't afford to be seen, pursued still further by reporters, resented still more by the hotel. Can't walk in the hall. Even the bloody rich person's bookstore in the basement is closed. It's Sunday—or rather Friday, which is Sunday here. Everything is closed. And our friends went to the country without us. We're too hot to travel. Certainly to travel with. And today it's dangerous, even to be in the street is forbidden us today—our friends insist upon it.

The chador parade. I had actually wanted to go see it. Watch politely from the curb. "You're nuts." "Then I'll wear a chador—Elaine gave us each one." "I will choke rather than wear a chador," Sophie says. "But they're pretty, given the right circumstances they're a beautiful garment. If you wore it 'cause you felt like it—" "That is the point, I don't feel like it." Every time we get dressed up in them, the rest of us, playing with them, playing dress-up—for many reasons: first of all to see what it feels like, something we need to know, and then for the fun of it, to see how we look, to see how the fabric accents the cheekbones, frames the brow, makes nearly all of us look Persian, even Semitic—and every time, Sophie refuses. "Maybe you wouldn't even look like a Scot, a Saxon." "I am not a Saxon, I am, like you are, nitwit, a Celt." "Well, you know what I mean—it would be an experience for you to see yourself in one." "No, it wouldn't. Not here. Not now. Maybe someday. But not now."

As if the cloth were magic, were contamination. Whereas I love my chador, or rather the two chadors Elaine lent us for protection, they are invaluable when room service knocks and one is in the bath; I am scheming to buy one of my own on a trip to the bazaar. "If we could go out I could buy one." "Listen, if you showed your crazy little face at the chador parade, they'd pull you to pieces." "But I'd be invisible." "If they found a foreigner disguised in a chador—they'd stomp you to death." "Understandable, in some respects." "Exactly." "But still, xenophobia, classic case." Sophie sniffs. She has spent a lot of time in the Near East. "Doesn't all this tribalistic business bore you, don't you find it silly, reactionary, narrow-assed? Masculine? Oppressive? Oppressively masculine?" "There's the question of Muslim independence." "Yeah, but the tribe just reinforces patriarchy. Nationalism always gives me the creeps that way." "Well, we're staying home." "Claudine and Sylvina are out there somewhere today, braving the masses." "They aren't in the papers yet, they can afford to." "But they look like foreigners, more than I do. And they have a movie camera." "They didn't go to the chador march; they're interviewing Iranian women now because they are going home tomorrow." "If only we could have gone to the country." "It was too dangerous to go to the country. Compose yourself. We're staying home." "Home, Sophie, don't you realize we're imprisoned here?" "At least it's comfortable."

But it isn't Persia. The mountain is Persia. Right beyond the window. And in an hour, or tomorrow, which is Saturday, a working day for officers of the state, cops, gunmen, I will be taken away from Persia without ever having seen it. I loved the revolution and it went away. But Persia is still there in the mountain. There are flowers on its sides, it is spring. I needed that day away from here. The miniatures are locked away behind glass in the shop downstairs, the museums have been closed for weeks. The rug museum is only next door, but it has been closed all along. Now even the people we know here cannot see us, be seen with us. And the mountain is all that's left. I have a special relationship with this mountain, talking to it in my mind, communicating with it as a living symbol, as it must have been for so many people here so many hundreds of years; the rulers good or bad or changing or falling from favor and a poet or a water carrier or a courtier or a poor woman talked to that mountain. And it heard. Or didn't hear and it didn't matter a damn because the talk was made, the wish, the heart sent upon the beam of the eye toward the great white mystic sum of Persia.

It will always be Persia to me. Not Iran. A good word too, even ancient, but tainted by government, recent Shahs, the Pahlavi dynasty, armies, tanks, oil and ambition. Persia is for sure: for sure the poets, the miniatures, courtly love and the rose. The rose came from Persia. Rugs, colors, pictures, the infinite grace of gestures, objects, the noble courtesy of this culture. The music in old songs we never heard, music having disappeared here now; but old songs from the West even, early music, Renaissance sounds, the tones of ancient instruments, the half-tones that came back with the Crusaders, minor modes. And this mountain. All that's left at the moment, for us. The last taste, the only morsel in view, the tantalizing hope. If one could run away to that mountain and stay awhile—the absurd fantasy occurring—so much I hate to leave. Without ever having had the place. No country, not even Japan, can withstand the assaults of a lover, close itself forever. After six months in Japan I nearly despaired of the language and the race and the culture standing between us. So I gambled. Even when my money was gone, I bet on three more months. And I did break through. After two years I went home rich in friends, a bar-Japanese lingo, even an exhibition there.

"You know, this is the first time I've ever been in the whole Near Eastern world and I get my ass kicked out of the country." "Mazeltov." "Here we are, dying to love the place and we meet all these wonderful women—" "And Vice Premier Entezam takes it into his head to toss us." "It's funny." "It's awful." "It is becoming very boring too." "Why don't you take a walk and go see yourself on television. ABC is rewinding that tape they did outside the hotel this morning. You might as well look at it; the film I did on the Bolex is probably going to end up on the floor of some cop shop or out at the airport." "Okay." "Just have a look at it, see if maybe they'll give us a strike when we get home. They said they'd be glad to show it to you, take them up on it."

Negotiating the corridors and the elevator and the looks in the elevator and then the media persons themselves: the nice woman who offered to show me the tape, the big shots eating their lunch with a real tablecloth and an ice bucket, and the technical man who knows so much he winds it on backwards and you must shut up until he gets it right and then watch yourself to see if you are getting better or if your chin is getting worse, your aging Irish chin. Forget your chin—see if you are learning how to speak, to persuade, to be honest and look it. You are tired and scared and you look it. Okay, are you quiet enough, centered enough, or all running off in nervous tangent? Bit of each. It's like drawing the nude—you never do learn it. A man talks loudly over my voice, a journalist kibitzing. I even have the nerve to ask him to let me listen to myself. Amazing egotism. But then, I gave these people this, my work, done with the most difficult effort and concentration: they are selling it along with orange juice and Coca-Cola and Chevrolets as entertainment. Like art dealers. Worse, I wonder if they will give me a copy of my own work which they now own and could forbid me even to see. Looking, through their benevolence, at the face on the box: now she's talking about the executions, justice and open trials, the threats to the rights of women, their struggle here. And then the little image, the postage-stamp face winds down, disappears into static.

Back again for one little extra take, a woman has come out of the crowd demanding all hear her—I remember her now, just at the end. Even the reporters shrugged and said she was a plant. Many refused to film her. This cameraman has her for only a few moments and even then her English—for she had to speak English to do this job right— undid her. So bad it was. So incoherent. Even a few words pronounced slowly and carefully would have done the trick for her, discredited me utterly. I was lucky. But I am also intrigued; the betrayal of women by women is always fascinating. Instructive. Even though you felt, didn't know for sure, but felt, with perfect assurance, that she was not merely part of fanatic Islam, but paid to do what she did: denounce the women's demonstrations, call the feminists prostitutes, communists, foreign agents, blame it all on foreigners. But when I looked her in the eye there was a flicker. I was not angry, only interested. Even sympathetic. That caused the flicker. Wondering what her life is like, what it was like to work with the men she must work with, what does she do with the money? How many children?

The women at the chador march are of course archetypal; they will look like her too, but in chador. Long files of black obedience, like nuns, like ravens, like hags—the centuries of that disguise. They will be the women of the attackers, some of the pious come from the mosques. Buses of them will come, the government boasts that one million people will come to this march. The women walking behind probably, since Islam frowns on mixed marching. Perhaps it was that the women in the insurrection were forced to march alone, by themselves, because women—that precipitated their consciousness of themselves as women and therefore the women's demonstrations which this demonstration is meant to contradict, outdraw and put an end to. Will it work?

Because today is to mark the end of the period of women's protest. The beginning of the end of possibilities for women was marked already by the protests themselves. If protest is hereafter discouraged, forbidden, made in some outright or even unconscious way no longer possible, viable—then what? As Kateh has pointed out, my expulsion is the first official act of this government against organized feminism. The women here are still looking for an office. Other feminists arrive on Monday. I have only to hold out till then.

Then someone else carries the ball, lifts the stone: we are democratic and we are many; no one is expected to go the distance. You have these jobs for a while and then another sister is there to do it: write the tract, talk on the radio, chair the meeting. You go back to your life as an artist. If you can stay out of jail. If they don't make an example of you in a foreign country which would not even require you break a law before you're busted, since they are not about to put up with your civil-liberties fussiness and could care less about your constitutional safeguards, lawyers and rigmarole. And therefore could do anything they wanted to you. Anything. Torture. Long sentences. The two together—you know the methods from before—you used to make speeches about them. Any indecency. Any immorality, against the spirit, the body, the mind. Anything by way of information, informing, turning in your friends here, any phone numbers, names, addresses.

So we have transcribed all contacts and phone numbers into code in a separate notebook, a code of Roman numerals, here in the home of the Arabic number. They are all in one notebook, the notebook of last resort. And they are safe. Childish scrawls, drawings of our friends only we can understand because the caricatures are agreed upon, the sobriquets, artful, nonsensical, a combination of childish reasoning and hippie dope talk and bohemian daubing. What is not safe is my address book itself, the four pages of Iranian names that we must save from arrest, destroy. The presence of mind to protect them, all of them, all the women. And the men too, the men of Caifi. In the code notebook, Bahram is a square, for example, because I decided his face had a squarish cast. Sophie hadn't even noticed it. And Kateh is "bright eyes" not only because her eyes are indeed bright, even sparkle, but because such an asinine name is safety, the showgirl trivia of it is a protection in itself. Nelufar is Sorbonne in honor of her education; her house is color crayon. We rehearse sentences in this silly code: Tough break we didn't shoot crayon and get the stained glass (moving pictures) before the fuzz hit the shit. A language of paranoia, put on, Terry and the Pirates and madhouse poetics. A joke growing earnest.

In the middle of the night trying to tell a friendly woman journalist (she is to buy pictures from Sophie, I am to write a piece for her or be interviewed and she needs another contact in case I am arrested) how to reach us through Nelufar and making her remember, over a bugged phone—so bugged that if you give out a number they disconnect you while the eavesdropper downstairs gets a pencil to write the number down—dragging this overwrought American female in her New York office into my necessarily paranoid conspiratorial line of thought, and like a kindergarten teacher explaining the Roman-numeral system to someone who has forgotten it. And since one says "Two" in English, I must talk her a picture of Two. "Think of a wedding cake," I say, frantic to think of a symbol (if only she had been in civil rights and knew "Green grow the rushes Ho" and the lily-white boys, this could be a delight). "What on earth are you talking about?" "A friend, I am talking about a friend, and you are interested and we are continuing this conversation in case I should become indisposed . . ." "Just tell me where you'll be." "This telephone resembles a sieve, do you follow me?" "No, I don't really." "Well, draw two parallel vertical lines on a piece of paper and concentrate. I must speak to you in poetry." "Huh?" "Poetry, a term of the mad or the cunning, follow me?" "Nope."

Probably thinks I'm bonkers. Has never been mad, has no appreciation of symbols, the language used in that frame of mind, as far as I can ascertain, the lay equivalent of poetry. "Let's try again. Wedding cake." "Huh?" "Just follow me patiently for a moment." It's four-thirty in the morning; she called me, I'm being patient, why can't she? "I'm trying to figure out what you're talking about." "For reasons of safety [if she were quicker I could say "sanitation" or "sanity," but forget it], I must talk to you in pictures. Think of a wedding cake." "Okay." "See it." "What d'ya mean?" "See a wedding cake, visualize the thing." Keep your temper. "All right." "At the top are a bride and groom. A pair." "Two of them?" "Shhh, a pair. Now make a mark for each of the pair." "Okay." "Did you? Are you looking at the lines?" "Yeah." "Okay, put a roof and a floor, top and bottom. No . . . don't say what you see, but realize it is a pictogram, a picture with symbolic meaning, like a letter or a numeral or Chinese characters." "Oh, it's a—" "Shhh. Now: wedding cake, wedding cake Victor." "Hah?" "Come on, you know Victor, the operator uses him to help you with exchanges, Victory, Viking." "But—" "It's like wedding cake. The Romans have a way with everything and you're into Latin now." "Boy, I just wish you'd tell me and get it over with—this is long distance." "Listen, buddy, this is longer distance than you think. Draw what I say and see it." Cursing people who cannot draw a straight line and see meaning in it, know nothing but numerals and words and can miss the whole world in between and land Nelufar in a cop car, her children watching, stunned figures by a doorway. Hermoz. I must protect them. On with it, till every digit of that phone number is safe.

For by now a handsome man Sophie burst in upon and discovered in his Jockey shorts, his face covered with shaving cream, a reporter from this woman's magazine, has smuggled all our stills back into America to be printed. Part of our work is already safe. The tapes and the movie film are still with Carole. Her French lady had tea but insufficient sympathy, and the diplomatic pouch is no longer safe in any case. Yesterday the letters of the French ambassador were opened, they say. We will go on waiting. We may still lose it. They may nab Carole, but she's chipper about it. Time. Patience and time.

Wending my way back to the room, nearly at the end of patience. The elevator will stop. I'll be trapped. No, it's fine, there's even a man on it with me, once my enemy, now curiously my friend. He who had been so obnoxious over the "Isn't Khomeini a male chauvinist pig?" question, bullying in his rather Mid-Atlantic accent, persisting so maliciously, so eager to skewer me. And today he is so different. Not even the journalistic buttering-up, the palsy-walsy so they can quote you as having said some frivolous unguarded thing; no, after today's press conference, having seen me alone there and so frightened and trying to do the thing with honor, there is now something kind about him. Almost respectful. The continuous difficulty of having to deal with people who treat one with persistent contempt. Saying good-bye at the elevator door, he no longer treated me with contempt.

That is still not quite enough for today's paranoia, however, I deliberately get off at the wrong floor so that our room will not be invaded. But then the elevator will not come to take me from six to seven. Walk. They are stuck again. Walk. Are there even stairs in this place? Fatigue under pressure producing a little mad episode; I am convinced there are no stairs. That they actually have hotels now without stairs. Belief in technology, blind idiot naiveté, has gone this far; you can see it everywhere, why not here, what with the Shah's worship of American "modernity"—they must have gone right ahead and built the damn thing without stairs, twenty floors. But in case of fire? It must be a law, everywhere it must be a law. My father was an engineer, he would have a fit—I am having one. Inconceivable. Finally an elevator. Just one floor. It takes forever. Will it jam, have they invented, finally, the perfect way for it to happen? I'll be alone. It will stop. And then they will recall it to the lobby, where the cop is waiting. It's going down. Fourth floor. They could do that too. Be waiting.

When I finally got back to the room, Sophie kindly took me into the hall and showed me the staircases. Two of them. Also a service elevator. A linen room. "Get a grip." "Sure, I'm sorry. I think I've already been to the worst place by now, I'll be all right from here on." Back in the room, watching the mountain. Grateful for that. Never mind that it is far. It is there. It is still there. From inside this glass box I can see Persia. Outside the streets teem with cars going home from the chador march which is not Persia, or is only what so long misrule has made it, folly and fanaticism, thugs walking the street; there will be a lot of people hurt today. The mountain watches back. It has seen worse; in a great civilization you see everything. Many times.

6

WE WILL HAVE to be careful, getting out of the car and walking the two blocks to Lahadji's office. We could be recognized, my picture has been in the news stories of our expulsion, It is not only the attackers who might go for me now, ruffians and outlaws; it is perhaps ordinary persons too, the persons who are generally curious or friendly with foreigners. Even the women, remembering how infallibly kind they were to a supporter in the marches. Now feminism is again a small band of devoted pioneers, the great numbers have not been built into a movement yet. But the office is coming; Kateh has had that on her mind all day. As well as our dilemma. Coming to the hotel this morning and taking charge of the great telephone marathon, our formal inquiry to the ministry. On Thursday their offices were shutting down for the afternoon as we tried to reach them, calling them as a last resort from Nasrin's. Then Friday, the holiday. Now, on Saturday morning, they should have a Monday morning's briskness—perhaps we will even be able to get through. For the ultimate frustration here is that the official telephones are always busy. One calls, and calls again, keeps calling, through coffee, trips to the bathroom, a glance at the paper; another ten minutes, another call. All calls must be placed through the leaky hotel switchboard. We joke that the hotel functionaries, who must have a better line, a private number, might just pass the message along: the culprits are trying to get through. Are breaking their necks to comply; are doubled over in servile compliance—how ridiculous that government makes itself inaccessible, redoubles its godlike power by issuing edicts and then making it impossible even to communicate one's willingness to obey. But we are still not on that plane. The last flights of the day are leaving now. As we place the call over and over again petitioning for a date, for some loophole, some dialogue. Dialogue is impossible when the busy signal lasts over two hours and forty minutes.

And then finally we do get through. I am holding the phone at the moment. I signal for Kateh, but meanwhile try in English to state my name and location. And ever so politely to broach the subject of clarification. "Give me your interpreter." "But, sir, you speak English." "I will only speak in Farsi." Funny guy, mean mood. "But surely it is possible to speak with me; am I not the one affected? I would take it as a great kindness if you would—" "Absolutely not," his voice furious, peremptory. "Your translator, or I will not speak." "Yes, sir." I hand over the receiver. "Here you are, Kateh, he's mad as hell."

She begins with the delicacy of a sparrow, the grace of a flower, listening to him, agreeing, enduring his tirade. She is charming, she is witty, she is infinitely respectful. He must be assuaged. But she is getting a word in. She is getting answers. "What's he say?" "So far he says you are expelled." Our hearts sink, this is confirmation from the office of the ministry itself; it is the press-conference remark bruited through the press and solidified now into a government order. Hard to take back, Kateh plays it for that now. And for time. For our excellent intentions to obey in everything, for our genial and eager desire to comply, to act in goodwill, with politesse. Only, if the government would be kind enough to state when it is they desire Miss Millett to leave? She is of course perfectly willing to do so, wishes only to avoid any awkwardness or embarrassment, unpleasantness of any kind. She is making her plans now—there is the matter of an invitation to speak at two different universities, surely you are aware she is a scholar of considerable repute?

The hell with that, one gathers from Kateh's expression at his reply, just as one gathers references from familiar names like Damovar and Tehran University, and the content from the tone itself: Kateh a nightingale, a court lady, a poet of elegant circumlocution. He is a bear. No—nothing—she signals, the play for time, the all or part of the next six days before the ticket is good. No concession. Well, what then? When does he want—what day? He will decide or confer and call back. But our attitude is established: we will be harder to get rid of because we are such conscientious objectors, our objections so soft and courteous, hardly objections at all.

And then it all takes a surreal swerve. Kateh must be arguing back. The arguments of a civil-rights fighter: legal, moral, political statements. From the hip. The head no longer bows, the automatic smile of the feminine, the well-bred, the female deferring before a powerful male. She holds her head straight while she talks, her eyes flash in anger or concentration on her argument, on his argument as he is making it and she is watching it for the points she will raise the second he has finished. She might be taking notes, so rapidly these brilliant eyes calculate. And then it goes further. She is talking louder. Then a retreat. A laugh, she has said something to make him laugh. But it is not the practiced servility of before, it is a laugh forced upon a man by a woman acting his equal. There is something shocking about it in these circumstances.

And now she's off, talking fast and hard and angrily, to the minister or subminister or subancillary aide to a minister or whatever he is, but she is telling him off. He is unjust and she can bear it no longer. I cross my fingers at the risk and forgive her whatever indiscretion this represents against our case. It is so beautifully on our behalf, the indignation such an act of friendship. And the fury is only our own, expressed for us. With a man who will order me out of the country while refusing even to condescend to talk to me. No paper, no written order, no charges laid.

This is what is being fought out now: the arbitrary extralegal character of their treatment of me. But he sails on righteously, he can order anyone out. Reasons needn't be given. But if you want some— she's an agent, a whatever. Kateh certainly won't let him get by with that. "Substantiate such charges." "Never." "You are absurd."

"Madam, you may consider yourself informed." And she sees it is hopeless, they are immovable—already I see her racing ahead to other solutions, informing him of our legal representation.

And like two contestants who have been in a clinch and then gone back to their corners, the final five minutes of this interminable phone call is winding down, subsiding, returning to official manners. "Get his name"—we hand the words to Kateh on a slip of paper. She tries again—for I had tried in the beginning and he refused ever to give his name or tell me what member or rank of the staff I spoke with. A thing bewildering: is no one responsible? And to my astonishment, it happens again—we have been ordered to depart by an official of the ministry who absolutely refuses to identify himself. To whom shall we refer then, later? Nobody. A nameless member of the ministry. High or low. Responsible or not. Nobody. Who also will not even tell us when. Or will tell us later today. So we should spend all of what little time is left us sitting by the phone. On Thursday we left several messages for calls to be returned from the ministry. They never were.

Moreover, I'd like to change hotels, move to the Park. The spying, the insolence here. And the reporters at every hour of the day and night, ringing our room, knocking on the door. The Park is quieter, better if we want to stay on, low-profile. This man should know that we may be at the Park if we are not here; Kateh conveys this as she rings off. Or rather, as he hangs up, the level of hostility mounting again, and I am not quite certain how it has ended, so outraged is Kateh, so annoyed, so embarrassed by her own—that odd way one can be embarrassed before others by the very officials one curses easily among compatriots.

It happens everywhere, we tell her: "Consider my case; I got married thanks to the United States Immigration Authority." "Since you are already married, perhaps that at least is not likely to happen here," Sophie laughs, pouring Kateh more coffee, the two of us consoling her as she consoles us. Because it's really trouble now, even Kateh's confidence is shaken, the optimism all the women here have been able to maintain. Bland, it had seemed at times to me and to Sophie; the Shah was gone, things had to be in order now, naive—with that naiveté one has about home—that they can make mistakes but can't really be that bad, even this government which none of them approves of, the old-guard bureaucracy. Now at least the civil forms would be respected, they believed. And they also believed, touchingly, that since I was a writer, a scholar, that would be honored in Iran. Of course it wouldn't mean a thing in America. But this is an older culture, more European than your New World, they seemed to imply: we are civilized. It was exactly the artists and scholars whom the Shah persecuted, even the religious dissenters—I would argue—ah, but that was the Shah, they would say, rolling their eyes, this is the new government, he is gone, the insurrection, this is a new government. And I see in Kateh's eyes, the future: she has met the new government on the phone. And it is not only my fate—tangential foreigner—but the chances for a movement of women here, those possibilities clouding over has put out the light in her eyes. I feel this sickening of hope keenly, like a sharp pain as I watch her.

But now she'll fight. She is back on the phone again. Lahadji himself. The man credited with stopping the executions as of yesterday. A great civil-rights lawyer here, a man who managed to stay alive under the Shah and to speak his mind as well, one of the heroes of the movement against the Shah, one of the bright lights around Martin Daftari. And Daftari, the one man who stands for constitutional government against the push from Khomeini, against the blank and probably tyrannous religious "constitution" that is to emerge after the mysterious Islamic republic is railroaded through a month from now. Endorsement of the undefined Islamic republic is virtually the only choice open to voters; the other ballot—the red one—would be to endorse the Shah. Something laughable, impossible now. So the little green counter (green for Islam) is to be handed in by all, literate and illiterate, the thing inspected and no secret. Only in Kurdistan will people refuse to vote at all. The Fedayeen protest the character of this election, but not strenuously enough. No other groups with any power denounce it. Except Daftari; if he were to regroup the liberal and radical element, if he were to be able to run for office . . . But there is now no mechanism for that. No one runs for office, there will be no election till after the "constitution" is written, many months from now, and the "constitution" is to be written by Khomeini and a pack of mullahs who will bypass democracy, constitutionality itself.

The old constitution of 1906, the only constitution—I hear Reza grumble in my head—the constitution he used to drone on about lovingly to bored little American undergraduates who weren't too certain just where Iran was and were incredulous of what he said about the Shah and his crimes, atrocities that nearly titillated them, so unreal they were—and the worst crime of all was what the Shah did to the constitution—at least to Reza it was—that document sacred to him as ours might be if we did not have the opportunity of taking it for granted . . . to Reza it was sacred writ, and justly so, because for two thousand years Persia had no social contract whatsoever between its rulers and its ruled and then in so few years to have the precious thing trampled by tyranny again.

And again now, new and fashionable tyranny, old and pietistic tyranny, medieval tyranny calling itself revolution, national dignity, freedom from evil colonial pillage. But really the same business wherein the individual again has no rights. And should the individual happen to be a woman . . . In the interim, we have the Bazargan bureaucracy, sinister as Kafka's imponderables. And perhaps as efficient in abuse as Savak. For all we know. But as labyrinthine in control as Stalin—we were soon to find. Trying to move over to the Park Hotel, we discover that they will not accept a reservation in the name of Kate Millett. Their front desk had been effusive hotelier courtesy as I asked about prices and rooms. As the arrangements drew to a close, I gave him my name—it is pointless to deceive them or pass this off, and it is of the essence that we act aboveboard, demonstrate our good faith to the government, even to the hotel that would house us, demonstrate it effusively. "May I ask why you will not take a reservation in this name?" "Madam, I am terribly sorry; we have government orders not to do so." "May I ask what official or what department has so ordered you, and when?" "But a moment ago. They left no name or rank."

"They operate like the Mafia," I say to Sophie. "Cowards," Kateh sneers. Centuries of her kind have said this and shrugged, certain spirits have always lived among lesser spirits, endured the oppression of their greater numbers, power, bigotry, rules, preventions. A Zoroastrian, to whom wine is part of family life, homemade wine, wine with meals, dinners with good wine your own mother makes—Kateh's has made it all her life—and now wine is forbidden to all because Islam frowns on it in the grimace of Imam. And Persian wine is excellent, centuries of cultivation of the stock, perfection in the art of the winemaker. "Of course," Kateh smiles. "It's crazy, isn't it?" "Crazy."

This afternoon we have an appointment with A. K. Lahadji. Nelufar will come in an hour to take us to our lawyer; Kateh will meet us there. Or rather at a certain corner near there. At one o'clock. Since I must not be seen in the street, we will meet in the car. "Be sure you stay in the car. Don't get out. Don't be seen. If I'm late . . ." We smile, having such an acquaintance of Kateh's lateness, everyone's lateness. "You understand it by now." "We do, really we do. So we'll just wait in the car." "Be inconspicuous." "We will, Nelufar will be with us, don't worry." She kisses us each good-bye. We become precious to each other.

So of course we are philosophy itself, waiting. Nelufar gets out and stands in the sun occasionally, looking up and down the road. Our last visit to Nelufar's house has shaken me. We stopped off on our way here, to have lunch, to say good-bye and take the last photographs of the "crayon room" where the meeting was held; this is our last chance to get them and we have a good courier to get them out of the country. To our astonishment, the room was transformed. It had been a bedroom, one of the girls' bedrooms, now it is a sitting room. As if everything in this house is conscious of the imminent arrival of the police. Lunch was very tense, Sophie wishing to film before the noon light went, Hermoz anxious we not let our asparagus grow cold. It is a delicacy that comes from afar; it is also all that he can do for us now, the last hospitality within his reach to extend since it is too dangerous for us to be his house guests. I am torn between the two of them, my duty to help Sophie and be sure we have the pictures, my compassion for Hermoz fussing over the asparagus. You're letting your asparagus get cold—how like one's mother he sounds, how like a nagging female relative. I love him for this last remnant of pride and dignity. But how pained he is, this handsome man, how terrible the pressure, the invasion of all our lives now by government, by fear, by waiting. Hermoz also has a bad gash on his forehead, an accident with the car yesterday. After lunch he and Nelufar go through documents and consult papers which seem to refer to their situation now, the possibility of her going into exile again. He seems to be protesting that they will fight it, there are lawyers, connections in politics, but he is clearly a brave man frightened, his life coming down around him. We are watching a family collapsing before the state. Leaving, I imagine the moment when officials will come up this walk, knock on the door by the cedar tree. Will they have to leave to prevent this, will they be able to get out in time?

Now we are waiting for Kateh. A busy street full of men, many of them young and with that aggressive hostility toward women which seems to increase here every day. Women of our kind. Women of Nelufar's kind. Or Kateh's. The telltale independence, the look of assurance or self-possession that is not the downward, erased look, the I-am-no-one look of invisibility and nonexistence, the only look condoned now. So we make ourselves small in the car, my back to the sidewalk, so that my face, either in its foreignness or in its familiarity from somewhere, will not be spotted. Sophie, who is fairer and more foreign-seeming, stays in the backseat, Nelufar alone venturing out to take an occasional hopeful look to see if Kateh is in sight.

Odd to be on the way to see a lawyer and huddling like culprits, not only from the police, whom we inform of our whereabouts moment to moment through the police auxiliary of the hotel desk and the frustrations of telephone messages to the ministry, but huddled like culprits from the very populace itself. Government makes you a pariah, elects to persecute you and in a day or so has the entire population hunting you. Or capable of doing so. The control assumed thus over human life. And so you smoke and avert your eyes from the normal curiosity of passersby, their curiosity, your own, the entertainment of the spectacle of a foreign place, days of seclusion in the fortress of the hotel, and now the liveliness, the delight of street life—is a threat as well. Turn your head away from the street and the handsome men striding by, mustaches, eyes—it is dangerous. Smoke and turn away from the boulevard, desultory talk with Sophie, there is nothing to talk about. Fear. A fear so engulfing it is ridiculous, demoralizing to face. You got yourself in one hell of a predicament. Keep your head toward the empty driver's seat, lower your eyes, rest your forehead on your arm as it rests on the back of the driver's seat. Sophie is invisible in the back, you are nearly invisible to the front and Nelufar alone ventures out to take an occasional hopeful look to see if Kateh is in sight. An hour of this and she is.

Lahadji is both impressive and comic. Correct with the rectitude of another culture, perhaps another century. The high starched collar is decidedly colonial. Bureaucratic. Like his card, like Elizabeth Street, the name of the street on his card, one is amused by the familiar British colonial ring to it, the Westernization. I am reminded of that amusement, always tinged with dismay, prompted by the signs on shops in Japan, signs in a kind of Ur English which is not English but an imitation that merely apes some lost model. Lahadji, on the other hand, has all his credentials in order, knows the law as well as any barrister, has worked with international committees, mentions Amnesty at once. I am flattered by his courtesy in regarding me as a colleague in civil-rights work. There are mutual congratulations upon work done in behalf of the political prisoners under the Shah. And my own admiration for the protection of rights he has undertaken here, surely a thing he is most courageous in doing, surely a thing unpopular with the new regime just now, surely a thing difficult to achieve. And he has just had a victory. His modesty shrugs it aside.

Why does he seem so old-fashioned, so foreign to Iran today, its mustached militia, its mullahs—does one have to look like the product of colonial education to stand for rationality here, the rights of man, eighteenth-century lucidity and measure? And a formality too. Of course he is acting as a legal adviser, a counselor to my indignation, a mediator to my hotheaded annoyance before what seems to me to be deliberate harassment—a counsel he is giving willingly, perhaps even for nothing (the situation is too grave to haggle over fees, probably no one else would even undertake what he is doing here) but there is soon the distance between us of the patient and the doctor, the choleric farmer arguing a fence line and the man of reason who attempts to negotiate.

And another curious note, the gallant, the paternal figure with the lady in distress. "Madam, have no fear." "But look, they could do anything they like with me. Could you outline for me exactly what my rights are at this time? Particularly at arrest." The high stiff collar, the thirties haircut; he is not that old a man, why does he seem so avuncular? He is perhaps three years younger than I. But a lawyer. Lawyers have that clerical way, that license to patronize. And I like him—yet I just can't get him to understand. "Of course you are upset." As if it were heartburn. "Of course. You know, the odd thing is that in all my work, in all these years of civil-rights work, I have, for some mysterious reason, never been arrested. So many times it was nearly inevitable, the antiwar movement particularly, yet by some accident I have never been taken into custody." "But of course you needn't worry about that." "But of course I do." "Madam, rest assured you will never be detained." Who is he kidding? Where is Ralph right now?— we have combed the world news for word of him. There is no sign of his landing in England as promised. "I'm sure you have nothing to worry about."

I am worried to death, I am frantic, my hands holding the foolish little tape recorder, then putting it on a desk so he is aware of it. And part of the conversation is entertaining enough to record: that disparity in perception between the bear caught in a trap and the mechanic observing the function of the snare and describing it. But the odd thing is that I like him. And admire him too. He has done the unpopular. And for all his "Westernization," he has stood for things one is proud of anywhere, whereas all other Western influences I see are corrupt, corrupting: contemptible popular trash, technological inhumanity. This man has drawn into his peculiar suit and collar, his antique haircut, some aura of integrity lost already to the West itself. He looks like a groom in an old photograph, upright.

But he cannot comprehend my terror. Nothing unpleasant will befall me if expelled, I will be taken at once to the airport. "And permitted to leave?" "But of course." "It is not an arrest?" "Not at all." "Then why was I not asked to leave, rather than ordered? Why not privately and personally, rather than the thing announced at a press conference?" "Well, I can't say. It may even be a bit of a mistake actually." He looks at Kateh and they worry the issue in Farsi. Her enormous respect for the man—marching here along the street she told me that in Lahadji I had one of the strongest men in Iran on my side; it is men like this who will end up running it all soon, did I not see his power in putting a stop to the executions, the news in today's paper? Kateh is now putting the case for women here: was it not misguided to expel a feminist, what provocation could government claim? His eyebrows lift, and his shoulder, a hand rattling the change in his pocket: the publicity about the demonstrations has annoyed them considerably, there are new restrictions on the press because of this. I would know what is being said. Delays and translations. But surely I am within my rights as well as performing a duty to a cause in publicizing those same demonstrations as much as possible and thereby preventing harm to the demonstrators. I put it to him, relishing the debate of it, a closet lawyer myself. "Surely, and there is also the issue," Kateh urging now, "that they embarrass themselves in attacking an author." She would spring me on "culture," always a line the women here take with men, government. I am not in politics, only in civil rights, and really a scholar, a literary person. This has some effect on Lahadji and he contemplates action.

Here I caution him, cards on the table. "Look, you are enormously kind to give me your time and advice. But I am not seeking to appeal expulsion or go to court to avoid deportation, waiting through hearings while I'm incarcerated, a little football between this regime, its several branches and stripes of government, secular, religious and popular, and whatever notice the American authorities take or fail to, while the media make copy of it all, a nightmare that could go on for weeks—or if I were lucky, rich and represented, I could go on living expensively on tenterhooks in a hotel which actually I could scarcely afford even if I succeeded in staying just those six days I'm asking for until my ticket is good." "You needn't worry about your ticket." "But I do." "There will be no problem of money." "Will the Iranian government pay the difference? I really don't have it with me." "I'm sure they can handle those things." "I'm sure they can too, but will they?" "You have nothing to fear." "I fear detention a great deal." "Nonsense."

Having to say it finally, so he will understand: I am a claustrophobe. It is not a word he is familiar with. After explanations, I feel he is still unable to grasp the meaning. I am trying to say that I have a particular fear of being confined, I might find it unbearable and would then worry about my ability to keep sane. Talking to a man who has talked to thousands of prisoners. They are probably all claustrophobes. Everybody in their right mind is probably a claustrophobe. And Lahadji knew the political prisoners better than I did. Though he is a man in a suit with influence in the government who may never have been a prisoner a moment in his life.

I am facing certain possibilities and insisting on a fear he denigrates.

"You have nothing to fear, your rights will be respected." What can he mean saying that? "I have a good knowledge of political imprisonment in this country and can have no such confidence." "But that was before." "How can you be so sure it has changed that much—there were still executions." "Until today." "How much of the Savak system is gone, its way of thinking?" "Surely you exaggerate." "Probably. But I came here to make a little speech at a rally, was surprised and delighted by demonstrations and now dread going home before my real work is done here. Historical work: tapes, documentary film, interviews with women. I wanted a little time, the time to finish my job and go when I wished, when I planned, just the few days until March 24, my reservation from the beginning coinciding with my visa and ticket. Six days aren't worth going through the hell of imprisonment for. If they will give me a date, a moment to leave, I shall do so exactly as they require. Only that—the hour . . .

"My god, Kateh—we were supposed to call them back." "Who?" "The ministry. I have the number in my pocket. They ordered us to call them back, the clerk at the Park Hotel had a message from them. We tried the number for an hour after you left. No answer, of course." The line is busy or ignored. You are ordered to call a number that doesn't answer. The perfect double bind. I must start to call them again. On Lahadji's phone. Embarrassed for the impertinence it represents. At his desk. The interruption, the use of his facilities. He has several phones on the desk and some more outside with his "man," a combination secretary-factotum who has already brought us tea, and who comes and goes with messages about other business probably far more urgent than ours. I feel like a fool, like a parolee checking in with a warden, but the command must be obeyed. "Don't bother, that's absurd," Lahadji deprecates. A lawyer telling me to ignore the order of the government. Never on my life. My very plan here is to obey them to the letter. "Their lines are engaged, it's a waste of time." "But it's an order, I must keep trying." Wondering if he's right, and embarrassed to borrow the telephone, nearly to demand it. It's either busy or it rings and no one answers because all the lines are busy at once, but you have to keep trying. Everyone is telling me to stop being silly. Kateh has other arguments to pursue. No one can figure out why I am being so intransigent over this petty thing. "Call when you get back to the hotel," they say. But their offices will close in twenty minutes. They can arrest me tonight for not having obeyed that order. Lahadji thinks I'm a maniac.

I get on the phone anyway. Feeling rude and a bit out of order. But acting from my deepest instinct that only pacifist correctness can save me. I can risk no error at all now, none. Even if I blunder here, even if the smart thing is to take on Lahadji's line, whatever it be: formal bureaucratic process, legal representation to power, a petition in writing—whatever—it must be in conjunction with and even in deference to whatever autocratic mean little signals are given from government. If the bully, nameless and faceless in the ministry, dictates I return a call to be given a date of departure, I must return that call even though I have to speak to another faceless bully and cannot refer even to the first by name. All right. But the line is busy.

Lahadji is adjusting his attitude a bit. In conference with Kateh, in response to her urging, maybe even through having watched my terror before this situation and its consequences. Evening approaching, the room filling with a light gray, a room as old-fashioned as he is, velvet chairs, little Persian table. He is beginning to churn toward some direct effort. He will call Entezam himself. All this has to be a mistake. There is no reason for this to be so upsetting. He knows the unlisted number of Entezam's home. My god, the old-boy system, I think, disillusioned. What if all you had to do was ring up the unlisted number of Entezam, know his wife or something? Is it all merely this ridiculous? Is that why one needs a lawyer, for the unlisted phone number? And Entezam will laugh and Lahadji will laugh and it was not quite a mistake but a complication that has to be "straightened out" and yes you are able to stay six days longer though it would be wise to keep your head down and not talk with reporters. A good girl.

I keep dialing the telephone number I was ordered to dial. It is the seventh time and I cannot get through. Lahadji, having tried a "really good number" for Entezam's own office and having left a message there for his call to be returned, begins now the portentous act of dialing Entezam's unlisted home phone. He talks to someone and hangs up. The lord is not in yet. He will soon be home for dinner and at that time will return Lahadji's call. Meanwhile—we have nothing to worry about—Lahadji is triumphant, quite as pleased as if he had gotten through. "Go back to the hotel and rest. Everything is in fine order. This will all be straightened out in an hour or two and I will phone you there at the hotel. There is nothing to worry about, not a thing in the world to fear."

Kateh is pleased. Sophie is pleased. I try to imitate their pleasure but know already that this is either a delusion or a travesty. The latter if all you do is call a crony; the former—how much more likely—if Lahadji's well-meant counsel is only the belief in influence I am already dubious will be permitted. It is not that he deceives us, it is that he deceives himself. Will his optimism about our rights being respected upon arrest be as unfounded? I feel a frozen despair, knowing the government offices will close in four more minutes.

7 ✻ ✻ ✻

I OPEN MY EYES. It must be late. We've made it. Another day. If they were coming they would have come by seven; even then you'll miss the eight- and nine-o'clock flights. If you are going to make the last flight at noon, you must be arrested early. They didn't come, we have another day. Maybe we'll get the next six days too; we're close now, this is the fourth day we have been expelled and we're still here. It's working. I smile and have a look at the mountain from where I lie, the nicest thing about this room, you can have the mountain in bed with you. Sophie, too, safely asleep. In a moment I'll order our breakfast. What shall we do today? Of course, go and visit the new office. Maybe we can give a hand and paint the place—I love painting walls—what will Iranian paint rollers be like? Fixing up a place, nothing more optimistic and satisfying than that.

Last night we celebrated the office, that the women's movement here has an office, today a telephone, soon materials to print. Everyone was here last night. It was St. Patrick's night as well. Wonderful party. Remarkably little hangover, considering the occasion. The hilarity of it, the communion, Carole and the Frenchwomen, nearly all the Iranian feminists we know. Tomorrow the international delegation arrives, already it looks like I can make it till then, perhaps even meet them and pass on what I've learned. Last night so much to rejoice in, such closeness, all of us in the room here have, in these last tense days, become better and dearer friends. The demonstrations, the establishment of a headquarters here. A good deal to drink, a lot of love, I think we even managed to find music. Some tapes from France, Iranian folk songs from the radio; I wonder if I lost my mind and did a jig—let's hope not.

Lighting a cigarette; in a moment the coffee. As I reach for the phone, it rings, the front desk announces a reporter is here to see me, two reporters. That's strange, I have no appointments today, don't plan to talk to reporters anymore anyway; keep it cool, I'm lasting here. Are they foreigners or Iranians? I ask. "Two Iranian gentlemen." "Would you tell them that as I have no appointment with them and have not yet had my breakfast, I will see them downstairs in an hour or so?" Curious nuisance. Now to breakfast. Having to wake Sophie to get her order, the pity of it. Let's have another half-hour just to snuggle. Not really a bad idea; this is the first day with leisure to sleep in. Time passes in the pleasant haze of half-asleep, half-awake: we must begin to set up our interviews with the women here, would Mimi give us some time today, she'd be the best to start off with— wonderful on camera. Sophie, what do you think? Sure.

The telephone again. I suppose it was too much to ask for. Those reporters probably. No. Immigration officials, the front desk says. I sit up, frightened, shaken. "They merely want to check your passports. It will take two minutes of your time. They apologize for the inconvenience but they say it is just a formality."

This could be good. Or it could be awful. They could be lowering the boom, or they could just be de-escalating the whole thing, letting us off the hook with bureaucratic visitation, the explanation of regulations, the establishment of our whereabouts, some little exercise of power that we would submit to like lambs and then have the whole day free to do as we like. It's just two moments, they say. "Don't believe them," Sophie says, jumping up. I feel my bowels churn, am I going to have diarrhea the moment I'm busted? And in bed—we are in bed— are we being caught in flagrante delicto, the haunting of a lifetime come to some unconscious crisis? Bounding around in search of clothes, the suitcases all unpacked, clothes in closets, tapes all over the chairs, silly tapes from last night. A performance of me and Kateh and the ministry done to entertain Carole. We didn't tape during the party, too noisy and too dangerous for the Iranian women. But somewhere in the early evening Derek Ives of Associated Press, London, stopped by and told me of the photographs he took when he went in with the demonstrators during the insurrection as the political prisoners were being liberated. No visible evidence of torture had come to light in the big prisons, he'd said, it must have been already put out of sight. But there was one place, a private house, a mansion really, same neighborhood as the American embassy, so posh that you could not believe what you saw downstairs in its cellar. He had seen it all, photographed it: "Like a medieval torture chamber, really, it was inconceivable," the outrage in his eyes still. So unlike your media cynic, a wonderful man. There were severed arms, he said, whole counters of dismembered limbs. An acid bath for disposing of corpses of the tortured. But a regime like that could have buried bodies anywhere, was absolute, I wondered at it. They did these things out of a love of cruelty, perhaps. Having lost their minds in it. That tape.

And the tape from Lahadji's office. The new notebook. Bring the notebook: forget the tape recorder.

Still there is nothing we cannot lose or are afraid to be found with. Front calls again, far less politeness—we are to come down at once. Of course, we're just coming. I cannot find my boots and so must go without them, in bedroom slippers. It is just for two minutes. And if they want to bust us we will have to come back up here to pack. Lahadji's card is right next to the phone, our *vade mecum*. I'll give a call and tell him what has happened. No answer. Too early. Lawyers don't save your neck till after nine in the morning, possibly not till ten. If there's any trouble, I can call again, keeping the card in my passport case. It's the best we can do. And one more call, to Trish Riley, a reporter Gloria has recommended to us as a sister. She's staying in one of the rooms we once stayed in and it amuses us all how many of our telephone calls she still gets. Meet us in the hall. We're going down now. If anything happens, you can get the word out.

The three of us like conspirators or schoolgirls or merely intimidated innocents going to meet trivial official tedium. Or the worst. But the whole message seemed so reassuring—the two moments, I cling to that. As two very rude and angry men confront us at the front desk. Were they the Iranian reporters of half an hour ago? Is it a trap?

Yes. The moment our passports are in their hands, we are pulled behind the desk into the private office behind. And then the bigger and more irascible of these men hands me a little package. A tape cassette. The evidence against us presumably. My blood freezes. It's like a movie, the murderer upon apprehension is presented with the bloody gloves he used—"The jig is up," the movie cop says—but this is real. Watching them, the men who have us now in their trap, it is like the taking of Volodin in *The First Circle*, suddenly the secret service are there. Joseph K woke up to find them in his boardinghouse.

And they have a document, they have a "display," an exhibit for court, fraudulent or forged or frivolous, a tangible shred against you that can be docketed, photographed for the papers—even still in its wrapper, untranscribed—it is enough for the superstitious. And what is it in our case? A tape. Which one? Proof that they have heard all, seen all as well as eavesdropped and followed? Did they bug the room? Stolen our words, our minds? Only in order to use them against us this terrible moment.

Hang on. What have you said in a tape that could ever incriminate, given that you now have criminal activities? Well, how about your lighter moments, that conversation with Carole, just before the party, you were making merry by arranging mock marriages, Carole having decided that the way to solve the predicament of women here was for feminists to make the supreme sacrifice, marry and convert the mullahs. Volunteering to immolate herself upon Khomeini, if I would take Tolerani to my bed. It's no problem, they're impotent for sure, merely a matter of keeping them warm at night a few months—a double wedding, think of it—what shall we wear? God knows what could be on any of those tapes. Our friends here, do they have their voices? Will they go now and find them, having followed them, numbered them, studied them already? Some voice-detector thing out of Stalinist fantasy. No, I have taken care to tape none of the women here since we have given our tapes to Carole for safekeeping. Except Kateh at Lahadji's, and that tape was in our room a moment ago. Who then? How did they get this tape? The Frenchwomen? Did Des Femmes make it out of here today as they were going to? Have they been arrested, searched? Is it some sign that he has them? Now holding the tape with frightened hands, fumbling, seeing that beneath the paper it is wrapped in it is indeed labeled in my handwriting. And it is labeled "Antoinette's message." How did they come by that? I had loaned it to Claudine to transcribe it for her reports, to translate back into French, since it was first given to me in English over the phone from Paris to my studio in New York.

We have come full circle. The joyousness with which that message was given to me to convey to Iranian women, a Frenchwoman and an American, two international feminists laughing and delighted and composing a manifesto of freedom, a greeting and congratulations to our sisters here, beginning a new movement of women, a movement that in so few days would become an avalanche. And then . . . a man holding that tape out to me in triumph, proof that I was captured. Proof, it seems, if I understand him, that my crime is established. Though never named. Five men stand around us. We are taken. The jig is up. There are no windows to the light. Only one door and it is guarded. The big windows onto the lobby are rolled down and slammed shut.

The hotel telephonists go on plying their switchboards in our ready-made prison, looking askance at us from time to time; probably they've seen all this before. Ralph, was it like this for you? Were you this afraid? There are five men around us. We are shoved further from the door and into chairs. Just as well, it is hard to stand. There are five men, sorting them out in my head. One is familiar. We have seen him in the hotel many times: gray-haired, handsome, upper-class look. A spy inside, Sophie says softly, watching him. Always agreeable in the elevator and the lobby, air of a wealthy traveler. "He's been on our case all along, I bet," she says during an instant they turn away to telephone their office. "Why didn't you come at once!" they all keep

shouting. "You have kept us waiting an hour!" "We came immediately," I try to say. "We came immediately we heard you were from
the immigration office." "No, you didn't," he bellows.

Why argue? Are they Immigration? Every one of them has a gun, it
is obvious even to me. Sophie has signaled by putting a hand under
her arm where their guns are carried. But I can even see one through
an unbuttoned suit coat. They move like men with guns, they yell like
that. "Immigration police," the big one screams at me. Yes, sir.
"Immigration police," he shouts again. And then grins at the others as
if there were a joke, a shared comedy among them. And they adore
their effect, our visible fear. Now I must do something asinine but
necessary. Itself a comedy. I must go through the civil-rights procedure and inquire for proof of their authority. Knowing, of course,
that the gun is their authority, the fist in their voices, knowing how
soon I may be slapped, beaten up by the whole gang of them for
"resistance." They are the ultimate power, there being no witnesses,
they are covered against any backchat, and my insistence can be
phrased just as they like, resisting arrest, resisting an agent of the
government, or however it would be termed if challenged. Who would
challenge them?

Riley, for one—somehow she has talked her way in here—"I am a
reporter and a personal friend and I am here to see that these women
are treated justly." "Bravo, Riley," I almost grin. Where did she come
from, how did she ever get in here? The big one, the meanest one, the
angriest and loudest one, his very rage and height dominating the
others—why in hell are they so pissed off? They can surely do their
job without this frenzy, or is it all part of the bullying, the intimidation—laughing, looking around and inviting the others to laugh, pulls
ceremoniously from his inner pocket a document in Farsi. Which, of
course, I cannot read, and he knows I cannot; it could be a license to
drive a bakery van for all I know. Though it has some official air about
it. And his picture. An interesting picture—the picture meaning
everything to me: he is in uniform. The uniform of the Shah's colonel.
Today he is in civilian clothes. But the uniform was the Shah's, just as
the picture is some two years old, by the look of it, the fading, the
graying of the paper within its cellophane folder. And the new regime
is only months old, the immigration authority probably no longer
wears uniforms, but surely that was a colonel of the Shah. Therefore
probably of Savak. The whole manner, the method of operation. The
deception of playing reporter so we would come down completely
unaware. Then the fury as we tarried when the summons came from a
government office. Then immediately rushing us to a place where we
were cornered, could not be reached by the press. Then the threat of

force. A threat exercised as we were rushed around the corner, not hit, but pushed. Pressed into chairs. Lunged at and screamed at, but still not struck, the guns present and presented. And the shouting, always the shouting, the great hubbub of anger, real or pretended, as if the big one is just by a hair of will preventing himself from striking me backhand across the face.

He has now, by a further effort of will, condescended to answer my outrageous request to see his document of authorization by turning it into a parody to amuse the others and keep face. Scared as I am, I realize this bully has rarely so conformed—in the old days things were different—but even now, confronted by a short woman scared out of her wits, even now he seems free to fall back on the past and just take fist to her. Daring to ask his name, then to ask it again so she can write it on the back of her cheap brown cardboard notebook. Colonel Ahab—one likes the Ahab, nothing could be better, more apropos than Ahab, humor fighting dread—Colonel Ahab Shawabi. No, Shaabi, perhaps that is closer, the delay further infuriating him and I try to write steadily, crossing out one shaky version and trying another and then another. Riley waits. "Tell, Riley, get the word out. We seem to be busted." She registers and focuses upon my notebook, where I have written Lahadji's telephone number for her to memorize. I have already been refused the use of the telephone by my captors.

And then they turn on her—in a second she is out of the room. I ask again to phone my lawyer, as I will ask over and over from now on. They refuse. And I ask again. And they say, "Later," when we get to their offices. And I say I would prefer to telephone now. Asking politely in a frightened voice. And they boom, "Later," and curse us for making them wait, they are late. Late for the plane? Late for jail? Where are they taking us?

Because they are. And they will not say where. They are taking us somewhere because suddenly, after one more of their many phone calls to some greater power, they order Sophie to stand and go upstairs to pack—it is this or they will pack for us—Sophie refused that categorically because of the movie camera. "We borrowed it, we can't take chances." And then I thought we could both go—what's more reasonable, there are now more than five armed men to guard us, two frightened women, surely we are not about to scoot away down a corridor. They control the whole hotel. Even have spies, two more of them jumping out of the two rooms adjoining our own as Sophie is led up the corridor and forced to pack, the whole lot of them watching her to see that she destroys nothing. Wonder if she'll get my boots. Wondering now, in a shock of fear, if I'll ever see her again, the fear so great now that one surrenders to it, all will to struggle evaporating, only survival, surviving, patient, childlike hope which almost clings to the tormentor, utter dependency setting in, the tormentor having got one into this labyrinth, only the tormentor can get one out. The way one waited for visits in the loony bin, visits from the very persons who put you there, but who might spring you.

Around me the hotel proceeds in a grim imitation of a hotel, the telephone operators, one of whom, a woman, smiles at me. That sympathy. Coffee is on my right, contributed from somewhere, the hand shakes raising the cup. A prisoner now, grateful. The eyes I direct toward the woman telephonist are the eyes of a jailbird, afraid to slip her a number; a dog wouldn't incriminate her. Use of the telephone in the intervening delay, while the packing is done, is forbidden again. I revive and point out that this is my lawyer and these are my rights. Further humor. Gentle insistence. Then they pretend, the big one and the little one—a bureaucrat in a real bureaucrat suit and nearer to forms and procedure and so I lean upon him, pulling the strings of whatever civil official might remain—they pretend now that they do not understand my English. The best speaker, the hotel dick, has gone with Sophie. This is the trick they resort to when shouting doesn't work, when peremptory refusal doesn't work. I concentrate on the big one for a while, the colonel— different tactics: cheery chitchat, personal inquiries, his children, the difficulties of his job, the weather, the green walnuts we have been buying from street vendors, showing him how I had written the Farsi word in my notebook, the Persian words *"chaghale badam."* Interesting the man in the correct suit as well, getting somewhere in establishing my harmlessness, my humanity, whatever will stay the hand, the gun, bring Sophie back. Inquiring sweetly after her, remarking on the delay, sidling up to the telephone issue again. These men have my life in their hands. Even whether or not I will see Sophie. They must bring her back if I am to live through whatever comes. Alone I may not be able to make it.

Whatever it is, the ego wriggling before the fate unannounced, and against that I must concentrate every power of personal persuasion to establish two things: that I am harmless, not only scared (that's easy) but so scared of them that I am completely helpless, a mere woman, a mere writer, a mere artist, a mere traveler, an incoherent rather silly person not much more than twelve years old. And, this is harder, but I must begin to establish it, that the person they have been sent to arrest is actually innocent, is incapable of whatever harm accused of, is righteous and upstanding, punctilious and in awe of authority, a model citizen somehow caught up in some kind of clerical error, bureaucratic shuffle, misunderstanding. In a short time it will all be rectified with gallantry and good humor as she eagerly mounts the stairway to her plane. Of course there will be a plane. They have said so. Of course I believe them without question. So it is merely a matter of explaining to me the business before us today. What office is it that they intend to bring us to? How long shall we be there? What plane is it they intend us to catch? Merely knowing all that would be so reassuring; of course, they will understand the anxiety of travelers.

Knowing already that it is getting on for ten o'clock. Why take us to an office when we must go directly to the airport if we are to get on the last plane, an hour's drive, tickets to fix, customs to get through. The fact that the colonel has handed me the tape probably taken from Claudine may mean that the women from Des Femmes have made their plane. Or it may mean that, having been searched, they are now in custody somewhere. Is that what they intend to do with us? Word has never reached us that Ralph arrived in London safely. We have asked reporters for news of him every day: perhaps it is only the difficulty of getting news here, perhaps Ralph never bothered to talk to the press when he arrived, perhaps they blacked him out. Or perhaps he is still being held here. Is that what they have in mind, and the occasional reassuring remarks about taking us to their office before the airport, which alternate with their shouting and bullying, are merely a trick? So that we will not seek further help here in the hotel, reporters one suspects asking already in the lobby, Riley's colleagues. The door to the lobby is so near me. And the colonel between me and that metal door. Forget it. They have Sophie. Only they can give her back to you.

Then suddenly we are leaving, I am to stand, grab my handbag, suddenly they are all standing, as all their movements are sudden, as if to throw you off balance, frighten you more—though if all they are doing is throwing me out of their country, I'm presently very eager to leave and would taxi to their airport this moment—hell, call me a cab; I'll flag one myself—if all they are doing is throwing me out, they could be informative about it. They could use the time to reserve space on a flight of their choice. They could bring Sophie back and wave us off from the front door. I asked when they wanted me to go and I understand the answer is "now, today." Fine. But why the obscurity, why trips to other places, why the mystery, why the brutality, why not bring Sophie? There is something wrong. I will not go without her.

Yes I will—they are making me. I gather all my tiny determination and inquire, trying not to seem afraid, trying also not to rile them— "But my friend?" speaking English now as they do, in a bewilderment of simple locution, indication, gesture; even this—language, articulation, nuance—must not be a threat to them. "She come!" they shout, as if to the deaf, the simple. "Where?" "She come!" the thing infinitely funny to them. A trap. A deceit. In the lobby I will have a chance, can pass the word to someone, Riley, someone will be glad enough to perform this mercy in return for whatever copy they can make of it.

But no, we are not going that way, the longed-for swinging metal door to the lobby locked at all moments since we have been put here. Only the moment they took Sophie out it. No, there is another door, a service door, it goes to parts of the building I have never seen before. Then an elevator. Going up to Sophie, she must be finished packing. No, feel it. Not going up. I can feel it going down, need not even look at the register above the door, a man on each side of me, holding me. All the times one sees prisoners in manacles on the backseats of airplanes, Mexicans being flown home, courtrooms with prisoners in cuffs; this is how I would look if there were someone else on the elevator which should be going to unite me with all my worldly belongings in an overpriced hotel room where my friend is held hostage—what have they done to her?—but we are not even going up. We are going down. The doors opening on storerooms, dark airless corridors. The meat must be kept down here, the linen, the food. And people? In addition to every other device of espionage, does this damned hotel have holding rooms? Under the Shah did they "question" people here? Will they still? How long? And where is she?

And then, at the very end a corridor, there is light. Natural light, the out-of-doors, freedom. Temporary or permanent. And Sophie is standing at the end of it, standing on a loading platform before a parking lot I did not even know existed. The most welcome sight in the world. The men who hold us captive laugh. A moment of pure fury—they have done this on purpose—they have refused to tell me she would be here, in the parking lot, rather than the room, failing to explain when I asked why we were going down rather than up, and relishing my insecurity through the underground passageways; they have deliberately misled me to imagine they were separating us. All so they could scare the rabbit, laugh at her fear. All utterly unnecessary. All sadism. The sadism they permit themselves so far. How much more when we are out of the hotel and civil territory and in their offices, their cars going to their offices? What offices? Where, how long? They have deliberately misled me to imagine they were separating us. But will they really do so? Never. Sophie waves. She too was fearing the worst. I have never loved her so much as this moment. The feeling makes a little balloon in my chest, I exhale involuntarily. Still running about in my bedroom slippers, keeping up with the pace of my guards—her slender figure against the light, smiling triumphantly, how wonderful she is—she holds up my boots.

8

EVEN WHEN YOU'RE IN CUSTODY, you have to pay your hotel bill. Perhaps especially then. The manager presents the dreaded total. In addition to our other embarrassments, we may not be able to meet it. Of course, we had not intended to pay up at just this moment, had counted on help from others now in Paris or America if the sum were to go over our heads, relying on the fact that bills incurred here can be paid at any other branch of the Intercontinental chain. No time for that now. Before our armed guards' impatience, we must ante up. The translation from rials to dollars seems to take forever—tell us the news—I watch the manager, holding my breath. Maybe we can go to jail for defaulting on our hotel bill too, a civil misdemeanor compounded to our other intangible unexplained crimes. Sophie is disarming our guards by finding the whole thing quaint and droll, remarking on the excellent weather, encouraging the clerk in his labored calculations. We all stand around doing sums, translating currency. For a moment we are ordinary people. It is exactly twenty-six thousand, nine hundred and eighty-six rials—but what is that in dollars? Four hundred and thirty-four.

And that is exactly what we have. Plus some ten dollars and forty-seven cents to last us the rest of our lives here. At least we made it. A little victory for our honor, our projected good-citizen plausibility. We are solid bourgeoisie, ladylike; we pay our bills.

Putting us into the car, our captors are almost gallant. Doors are opened—they would be anyway, but they are opened with a little ceremony, some avuncular goodwill. We play it for all we can, Sophie a determined and flourishing conversationalist as we go along. The great question, of course, is where are we going? It has never been answered beyond "our office." And what office would that be, and where? And how long shall we be there? Vital questions she approaches sideways with inquiries about their length of service, how arduous they find their work. Feminine stroking. All the everyday equipment of female survival operated now on an emergency basis, its effectiveness impressive. They answer, disarmed by attention to their very selves, the flattery of it, the kindness with which she inquires, the sympathy, the understanding. Listening to this performance, thinking how oddly pacific this approach to another human being really is, how essentially good-willed. Even applied deliberately, as now, it has no malice in it. And we are succeeding in establishing ourselves in their minds as human beings, even pleasant women. Less and less can they imagine us enemies of the state, the people, the revolution—whatever the charge—and though their orders of course still hold, they can now be carried out with civility. We are resigned to expulsion, even to whatever else befalls us, but we must neutralize the dominant who have our fate in their hands. Who were an hour ago fanatic in their hatred. We were then a thing; now we have arrived at personhood. And better chances.

But still so little information. The one with us in the backseat, the one whom I call the civil servant, elderly, respectable, the proper suit, the steel-rim glasses—he's the one to work on. But keep the Colonel in good form, his huge bullying shape up in the front seat with the goon-type driver—but do what you can for him too, remarks on the traffic, questions about the car—whatever you do, keep the Colonel in good form. He is the military arm, the origin of force. And meanwhile, insinuate yourself in the reasonable mentality of the civil servant. Loath as everyone is to acknowledge that you have certain rights, a civil servant is aware of them and, provided you do not ruffle his sense of authority over you, he can, if coddled properly, dispense as mercy what is really your due.

Where are you taking us? we had asked before, trembling in the hotel's back room. Please, if you would only tell us . . . The answer was, "to the airport" one time, "to the office" another, and "you will see" a third. With laughter. At us, their dupes. At our stupidity. At our anxiety. We were clearly two women afraid. It is our weakness, we will make it our strength. They will tire of terrorizing us if we can make it uninteresting, tasteless enough. If we can smother that nasty impulse with our goodwill, if we can make them act like men rather than mean little boys. If we can, without making them dig in their heels by challenging their almighty authority with refusal or downright insistence upon rights they may never acknowledge or even be under no obligation to admit, if we can slowly bring them back from military and political orientation to civil law and process, we may make it. We may get in and out of their bloody offices without being hurt or interrogated. And get from there to an airport rather than a jail.

Because the interrogation business may be in store. Not that its first indications show much promise. "You know Angela Davis?" the

Colonel demands of both of us. Sophie admits to knowing of Angela Davis but not to knowing her. That takes a moment to clarify. I must admit to knowing Angela Davis, was for six weeks a supporter at her trial. Having meant to stop in and stay for two days while on a trip to California. Then I saw the horror of her predicament, one individual at the mercy of the full powers of the state, a state intent upon taking her life—so I stayed on week after week, sleeping on my friend Sherman's couch as week gave way to week and the beauty of Angela's courage made it impossible to leave her side. The hour of her acquittal I walked next to her, proud to be one of her bodyguard against the expected bullets of assassins, some twenty-eight of whom had telephoned offers to kill her that very afternoon. Yes, I know Angela Davis. But why do you ask? Is she a culture hero, an American woman whose name he has heard of? Will he ask next about Jane Fonda? Or will it be Janis Joplin? What's on his mind? "Communist?" he asks. I mustn't giggle. There is an old CIA file in his mind, perhaps even on his desk. It probably mentions the two pieces I published on Angela. I must remember to send for my files again. The last time I ordered them up under the Freedom of Information Act, they gave me only mediocre book reviews, a page or two with blacked-out names—informants?—and little else. Apparently one has to persist before the meatier items surface, the full dossier. Provided probably as a matter of course to old allies in Savak under the Shah and, I'm told, still rattling around in the offices of political police. Perhaps even newly furnished, updated, or courteously extended as the fruit of recent inquiry.

Are we going to jail or to Immigration? Surprised to find that Immigration is a kind of jail itself. One expects the monotony of an office building like the one where I spent a summer standing in lines to save Fumio from deportation before ending up in City Hall with two witnesses. Almost reassuring in retrospect as we look at the fortress we are being forced into now. It has huge iron gates, iron that extends to the very top of the entrance cavity; you could never get out of here. Claustrophobia. And the fear of prison. The gates are jammed with supplicants, the halls are packed with human freight, dark faces of destitute Pakistanis thronging to enter Iran in the hope of work. In a stalled economy they are given the consideration of roaches; the Colonel strides through, scattering them. Their faces are sorrow, waiting. We are whisked through like important persons. I look at the Pakistani, petitioners to remain in this country as we are leaving it, seeing them with pity and a terrible anger at how they are treated. Of course they could still leave the building, are not in custody to anything but their need, they still have liberty of person, they are not political, only poor. As if that were not political imprisonment in itself.

And perhaps they are prisoners too—who sleeps on the beds we pass on the first landing, a terrible cage of a hall, all barred? Is this some holding cell, some pen for immigration offenders, the destitute? Passing it, I am almost sick considering it our fate, imagining our night here tonight. We go further up, scattering old women who beg for their children's entry, the aged and indigent approaching the Colonel timidly as he brings us along. Offices now, fewer crowds, the higher floors, the more swollen and important officials. The Colonel himself. We are deposited in an office. He has done his job, he is off to run this zoo of misery; we remain with the civil servant. An improvement. Even tea.

Maybe it's just some dumb form to fill out and then the plane. Lovely. But the plane is leaving in less than an hour—hurry. Asking ever so gently if reservations have been made, space saved for us, the airlines notified that the government wishes to put two passengers on. Will they hold the plane, will the government let it go without us? Are they doing this on purpose? And if so, where will they put us till the next plane—or is the plane a ruse to get us to sign papers? Have they all along intended to put us in jail and this is only a place where we will be interrogated? Apparently not. I wait for the inevitable questions about my comrades, knowing I will not betray them through mere words or tricks, but not knowing how long I would last if it came to blows. Soldiers and guns are everywhere.

Doltish and amateur young militiamen, big young overgrown louts with submachine guns, stand in the door staring at us. They gape awhile and then call a friend to come see "them," grin or spit or curse or even smile back at our intended serene and smiling aplomb. Even they must conclude we're human, harmless. Maybe it's a mistake after all to arrest us, maybe Lahadji is chattering away with Entezam or Mrs. Entezam at this moment—don't we ourselves possess (gifts from well-wishers) the telephone number of Khomeini's daughter and Bazargan's wife—surreal recollections in this surreal place. Kafka wrote *The Castle* for this building and *The Trial* for our civil servant at this desk. Whereon now lie our passports and airline tickets. Even our money, such as it is. For some two hours now we have been prisoners not only in body but because the authorities have our papers and without that passport we cannot go home even if they let us. Also the ticket. And the paper money. I want them all. Especially I want the passport. Things are now being done to it. Presumably my visa is being examined. Valid as gold, and for extra gold, I have my letter of invitation on Caifi stationery, but because it is tarnished by prejudice at the moment—moment to moment, who knows here—I will just hold on to it, the letter folded into my notebook, until further verification is required. It isn't.

What is required is that we sign a document, a piece of paper—just a piece of paper—the civil servant says, coming and going in great haste and importance and on and off the phone and in and out of the room. I try to read the piece of paper. Failing to comprehend. Lots of Farsi, smatterings of French, insufficient to explain itself. "Why bother? You're going to have to sign it," Sophie says. "We've got to understand the damn thing." "It's Immigration, it's not a confession, come on." My name has already been written out for me in script; who would know it is not my signature? Civil servant comes back, rather uncivil now and demanding we sign or we cannot leave. It's signed.

More calls, hopefulness that we are leaving. Our horrible luggage has been dragged up three flights by soldiers. Why do that? Why not leave it in the car if we are going to the airport? "You will go now with the others." "Who? Where will they take us?" The pleading in these questions. "The airport." "Do you promise that?" "You will go." "All right, of course we will go, but we will be so grateful if they will let us get there in time so that we do not miss the plane, of course you understand that the last plane is leaving very soon?" "We understand everything"—placing our passports in the hands of new guards. The form we signed was a trick; it was an application for renewal of visa, an odd thing to be doing when leaving, and it bewildered me. But they have processed the application only in order to deny it—in big red letters, so that we can never attempt to enter the country again. Gratitude giving way to betrayal when we see the red stamp of outlawry. We are expelled by the police. It is now in our record forever, records that we shall carry ourselves, available to our own governments, records that will be kept to the end of time here. So that we can never return. Persia is lost now.

It still stings in the car. Watching the avenues go by. After the almost cheerful way that our new guards, persons more civilian somehow, relaxed, decent to us, crammed our big luggage into their little car, the hated duffel bag resisting to the end. There are magazines on the seat of the car, somehow that is reassuring, magazines are ordinary life. A car radio, infinitely reassuring. How beautiful music is at this moment, after this terror. Tell yourself you are going to the airport, not to jail. And believe it, because the two men driving us feel like that is what they are doing. Not once have they laughed at us, sneered that sneer of cop and culprit. They even ask if we like the program, Persian classical music. Sophie has discovered that they are not police; they are Komiteh, neighborhood men who live in alliances of their district or profession. The man who drives us is an engineer. My father was a civil engineer, something relaxes in me.

And being relaxed, we can stop having to butter them up, the doe eyes of our harmless questions and diagonal inquiries. Fine. They drive. We sit back and think. Recover. A new pain entering in the knowledge of our expulsion's finality; we are leaving this place, without ever having seen it, experienced it, known it, without having finished our work and our learning of it. And we can never come back. Persia, how I wanted to love you, how you are ripped away, the mountains glowing around the city, like clouds of glory they are always, the world below them is for us only the public avenues speeding by now—this city and the days in this city, the euphoria of certain hours here. It hits hard, passing Freedom Square, the place of the great march, the enormous sculptures shining in the sun. "Never got to the bazaar, did we?" I say to Sophie, suppressing tears with trivia. She squeezes my hand. We watch bleakly as banners are erected for tomorrow's mass demonstration of the Army. They expect millions. It's a bad omen. Almost full circle, it began against the Army. Only a matter of months. But it's not over yet. "Think of the guts they had in February, they'll make it someday." "I hope so—and the women." "The delegation arrives tomorrow; if they just keep coming."

Along Shah Reza, near the university, we turned a corner and heard the muezzin shout out the midday prayers. From a loudspeaker. But even the blur of technology cannot take the power from it, even the fact that everyone keeps right on walking, honking their horns, reading the newspaper at the wheel in stalled traffic. The ambivalence one feels before the force of this religion, before organized religion itself. The admiration and respect. Out of deference to those who do believe, their faith and piety and care. And an objective respect for its aesthetic, occasionally for its ethic. Though not always; one is forced to dislike its bigotry, narrow-mindedness, puritanism, the hold of these things over the lives and loves of those who subscribe as well as those who don't. The abuses of its power. Especially here, for as Islamic political consciousness rises here and throughout the world, Islamism, so too is a threat posed against women. Women within Islam. Even those without.

For the patriarchal feeling in this, the youngest religion (paradox that the newest world religion, the most recent, should also be the most virulent in patriarchal sentiment and animosity) cannot but have a deleterious effect upon women's hopes throughout the world. And Islam is growing, the only major religion to grow and go on growing, spreading and solidifying through Africa and the Near East, spreading beyond that too, East and West. And in the diplomacy of oil and money and guns and third world versus Western confrontation, the Muslim brings his religion to battle now like a sword; the prophet makes him right, the prophet makes him master too. Surely over "his woman." His serf as he was once the serf of the colonizer. He will keep that hierarchy, it is built into his bitterest experience. And hallowed by an even older tradition. He is armed by God. The price of his freedom is the enslavement of his women.

And as patriarch faces patriarch for power, as a new and revitalized Islamic chauvinism enters the battle of national chauvinism, the male chauvinism of Islam may shame the West back into its own; at the moment it might have felt easy in shrugging it off, it will be reminded, enticed, even compelled to assume it again. Lest it offend the new might it faces, lest it be called less than a man, lest it be embarrassed without its own arrogance to protect its ego.

Will it go harder for women here? Will it go harder for all of us? Unless a stand is made such as women have made here. But how will that proceed when, as one woman here reminded me, her voice persisting still in my mind, "If we are isolated, you see, we will not be able to endure." That cannot happen. But will it, anyway?

The man who is driving us calls our attention to the muezzin, charming us, explaining it to us; Allah is great, the other man says with a smile. We smile too, there being no option in the churn of conflicting emotions. The mosque we pass is a very ordinary building, but still full of meaning to the faithful. All the loveliness of mosques we did not see, the superb plates in my books. And the university is just beyond, where we spent so much time. And then the road is open at last and we are for the airport. We will make the plane, just. We will have to leave, but will also get out of here without going to jail. Faster and faster, racing the clock now, pulling up before the airport in a flurry of gravel.

Just as a whole load of reporters pulls up too. There's Derek Ives, how good of him. And the American who got our pictures out for us. But the airport is deserted. The plane must have left. It is only noon, or is it past? is it five past? fifteen past? Running with our guards, door after door automatically shut against us. Political posters pasted on them. Khomeini's endless face, and another who seems to have fallen from favor and is now painted out with an X. Khomeini again smiling with Arafat. Khomeini frowning all by himself. Let me in, old man, let me through the door out of your automated police state, I curse. All the doors are locked saved one, a block away, we run there, reporters running after, the men who drove us here looking stupid and even malicious—did they always know we'd miss the plane? How could the whole pack of them have been such ninnies—if they had taken us right from the hotel to the airport we could have made it—why not do your idiot bureaucratic silliness, your fussing with papers right out here at the airport, why intimidate us in hotels and offices for three unnecessary hours and make us miss the plane? If you kick us out, don't lock the door first. How the devil does one get out of this country?

9

SO MAYBE YOU'RE NOT going to get out after all. The reporters feel it too. "Where are they taking you?" "We don't know." "Are they taking you to jail?" Running behind us, as we are marched across the tundra of the airport lobbies, "Do you have a statement?" Then, on closer range, "Is there anyone you'd like us to contact?" I look at them, they look at me—there is so much to say if one dared. But our guards must turn us over to other guards and are restive now, afraid of reproof. And the main thing is to catch the plane if we still can. The airport deserted, surely it's gone. Look, there is a man cleaning the floor with an enormous machine, "Clark" it is labeled, made in America for the Shah. Along with this vast expensive rubber floor, the acoustical-tiled ceiling which seems only to exaggerate the noise when the airport is full as it is during flying hours. Now at noon, it is completely empty, a desert awaiting the night planes from the West, hours from now, its international surface beguiling you into imagining you are at liberty, civilian existence, luggage and tickets. When in reality you have only entered another police state, the world beyond the Do Not Enter signs, a world that must exist in every airport now though you never knew it before. Where the police reside, the immigration police, the civil police. And the Komiteh. Represented not only by our drivers, but by others, bigger and smaller. There is also the Army. And the Air Force. We are rushed into a room with a counter, where the whole pack of them begins operating upon us. The reporters are chased away. The nice guy who helped smuggle our pictures. And Derek Ives. Derek something of a friend by now, the others supportive, and as their consternation grows at the arbitrary way they are treated, more supportive. They are also reporters on a story. Odd to feel you are a story when you are actually a frightened woman concerned for her life. Though seen in the light of a story by the only people who can help you now, can get the word out as you are dragged away from them and into a blocked-off area they cannot enter. Reporters hovering at a distance, in attendance, abeyance, just out of reach as you are out of theirs. The thing is absurd. And is getting worse.

There is definitely no plane. Not till tomorrow. Even the question of a special plane is considered. Iran Air, a short trip that would put us beyond the border, Istanbul, Karachi. A momentary euphoria until they all decide that getting rid of us is too expensive. No. There will be no other plane leaving for anywhere today. Under any circumstances. Then what will they do with us? Will they park us in jail overnight? No, please, no, the terror rising. Will they put us in jail, nominally overnight, and then neglect to get us out in the morning, decide to keep us, factions arguing, charges laid. If it takes no time to get into jail, how long does it take to get out? Once in, we could become the football of all the groups now already contending for us. The Air Force. The civil police. A military type of police. The Komiteh. The militia. Certain fanatical types who keep coming and going, representing more hostile elements of outraged religious sentiment. If the right got hold of us . . . I see Derek out of the corner of my eye. He and the American fellow have jumped the Do Not Enter section and are now trying to edge closer. One reporter has actually managed to get into the room with us and is sitting quietly in a chair, behaving beautifully, behaving like an invisible man, behaving like a schoolboy playing a prank, sitting in one of those grade-school chairs that has a large arm to one side for writing on. If he speaks, they will catch him. So far he hasn't.

There is something funny in all this, something exasperating, as arrangements here generally are, the authoritarian front penetrated by a thousand negligences, unnoticed bits of inefficiency, oversight, incompletion, even humanity. Mortal human folly. But the man behind the desk now is everything we dread, a big shot, punitive, revengeful for whatever crime I am supposed to have committed. And so I ask him again if he could explain my expulsion to me. Provide some reason. Since there is no plane till tomorrow, may I just spend the intervening time in a hotel, surely there is one right out here by the airport, you will know my whereabouts, you can even post a guard. But we would be comfortable. "You will be comfortable here. Right here." He is furious. There are rooms here? Holding rooms? Cells? Is it jail here or jail back in the city, buried in some neighborhood precinct. I see a shabby street, a dirty jail, an eternal cell. After tomorrow there may be contention, unfavorable publicity—they may hold on to me while keeping face against the press clamor and activities on my behalf as well as against me by lawyers, factions in conflict: the Bazargan bureaucrats, the Komiteh, the religious party, even the fanatics. This I don't need. Just let me out as soon as possible and until then let me stay as close to the door of the country, its airport, as possible.

The reporter is discovered. They are all angry now—we will be moved to further fastnesses, deeper into the maze of offices, the police and government nest behind the serene commercial international tourist veneer of the front, the airport most people see. "Are they taking you to jail?" the voices of reporters, English speakers, Westerners. Media, the ambivalence one feels toward them. And the only hope. Riley has got them out here. Has the news reached the Iranian feminists? Could one trust one of these with a telephone number? Which one? Derek. Yet it is not Derek who is sly enough to follow us down a hall into an office, but the American who saved our pictures. A uniformed civil policeman orders us to stay here and guards the door. This will be our cell. His English is very rudimentary; it is possible to talk in various American codes quietly or over his head. It is also very easy for Sophie and me to amuse ourselves with fanciful schemes of how we will spend the night rearranging their files in the big cabinets that take up half the room. "I started life as a file clerk." "Make a mess out of these and you'll end as one too." "Do they expect us to sleep on the desks?" "Either that or the floor." "Our luggage is here, we have lots of nice soft clothes, be very comfortable." "When we're bored, we can have a costume party or fashion shows for each other. Our clothes are all we have to entertain ourselves in the world now." "By no means, I have my entire library, this is a perfect chance to read. I can play the scholar and appeal to Oriental reverence for learning."

We are safe, this really is just an office, not a jail. They will need it tomorrow so they will simply put us on a plane and return to business as normal, even police business. Unless they take us to jail. But it is less likely now; we have stayed in the airport. Things are not that bad at all. The American reporter, our buddy, is in the hall, gesturing, just out of sight of our policeman. But I think I'll just behave and go along with my captors for a while; news coverage gives them the hives. There is nothing I want to say at the moment, and I know no more than anyone else about my disposition, probably less. Just pass up this occasion to rile the policeman, realizing suddenly, going through my purse, that the address book is still there, complete with every connection I have in Iran. I should have destroyed the three pages of Iranian names back in the hotel when we were first called downstairs. How green I was in the spy business. I believed the ruse about two minutes. A fatal mistake. Since then we have been watched every moment. Nor can I do it here.

I have had Kateh's number in my mind all day, memorized like the others, but somehow insisting the hardest. Do I dare to tell it to our friend out in the hall and ask him to call her? Check it again from the book. Writing the number out on the cuff of my white Mexican shirt—there may still be time to destroy the pages, but this number must be reached by someone I can trust. And the guard is right in the room with us.

There is a way to say numbers fast, so fast they they are like a ball thrown to one who can catch past someone else who cannot. The "pickle" we called this figure when we played "keepaway" in childhood. And I fire the number. The policeman never looks up, he could never write it down if he heard it. So fast. Kateh's number—she will get Lahadji, she will tell the others. For I would say good-bye somehow. "Say it's good-bye for a while. Send my love." And then he's gone. Trusting the kindness of strangers, taking a calculated risk, hoping I have not been foolish.

And then feeling more than idiotic pretending to look at a book while licking the ball-point figures on my shirtcuff into a large blue permanent stain. But you can't read it, my eyes meeting those of the young policeman watching me. Quizzical? Accusatory? Amused? It is very difficult to tell, but in a while he has brought us tea and we have settled down as roommates for the duration. Sophie at her desk, the policeman at his desk by the door, I at my desk surrounded with the art books recovered from our bags, several history texts, even the long-vanished Persian poets. Their time has come. The mind is not up to history texts, the pursuit of narrative through time. Pictures comfort more than anything I can imagine in the world just now. And, angry at Iran, in the person of its police, dictatorial government officials and such, it is a particular comfort to batten on Iran as lyric, Persia as pictures, miniatures, mosques. The flirtation of poets. In a while I have left our present circumstances and ensconced myself very pleasantly in another century.

Until the entrance of the hero. An Air Force captain whose great work it will be to search us. Fine. Search. "I will not search without your permission." He smiles, even in a man so attractive it is a leer. Sophie and I consult with our eyes. "What choice do we have?" she asks. He shrugs; none, of course. "Then why ask?" "I must ask, and I must not search without your permission." "If we deny it?" "You cannot leave without being searched." "Then search. We are anxious to leave." Hoping, of course, that this is the reason of the search. Or is it a formality to find something with which to accuse us so that we may not leave? So that we will be sent to prison, the sentiment that we should being that of most of the men around us. Particularly the civil police. But our Captain is Air Force. The Air Force, we are given to understand, is responsible for the favor of our staying here in the airport and not going to jail. Refuse the Air Force and you are turned over to the police and prison. Of course, let us be searched, customs searches all. And if the search unearths something, would that something be turned over by the Air Force to the police or to the government? Don't ask; be searched, it is the test now of freedom.

Letting him search as Sophie watches from her desk, the policeman from his. I return to my own desk, needing my books now, no longer pastime but food, rescue for the mind as it spins off its course in fear, intrigue. There is the address book for him to find. But he goes right through my purse, ignoring it. Or sparing it. One never knows with this man. Dashing figure that he is, remarkably handsome, remarkably vain. And strangely kind. As well as cruel. I ponder the mosque of Ibn Tulun, the tower of Gunbad-i-Kabus, wonderful color plates. To stay alive on art, the most ridiculous thing in the world. But what else would sustain one in these straits? In a moment he will come upon tapes, the last tapes, and confiscate them. So be it. There is nothing on them which shames or incriminates me or anyone else. If they are fair. If they aren't, they can hang you on your laundry ticket. Four hours of English, room tone and extrania. As for the tape with Lahadji, how fitting it should be confiscated, it was intended for government ears and now will reach its destination. If they ever bother to listen to it.

Despite overlooking my address book and every political contact I have with feminists all over the world, my Captain is now doggedly pursuing a scrap of paper negligently stuck in a pocket, the name and phone number of a famous woman poet here, Simone Danishvar. Someone had offered to introduce me, it was one of the interviews I had looked forward to in my last days. Vita Tabrizi I had hoped to meet too, a woman we in Caifi worked so long to rescue from the Shah's torturers and now a heroine of the revolution. "How do you know this woman?" "I don't know her; someone offered to introduce us, there never was time." How interesting that a soldier would know the name of a poet. He is excited by this scrap of paper, does it have sinister political importance to him? Have I got her in trouble in this innocent way, or is he a fan? The paper is confiscated. He's being silly, I think, returning to my pictures as he starts on Sophie.

The less we protest, the better; the more unconcerned we are, the better. Passing myself off as a pedant who cannot be pried away from her book, an art historian with evangelical tendencies, involving my policeman from time to time in particular gems, fine view of the Friday Mosque in Isfahan, the Mausoleum of the Samanids in Bukhara. Even the Captain stops for a second to have a look at a brush drawing of *Quarun Swallowed by the Earth,* circa 1306; much the same finesse and delicacy as a Hakuin, I'd like to point out. I invite comment. Sophie tends to business, the Mahatma act is not her cup of tea. But for all the flamboyance of my academic humility, it takes over: I may be about to be filed away in a cell for who knows how long—if I lose my temper, act nervous or suspicious, insist on keeping my materials—the Captain is flinging through my last notebook at the moment—a thing infinitely precious to me, the little cue words through which I remember a scene, my clues toward remaking this very moment—and if I make a fuss, I may lose it. And if I lose it I may go to jail for some silly shorthand, the name of a green walnut or a colonel, a phone number, scribbled down between calls to the ministry, random jottings at Lahadji's: "I chew on the sugar cube that came with the tea, and refuse the possibility of going directly to the ministry—might get busted." "Everybody (Kateh, Lahadji) believes democracy is still the rule here. The tragedy of that smugness." Sophie's comment, having taken the book into her own hands: "There is still an old-boy network in existence. We are the victims of it. Of course we should have called the ministry number at once. Never allow anyone to decide anything for you. Let's wait a few more minutes and call the hotel. Persian time—allow just a bit for that and we're safe." There is even a plan for a press conference in Rome if expelled and put on our own Pan Am flight that goes through Rome. I could meet Alma Sabatini in the duty-free shop, speak to the European press before the American, a thing I prefer, a call having been made already to Alma, alerting her should we be routed back that way rather than Iran Air or the French flight via Paris.

Sophie chattering our usual chatter about which airplane we might be taking, would the Captain know, would it have been decided by now? My family are concerned, distracting him from my notebook, this largely empty and messy collection of scribbles, distracting in itself by the frivolity of a flower scrawled on its cover. Dumb. Childish. Female. Arty. He doesn't want it, he puts it down. And goes for Sophie. Having spared the one, he must hurt the other; he demands her film. It has not been processed yet. He either doesn't know what that means or pretends not to.

He wants to open every box. Even the unused film. That's forty dollars' worth of film. Let him, I think, it's just money. I bought it, but

I'd rather get out of here than oppose him and go to jail. Sophie goes on, reason itself. She has almost made him understand that it is unused, the boxes are still sealed. Processing, however, is more complicated. How can they have people conducting searches who are so ignorant? she fumes. Let him, I gesture. What's in it? Nothing. Let him wreck it—we can trade that for something more important. Sensing the bargaining of it. Sensing how he senses what is precious. And what is culpable. Nothing we have is culpable, I figure. Going back to my picture book, refusing now in truly sage disaffection, I understand more about Zen. Even about Gandhi. He would never have taken an interest in this rape. Everything we own is strung out around this office, even the Tampax. But when another officer enters, more boorish, the Captain puts our Tampax away. Discretion. Or disgust. Sophie is disgusted. I am interested in my pictures. In the Captain. In my own new ability to shut up and be wise.

Now, there is an argument. Sophie is insisting he cannot open and ruin her movie film. "It is my work. I have rights." I love her, I love it. That she would just tell him off in this English-lady voice, a free Canadian spirit who will not be pushed around. Yet I worry if it will work. But it does. He leaves her alone. Touched a nerve of integrity. Who knows? The next moment he is rifling my black passport case, all its lovely red grosgrain-ribbon pockets. Until he comes upon the little drawing I made that night at dinner with Dakota Rosie by candlelight in Colorado, the evening of the day we first saw some land and decided to buy it and build a cabin on it. That very day Robin Morgan was calling all over the Western United States to tell me the news that Sita had committed suicide. Some kids came upon me in the wilderness around noon and told me to call Robin, but I never suspected why. And did not know till the next morning. Sita was dead, someone else got the land, but I kept the drawing, the back of a restaurant check, pulp paper, crinkled and faded and browning already though only a year. Because that cabin was a dream of owning something together, this old lover and I. That sketch means a lot to me.

Sophie is sympathetic as I wince, seeing the Captain pounce on it. Evidence of a bomb plot? I wonder. The ball-point lines marking the road and the lake and proclaiming "photog" and "writing" and "liv room" and "garden." A log cabin we could go on building forever, the two of us high on wine and mountain air and land in the wilderness. The next day Robin Morgan telephoned that Sita was dead by suicide. It seemed more important than ever to buy something with someone still living. Dakota and I went to a land agent and bought an option. Another buyer was ahead of us and got the land.

So all I have left of this adventure, this love of the Rockies and one of the times of my life, is a piece of paper now joining the tapes, Jacqui Ceballos' telegram cheering on the marchers, one roll of color film still unprocessed and one roll of black-and-white with pictures of a little girl Sophie came upon in the road.

Now the Captain picks up my notebook again. I am feeling pushed. I happen to need that. The fine arts are beginning to lose their ability to sustain the philosophic mind in the open book of color plates before me on the desk. I need that notebook in order to write about these last two days. I need it still more if I'm going to do any writing from now on. Tonight or in jail or however long I may be here. And I will not go without paper. Sophie protests that the notebook is my work, I am a writer. He is dubious. As long as they don't take my pen, it has also occurred to me that I could still take notes in the endpapers of the books I have with me. It would ruin them. So what, acts of impiety against published books are always necessary in making new ones. The Captain wavers. I urge ever so gently, showing him a lovely garden scene of a prince entertaining a lady. Actually my favorite. In doing so I am giving him something dear to me but of his own culture and therefore dear to him. He takes pride in it. He relinquishes my notebook. It is a civilized exchange.

We have been searched and found innocent? Or will the trivia he has taken from us now be construed as evidence of terrible wrongdoing? Dakota's cabin in the woods, now entering my permanent file for espionage or whatever, right behind a copy of the police stamp declaring me to be expelled forever, all visas denied me for eternity. Persia, the heart aches for you. Not least for the folly; taxes upon the people will pay for this travesty, perpetuate it. Should I reappeal someday, this diagram of a little cabin will peek out of the ream of secret documents, evidence of some plot, breathed out of smoke by a genie (Beria would have loved this, the Shah, Savak itself), docketed and preserved out of stupid and suspicious habit by my good Captain, then authenticated by his superiors, their eyes passing casually over this incriminating scrawl, their stamps stamping it, their files holding it. Ready for recall whenever I petition to return.

I think of this sketch often, first to mourn it, a personal loss, a souvenir, then to laugh at its present political role. And finally to be saddened that a Colorado shack which never even got built should be laid by as a bar to my ever seeing Persia again. You cannot see the mountains from this room, there are no windows. Maybe we will never see them again. One way or another, either from the land or the sky. Time goes on in the little room.

10 ✻ ✻ ✻

AND THEN AN EXPLOSION. An entire network television crew are at and then inside the door. How? Who's permitting them? "Will you be interviewed?" "Only if you have permission." But permission is clearly right beside the interviewer, Bob Dykes of ABC, in the form of a young policeman, Air Force man. The uniforms confuse me, also the rank and degree of authority. But this man has obviously granted permission for the very American team who now completely fill our little office. There is even a Japanese soundman, American as I am, but still bringing Fumio to me in this place, suddenly as strong as tears, a lovable boy's head, a beatific smile full of humor and mischief. Neisei or Isei, I wonder, what if he were born in America and talks less Japanese than I and would therefore resent mine? But impossible, in this surreal place, not to show off and greet him, foreknowing his astonishment, that of the others—fun. *"Nihonjin, des'ka?"* I say in a barroom growl that will make him laugh. If he's not really Chinese after all, or Korean. *"Soooooo'h!"* he laughs like a bandit. *"Shiboraku,"* one wants to say next, like the brigands meeting in the night in a Kabuki play, *"Shiboraku—*it's been a long time, man," as pantomime artists used to love doing over there, Fumio and I still love to clown it when we dine together at my loft, the fire burning in the Franklin stove. A million miles away.

I love this soundman, he makes me happy, able to stop shaking and talk, knowing very well how dangerous it is for me to talk, how necessary. I am sat in a chair. To lecture on civil rights, the lecture of my life, what injustice feels like, what it's like to be suddenly a prisoner, my own rights so little respected in my arrest, the arrest so unnecessary, arbitrary. Getting to say it all. To speak my piece. Feeling the principle so keenly, personally; if I could get on television the ideas themselves, teach something, not just serve my own purpose, the Americans I speak to from this little room in Tehran, so unthinking, so sheeplike before all government power. Somehow having my mother in mind, not only that she might see me and know I'm still all right, but a larger purpose too, for if you could communicate to her kind of people, less astute than she, but her neighbors, her eighty-six cousins—who are America—you could challenge a great deal that they now take for granted. Simply because you are a reasonable person who has done nothing wrong yet so fearful now because so unfairly treated.

It is the chance of a lifetime to say things I care about. And I give it all I can. Nor does he interrupt or harry me, Dykes, the interviewer; he wants to let me speak. How did he ever manage it, I ask afterwards, how did he ever penetrate this place? And will he get it out of here and will he ever get it on the air? Converting back to Japanese with my soundman, adoring him and the moments of our banter as I adore Fumio, the brother, the buddy, the fun of it, this small lively person so precious to me, surrogate for so much that I love and miss, the whimsy such a relief from the big solemn American men, the enormous weight of the network on them, the institution they represent, so powerful it is almost a branch of government. They are nearly official America. Whereas the immigrant soundman is America to me, also Japan, also what delights me in men—or one of the things— playfulness. Playing with him as long as I can while the equipment is packed up, watching the departure with regret; their leaving signals our return to prison, to being prisoners. Again we cannot speak to anyone, and as always are not permitted to use the phone. We are being held incommunicado—so how on earth is television permitted? Iranian mysteries. The sound cords are folded neatly and put into their cases. *"Ja-matta,"* we say, like old cronies, pretending it's just "so long, see you later." The tripod is slowly being folded into its box, the cameraman taking longer.

He bends over, loosening the knobs that will permit it to fold; watching him, memories of filming—if we could ever get a copy of this . . . when suddenly there is shouting in the hall. Three uniformed men burst into the room, furious. "Get out of here, you will get out of here." "Wait a moment, we had permission." "You did not." "We did," Dykes confident, a confidence real or pretended. A great network. Within his rights. Powerful connections here in government, too, the universal respect of the press, its liberty. How could it be that the officer is seizing his film—he has no right to do that—Dykes really angry now. In that box which has just been confiscated is something precious of my life, my work, too. I gave it away. And now it is stolen. We sit in the little room, recovering. I smoke. I try to read. Time goes on again.

Only a little time. Until the same men are at the door again. We are summoned. Dykes has been taken to the front of the empty airport by several officers. Arguments and threats. Now they have returned for us. Now we are the malefactors. We probably cooked this up with him. We are exercising free speech in captivity, we are poisoning the ears of the multitudes, we are breaking our arrest. Further punishment is now in order for us. The guards are harsh, we are led roughly along corridors toward the front. There are soldiers all around us. Air Force. And also the regular civil police. The latter have their office across an empty space to the right, just next to the so-tantalizing door, the big sliding door of the airport where, every now and again—even though the airport is virtually closed at this midafternoon hour and until the next planes come at evening—an occasional person strolls through the automatic door, generally military or Komiteh, but there is still the air of outdoors, the cool of it on our foreheads a few seconds till the door closes.

Civil police and Air Force face each other across a great distance. First we go to Air Force since we are in their charge—our good fortune and may it remain so. But it is made clear to us—any bad behavior and we will be turned over to the civil police. Who will imprison us. Who knows how long—a question we ask repeatedly but which is never answered.

Part sadism, part reality; once in jail, no one can guess how long, processes once set in order. Why was I expelled? I asked an Air Force man once, and he shrugged, "Why is the sky high?" But there was some charm to the performance. There is little charm to the police. And it is toward them we are now being led. We remonstrate, beg even. No avail. This is it, then? My legs turn to water. Did the interview constitute bad behavior? We have been warned, they say. Still not fair—I gave the interview on the understanding it was permitted—one of you brought those men to where we were being held. You caused the interview to take place, not me. Arguing for dear life, but gently, slightly disingenuously, since the interview was a moral responsibility to perform, work in other words, political work. But I am their prisoner, not their slave, and all opportunities to oppose them peacefully are to be seized on as calculated risks against further and longer imprisonment. And it seems I missed a bet again.

Yet I am still afraid of the consequences. A personal thing, claustrophobia. A political thing, too. But a bit overdeveloped in me, a weakness, a secret weakness I hope they will never listen to the tape with Lahadji to discover. It would be all up with me if they used that knowledge. The rats in *1984* for the man who feared rats. But we all fear. Sit straight before the policeman as he begins to make the papers of your jail. Writing down the numbers on my impounded passport. Now he will hold you by other bonds as well. No mere office turned into a cell, a real cell now. A long drive back into the city. A street whose name you'll never know. Whose name you cannot tell to Kateh. Or Lahadji. You will disappear. As people do all over the world. And maybe you'll surface sometime—but you will have no control over it at all. You are now really a slave. The "I would like to telephone my lawyer" routine. Routinely denied. Sophie sits by me, numb with her own courage.

And then the whole crazy thing changes again. An Air Force man comes and fetches us over to his side of the vast room. Where we sit like much freer people, not on hard little office chairs being booked, but on real civilian leather sofas with the officers and gentlemen spectators of the struggle of Bob Dykes of ABC. Dykes has refused to leave the airport without his film. Calls are being made to Entezam's office; Dykes feels he can win his point only if he talks to the minister. These are mere soldiers, he will go to the top. I watch him, a big man growing tired, his face finally afraid it may lose. And more than just one interview. All foreign press in Tehran walk a fine line; there is always talk of their expulsion, jokes about it, another week, they say, maybe two—still it seems inconceivable that a place now the center of so much news could black out, refuse to permit coverage for good and all: either the favors of big media, hoopla, propaganda, self-impor-tance and corruption, or the freedom of information which a free press does provide, vital to civilization.

I watch him dialing and dialing again. He cannot get through. Neither could I. I watch someone learning by becoming as I learned. But he is still free to leave. I am not. Once I was, but I gambled on staying and getting my work before I left, getting it finished and under my arm by a certain date, even someone else's arm, as long as they still got the word out. And I lost the gamble. Dykes is betting higher and higher now, he has sent his crew back so that they will be free in case he gets arrested—because he will not stir from this spot or this telephone until his film is returned. The Air Force shrug. I sit uneasily next to one on a couch, watching Dykes go on dialing the phone. As he acts, so will we be judged, if they decide we are in collusion. If they decide that all Sophie and I want is to go home and interviews are not being secretly arranged—then maybe we can just go back to our cell.

I watch Dykes with sympathy, even respect; big red-faced American that he is being just now, that he must appear to the men in their proud blue uniforms next to me. They made a revolution, the Air Force, the cream. A revolution against America and ABC, and they even won it. Because I love that revolution, I love something in them. But because the revolution is becoming counterrevolution, I know the boys in blue are becoming what boys in blue always can be—bullies. They are bullying now, but quietly. Bullying someone much bigger in size, connection, reach, but also, it must be admitted, permitting him to use the phone. I wish I could call my lawyer.

And Dykes is blustering as one who is being bullied blusters, but he is also being unjustly treated; some junior noddy actually did permit him into that room. And they ought to admit that. And still deny him the film? Thwart a free press? How about the prisoner's right to speak, that's the interview? Listen, kid, you can't even call your lawyer. When do we arrive at a point when the accused can defend herself? When do we even get presented with charges? When will officials ever admit an error? In denying Dykes the film, they don't even concede that the permission granted to shoot it was given erroneously.

Talking to Dykes in my mind. I hope you get your film. I hope I get to call my lawyer someday. I wish I could talk to you, miles away in medialand, only six feet from me at a counter with your telephone, the two of us forbidden now by circumstance to speak—why? I wonder. Because we will be overheard and understood? Because further talk with you will get me in trouble just as further talk with me will even get you in trouble. Or do we add to that the other unspoken dimension planted between any safe citizen and the wretch arrested? the poor bugger braceleted to a cop whom one never thinks to ask what the fellow did, that pariah state whereby the unfortunate are paraded before ordinary citizens, which contributes so generously to timid obedience before all forms of tyranny.

Dykes is going to Entezam's office, he will present himself in person to have the film released. Bluster or optimism. There is no time even to say good-bye, we are led away still not knowing the fate of our film, the message this man had so enterprisingly and gallantly gathered, only to see it wrested from our hands to fall dead somewhere in an office where no one will ever develop and project it. Discouraging.

The Air Force men turn to us; do we want to remain with them or be turned over to the police? Of course we will stay with them. A little congratulation in the choice on both sides. But there is uncertainty now if they can keep us. The police are demanding us as wrongdoers, dangerous persons who must not be this much at loose. We promise good behavior, in good faith. Still, the police are insisting. We go again from the Air Force corner toward the police corner, or we start to go. Then both of us beg the officers, with all the dignity we can still cover ourselves with, that we not go to jail. It works. However, there is also the Komiteh. They hang out at the police side near the door, coming and going and busy as any grass-roots democratic agency would be. With different opinions, some favorable to us, some extremely hostile.

There is an indication that still another group, right-wing and religious, either on its own or with Komiteh connections, would like us not only in jail, but perhaps in some prison of its own devising. That is scary. Not just time but ill treatment is at issue here. Forget the Komiteh and all its rainbow possibilities. Stick with the Air Force. Watching the men at the doors, their menacing or reasonable expressions, the eye traveling to the right of them and finding the police at the ready before their office—in a whiff they could take us and perhaps satisfy all elements. The Air Force are the left wing in this paradigm. They are also right here in the airport and near a plane and maybe sufficiently disciplined to get us on one, sufficiently imaginative not to lock us up for a long boring while in a civil jail, and through their experience in this revolution as well as their training before it, not as prone to dangerous ideological fads and bigotries as the Komiteh and the pious, nor as experimental in their treatment of prisoners.

The Air Force, then. Appealing with genuine charm born of the most authentic need in the world; we are happiest with you. Accepted as a compliment. We feel safest here, having the most trust that we will be permitted to leave on an airplane tomorrow. "But don't sleep tonight," one young lieutenant says to us. We are sitting alone with him, a moment after the decision is made and while the usual inefficiency is rousing itself to deputize someone to take us to another office, an Air Force office (the last belonged to the police) here in the airport—actually it is a holding room of Immigration but now supervised by Air Force men. "Don't sleep, one of you should stay awake." It is odd to hear a man warning against other men. Odd because it is so many years now since fathers and husbands used to issue statements about self-defense and attacking at the groin when dealing with their own kind. And this thoroughly serious young man is putting us on guard against his comrades and subordinates. Horror stories and rape. Is he putting us on? Or are we going to be subjected to a gang of clods, louts, patriots? The politics of rape. The lack of same, the sheer patriarchal cruelty. No, it's too much to take in. I have a better opinion of these men than they have of themselves? I really cannot entertain the kind of fear that watches all night waiting the attack.

And yet we did. Not really quite meaning to. But one or the other of us was awake all night. We took turns. Yet it was not attack we feared, but discovery. Not even that we hid what we were doing, we simply disguised it. As any kind of writing. What a writer did—write. Right in front of their noses. The three on the bench through the wide-open door, rhetorically, needlessly, pointing their three automatic machine guns at us. You don't say no to that in the hands of a rapist. Yet we are so intent on what we were doing, the work. That the fear never came to a head, nor could be heard.

Around the time we were going to be given something to eat—four cups of tea and one long-gone hotel coffee were all we'd had by nightfall—another lieutenant of the Air Force paid us a visit. With him a mysterious man who said he was a journalist. Writing his name for me in my notebook, but not saying it aloud. A Persian name, Adimi. He is with the Tehran *Journal,* his card says. He is a friend of the officer's. Indeed, one might take him for the younger man's mentor, teacher, some respected old family connection. Their courtesy toward one another has something lovely in it, affectionate, a Near Eastern tenderness in friendship. Adimi is an interesting man, handsome, impressive old face, the look of a man of culture, one thinks of an artist, a musician, even a conductor. Pride, some authority. Though clearly he is in some trepidation in being here, an indiscretion he has risked nevertheless. And the officer with him, risking a lot. "Do you have some message for the Iranian women you leave here?" "Why do you ask?" "I am with the Tehran *Journal.* I could convey a message for you." I am baffled; how could a reporter get back in here for such a message, am I licensed to speak, is this a trap? "I know some of your friends." "Would you happen to know my lawyer, sir?" "Yes, I do, I even know his address on Elizabeth Street."

It is enough. Or is it? If he takes a risk, why shouldn't I? Because you have a lot to lose right now. You're winning just now, you're leaving tomorrow. Maybe. So don't prejudice that. But the opportunity to tell Kateh and the women, Lahadji, to clear myself with the Iranian people who have nothing but snide notices that a spy, foreign agent, got tossed. Which discredits the movement. It would go better if I could exonerate myself. Some sense of honor, of innocence, rages for it. "A message to the women?" "Yes, and one for your lawyer, an account of the matter. Letters to attorneys are often published here as essays clarifying cases, publishing the truth where persons are falsely accused, writers and others; it is rather a tradition. A tradition everywhere, I believe, to address oneself to one's attorney as a formal expression of the facts in a matter. Such letters are printed in journals as a diplomatic act, a formal explanation, if you like."

"I could write it tonight. Both messages." "Good. I will come for them in the morning. Either I will come or I will send someone." He turns to the Lieutenant. "I will come myself if I can, if it is advisable." "I thank you, sir, with my heart." "It is nothing, these things must always be done if they can, if they can be arranged."

And so when the Iranian fast food appeared, some chicken

dismembered over pink rice, the whole thing cold and stale and wrapped in tinfoil, a dreadful mess that passes for food, the soldiers presenting it in perfect confidence that it is food—we grab a bite of it and begin writing. I start the first draft while Sophie makes a great display of folding and repacking our clothes, giving the guards some activity to watch over while I go on writing in the brown notebook, patiently, with enormous care and concentration against our surroundings, yet out of their energy telling, telling carefully, but with great restraint. Sitting in a corner where the soldiers can see me if they try—I am not hiding what I do—but where I see less or little of them. So I can do it without being afraid to do it. Because this document, if confiscated—and therefore it must seem to be just the most ordinary journal entry, interrupted by laconic spoken exchanges, relaxed unimportant chatter—could get us arrested for sure. Since it could so easily be said to accuse, when speaking to Lahadji (what could be more seditious than innocence?), and to incite, when speaking to the women.

I have just finished the first message, short, simple, but full of a bewildered regret, when I am peremptorily called to the phone. Entezam himself will talk to me, I am told. A guard bringing me all through the airport to the central telephone switchboard. As we go along the long corridors I memorize a series of old photographs, mosques, icons they seem, gravures you hold on to against catastrophe: what will this man say to me? An explanation for my expulsion? The order for my arrest and further detention? The public area of the airport is full of people. Stares. Recognition. The guard at my side proclaims my imprisonment, or maybe he protects me. The faces seem curious, but not hostile. When I reach the telephone, my anxiety is rewarded with a typical event; the connection is broken. For an hour we wait while the ministry reaches us, only to be disconnected again, the bullying voice at the other end demanding if I am Kate Millett. Yes, I say, then we are cut off again. The Air Force dials back. Disconnection again. This would be funny if it were not so torturous. And boring. A call comes in for me, I take it, and am dumbfounded to find that it is not the ministry but some reporter calling from Australia wanting a statement. I have nothing to say to him—but how curious that this is permitted. It gives one ideas. My guard chats with other guards, giving me a few feet of rope. I could get a phone call out of this if I play it smart. We wait some more. Calls and disconnections. Delay. Cigarettes all round. The guard is more interested in his companions than in me. I have noticed a number of women at the switchboard, they seem friendly. Would it be all right if I just sat with these ladies, while we're waiting. The guard nods, he is nonchalant, it will take longer to get through, I will be right in his view through the glass. And once established with the women, once calm and polite and drinking their tea, it is no great difficulty to beg a phone. Wonderful. A whole day incommunicado and then one is given a switchboard. But Kateh is not home. Nelufar is out, her housekeeper bewilders me in Farsi. My big chance at a phone and no luck. Lahadji's office is closed for the night. Riley, then. Not in her room. What other American media ladies would help? The woman from ABC cannot quite fathom how I am imprisoned in the airport incommunicado and still playing with the phone this way, she'll call anyone for me—would I like the embassy informed? Rather complicated emotions over this one. Ambassador Sullivan, the reputation of CIA this particular mission has, I would not like to beg their help, but if she were, on her own, rather than at my instance, to call them: "Do whatever you think you should." More interested in my lawyer and my friends and in how Riley has managed to coordinate things, having to put so much trust and responsibility on women I hardly know, women who are reporters and Americans, finally having to fly blind since my guard is waving me back to the phone where the ministry is coming in once again. Only to be disconnected several more times. A whimsical thought crosses my mind regarding the switchboard women; they pull the plugs. But I will never know now, I am being marched back to my cell. Past the stares and the murmurings that sound like my own name. And then a very odd sound, the word "lesbian," an English word, a word I do not even know in Farsi, so it must have been "lesbian." From a man who bumps against us as we turn up the ramp. It is said bitterly. I look at my guard in a different light, wondering if I need him. If lesbian is now part of the charge, spoken, unspoken, published or unpublished, rumored, fantasized—how did it become so? The hotel clerk? That was the only brush in Tehran. It is a general thing known about me, part of my work, printed in my own books, trumpeted proudly in years of gay liberation—but here, where homosexuals are executed? What could it come to mean here if I stay on, am detained, jailed? A shiver. The last fear.

I go back to finish my letter to Lahadji, a citizen's complaint against the abuse of rights in the forceful expulsion of one who had agreed to comply with a government order to begin with—correct, punctilious even—yet there is risk even in writing it. It seems less of one now, knowing that as a lesbian I have no rights at all, am anathema, probably worthy of death under the law. How soon can I get out of here?

By morning we have it finished. Taking turns at copying, recopying, revising, fretting over spellings. All the long cold night hours, one of us sleeping, one keeping watch, a stiff back against the wall. They have given us two cots. We ended up using the same one. But never at the same time. That would be madness to risk. Probably this is, too, these three pages we must now convey to Adimi or whomever he sends. A copy for him, a copy for ourselves—we too can have it printed if we get free. If we don't, maybe he still will. If not, the rest is silence. It is a lot to risk. But if we draw no attention to the pages, keep them in a book, the notebook itself. Or perhaps a magazine, we'll just hand him the magazine. It is in Sophie's hands, an old copy of *Time*. I am watching the magazine, anxious that our guard has perhaps already seen the gesture that inserted the loose-leaf pages into the gaudy cover. I think I have seen him out of the corner of my eye. I signal Sophie and she quietly rearranges all the magazines on the bed, removing the pages. They must stay in her purse where they are safer. Our purses are sacred, go everywhere with us.

We were too confident. Too confident they spoke little English, since their replies to our requests to use the bathroom were so primitive, visits under guard and with the guard pounding on the door if you brush your teeth too long. A malicious pounding that seems convinced we are escaping the windowless filthy room through a drain or practicing what his expression, when we open the door, proclaims as perversion. Not on your life. Not in this insalubrious place. It is not a bathroom, there is no bath, only cold-water sinks and toilets where you put a foot on each side of squat-down bowls without water to flush them. A remarkable comment on the achievements of modern Iran, the glories of the Shah and the fabled modernization one hears of in his defense. One must accept this as the crown of the Pahlavi dynasty's highly techno-industrial international airport. Rather a poor showing, if you consider the traditional Persian pot, dug over real earth and rinsed from a lovely pitcher after use. Here no one has rinsed. Why bother, it's supposed to be a flush toilet. Only it doesn't flush. And no one fills the pitcher. Just as no one turns off the cold water in the sinks. Which now leak, need washers, and have rusted, ugly dirty-feeling bowls.

Where Sophie is now trying to wash her hair. "You're crazy." "If we're really getting out of here, I want my hair clean." The guard knocks. "You'll catch pneumonia." "I'll have clean hair, in any case." The guard knocks again. "I love you." "I love you too—how am I ever going to get it dry?" Now he's shouting. I leave. He has to decide whether to escort me, leaving Sophie, or to let me go back by myself. The other guard can see me across the open space of a lobby. I proceed. I don't want to miss Adimi. "Halt." I halt. We all wait till Sophie emerges. When will Adimi come? Will he come? The papers are safe in Sophie's purse, ready for him. It is no longer that early, we begin to worry. We can hear the crowd now entering the airport, the first planes disembarking, the voices of travelers reaching us as a great wave of water surging past our little room.

They are not that far away, and yet they are forever away. This morning the delegation arrived, it is their voices we hear. If they did arrive, if their visas are still good, if our expulsion (and Claudine and Sylvina's—for they were on the list too, the Colonel told us on the ride to Immigration—though they had already beat the rap by leaving that morning) has not caused the government to withdraw permission for other feminists to enter. If Claude Servan-Schreiber and the others are among those voices we hear now coming into Iran, we have made it, bridged the gap, completed the relay. There is only Adimi left to wait for. And then we have completed the whole of our mission. And can leave. But it's getting awfully late—if they plan to let us board one of today's planes, they'd better get going.

11 ❋ ❋ ❋

OUR GUARD ENTERS. And sits down on Sophie's bed. He picks up the magazines, leafs through, shakes them. Looking for something. We all three know what. He examines them and shakes them again. Nothing falls out. It is an eternity in this little room. The big soldier sitting on Sophie's bed, making himself at home. The Lieutenant enters and orders him to leave. Adimi's lieutenant, but where is Adimi? The Lieutenant knows I am asking this, it is clear I should ask it silently and not aloud. "My friend has been detained." "Of course. We had something for him." "It is not a good idea. Your plane will be boarding soon. I wish you both much happiness."

It never happened. He's gone. He could not receive the papers. Adimi couldn't come—it has all broken down. The whole night's work. Because the soldier saw, he has alerted others, we are being watched now, the Lieutenant cannot make a move, introduce Adimi here again; he would be too compromised receiving the papers himself. "Publish it somewhere else then, when we get out." "Rome maybe."

"Paris maybe. Maybe they'll send us to Paris." "Maybe there'll be someone else to give it to before we leave here." Sophie goes on cheering me up with Paris, knowing how I love it, and because we have talked all night of staying abroad the last week of our ticket, devoting that time to serving the Iranian women in Europe by drumming up support for them there, telling their story in France and Italy. "Listen, if we could go first to Paris rather than Rome . . ." "Where we have to go anyway to catch our plane to New York, 'cause that's the routing on our ticket . . ." "Then we could do a week's work in Paris, team up with the delegation's offices there, the women's press there, Des Femmes." "And your usual publisher in France, Stock, they'd help, we can give a press conference in Paris . . ."

On and on, the two of us, like travel addicts. Stuck in our cell as the hours go by. They are not letting us out today. It will be like yesterday, a joke. A joke on us, our gullibility, optimism, trust: good faith met with bad. And when the last plane has left, then they will put us in jail. The charade will be over. The delegation, running in the delighted voices of the crowds filling the lobbies outside our door, the door they have shut now, the armed guards sitting innocently on a bench outside an office, as if they were resting or merely passing the time. And our friends and sisters are there somewhere in that din of happy voices. Having no idea where we are, imagining us back in New York. If they've heard we were expelled. If they haven't, Carole will tell them, and they will all be sure we're back in New York. And by the time they are settled in the Park Hotel, where Carole will play diplomat and liaison, the work of bridging factions I always aspire to, by the time they have the coffee before them, the police will have triumphed over the Air Force—the police who are probably pulling a fast one by now—everyone studiously ignoring our last five requests for information on our flight. And we'll be going through that office by the door, the police office, the lobby empty by then, the planes gone, the car waiting to take us to jail.

We have got to do something. It's ten o'clock. There are only two more planes today—Air France (what if we got on Air France and went to Paris, to paradise) and Air Iran to who knows where. But anywhere is fine. Anywhere at all, Holland, or Italy or even Istanbul. Just out. "Cool it." "But, Sophie, we're going to have to insist now." "I know it, they don't plan to let us go. No one's been in here in over an hour." So we insist, we even interest the Iran Air man who is providing sugar now for our tea from over his partition. Would he make a phone call to our lawyer? No dice. Use the phone? Next office. We can't go to the next office, our guards are right outside the door. Then we're just going to have to make a little scene with them and demand they get their officer and we get out of here.

"They could shoot us," "They can always shoot us. They could take us anywhere and shoot us." "But they're kids, you know, country boys, they're scared too, they could shoot from just getting nervous." "Crap, I happen to be as nervous as I intend to get, myself—and we have to make it out of here." "Okay, let's go." For all along we have maintained the crazy decorum imposed on culprits, we have acted like culprits. Who needed to be kept hidden, discreetly imprisoned in a little room. Who are guarded by three automatic machine guns but who are so polite and respectable that they keep their door shut in a ladylike manner, cooperating, never embarrassing their captors.

"You must get back inside." The muzzle of a gun. "We are not staying here unless you get your officers; we must speak to the Captain or the Lieutenant. Air Force." Instead we get police, Army and some extraneous man from an airline. We are conferred over. We protest we must leave. "If we are expelled, expel us. Let us get out of here." "Madam, you must be quiet this moment!" "Not until we know our flight." They promise to get one in higher authority. We wait. Another half-hour. "They never intended to let us leave." "Open the door again."

He's still there; Westerner, probably American, strikingly handsome man, looks Irish in my Celtic radar, could we get him to get out of his safe legal civilian seat and take a message? Psst, I think—like a schoolgirl. Speaking English loudly with the guard, protesting my condition—if he knows English he will turn around. And he does. Watches. I gesture to him—I am past caring about the spectacle we make, even the trouble we'll get into. As he comes near our door I begin explaining to him. He seems to know about it. He happens to be with the United States embassy here, he says. Happens, remarkable happening—have they bothered to send someone to help me? No, actually he happens to be in the airport at this moment only because he is going on leave and waiting for a plane to Holland.

"Were we in the papers?" I wonder, not having seen the papers since the issue where I was expelled in a few lines, one might easily fail to notice. "What is your name?" He even has a card. Finnegan, something like that, wonderfully Irish, the card presented with a gentry air. He is beautiful and exasperating, cool as a mist, refreshing as hope. He even speaks Farsi and begins to explain to the guard what I want. Of course, the guard knows but he seems to get the message better from Finnegan. There are now the promised authorities we have begged all morning to see, to question, to petition our tickets and passports from, to plead with for release. Finnegan is a marvel of expression to them. Not only the Farsi I envy him, the facility and grace in this language I would love to learn, need to know right now, the words flying back and forth, the circle of men deliberating our case. How men understand men, how businesslike and reasonable they are with each other, officials, authorities. It is infuriating to watch them give the answers for our lives to Finnegan—when the whole time we have been in custody they have refused to give them to us, never answering our simplest question, denying often that they know English, yet eavesdropping on us at every opportunity. All the reason we have asked for in vain is given to Finnegan. It looks like Finnegan will prevail—it looks like they may even give in and let us go. It also looks like the old business of the police versus the Air Force versus the Komiteh, or rather, that all of them might even be arriving at partial agreement to release us, it is just so damn complicated for them to coordinate their tedious inefficient efforts and that the last plane will leave before we're on it. And then the police will reassert their case.

A television crew bears down on us. The last thing I need at this delicate juncture. Or maybe, everything going awry again, one calls for help through the media? Don't chance it. The police are already furious. Even the Air Force. Finnegan has disappeared. "Sorry, I can't risk talking to you just now. Later. When I'm free." If I get free. The lines begin to form for the buses which carry travelers from the airport to the plane. Just there is the door to freedom. We are within five yards of being on those lines. The civilians, the lucky, their bags on their shoulders, their expectations. Finnegan is on one of those lines going to Holland. Another forms for Air France. If we could just get on that. If we could go to Paris. Anywhere. But Paris: it shines like light, the word in the mouth or the mind. New York. Home. But home is the end of the mission and there are days left till the twenty-fourth, days I owe to the Iranian women who bought this ticket. If we could get to Europe, we could give them their money's worth. If we could get out of here at all. The television crew have brought about a setback; it seems to have been decided that we will be held. Again. More. Another day. The police bridling in importance, ready to win.

And then comes our Captain, his paratrooper jumpsuit, his fancy revolver. Captain Jack. I can't help but smile, liking him, even the moments we hated him, his vanity is somehow endearing, compels admiration, his beauty and dash, even past our perception of its superficiality, he still represents something of the revolution, the time gone by, the flair and optimism that armed a people rising up against a tyrant. And against all the fat officials, the stubborn police, the heavy bumpkins with machine guns, he performs our rescue. We will board. They argue. Another moment of this and one would go mad and stay there. They disagree and step off a ways to hammer at each other.

Invade and retreat, waver to and fro, dispatch someone to telephone, another to summon an airline official. Iran Air it will be, the least pleasant alternative, of course, but a plane, any plane, even if we're captive all the way home, we will be aloft. Do the governments presume to own the air? I wonder. "The Ayatollah will certainly scratch cocktails." "Never mind, we'll still be going somewhere." In fact we are already; Captain Jack is ushering us toward the door.

Not the door where regular people wait for a bus. No, the door at the far end. How come? Maybe they aren't taking us to the plane at all, maybe it's a trick again. Jack's smiling, he's proud of himself. We ask again, where are we going? The old hopeless question. "To the plane." "Why not in the bus?" "A car will take you." Five men armed with submachine guns will take you. But where? A newsman shoots a picture of my dismay and fatigue which will represent me around the world. I look like I have swallowed the hindquarters of a rat, but it is surely authentic; it "happened," as documentarians say. And now suddenly there's a rush. We can't talk to anyone, but we whisper a last message to a reporter, "Watch to see if we turn up somewhere." The driver, machine gun between his legs at the driver's seat; you could do yourself a bit of damage that way, I think, looking into the barrels of two more machine guns who have crowded into the back seat with us. The hurry is either because we are missing the plane or because they are taking us somewhere else and want to get on with it and away from the press.

The absurdity is that the driver can't start the car. Wrong key. Sophie and I exchange a look which represents our certainty we could do rather better running our own lives. "What if we just took the bus with the others?" I ask, sweet reason itself. "No, no, impossible." They all laugh. Then we are not going to the airplane, after all. So near. And so helplessly far away. Another key is brought out and tried. But it isn't the key, it's the battery. Jesus. Then we can't help but laugh too, the whole car of us laughing, prisoners and machine guns and captors. As they get out and shove the car to start it. While we just ride along, laughing with the driver, who's steering and waiting to pop it into gear, then the wheels turning and the soldiers running like boys and hopping back in through the doors as it takes off and we laugh and I want to sing, to ride along singing with these guys—'cause we really are going to the plane—I can see it.

Of course, there's one more scare while they fumble and dither over our luggage, it wasn't ticketed, it is still in the terminal and we sit waiting for it to crawl toward us; forget it, we'll go without it, the hell with it, just to get out of this godforsaken place.

No, not on that note; it's ungracious to leave without goodwill, friends. You want to take back the words, you want to thank someone and shake their hands; pity Captain Jack isn't on hand, we'd kiss him. I watch my boot, feeling it on the stair to the plane, mounting in gratitude for deliverance as miraculous as this ascension. A few moments and this great machine will move, the mind moving the wheels faster and faster and up, taking off, it will do the unbelievable and the eyes will look down and see the earth leaving while we speed toward the heavens. And not till then will they tell us where we are going. Because that is the rule. Five miles up, the steward has said, and we will be free. And may finally know our destination. The absurdity of our captors' steadfast refusal ever to tell us.

Meanwhile we have pillows and blankets and, as the No Smoking light goes off, cigarettes, courtesy and hospitality and the decency accorded the ordinary citizen. The pall of custody falls away, accusation, deprivation. And the contempt with which this newspaper on my lap describes our departure, declaring it to have taken place yesterday. We know what we know and can tell it in New York or Rome or Paris, but cannot tell it in Iran, as it floats away below us. We can never tell it how we loved Persia and missed it. Or tell our friends there anything—they must take us on faith still. The mountains, they will be there forever and next time, if there is a next time, tearing oneself into the present while the eyes still caress the mountains, the heart pulled back to earth. To a Persia that is not a jail; pray for it. And the revolution, may it be completed and not fail, may it be for all: the poor, the women, the prisoners of all kinds, even those who are guilty—let the executions cease. For they have begun again, the paper says, prohibitions are strengthened, life is more and more unendurable by the withdrawal of pleasures, even those of wine and music, incursions into the privacy of life, the stigmatizing of sex, of women, of "adultery," of homosexuality—not even remembering how to make love until three days later in Paris sleeping on the floor of a friend's apartment with the best view of the roofs of the Latin Quarter and we saw the moon, only then were we really free.

Because we are five miles up now and the steward has come to say that this plane lands first in Paris. Then it goes to London. Then it goes to New York. "May we disembark at Paris?" "Of course. Your luggage will go on to New York, however, I fear, since the officials have directed it there." Having never consulted us about what we might like, they have decided for us: we should go right home to New York like good girls. "May we have it sent back to Paris on your next plane?" "Yes, you will receive it in a few days." And in only five hours we will be in Paris. Eating lunch at Balzar, the lunch hour stayed for us by the change of time zone. That you can go from a cell and

Iranian women in protest

submachine guns to a brasserie in the Latin Quarter . . . because of airplanes. Because the madness in one place is not the madness of another. If there is an airplane, as long as there is an airplane, as long as you can get on it, and they'll let you—the governments, the limiters of freedom, the appropriators of imagination and possibility, the unquestioned thieves of human life, liberty and pursuit of happiness. If they permit, and as long as they do—so guard what is left of that liberty—you may not only go home, you may go to Paris. "Which is better than home, it's heaven," we laugh and jump up and down in our seats, having received the greatest present, the grandest surprise, prisoners some twenty minutes ago and now winging our way, flying like birds or angels, the wonder of it, the inconceivable freedom of it— to fly. To the city of light streaming in the sun-filled sky, Paris. The happiness in that word.